Doggin'

100 Ideas For Great Outdoor Vacations To Take With Your Dog

Doug Gelbert

illustrations by

Andrew Chesworth

Cruden Bay Books

DOGGIN' AMERICA: 100 IDEAS FOR GREAT OUTDOOR VACATIONS TO TAKE WITH YOUR DOG

Copyright 2009 by Cruden Bay Books

Cruden Bay Books
PO Box 467
Montchanin, DE 19710

www.hikewithyourdog.com

International Standard Book Number 978-0-9815346-8-8

Up Ahead...

3. *Road Trippin' With Your Dog*

4.   *Doggin' American History*

INTRODUCTION

Every year an estimated 15 million people travel with their dogs. In recent years, mercifully, it has become much easier to do so with more and more lodging facilities becoming pet-friendly. But what happens when you actually want to leave the hotel room with your dog?

Our national parks are notoriously unfriendly to dogs. Of the more than 1,500 public beaches in the United States more than half don't allow dogs at all and most of the rest have some sort of restrictions. But there are rewarding outdoor vacations to be had out there that can include your dog.

This book is not about traveling with your dog to tiny, fenced in dog parks or disappearing into the wilderness; it is about places you want to see, and taking your dog to share your fun.

How To Use This Book

The 100 Vacation Ideas are presented as "Destinations" or "Tours." A destination is a place to to set up base camp and explore the area with your dog; tours, usually based around a common theme, take your dog from site to site. There is some overlap so when you take an idea to start planning a vacation with your dog, use the state-by-state index to identify tail-friendly sites in your targeted destination.

Where Are The Maps?

In this age of MapQuest and Google Maps and GPS, no tiny map printed in a book can compete. Contact information includes websites where applicable to provide the nuts-and-bolts for the more than 500 destinations for your dog listed within. Besides,not printing maps saves a few extra trees for your dog to enjoy.

It is sometimes hard for we dog owners to believe, but not everyone loves dogs. We are, in fact, in the minority when compared with our non-dog-owning neighbors. So when visiting a park always keep your dog under control and clean up any messes and we can expect these great parks to remain open to our dogs. And maybe some others will see the light as well. Remember, every time you go out with your dog you are an ambassador for all dog owners.

So, plan that next vacation to include your dog, grab that leash and get going!

1
DOGGIN'
AMERICA'S
PUBLIC LANDS

DESTINATION
IDEA #1: THE 5 BEST NATIONAL PARKS FOR DOGS

The welcome mat in our National Park System rolls up when we drive in with our dogs. Very few national parks allow dogs on hiking trails. In Yellowstone National Park dogs are not allowed more than 100 feet from roads, parking areas and campgrounds. In Yosemite National Park dogs can walk the paved paths of the Valley floor but are not permitted on any trail or slope. At the Grand Canyon dogs can walk along the South Rim in developed areas but can not go on any trail below the rim. At Zion National Park dogs are permitted on one mild trail.

And on and on. So, while most of America is making plans to visit our national natural treasures, we dog owners must be a bit more creative. Here are the 5 best national parks to take your dog...

1. Acadia National Park (Maine)

Acadia National Park is certainly one of the crown jewels in the National Park Service and dogs will not bark in dissent - this is the best national park to bring your dog for outdoor adventure. Except for the swimming beaches and ladder hiking trails like the *Precipice Trail*, dogs are allowed throughout the park.

Much of your time with your dog in Acadia will be spent on its intricate network of carriage roads. Mount Desert Island, named by French explorer Samuel Champlain in 1604, was once the summer playground of America's rich and famous. When John D. Rockefeller, Jr., no great fan of the horseless carriage, visited the Maine coast he enjoyed outings with his team of horses and open coaches. He painstakingly directed the construction of wide, motor-free carriage roads twisting through the island mountains. Forty-five miles of rustic broken stone roads were eventually built between 1913 and 1940 and the hand-built byways are the best examples of the construction technique still in use in America. In addition to the stone roads and stone guardrails, irregularly spaced granite slabs known locally as "Rockefeller's Teeth," there are 16 stone-faced bridges - each unique in design.

One of the wealthy elite, George B. Dorr, devoted 43 years and much of his family fortune to preserving the island. He offered more than 6,000 acres to the federal government and in 1916, Woodrow Wilson established the Sieur de Monts National Monument. Three years later Lafayette National Park became the first national park east of the Mississippi River. Honoring its Acadian heritage, the park became Acadia National Park in 1929.

Several park highlights come with little purchase for your dog. The *Jordan Pond Nature Trail* is a mile-long loop leading to views of glacial mountains reflecting in the pond waters. The rounded mountains, known as the Bubbles, can be climbed on short trails. Other easy hikes include the *Ocean Trail* to Otter Cliffs that clings to the edge of lands' end over the Atlantic surf and exploratory walks atop Cadillac Mountain. The 1530-foot summit is the highest point on the Atlantic Ocean north of Rio de Janeiro, Brazil and sunrise hikes here will be the first to be illuminated in America. The *Great Head Trail* loops across Sand Beach and most people go right at the head of the loop. But going left into the maritime forest saves the spectacular coastal views from one of America's highest headlands until the end. All these trails are easily accessed from the Park Loop Road and can get busy. Seek out trails across Somes Sound - America's only fjord - in the western reaches of the park to find fewer paw prints.

Bar Harbor, Maine
(207) 288-3338
www.nps.gov/acad/

2. Catoctin Mountain Park (Maryland)

"Any man who does not like dogs and want them about does not deserve to be in the White House," President Calvin Coolidge said. Coolidge himself had at least 12 dogs. Future office holders have taken the 29th American President's words to heart - every single one has shared the Oval Office with a canine friend - and one of President-elect Barrack Obama's first orders of business was to get a family dog.

How would you like to hike with your dog where Presidents hike with their dogs? When an American President leaves the White House for the presidential retreat of Camp David, there is almost always an eager dog in tow. Franklin Roosevelt's Scottish Terrier, Fala, was the first in a steady procession of Presidential pups to romp in the woods of Camp David. Ronald Reagan once complained that when he took a break at Camp David, his dog Rex would beat him to the window seat in the helicopter.

Everyone has heard of Camp David but where exactly it is? Surprisingly it is located deep inside a national park called Catoctin Mountain Park. When you take your dog there, you will never see Camp David or any evidence that the presidential compound is hidden among the trees but the trails you can hike on are of Presidential quality nonetheless. Just don't expect to see any First Dogs.

You could fill up a day of canine hiking at Catoctin Mountain Park just by checking off the many easy self-guiding interpretive trails as you learn about mountain culture and forest ecology. There is plenty of more challenging fare in the park as well. Three of the best vistas - Wolf Rock, Chimney Rock and Cat Rock - are connected by a roller-coaster trail on the eastern edge of the mountain. There is little understory in the woods and views are long. Many of the mountain slope trails are rocky and footing can be uncertain under paw on climbs to 1,500 feet.

In the western region of Catoctin Mountain, near the Owens Creek campground, are wide horse trails ideal for contemplative canine hiking. The grades are gentler for long hikes through mixed hardwoods of chestnut oak, hickory, black birch and yellow poplar. Dogs are allowed in the campground and on all national park trails but not across the road in popular Cunningham Falls State Park.

The forests deep in the rugged Catoctin Mountains provided ideal cover for a moonshining still, made illegal by the onset of Prohibition in 1919. On a steaming July day in 1929 Federal agents raided the Blue Blazes Whiskey Still and confiscated more than 25,000 gallons of mash. Today the airy, wooded *Blue Blazes Whiskey Trail* along Distillery Run leads to a recreated working still and interprets the history of whiskey making in the backwoods of Appalachia.

Thurmont, Maryland
(301) 663-9330
www.nps.gov/cato/

3. Cuyahoga Valley National Park (Ohio)

Raise your hand if you knew that America's first national park of the 21st Century was created in..............Cleveland? To the first people who came here 12,000 years ago the Cuyahoga was the "crooked river." Its steep valley walls inhibited settlement as easterners poked into the region in the late 1700s. But a navigable water link between Lake Erie and the Ohio River was a priority in the early American Canal Age and in 1832 the Ohio & Erie Canal became a reality. Ohio boomed and settlers poured into the area. The canal was put out of business by the Great Flood of 1913 and the Cuyahoga Valley was left to recreational purposes. The 33,000 acres along the banks of the Cuyahoga River were protected as a national recreation area so the heavy lifting for creating the park was done before its designation as a national park in 2000.

As befits its history as a recreation destination, Cuyahoga is a national park that permits dogs on its trails. It doesn't have the feel of the grand American national parks but instead evokes an intimate feel on the trails that are squeezed between highways, farmlands and neighborhoods.

The main trail through the park is the nearly 20 miles of the *Towpath Trail* along the route of the historic canal. Ten trailheads make it easy to hike the crushed limestone path in biscuit-size chunks. The trail is a mix of meadows and forests and the remnants of locks and villages. Another long distance adventure through the park is the *Buckeye Trail* that circles the entire state of Ohio for over 1200 miles. About 33 miles of the blue-blazed pathway cover the ravines and ridges of the valley.

Some of the best outings with your dog in the park are in the north end of the Cuyahoga Valley, in the Bradford Reservation. A five-mile all-purpose trail traverses the Tinkers Creek Gorge area, exploring Ohio's most spectacular canyon. The gorge is a National Natural Landmark, noted for its virgin hemlock forests. Short detours off the main trail include an easy walk to Bridal Veil Falls and the *Hemlock Creek Loop Trail*.

Other highlights include the dark and mysterious 2.2-mile ramble around the Ledges (from the Happy Day camp) and a short 1.25-mile loop through the Brandywine Gorge that takes your dog to the lip of Brandywine Falls and 160 feet down to the water level.

Brecksville, Ohio
(216) 524-1497
www.nps.gov/cuva/

4. Hot Springs National Park (Arkansas)

The water that bubbles to the ground at 143 degrees Farenheit fell to earth 4,000 years ago, percolating deep into the earth and heating four degrees every 300 feet before seeping out of the lower west slope of Hot Springs Mountain. Spanish explorers and French trappers visited the springs for centuries. In 1832 the Federal Government reserved land around the springs - the first "national park" to protect a natural resource. There was little done to administer the reserve, however, and private bathhouses sprung up to cater to tourists visiting to relax in the "healing" waters. Finally in 1921, Hot Springs became a true National

Park, a unique blend of a highly developed small city set in low-lying, rounded mountains.

There are over 30 miles of top-notch hiking trails available in Hot Springs, mostly on short, inter-connecting jogs on Hot Springs Mountain and West Mountain that flank the city. Many of these paths were carved for visitors who were encouraged to walk daily in addition to their baths as part of an all-encompassing healthy routine at the spas. Most were constructed wide enough to handle carriages and are still roomy today. Although the mountains only top out at little more than 1,000 feet expect to find some climbs that will leave you and your dog panting. Also, there aren't many streams so make sure you carry plenty of cooling water for your dog on a summer afternoon's outing.

For extended canine hiking head out on the *Sunset Trail* that leaves West Mountain and tags Music Mountain at 1,405 feet (the highest spot in the park) before doubling back onto Sugarloaf Mountain. This trail doesn't loop and is a good candidate for a car shuttle. Back in town you can take your dog on a tour of Bathhouse Row with a half-mile saunter down the Promenade, visiting several of the 47 springs that flow at an average rate of 850,000 gallons a day.

The one place you can't take your dog in Hot Springs are the centerpiece bathhouses but across from Bathhouse Row you can catch a ride on a Duck Boat, an amphibious vehicle that drives south of town for a cruise on Lake Hamilton. Dogs are allowed to ride on the top deck.

Hot Springs, Arkansas
(501) 620-6715
www.nps.gov/hosp/

5. Shenandoah National Park (Virginia)

The Blue Ridge Mountains that host Shenandoah National Park are the oldest rocks on earth. A billion years ago these mountains were higher than the Rockies when they were created. Time has weathered and rounded the peaks and valley that we see today. But what we see in Shenandoah has not been left to the hand of nature, as we have come to expect in our national parks.

Shenandoah is very much a planned national park. Herbert Hoover established a Summer White House on the Rapidan River (the park is only 75 miles from Washington DC) helping to trigger wilderness development. During the Great Depression Shenandoah was officially designated a national park and Franklin Roosevelt's "Tree Army" planted hundreds of thousands of trees on today the only public road in Shenandoah National Park. Your dog is welcome at just about every stop along the way - only 20 of the more than 500 miles of hiking trails are off-limits for dogs. These are some trails involving awkward passages and rock climbs but for the most part these routes are suitable for any level of canine hiker. Unfortunately one such trail that can't be on your favorite trail companion's "to-do" list is on Old Rag Mountain, a climb so fine that it is considered by many to be the best hike on the East Coast. But generally your dog will be able to visit the best views and waterfalls in Shenandoah National Park.

Luray, Virginia
(540) 999-3500
www.nps.gov/shen/

DESTINATION
IDEA #2: THE BEST ALTERNATIVES TO NATIONAL PARKS FOR DOGS

So traveling with your dog across the United States can indeed be frustrating for the active dog owner. But that national park experience can for dog owners with a little extra effort; your dog need not be shut out from America's natural splendors. If you have to drive past a tempting national park with your dog, don't go too fast. Here are some excellent choices right next door...

Catalina State Park/Saguaro National Park (Arizona)

Your dog won't be able to trot among the giant cacti in Saguaro National Park or in the Sonoran Desert in the expansive Tucson Mountain Park but she can experience this one-of-a-kind ecosystem nearby, nine miles north of Tucson, in Catalina State Park and see the same iconic cacti.

A small Hohokam Indian village was established on a wide ridge above Sutherland Wash, now known as Romero Ruin, about 1,500 years ago. The small community flourished for more than 1,000 years before being abandoned. The early Spaniards called the Santa Catalina Mountains "La Inglesia" for their cathedral-like appearance. The first European settlement in these foothills came around 1850 when cattle ranchers Francisco and Victoriana Romero established a homestead along the wash. The ranch grew to 5,000 acres but did not survive two generations. Gradually the forgotten property came to the attention of scientists and historians. In 1983 Catalina State Park, sprawling across 5,483 acres, was established, including 34 distinct archeological sites.

Eight trails of varying length and difficulty traverse the park's more than eight square miles. Most - including the longer and most strenuous hikes - are off-limits to dogs. The best canine hike at Catalina State Park is the 2.3-mile *Canyon Loop Trail* that visits the differing habitat types found in this beautiful desert terrain. The trail rolls gently up and down through riparian arroyos and past stands of stately saguaros. Keep an eye to the sky for a chance to see any of the more than 170 species of birds that call the park home. The loop winds up with an unexpected hidden stream complete with a delightful doggie swimming hole.

Tucson, Arizona
(520) 628-5798
www.azstateparks.com/Parks/CATA/index.html

Colorado Riverway Recreation Area/Arches National Park (Utah)

Your dog won't be able to walk under the magnificent natural arches in Arches National Park but he can play under the sixth longest natural rock span in the United States. East of Moab the Colorado Riverway Recreation Area serves up a red rock wonderland that looks just like the moonscape your dog is missing over at Arches. The packed-sand *Negro Bill Canyon Trail* climbs gently up a scenic canyon, crossing and tracing a clear-flowing stream for two miles to reach the Morning Glory Natural Bridge. The pool under the bridge makes an ideal doggie swimming pool but be careful of the flourishing poison ivy growing nearby.

After making your way back through the colorful cliffs and river-carved canyon you can camp with your dog at one of several first come-first served campsites directly on the swift-flowing Colorado River.

Moab, Utah
www.discovermoab.com/blm_riverway.htm

Converse Basin/Sequoia National Park (California)

Like Yosemite, its neighbors to the south, Kings Canyon and Sequoia national parks, boasting the largest concentration of giant sequoias in the world, do not allow dogs on the trail. About five miles north of Kings Canyon National Park and the famous General Grant Grove, however, is the Converse Basin Grove where your dog can mosey close to a famous giant sequoia, the Boole Tree.

Converse Basin is a giant sequoia graveyard. This area was once quite possibly the finest sequoia grove that ever was. Massive trees over 300 feet high were enthusiastically felled by loggers - often for little more than shingles. One 285-foot sequoia known as the General Noble Tree was cut in 1893 to display at the Columbian Exposition in Chicago and the Chicago Stump can be seen today. Among the trees destroyed in the Converse Basin was the oldest known giant sequoia to have been cut down - 3,200 annual growth rings were counted. So many trees were taken that the area is known as Stump Meadow.

The hiking trail in the Converse Basin is a 2.5-mile loop to reach the Boole Tree. Leading straight out from the parking lot you are quickly on the edge of Kings Canyon and you'll enjoy open, sweeping views as you switchback up the ridge. Shortly after finishing your climb you reach a short side trail that leads into a depression containing the Boole Tree, once thought to be the largest giant sequoia in the world but more exacting measurements have placed it eighth. No one knows why this great tree was spared when equally large trees were brought down.

If you have spent the day looking at giant sequoias in the landscaped national parks, your encounter with the Boole Tree might come as a bit of a shock. It is related to its brothers in Kings Canyon National Park like the wolf is to your dog. Surrounded by dense forest growth, it is actually possible to not immediately recognize the Boole Tree from the main trail. But once you see your dog up against its massive trunk - its ground perimeter of 113 feet is the greatest of all giant sequoias - there is no mistaking this special tree.

Visalia, California
(559) 784-1500
www.fs.fed.us/r5/sequoia/converse_basin/converse_basin.html

Dead Horse Point State Park /Canyonlands National Park (Utah)

Most of us have seen the spectacular scenery around Moab without realizing it - the landscape has often been used as the setting for Hollywood westerns. Before that, popular Western novelist Zane Grey stoked the imaginations of readers with action placed in Moab. Real people started coming to the Colorado River town in the 1950s when uranium was discovered nearby. Even though the mines have since played out, the town has never returned to its sleepy agricultural days. Today Moab is an outdoors mecca at the foot of the La Salle Mountains and the gateway to southeastern Utah's canyon country with national parks at Canyonlands and Arches. In these parks dogs are not allowed in the backcountry, on trails or on rivers within the park. Still, there are plenty of other opportunities here that make Moab a prime destination for canine adventurers.

Legend has it that cowboys once herded wild mustangs onto to the top of this isolated mesa - 2,000 feet above the Colorado River - and blocked escape across a narrow neck of land with branches and brush, thus creating a natural corral. One time the horses in the corral were forgotten about and died of thirst while looking at the unaccessible Colorado River below. In 1959 more than 5,000 acres, most of which are on the mesa top, were designated Dead Horse Point State Park. While your dog will never trot the trails of Canyonlands National Park and look straight down 1,000 feet at the confluence of the Green and Colorado rivers, she can get the same kind of experience next door in Dead Horse Point State Park.

Two loops, connected by the Visitor Center, skirt the edges of the rim of the rock peninsula. Numerous short spur trails poke out to promontories overlooking the canyonlands (most are unfenced and provide no protection for overcurious canines). This is sparse desert land on top of the mesa and during a hot summer day there is little shade and no natural drinking water on the trails for thirsty dogs. All told there are ten miles of paved and primitive trail at Dead Horse Point, most on hard, rocky paths.

Moab, Utah
(435) 259-2614
www.utah.com/stateparks/dead_horse.htm

Gallatin National Forest/Yellowstone National Park (Montana)

John Bozeman opened the first wagon trail through a break in the mountains that American Indians called "Valley of the Flowers." Revered as a sacred hunting ground, the Sioux killed Bozeman and no one dared try his trail again for nine years. Eventually in 1899 President William McKinley established the Gallatin National Forest by setting aside 45,000 acres that has grown to 1.8 million acres, including most of the northern and western boundaries of Yellowstone National Park and six mountain ranges. Gallatin shares much of the restless geology of its famous neighbor - on August 17, 1959, at 23 minutes before midnight, two massive blocks of the earth's crust dropped 10 feet tilting lakes, dropping houses into giant sinkholes and triggering a landslide that buried 19 campers.

The city bearing John Bozeman's name is a gateway for approaching Yellowstone Park from the north and a base point for exploring the Gallatin National Forest. Around Bozeman, check out Peet's Hill, a ridgeline trail designed for dogs to be walked under voice control. North of town, on the flank of Mount Baldy is a great letter "M," constructed of rocks by the Montana State University Class of 1918. Two trails, each about one mile in length, lead to the highly visible landmark that requires 80 gallons of white paint each year.

Any type of canine hike can be sculpted on the more than 2,000 miles of trails in the Gallatin National Forest. Popular short trails penetrate the Hyalite Canyon (out of Bozeman on South 19th Avenue) to reach refreshing waterfalls. The hikes can be extended to take as much of a mountain ascent as you want; the *Hyalite Peak Trail* leaves a deep glaciated valley at 7,000 feet and tops out on the summit seven miles later at 10,299 feet. Grotto Falls is two miles into this trek and Hyalite Lake comes another three miles up the trail.

One of the marquee canine hikes near Bozeman is the 3.5-mile journey to Lava Lake (south of town off US 191). It is a steady climb along Cascade Creek on a rocky path - sturdy wooden bridges over energetic mountain streams make appealing rest stops. Your destination is a secluded alpine lake tucked into the Spanish Peaks. For mountain-climbing canines the tallest peak in the Bridger Range, 9,670-foot Sacajawea, can be tagged by a steep, 2-mile climb at the Fairy Lake Campground.

Bozeman, Montana
(406) 587-6701
www.fs.fed.us/r1/gallatin/

Nelder Grove / Yosemite National Park (California)

One of the star attractions of Yosemite National Park is the Mariposa Grove of Giant Sequoias. It was these massive cinnamon-colored trees, the largest living things on earth, that inspired our national park system. In 1864 Abraham Lincoln set aside the Mariposa Grove as a protected state reserve "for the pleasuring of the people." Eight years later the world's first national park was created at Yellowstone and Yosemite was transferred to national guidance in 1890. Your dog can't get on the trail through the Mariposa Grove but the closest place to get him to walk among giant sequoias is five miles south of Yosemite in the Nelder Grove. Naturalist John Muir discovered this redwood grove in 1875 and as he investigated he happened upon a retired miner named John Nelder who was homesteading there. The area was heavily logged thereafter, mostly sugar pines, firs and cedar and the largest sequoias still stand.

The *Shadow of the Giants Trail*, now a National Recreational Trail, was built in 1965. The self-guiding interpretive path meanders for about a mile through the Nelder Grove, one of eight (the most famous is the Mariposa Grove) growing above the Kings River. Unlike sequoias in national parks, the 100 giants here remain in dense forest and you can walk right up to the largest trees. Those would be Old Granddad and the Kids, a grouping of giant sequoias on a ridgeline and Bull Buck, one of the world's five largest arboreal monarchs. After a half-mile hike from the lower campground you reach Bull Buck, nearly 250 feet tall, 99 feet around at the base and probably 2,700 years old.

Oakhurst, California
www.yosemitehikes.com/not-yosemite/nelder-grove/nelder-grove.htm

Oglala National Grasslands/Badlands National Park (Nebraska)

America's badlands received their ominous name when early settlers found it impossible to safely roll a wagon through the cracked lunar landscape in the Upper Midwest. Our most famous badlands are preserved in national parks in the Dakotas - and off limits to canine hikers.

To give your dog a chance to explore these unique lands of sculpted rock, head south from the Dakotas to the lesser-known "Little Badlands" of the Nebraska panhandle. Here in the Oglala National Grasslands you will find Toadstool Geologic Park where the relentless tag-team of water and wind has carved fanciful rock formations into the stark hills.

The "toadstools" form when underlying soft claystone erodes faster than the hard sandstone that caps it. A marked, mile-long interpretive loop creates an educational adventure through these badlands. Your dog is welcome on the hard rock trail but you can also explore off the path for close-up looks in the gullies at fossil bone fragments that lace the rocks and 30-million year-old footprints preserved in the stone.

For extended hikes with your dog, Toadstool Park connects to the world-renowned Hudson-Meng Bison Boneyard via a three-mile trail. This archeological site seeks to unravel the mystery of how over 600 bison died nearly 10,000 years ago in an area about the size of a football stadium. Human predation is the leading suspect.

Crawford, Nebraska
(308) 432-0300
www.fs.fed.us/r2/nebraska/recreation/by_unit/ong.shtml

Quinault Rain Forest/Olympic National Park (Washington)

All year long cool ocean currents brew Pacific storms that are powered onto the Washington coast on the prevailing westerly winds. Reaching shore, the storm clouds quickly slam into the Olympic Mountains and go no further. And so the state's northwestern coast is drenched in an average of 140 inches of rain every year, blanketing the region in some of America's largest and greenest trees. Visitors flock to Olympic National Park's Hoh Rain Forest to marvel at one of the best examples of the country's rare temperate rain forest ecosystem. Dogs aren't welcome here but you can still hike through a verdant rain forest with your favorite trail companion. Surrounding the national park is the generally dog-friendly Olympic National Forest.

Best explored on two loop trails off South Shore Road at Lake Quinault, the *Quinault Rain Forest Trail* penetrates deep into an old-growth forest where firs and spruce can tickle 300 feet in height. Clubmoss draping branches and thick canopies suffocate the light on the forest floor of this four-mile canine hike.

In a half-mile loop the *Rain Forest Nature Trail* interprets the creation of this lush arboreal paradise. At one magical turn in the trail you stand with your dog beneath all four titans of the Pacific rain forest - Western red cedar, Sitka spruce, Douglas fir and Western hemlock - growing in a row. Giant trees can often be seen growing in orderly rows. This is the result of their propagating on the mossy safety of large ancestors fallen on the forest floor. When the nurse logs decay completely their thriving wards are left with a distinctive hollow root pattern.

If this has only whetted your appetite for rain forests you can take the dog on a rough-and-tumble hike on the *Dry Creek Trail #872*. Other routes in the Quinault National Recreation Trail System lead to a cedar bog, waterfalls and along the lakeshore. Lake Quinault bills itself as the "Valley of the Rain Forest Giants" and several short spurs reveal several charter members, including the Worlds' Largest Spruce Tree. This monster soars 191 feet high with a circumference only a few whiskers shy of 59 feet around. On the North Shore a half-mile trail takes you to a gnarled big cedar that is believed to be over 1,000 years old. You can easily stand inside the ancient wonder with your dog.

Amanda Park, Washington
(360) 288-0571
www.quinaultrainforest.com/

Ross Lake National Recreation Area/North Cascades National Park (Washington)

This is glacier country - the North Cascades is the most heavily glaciated area in the continental United States. The current park glacier census stands at 318 with countless more snowfields that are fed by some of the heaviest snowfalls in the world, between 400 and 700 inches in an average year. The millions of North Cascades acres have been carved up among various federal agencies since 1968 but most of the region - 93% - has been designated as the Stephen Mather Wilderness Area, named after the first director of the National Park Service.

Dog owners must approach the North Cascades like working a jigsaw puzzle. Dogs are banned from the North Cascades National Park North Unit and South Unit (except on the *Pacific Crest National Scenic Trail*) but are permitted in the Ross Lake National Recreation Area sandwiched between. Dogs are also allowed in the limited-access Lake Chelan National Recreation Area to the south. The only paved access road to the area is Washington State Route 20, the North Cascades Highway that, to the good fortune of canine hikers, runs across the dog-friendly Ross Lake National Recreation Area (NRA), splatterd with outings from long day hikes to overnight expeditions.

Quick leg stretchers introduce the natural and human history of the mountains at the Visitor Center in the Newhalem Area. The *River Loop* picks its way through alpine forests to a free-flowing section of the Skagit River. Diablo Lake, with its rich turquoise waters, is the central jewel of the Ross Lake NRA and several canine hiking opportunities exist here. The *Diablo Lake Trail* on the north shore is an out-and-back affair of nearly four miles with just a modest elevation gain. Thunder Creek, that feeds the lake with fine glacial sediment, is shadowed by a 38-mile trail but the first steps are an easy canine hike of less than a mile to a crossing suspension bridge. The popular *Thunder Knob Trail* crawls through dry forest terrain to views of Diablo Lake and surrounding peaks.

More long-distance outings are available upstream at Ross Lake, the largest of the three man-made reservoirs on the Skagit River. The *East Bank Trail* runs 17 non-strenuous miles along the shore of the lake. At Ross Dam a short walk of less than a mile leads down to the 540-foot tall dam and across the road the *Happy Creek Forest Walk* takes a short stroll through an ancient creekside forest.

Diablo, Washington
(360) 854-7200
www.nps.gov/rola/

DESTINATION
IDEA #3: 6 CAN'T MISS CANADIAN NATIONAL PARKS FOR DOGS

Why are dogs not allowed much past the parking lot in our national parks? We have all heard the common refrains - dogs will bother the people, dogs will scare the wildlife, it is not safe for dogs. Canadian national parks attract just as many visitors - Banff and Jasper count theirs in the millions - and support just as much wildlife as their American counterparts. Yet dogs are allowed nearly everywhere in Canadian national parks. It's still North America and your dog won't want to miss these, so let's slip over the border to visit 6 great Canadian parks...

1. Banff National Park (Alberta)

In the fall of 1883, three Canadian Pacific Railway construction workers stumbled across a cave containing hot springs at the foot of Sulphur Mountain, known today as the Cave and Basin. Almost immediately the area was protected as a federal reserve and in 1887 "Rocky Mountains Park" was increased to 673 square kilometers to become Canada's first national park and the world's third. A town was built to entice tourists to the area and named Banff after "Banffshire," a village in Scotland that was the birthplace of two Canadian Pacific Railway officials.

Banff National Park is an outdoor wonderland, containing over 1,600 kilometers (1,000 miles) of trails, more than any other mountain park. Your dog's list of favorites will include...

* *Fairview Mountain Lookout Trail.* This healthy climb up a forested trail with a steep descent to the South shore of fabled Lake Louise is a good trail to get away from the crush of people you will find in the parking lot. This wide and soft dirt trail narrows as it jaunts along the lake with excellent water access for your dog.

* *Johnston Canyon.* This popular tourist walk uses boardwalks clinging to canyon walls early on; it leads to Lower Falls and Upper Falls and can go further up Johnston Creek into woodlands and meadows.

* *Moraine Lakeshore.* An easy, flat walk along the north shore of Moraine Lake stares into of the Valley of Ten Peaks. The trail stays right on water most of the way. You can also take the dog on the Rockpile with large boulders to scramble on at east end of lake.

* *Mistaya Canyon.* This short, paved descent into a limestone gorge sculpted

by rushing meltwaters of Mistaya River is worth having to navigate your dog through the tourists.

   * *Parker Ridge.* This is a steep, open climb through rocky tundra that switches 800 feet up the mountain to a treeless ridge with spectacular views of Saskatchewan Glacier. The rocks scattered along the trail contain fossil corals indicative of an ancient seabed.

   * *Sunshine Meadows.* This is a ski area accessed by shuttle bus. You can walk your dog up the road to the ski lodge and pick up the trails from there. Save this effort for athletic dogs ready for a long, rewarding day on the trail. These trails skip over ridges of the Great Divide, completely above the treeline with flower-filled meadows, eventually leading to Rock Isle Lake and loops around for a trip of several miles.

Banff, Alberta
(403) 762-1550
www.pc.gc.ca/pn-np/ab/banff/index_E.asp

2. Cape Breton Highlands National Park (Nova Scotia)

   Stretching from coast-to-coast across the northern tip of Cape Breton Island, the national park embraces 366 square miles of highland wilderness and dramatic coastlines. Cape Breton Highlands is known for its scenic kinship with the coastal regions of Scotland. The Cabot Trail, one of the world's great driving roads, tickles the edges of the park from the eastern shore to the western sea and travels along the picturesque Margaree Valley in the south. When the Canadian government decided to establish the first national park in the Atlantic provinces, Cape Breton Highlands was a natural choice.

   Dog owners accustomed to the restrictive policies of American national parks will encounter a dog-friendly paradise at Cape Breton Highlands. Of the 26 marked and named hiking trails in the park only one, the *Skyline Trail*, is off-limits to dogs. (This trail, restricted due to heavy concentration of moose, is a flat two-mile walk to exposed headland cliffs and well-worth giving the dog a rest in the car in the normally cool weather). Some of the highlights include:

   * *L'Acadien Trail.* The marquee trail of the park's west side, the 6-mile loop climbs steadily beside the Robert Brook to an elevation over 1,000 feet to a windswept landscape of stunted trees and panoramic views of the Gulf of St. Lawrence coast to the west and the highlands to the east.

   * *Bog Trail.* A chance to stop and experience the interior plateau of the park,

this trail is a half-mile boardwalk around a nutrient-starved alpine bog where specialized plants, including several carnivorous ones, have adapted to a hostile life.

 * *Lone Shieling.* This is a quiet half-mile descent into a 300-year old hardwood forest where more than 90% of the trees are vibrant sugar maples. Highlights include a replica of a Scottish sheep-crofter's hut and a roiling stream that makes an excellent doggie whirlpool.

 * *Coastal.* A short wooded hike leads to a generally deserted sandy beach for good Atlantic Ocean dog swimming (dogs are not allowed at the main swimming beach in Cape Breton Highlands National Park) and then heads along the coast for three miles. A good place to turn around on this linear trek is a large beach covered with smooth, egg-shaped cobbles.

 * *Jack Pine.* This 1.7-mile loop travels through a forest of pioneering jack pines that grow tenaciously on the hard rocky surface and pops out onto the rocky Atlantic coast where your dog will be treated to impressive blowholes.

 * *Franey.* One of the star trails on Cape Breton, the Franey trail climbs 366 meters (almost 1200 feet) in 3 kilometers, ending on rocky summits with the best overlooks of the Atlantic Ocean, Middle Head and Ignonish Beach. The descent is totally on an old access road and uninspiring in comparison.

 * *Middle Head.* An easy-walking 2.5-mile loop leads out into the Atlantic Ocean where spruce woodlands give way to grassy headlands. You'll get surf and mountain views on both sides of the loop.

 Cape Breton Highlands National Park is home to the Highland Links, a masterpiece by legendary course designer Stanley Thompson. He called this 1939 creation his "mountains and ocean course" and is often ranked the top golf course in Canada. Since it is in the national park, the same rules apply for the golf course as the hiking trails and your dog is welcome to join your foursome as you play.

Ignonish Beach, Nova Scotia
(902) 224-2306
www.pc.gc.ca/pn-np/ns/cbreton/index_E.asp

3. Forillon National Park (Quebec)

 Jacques Cartier sailed along the snakehead-shaped Gaspé Peninsula in 1534 to claim the territory for France. Named for the Mi'kmaq Indian word meaning "land's end," the Appalachian Mountains tumble into the sea in Forillon National Park on the peninsula's northeast tip.

Dogs are welcome on all nine trails across Forillon's 95 square miles. The marquee walk is *Les Graves Trail*, a linear route that can be accessed by car at several points along its 8.9 kilometers. It bounds along Gaspé Bay through light forests and meadows, drops onto sandy beach coves for canine swimming and passes through Grande-Grove National Historic Site where the homestead of generations of fisherman-farmers is preserved. The route also tracks through two historic cemeteries.

Les Graves Trail then climbs into the thick forest and finishes up on the last steps of the *International Appalachian Trail* that ends (or begins) its 4,555-kilometer journey at the very tip of Cap-Gaspé after beginning in Georgia. At the very end of *Les Graves Trail* another trail leads downhill for a kilometer to a small observation deck where you can see the very end of the Appalachian Mountains as the world's oldest mountain range cascades beneath the sea. In the waters off-shore you and your dog can watch some of the seven species of whales that haunt the region and maybe spy a harbor seal on the rocks.

The *Mont-Saint Alban Trail* visits both sides of the peninsula in its 8.5-kilometer loop ("boucle" in French) and passes an 80-foot high observation tower. The tower, whose wide steps can be climbed by a dog, overlooks the Gulf of St. Lawrence with a 360-degree view. Although named for the waterfall traversed top and bottom by the trail boardwalk, *La Chute Trail* is actually worth a visit more for its vibrant maple forest than the tumbling waters.

Gaspé, Quebec
(418) 368-5505
www.pc.gc.ca/pn-np/qc/forillon/index_E.asp

4. Fundy National Park (New Brunswick)

Fundy National Park was created to protect an 80-square mile swath of the Maritime Acadian Highlands. This is an area where the deep green forests of the Caledonia Highlands sweep across a rolling plateau to reach the highest tides in the world at the Bay of Fundy. You can watch the water level change as much as 40 feet between low and high tides.

Fundy National Park features 25 dog-friendly trails, most of which are quite sporty. The trails are broken out for canine hikers by the natural features they highlight: coastal trails, waterfall trails, river valley trails, forest trails and lake trails. Only a handful loop, although there are many combinations to be crafted to create ambitious journeys with your dog. The Fundy Circuit links seven hiking trails and covers 30 miles, including four campsites.

While the big attraction of Fundy is its great tides, most of the trails offer only sporadic views of the famous bay. Some of the best come on the *Matthews Head Trail*, a 3-mile loop that begins and ends in open meadow and in between dips into thick red spruce forests. Nearby is the eerie *Devil's Half Acre* loop. Its dark mossy crevasses, nooks and crannies are the park's best testament to the region's ultra-moist climate.

Away from the coast, fast-flowing streams have been busy cutting valleys and canyons through the plateau. Look for hardy climbs through hardwood and spruce forests here. Wooden steps have been added on several trails to help out. One, the *Dickson Falls Loop*, is completely built on boardwalk from the top of the falls into a valley cooled by cascading water.

Several beaches are accessible from the trails to experience the phenomenal tides of the Bay of Fundy. The *Point Wolfe Beach Trail* is a short descent to a long beach (at low tide) where your dog can frolic in the receding (or oncoming) waves.

Alma, New Brunswick
(506) 887-6000
www.pc.gc.ca/pn-np/nb/fundy/index_e.asp

5.   Jasper National Park

Fur trader David Thompson explored the Athabasca Pass in 1811 and helped establish Canada's first transcontinental route. The park began in 1907 as Jasper Forest Park, named for longtime trading post clerk Jasper Hawes. In 1930, with the passage of the National Parks Act, Jasper became an official national park. It is the largest of Canada's four Rocky Mountain national parks - there are 660 miles of trails in more than 400 square miles. Located on the eastern slope of the Continental Divide, the landscape is characterized by plunging valleys, deep forests and broad alpine meadows.

Dogs are allowed throughout this magnificent park - even crowded trails, such as the dirt Maligne Canyon footpath up the limestone gorge carved by the Maligne River. Canine hikers can bypass the multitudes on the return trip by crossing the gorge on roads at either end and using an unblazed trail on the opposite side.

Mountain climbing dogs will pant over *Whistlers Trail*, a steep and narrow route that gains 4,000 feet in elevation to unobstructed views of the Miette

Valley and Athabasca Valley high above the treeline. Near the town of Jasper
is an extensive trail system leading to Pyramid Lake and Patricia Lake; a wide
climb from the back of the town leads to overlooks from Pyramid Bench, and
another convenient canine hike is the Valley of Five Lakes. After walking through
a lodgepole pine forest and across a boardwalk through Wabasso Creek wetlands,
this trail loops around a series of secluded bluegreen lakes, each a different depth
and hue.

South of the park, and on the road to Banff, is Athabasca Glacier, the most
accessible glacier in North America. A short, barren walk on the *Forefield Trail*
will take you and the dog to the toe of the glacier in the Columbia Icefield. The
Columbia Icefield is the hydrographic apex of the continent where water flows to
three different oceans from a single point.

Jasper, Alberta
(780) 852-6176
www.pc.gc.ca/pn-np/ab/jasper/index_e.asp

6. Prince Edward Island National Park (Prince Edward Island)

Lucy Maud Montgomery introduced the world to the Cavendish region of
Prince Edward Island in her much-beloved coming-of-age tale, Anne of Green
Gables. Montgomery waxed rhapsodic over the Cavendish shoreline on the Gulf
of St. Lawrence, calling the sandy beaches framed in red sandstone the prettiest
in the world. Many visitors since the book's publication in 1908 have agreed with
her.

Canada established Prince Edward Island National Park in 1937, preserving
forever 25 miles of the island's north shore. In addition to protecting salt marshes,
sandstone cliffs, dune-fringed beaches and Acadian woodlands, the park service
oversees the original Green Gables House of Montgomery's childhood. She came
here at the age of 21 months to live with her grandparents. Further east, a separate
section of the park was established on the western tip of Greenwich, a peninsula
that separates St. Peters Bay from the Gulf of St. Lawrence. Here, a rare parabolic
sand dune sweeps along the coast inundating forests and leaving blanched, skeletal
remains in its wake.

There are 11 trails at Prince Edward Island National Park, ten of which
welcome dogs. Dogs can also visit park beaches but must wait until the off-season
on October 15. All of the hiking on these trails is easy going - the elevation in
the park tops out at 160 feet. The longest of the walks at Prince Edward Island is

Homestead, kicking off just outside the campground. It is a stacked loop of either 3.4 miles or 5 miles that plunges into woodlands before emerging on open paths along New London Bay. Driving across the island the urge to stop the car and romp across the impossibly green fields will grow steadily and this trail will satiate that yearning. Most of this land was cleared by 1900 for farms, stripping the original Acadian forest mix of hardwood and softwood species.

Trails through the regenerating forests can be enjoyed in the Brackley section of the park. Also here is a quiet trip along the *Reeds and Rushes Trail* into the heart of a vibrant salt water marsh community. Dogs are barred from the main *Greenwich Dunes Trail* but you can get a brief feel of the power of the shifting sands in a parabolic dune on the adjacent *Tlagatik Loop*. Out in the warm waters of St. Peters Bay you can see the oyster lines of aquafarmers.

Cavendish, Prince Edward Island
(902) 672-6350
www.pc.gc.ca/pn-np/pe/pei-ipe/index_e.asp

DESTINATION
IDEA #4: DOGGIN' AMERICA'S NATIONAL RECREATION AREAS

National parks are created with the dual missions of preservation and education. Dogs do not fit easily into that equation. More appropriate destinations across the American landscape for dog owners are the national recreation areas that are lands set aside for boating, hiking, off-roading and more. Here are five great choices for your dog...

Big South Fork National Recreation Area (Tennessee/Kentucky)

Flowing north from Tennessee into Kentucky, the Big South Fork of the Cumberland River and its tributaries have been carving up the Cumberland Plateau into cliffs, natural arches and rock shelters for tens of thousands of years. In 1974 Congress placed 123,000 acres of wilderness under the management of the National Park Service in the Big South Fork National River and Recreation Area. The centerpiece of the park is the Big South Fork River with 90 miles of free-flowing, navigable water through gorges and valleys.

Straddling the Tennessee-Kentucky border, the 150 miles of hiking trails through mixed hardwood and pine forests are uncrowded - in stark contrast to Great Smokey Mountains National Park, America's most-visited national park (where dogs are not allowed on trails), to the southeast.

Save for the 6.5-mile *Blue Heron Loop*, the top hikes at Big South Fork are in the Tennessee portion of the park near the Bandy Creek Visitor Center. At the Visitor Center is the *Oscar Blevin Trail*, an easy 3.2-ramble loop through mature forest to an historic farmstead that was worked until the National Park Service took over into 1974.

To the east of Bandy Creek is the Leatherwood Ford, the trailhead for the popular *Angel Falls Trail*, a small segment of the *John Muir Trail* which stretches 50 miles across the park. This easy two-miler along the west bank of the Big South Fork Cumberland River winds to the top of a limestone bluff with a commanding view of Angel Falls, actually a series of rapids. The cliffs are unprotected but the climb can be negotiated by an agile dog.

In the remote western region of Big South Fork National River and Recreation Area are a sandstone double archway known as the Twin Arches. A short, but hardy, trek of less than a mile leads to the largest natural sandstone bridges in Tennessee. Rock shelters like these deep in the woods were once popular harbors for moonshine stills and old still equipment is on display in the park.

Oneida, Tennessee
(423) 569-9778
www.nps.gov/biso/

Chattahoochee River National Recreation Area (Georgia)

Most rivers meander and change course over time but the Chattahoochee River is locked in place by the 320-mile Brevard Fault that divides the Appalachian Mountains and the Piedmont Plateau. President Jimmy Carter created the Chattahoochee River National Recreation Area (NRA) in his home state to protect 48 miles of the slow-moving waters south of Lake Lanier. Today the 4,100-acre preserve is one of the most popular destinations in the national park system, attracting more than three million visitors each year.

Two visitor centers, Paces Mill at the southern access and Island Ford near the center, service the Chattahoochee River NRA's 14 land units and more than 50 miles of trails. Much of the canine hiking on these day-use trails is easy, through meadows and wooded gorges along the river. Expect a cool swim for your dog when she plunges in - the water temperature rarely warms to more than 50 degrees. One of the premier hikes is the *Jones Bridge Trail*, a 2.6-mile jaunt that hugs the Chattahoochee for most of its length before ascending a small ridge.

Sandy Springs, Georgia
(678) 538-1200
www.nps.gov/chat/

Delaware Water Gap National Recreation Area (Pennsylvania)

The Delaware Water Gap, a mile-wide break in the spine of the Appalachian Mountains, is renowned for its depth, width and memorable beauty. Travelers and settlers have long taken advantage of the breach, caused by a combination of continental drift, ages of mountain building and the relentless action of determined rivers. A 40-mile stretch of the Delaware River, one of the last free-flowing rivers in the eastern United States, was declared a National Recreation Area in 1965. More than five million people come each year to explore the park's 70,000 acres.

Sixty miles of trails are available to satisfy any taste in canine hiking - dogs are welcome on all trails and most anywhere in the park, save for the beach areas. On the Pennsylvania side of the Delaware River are a variety of shorter trails leading to hemlock-filled ravines and waterfalls. In New Jersey, the going is more strenuous. Day hikers can travel along 25 miles of the *Appalachian Trail* that skirts the Kittatinny Ridge and passes Sunfish Pond, one of New Jersey's "7 Natural Wonders."

Challenging canine hiking awaits at the southern end of the park where the Delaware River courses through the Gap. In Pennsylvania an old fire road climbs more than 1,000 feet to the top of 1,463-foot Mt. Minsi. The hike can be combined with the *Appalachian Trail* to form a four-mile loop. Its New Jersey twin, 1,527-foot Mt. Tammany, is ascended from the parking lot by the twisting *Red Dot Trail* that switches steeply up the rocky slopes for 1.5 miles. Both peaks serve up superlative views of the Delaware Water Gap below. A trail system leads off Mt. Tammany to join the *Appalachian Trail* where your dog can cool off in merry Dunnefield Creek. Trails also take advantage of old railroad lines and historic military roads for easier canine hiking along the Delaware River in the Gap.

Bushkill, Pennsylvania
(570) 828-2253
www.nps.gov/dewa/

Hells Canyon National Recreation Area (Idaho/Oregon)

Along the Idaho-Oregon border the Snake River has carved the continent's deepest gorge. The East Rim of Hells Canyon is 8,043 feet above the river and in places can be 10 miles across from rim to rim. Established in 1975, the Hells Canyon National Recreation Area showcases 652,488 acres of remote, rugged landscape.

The Hells Canyon trail system is extensive - more than 900 miles - but doesn't lend itself easily to day hikes. Trailheads are often at the end of steep, single-lane unimproved roads and many trails are multi-day affairs on both sides of the canyon. The easiest way to hike into Hells Canyon with your dog is to drive up the paved Snake River Road to Hells Canyon Dam. Here, a narrow band of dirt pushes into the canyon downstream from the visitor center. Beware of rattlesnakes that live in the rocky terrain.

The best access to rim trails is on the Idaho side of the gorge at Pittsburgh Landing on Deer Creek Road, Forest Road #493. At the Upper Pittsburg Landing Campground you'll find the trailhead for the *Snake River National Recreation Trail #102*. The path traces the Wild and Scenic Snake River upstream for 26.6 miles to Granite Creek, keeping the water in view during most of the hike. The trail starts at 1,200 feet in elevation and dips down to the shoreline in several places.

Heaven's Gate Overlook at the end of Forest Road #517, where a 660-yard trail climbs sharply to views of Hells Canyon and parts of four states, is a popular jumping off point for hikes into the canyon. Deep in the Seven Devils Mountains, this is the area of highest elevation above the water. *Little Granite Trail* is the shortest route from this alpine country to the Snake River, a steep canine hike of six miles that drops 5,710 feet. Another wilderness trail to try is the 2.1-mile trek to Dry Giggins Lookout, one of the few places above Hells Canyon where you can actually see the Snake River. Your dog will sleep well indeed after a day's exploration of Hells Canyon.

Riggins, Idaho
(208) 628-3916
www.fs.fed.us/hellscanyon/

New River Gorge National River (West Virginia)

Like Greenland, the New River as a geographic name is an oxymoron. This may be the oldest river in North America, flowing in its present course for at least 65 million years. The New River falls 750 feet in 50 miles, creating the best whitewater rafting in the Eastern United States. Your dog won't experience the thrills of riding the New River but she will find a variety of attractions on shore where national parks protect 53 miles of the New River and 72,000 surrounding acres.

An 83-mile driving loop will take you and your dog through a cornucopia of man-made and natural wonders around the New River. Beginning in the north at the Canyon Rim Visitor Center, one of America's most remarkable bridges starts your tour with a bang - the New River Gorge Bridge is the longest steel span in the western hemisphere and the second highest in the United States. On the south side of the gorge the *Kaymoor Miners Trail* descends steeply to an abandoned coal mine. To reach the river level your dog must bound down 820 steps along the haulage for great swimming before a strenuous return climb.

Traveling to the south, a spur from US 19 leads to the Thurmond Historic District on the river. Once a thriving railroad depot in the heart of the gorge, short interpretive trails now lead to highlights of the virtual ghost town. Be careful when hiking with your dog around the tracks, however, since Chesapeake & Ohio freight trains still rumble through Thurmond.

Turning east on I-64, your next scenic spur leads to Grandview, with wooded trails culminating in panoramic looks down to the New River as it doubles back on itself in a wide parabola. These are easy dirt paths for your dog to amble along radiating out from an expansive picnic area.

A long detour south from I-64 is rewarded by the largest waterfall on the New River - Sandstone Falls which tumble across the width of the river. An easy island nature trail gives your dog plenty of chances for a doggie dip. Also on this detour is the impressive Brooks Falls that power over ledges in the riverbed.

Heading back up the east side of the river, your destination of choice is Babcock State Park, one of the oldest parks in West Virginia. Here your dog can enjoy wooded trails and pose in front of a rustic operating grist mill on Glade Creek, one of the most photographed spots in Appalachia.

Glen Jean, West Virginia
(304) 465-0508
www.nps.gov/neri/

TOUR
IDEA #5: DOGGIN' AMERICA'S NATIONAL WILDLIFE REFUGES

One of the reasons often given for keeping dogs off trails in National Parks is that dogs disturb wildlife. So you might be surprised to learn about some of the best lands our federal government maintains where you can hike with your dog - our National Wildlife Refuges.

President Theodore Roosevelt created America's first wildlife refuge on tiny Pelican Island in Florida in 1903 and a hundred years later there are now more than 500 national wildlife refuges. There is at least one in every state and one within an hour's drive of every major city in the country. In fact there are wildlife refuges in two cities: San Francisco and Philadelphia.

While the priority of National Wildlife Refuges is to manage lands for the benefit of wildlife, human visitors are welcome in 98 percent of the refuges. And most will welcome your dog in as well. Not all, so check the U.S. Fish and Wildlife Service for details on specific refuges in the areas you plan to travel - **www.fws.gov/refuges/**.

What can you expect when you take your dog to a National Wildlife Refuge? The first thing you will notice is that you may have the place to yourself - especially if you come in the off-season. I don't know if I've ever seen 10 cars in a National Wildlife Refuge parking lot.

At many refuges you will be hiking with your dog on dirt roads; if there are trails they are typically short and highlight the diversity of the property. You won't often find trails of several hours' duration in a National Wildlife Refuge like are common in many recreation parks.

Don't limit your explorations with your dog to national wildlife refuges. Most states maintain their own conservation departments and have wildlife refuges open to the public. There are plenty of hidden gems for your dog to be discovered here. Here are some examples of what you will encounter when you plan a tour of wildlife refuges with your dog...

Aransas National Wildlife Refuge (Texas)

Aransas is a stronghold for North America's tallest birds with the continent's largest flock of wintering whooping cranes but the 115,000-acre complex is a good example of refuge as park. Bicycling is encouraged here, fishing is allowed and there is even a picnic area with tables and barbecue grills.

Your dog can stretch her legs on several short trails, across varied terrains and ecosystems. The *Heron Flats Trail* meanders from freshwater sloughs to marshy salt flats; while your dog is sniffing relentlessly you can take advantage of observation platforms equipped with telescopes to peek in on wading birds and pelicans. The *Dagger Point Trail* ascends one of the few hills at Aransas on a sandy trail through an oak/redbay forest and looks out over San Antonio Bay. It also touches on the shoreline where your dog can get a refreshing dip. The *Big Tree Trail* is a wide, easy trot for your dog under some of the refuge's largest live oak trees before popping out in a salt marsh that is a prime location for observing whooping cranes from late October to mid-April.

Austwell, Texas
(361) 286-3559
www.fws.gov/refuges/texas/aransas/

Eastern Shore of Virginia National Wildlife Refuge (Virginia)

The Eastern Shore of Virginia National Wildlife Refuge, located at the southern tip of the Delmarva Peninsula, was established in 1984 for migratory and endangered species management and for wildlife oriented recreation. The 1,153 acres of maritime forest, myrtle and bayberry thickets, grasslands, croplands, and fresh and brackish ponds provide important habitat for wildlife.

Canine hiking in the refuge takes place on a pair of wide, grassy trails and lightly traveled sandy dirt park roads providing a pleasing mix of open air hiking and woodsy walking. The half-mile *Interpretive Trail* loops through mixed hardwoods, past an old cemetery, and out to a saltmarsh overlook. The peripatetic *Butterfly Trail* winds through a field of flowers, brambles, grasses and shrubs.

This was once a military installation, part of America's coastal defenses during World II. Traces of its less idyllic past remain and you can scramble to the top of an old bunker with your dog that affords a panoramic view of refuge.

Cape Charles, Virginia
(757) 331-3425
easternshore.fws.gov/

Montezuma National Wildlife Refuge (New York)

The name "Montezuma" was first used in 1806 when Dr. Peter Clark named his hilltop home after the Aztec Emperor Montezuma. Eventually the Marsh, the Village, and the Refuge all acquired the name. The wetlands survived the building of the Erie Canal to its north but the Seneca River was dramatically altered by the expansion of the Cayuga extension to the canal in 1910. The level of the river plunged eight feet and the water drained from the marshes.

In 1937 the Bureau of Biological Survey, which later became the U.S. Fish and Wildlife Service, purchased 6,432 acres of the former marsh and set about building dikes to restore the marsh habitat. In 1938, Montezuma Migratory Bird Refuge was established to provide resting, nesting, and feeding habitat for waterfowl and other migratory birds. Since its opening 320 species of birds have been identified here.

Unlike many wildlife refuges you can hike on more than park roads here. In fact, there is no walking on Wildlife Drive. The marquee dog hike is on the *Esker Brook Nature Trail*, actually a series of three parallel paths that combine into a 1.5-mile loop. Your dog will be trotting along a glacially formed ridge, through a long-gone apple orchard and down to the views across man-made ponds. This is easy going through light woods on natural dirt and gravel footpaths. For a sensuous open-air excursion, guide your dog around the .75-mile *Oxbow Trail* on wide mown paths in a refuge grassland. The route visits the edge of the water where you can see carp in the stream and adjacent canal.

Seneca Falls, New York
(315) 568-5987
www.fws.gov/r5mnwr/

Moosehorn National Wildlife Refuge (Maine)

Moosehorn, near the port of Calais at the mouth of the St. Croix River, is typical of the experience awaiting you when you vacation with your dog in America's wildlife refuges. There is only one former nature trail - an interpretive wooded path of a little over a mile - but there are another 50 miles of dirt roads to wander with your dog. The refuge roads are closed to private vehicles and in the wilderness area, nothing mechanical is allowed on the spiderweb of old logging roads so you get ideal quiet, roomy hiking paths.

This is one of the first National Wildlife Refuges created, back in 1937, shortly after a widespread fire burned large swaths of woodlands. Before that Moosehorn's nearly 30,000 acres were logged not once, but twice. This is one of the northernmost wildlife refuges on the famous Atlantic Flyway migratory route and more than 200 species of birds have been recorded here. A special trail has been carved out for the mottled brown American woodcock, a long-time favorite of birdwatchers who cherish its unique courtship display. In springtime, at dusk, males arrive at "singing grounds" and begin flying in upward spiraling circles before swooping back to earth where they herald their flights in song.

Baring, Maine
9207) 454-7161
www.fws.gov/refuges/profiles/index.cfm?id=53530

Noxubee National Wildlife Refuge (Mississippi)

You may feel like re-checking the entrance sign when you pull into Noxubee National Wildlife Refuge - only 3,000 of the more than 48,000 acres in the refuge are designated as a sanctuary. In fact, one of the big activities here is hunting so pack some day-glow orange for your dog if you arrive during shooting season in November and December when tens of thousands of waterfowl invade the reservoirs, lakes, impoundments and wetlands of the refuge. If you and your dog aren't birdwatchers plan your visit for a different time.

The refuge is saturated with gravelly roads and seven hiking trails, most of comfortable duration. The *Bluff Lake Boardwalk* thrusts across a cypress island to the water's edge and a large cattle egret rookery. The *Morgan Hill Overlook Trail* serves up a demonstration prairie environment and panoramic vistas. The star canine hike at Noxubee is the four-mile round trip through bottomland hardwoods on the *Trail of Big Trees*. The destination is a sobering visit to a former National Champion Shumard oak tree recently felled by the wind. Hurricanes Katrina and Rita felled many trees in this wilderness area - no management within the past 80 years - so check on trail clearance before you set off.

Oh, in addition to being free, with a variety of interesting, uncrowded trails, your well-behaved dog can trot off-leash under voice control. Who says the federal government can't be welcoming to dogs?

Brooksville, Mississippi
(662) 323-5548
www.fws.gov/Refuges/profiles/index.cfm?id=43620

Prime Hook National Wildlife Refuge (Delaware)

When Dutch settlers first pushed onto these shores nearly 400 years ago they discovered an abundance of purple beach plums and named that area Priume Hoek, meaning "Plum Point." In 1963, the United States Fish & Wildlife Service created the refuge to protect more than 10,000 acres of fresh and saltwater wetlands from Slaughter Beach to the Broadkill River.

Prime Hook features four walking trails that visit fields, forest and marshlands. All four, located off the main road, can be completed comfortably in an afternoon's visit. The *Pine Grove Trail* follows a serpentine path between Turkle and Fleetwood ponds. The trail is just under one mile long. Up the road is the *Black Farm Trail* that skirts wooded uplands and marshes as it travels around former farm fields. A trail extension leads to a photography blind. This is flat, easy canine hiking. At the park office are two adjoining walks that explore a freshwater marsh. The *Dike Trail* travels atop the spoil from the digging of the Headquarters Ditch straight out for a half-mile and the *Boardwalk Trail* slips across the water after passing by the Morris family cemetery, where eight family members are buried.

The soft pine straw-and leaf surface beneath mature loblolly pines is extremely easy on the paw. And when your dog craves a swim there are few better places than the often deserted Broadkill Beach on the Delaware Bay. Here you'll find deep, soft sand, gentle waves, plenty of driftwood for a game of fetch and a long, sparsely populated beachfront for walks with your dog.

Milton, Delaware
(302) 684-8419
primehook.fws.gov/

DESTINATION
IDEA #6: 10 GREAT STATE PARKS FOR DOGS

Sometimes the best vacation you can take with your dog is to bypass federal lands altogether and head for a state park. State parks are much more welcoming to dogs than their national big brothers but the red carpet is far from universal. Some states don't allow dogs in their campgrounds, for example, and others keep dogs out of certain parks altogether. Hunting for state parks is typically more fertile east of the Mississippi River where the federal government doesn't own as much land as it does out West. Most states do a good job with their websites at describing their parks and rules for dogs but here are 10 you can't miss with...

1. Cumberland Falls State Resort Park (Kentucky)

Cumberland Falls is located west of Corbin (birthplace of Kentucky Fried Chicken) and is the largest waterfall on the Cumberland River. Known as the "Niagara of the South," the thundering waters of Cumberland Falls are 65 feet high and 125 feet in width. When the Cumberland River is at flood stage the width of the falls can quickly expand to 300 feet. The view is dramatic during the day but is truly special at night.

On clear, moonlit evenings during a full moon a moonbow rises across the river from beneath the falls. This is the only place in the Western Hemisphere where this phenomenon occurs and is said to only be duplicated at Victoria Falls in Africa. This truly awesome sight takes place only two days before and two days after the night of a full moon.

Most visitors will observe the moonbow from the viewing platforms built at the Cumberland Falls State Resort Park Visitor Center. But adventurous dog owners will want to go to the other side of the river where *Trail 9* offers some of the best views of the falls. At 1.5 miles, this natural surface trail seems benign enough but if you complete all of *Trail 9* your dog will know he's had a workout.

About a half-mile from the trailhead you get a view of the Cumberland Gorge below the falls. Next comes a spur that drops all the way to the river level and picks its way over rocks to Eagles Fall, a worthy hydrospectacular in its own right. Your dog will be able to play in the plunge pool here so you won't be in any hurry to start back up. The upper trail traces Eagle Creek upstream to a ridge as the hike becomes very rugged in a spectacular forest. The loop closes before reaching Cumberland Falls so your dog will get one last look before a well-earned return to your car.

Cumberland State Falls is one of 17 Kentucky resort parks with expanded facilities. Dogs can't bed down in the lodges or cabins but they are welcome in the campsites. With 17 miles of trails and connectors into the Daniel Boone National Forest and its 500 miles of trails your tent stakes could be planted quite a while here.

Corbin, Kentucky
(606) 528-4121
parks.ky.gov/findparks/resortparks/cf/

2. Custer State Park (South Dakota)

General George Armstrong Custer led an expedition into the Black Hills in 1874, then considered one of the last unexplored regions of the United States. Custer and his men discovered gold and the region was a secret no more. Precious metals are just part of the cornucopia of riches found in the Black Hills. Custer State Park, the largest state park in the Continental United States, is able to support its 73,000 acres without government money. Entrance fees are supplemented by harvesting timber, selling special hunting licenses for unique game like big horn sheep and buffalo, and renting park attractions to private concessionaires. The park's annual buffalo sale can yield $250,000 alone.

The bounty at Custer State Park extends to canine adventurers as well. In the main body of Custer State Park, you will find the French Creek Natural Area at its center. There are no marked trails along this 2,200-acre swath of protected land but paths meander along the creek. There are many stream crossings and the sheer canyon walls narrow practically to the width of a greyhound at one point. One of the biggest attractions in Custer State Park is one of the world's largest free-ranging buffalo herds that grazes on over 18,000 acres of mixed prairie grasslands. The 3-mile hillside *Prairie Trail* off the Wildlife Loop Road is a rolling loop that explodes into a spectacular wildflower display in the summer.

In the summer of 1927, with the White House under renovation, President Calvin Coolidge was looking to get out of hot and buggy Washington. He set up his "Summer White House" in Custer State Park. South Dakota was thrilled to have him and went overboard in welcoming the Coolidges. They showered the First Couple with gifts and overstocked the creek with so much trout that the President, a novice fisherman, could scarcely get his line in the water before getting a strike. The Grace Coolidge Creek that spills out of Center Lake is named for the First Lady and features an easy three-mile walk on a dirt path past seven lowhead dams. The Coolidge family loved their pets and historic photographs often feature their white collies, Rob Roy and Prudence Prim. Other dogs in the Presidential menagerie included Blackberry and Tiny Tim - both Chows; Bessie, a Yellow Collie; Boston Beans, a Bulldog; Calamity Jane, a Shetland Sheepdog; Paul Pry, an Airedale; Peter Pan, a Terrier; Ruby Rough, a Brown Collie.

Custer, South Dakota
(605) 255-4515
www.custerstatepark.info/

3. DeSoto State Park (Alabama)

Little River is one of America's longest rivers that spends its entire life atop a mountain. The water begins flowing at 1,900 feet above sea level on Lookout Mountain before rushing off the Cumberland Plateau into Weiss Lake at 650 feet high. Along the way Little River has carved a 12-mile long canyon as deep as

700 feet in places. DeSoto State Park, on the West Fork of the Little River, is the gateway to one of the most impressive canyon landscapes in the Southeast.

Much of the work done to create DeSoto took place during the 1930s when the Civilian Conservation Corps built what was Alabama's largest state park at the time. Most of the structures on the grounds date to that time, including a magnificent stone bridge that was unfinished due to the outbreak of World War II. Equally impressive is nature's handiwork atop Lookout Mountain, including the powerful 100-foot plunge of DeSoto Falls, north of the main park. Several looping hiking trails lead your dog past additional waterfalls such as the Azaela Cascade, Lost Falls and Laurel Falls. Lost Falls in particular, reached via the *Blue Trail* or *Orange Trail*, has a delightful plunge pool where your dog can swim.

Little River Canyon is experienced mostly from overlooks on an 11-mile scenic road along the west rim. Hiking into the canyon is possible down steep, winding paths. Your best choice for this exploration is at Eberhart Point near the center of the canyon road. When accessible a day-use area at Canyon Mouth supports excursions into the lower canyon with its impressive rapids and boulder fields.

Fort Payne, Alabama
(256) 845-5380
www.desotostatepark.com/

4. First Landing State Park (Virginia)

It has been almost 400 years now since the first English settlers came ashore here at the bottom of the Chesapeake Bay. The Commonwealth of Virginia obtained more than 2,000 acres near Cape Henry in 1933 at the cost of $157,000. Depression-era public work programs set out to shape the land into the park that was dedicated in 1936. In 1965, First Landing State Park was included in the National Register of Natural Landmarks as the northernmost location on the East Coast where subtropical and temperate plants grow and thrive together.

The trail system, designated as part of the National Recreation Trail System, features 19 miles of dog-friendly hiking. The marquee walk is the *Bald Cypress Trail* that circles a cypress swamp for 1.5 miles, much of the way on elevated boardwalks. Airborne Spanish moss drapes many of the ancient giants. Looping off that path is the 3.1-mile blue *Osmanthus Trail*, named for the American olive tree that grows abundantly on the fringes of the dark lagoon along the trail. Another worthwhile detour is the quarter-mile *High Dune Trail* that uses wooden sleeper-steps to ascend a steep, wooded dune. It is easy walking for your dog on these packed sand and soft dirt trails that are further cushioned to the paw by pine straw from towering loblolly pines. There are gentle undulations that spice up the flat canine hiking along the eight hiker-only trails and the 6-mile *Cape Henry multi-use trail.*

First Landing State Park stretches to the edge of the Chesapeake Bay where swimming is allowed on unguarded sandy beaches. Dogs are allowed on this beach year-round, the only such Virginia state park allowing dogs in the beach/swimming areas. Just off-shore are views of the Chesapeake Bay Bridge-Tunnel, one of the seven modern engineering marvels of the world. Each span of the 17.6-mile crossing utilizes more than 2,500 concrete piles to support the trestles. Construction of the bridge-tunnel complex required undertaking a project of more than 12 miles of low-level trestles, two 1-mile tunnels, two bridges, almost 2 miles of causeway, four manmade islands and 5-1/2 miles of approach roads, totaling 23 miles.

Virginia Beach, Virginia
(757) 412-2300
www.dcr.virginia.gov/state_parks/fir.shtml

5. Harriman State Park (New York)

As development slowly crept into the Hudson Highlands around the turn of the 20th century, efforts were made to preserve the area but it was not until the State of New York tried to relocate Sing Sing Prison to Bear Mountain - so named for its resemblance to a bear in repose - that conservation forces truly mobilized. Railroad magnate E.H. Harriman and others donated land and vast sums of money to save the Highlands and in 1910 Bear Mountain-Harriman State Park was dedicated. Within five years it was hosting more than one million visitors per year and 100 years later more people come to the state park, New York's second largest, than Yellowstone National Park.

Harriman is one of the best parks around for all-day hikes with your dog - the first segment of America's most famous trail, the *Appalachian Trail* was carved across Bear Mountain in the 1920s. There are more than 200 miles of marked hiking trails through Harriman State Park and many more in adjacent Bear Mountain State Park. Even so, the crush of visitors can be so great that designated hiker-only parking lots fill up quickly. Arrive early or face difficult access to trailheads in good weather.

The *Timp Hike* is a popular introduction to the Hudson Highlands, starting directly on Route 9W that runs along the Hudson River opposite of Jones Point, just south of Bear Mountain. The trailhead is an unpromising break in the weeds just south of the parking lot but things pick up once your dog negotiates the awkward, rocky steps in the early stages of the journey. The hike splits into the *Ramapo-Dunderberg Trail* (red blazes) and *Timp-Torne Trail* (blue blazes). From here, heading up the red trail, you break out to views of the Hudson River and roll up and down mountains through boulder foundations until the Timp, a peak overlooking the interior of the Highlands. Climb back down the Timp and return on the blue trail to complete a rewarding 9-mile loop.

In general, the hiking in the west region of the park is more paw-friendly. Dirt trails move through forests with little understory and long sightlines. The trails crisscross often and there is plenty of up-and-down hiking. It is not unusual to have tagged four or five small peaks in a two-hour trip. Make sure to find a trail map before heading out. Oh, and dogs aren't allowed in park campgrounds so you'll have to leave and come back each day of canine hiking.

Bear Mountain, New York
(845) 786-2701
nysparks.state.ny.us/parks/info.asp?parkID=143

6. Hither Hills State Park (New York)

In 1879, ten years before his death, Arthur W. Benson, of Brooklyn Gas & Light and Bensonhurst fame, purchased 10,000 acres of government land around Montauk for a little more than $15 an acre. He envisioned his new lands as a playground for the rich. A generation later Robert Moses, the visionary New York land planner, saw a different future for Montauk. He wanted a necklace of public parks along the Montauk shores and in 1924 announced plans to condemn 1700 Benson estate acres for the fledgling New York State Parks system. It took a three-year court battle that wound its way to the New York Supreme Court but Moses prevailed. The enduring jewel of his struggle is Hither Hills State Park that stretches from ocean to bay and is the largest state park in Montauk.

For most visitors, Hither Hills is a mile of pristine, dune-backed Atlantic Ocean beach and top-rated campground. With such delights, the 1,755-acre park's interior that stretches to Napeague Bay is often overlooked. All the better for canine hikers, who are not welcome on the beach anyway. Miles of informal sandy trails and jeep roads pick through the pitch pine, scrub oak and beach heather.

Of the marked trails, the long-distance *Paumanok Path* that crosses to Montauk is the most prominent. It can be combined with the *Serpent's Back Trail* and others to form sporty hiking loops that will delight your dog for hours. Expect plenty of ups and downs as you twist through the pine barrens. Highlights include the bass-stuffed Fresh Pond, panoramic overlooks and the sandy/cobbly shore of Napeague Bay. Dogs are not permitted anywhere south of Route 27 including the beach and campground but can hike east of Napeague Harbor and south of Napeague Bay.

Hither Hills is home to the unique walking dunes - 80-foot high piles of sand that are blown more than three feet each year by the strong westerly winds. As the sands shift they completely bury trees and vegetation, eventually moving on and leaving phantom forests of dead trees. A 3/4-mile trail loops through the dunes and giant bowls for you and your dog to explore the bogs and coastal shrubs up close. Further explorations can take place along the shore of Napeague Harbor and around Goff Point. Parking for the Walking Dunes is at the end of Napeague Harbor Road and is limited to a few cars.

Montauk, New York
(631) 668-2554
nysparks.state.ny.us/parks/info.asp?parkID=48

7. Hocking Hills State Park (Ohio)

Much of the bedrock in this area of Ohio was deposited 350 million years ago as the delta of a shallow ancient ocean. The sandstone is of varying hardness that has cracked and eroded into fascinating rock formations and caves. When the first settlers sought shelter in these recesses more than 7,000 years ago they found vegetation deep in the gorges that still hearkened back to the last ice age - stately eastern hemlocks and Canadian yew and birches thriving in the moist, cool environment. The tribes of the Wyandot, Delaware and Shawnee knew the valley as "Hockhocking" for its bottle shape, created when glacial ice plugged the Hocking River. The state of Ohio began preserving this unique natural area in 1924 with a purchase of 146 acres.

Hocking Hills State Park is a superb destination for any dog, but is especially delightful for the canine hiker who is a few hikes beyond those days of the 10-mile treks. There are six distinct areas in the park - five for canine exploring: no dogs are permitted in the Conkles Hollow state nature preserve in the center of

Hocking Hills.

The star of Hocking Hills is Old Man's Cave tucked into a heavily wooded, twisting ravine. The Old Man was Richard Rowe who moved to the area some time around 1796 to establish a trading post. Upon arriving in Hocking Hills he stayed and lived out his life here, traveling with his two dogs in search of game. Rowe is buried beneath the ledge of the main recess cave. An easy, one-mile trail works its way into and around the primeval gorge; wooden steps and bridges smooth the way. Your dog will enjoy a dip in Old Man's Creek, especially in the pool beneath the Upper Falls. Additional attractions near Old Man's Cave are Cedar Falls and Ash Cave. Both can be accessed by car and a short walk from the parking lots. For heartier visitors, a 6-mile trail connects all three natural attractions. There is more great dog-paddling under Cedar Falls and nearby Rose Lake.

In the north sections of Hocking Hills the trails explore impressive cliff formations on trails less than one mile long. Wide and graded with easy footing, your dog makes her way from the rim to the floor at the Rock House and Cantwell Cliffs. The Rock House is a perpendicular cliff that features hollowed-out rooms at the bottom. At Cantwell Cliffs your dog will enjoy navigating through separated pillars of sandstone that have left narrow openings with colorful names like Fat Woman's Squeeze.

Logan, Ohio
(740) 385.6842
www.dnr.state.oh.us/parks/parks/hocking.htm

8. Petit Jean State Park (Arkansas)

This was Arkansas' first state park, a slice of land between the Ozark and Ouachita mountain ranges considered so beautiful it was under consideration to be a national park before being deemed too small. Petit Jean was a young French girl who disguised herself as a cabin boy so she could secretly sail with her lover to America. Once on these shores she fell ill and requested to be buried here before she died.

The park, where dogs are permitted everywhere but in the lodges, is an enchanting mix of eroded bluffs and forested canyons lubricated by Cedar Creek. There are more than 20 miles of trails across more than 2,500 acres but you will likely steer your dog towards the three that have been awarded National Trail designation. The most popular is a one-mile trek down into Cedar Creek Canyon (rock steps and wooden walkways constructed by the Civilian Conservation Corps in the 1930s will ease the journey) that climaxes at Cedar Falls. The wide plunge pool in the rock amphitheater is a perfect spot for your dog to swim under the 94-foot cascade.

The *Seven Hollow Trail* (you actually only visit four) takes your dog from lush hardwood forests to stark, open air rock fields in its 4.5-mile loop. Each hollow on this sporty canine hike has its own delights, from a natural rock bridge to a secluded watery grotto beneath a rock overhang. The *Cedar Creek Trail* launches form the rough hewn pine cabin constructed by John Walker, Petit Jean's first settler, in 1845. This interpretive loop of a few hops over a mile envelops your dog in the thickly vegetated stream corridor.

Morrilton, Arkansas
(501) 727-5441
www.petitjeanstatepark.com/

9. Pickett State Park (Tennessee)

Situated in a remote section of the upper Cumberland Mountains, the 17,000 acres of Pickett State Park and Forest, once owned by the massive Stearns Coal & Lumber Company, became one of Tennessee's earliest state parks in the 1930s. Here are botanical and geological wonders found nowhere else in Tennessee. The Civilian Conservation Corps set up shop in the dark forest during the Depression and crafted enough buildings of locally quarried sandstone that the park is listed on the National Register of Historic Places.

With 58 miles of hiking trails you could hunker down with your dog for a week in these hollows but the attraction of Pickett for most canine adventurers is that most of the more accessible trails are short, ranging from a quarter-mile to three miles so you can sample many of them in a short visit. One of the jewels of Pickett State Park is the *Hidden Passage Trail* that ducks in and out of rock houses and slides past trickling waterfalls. Pickett is a wild place and trail maintenance may be spottier than on the groomed pathways of some parks; also make sure you secure a good map to help with the abundance of spur trails. Other highlights include the 3/4-mile *Lake View Trail* along still, dark green waters accessed by a swinging bridge and the 1.5-mile loop through dense foliage to a memorable conclusion at a natural bridge.

Jamestown, Tennessee
(931) 879-5821
www.state.tn.us/environment/parks/Pickett/

10. Stokes State Forest (New Jersey)

The State of New Jersey began buying land for Stokes Forest in 1907 - sometimes paying a whole dollar an acre. The forest is named for Edward Casper Stokes who served one term as Republican governor from 1905 until 1908, forming the New Jersey Forest Commission during his tenure. He donated the first 500 acres.

After he left office Stokes remained active in politics, failing in three bids to win a U.S. Senate seat and another term as governor. In 2001, lightning struck his mausoleum in the Mount Pleasant Cemetery in Millville. The lightning blasted through the mausoleum's roof and littered the floor with shattered marble, blowing a 6-inch hole in the governor's crypt. His casket was not damaged.

Stokes Forest is the chunk of land between the Delaware Water Gap National Recreation Area to the south and High Point State Park to the north giving New Jersey about 30 miles of uninterrupted parkland along the Kittatinny Ridge of the Appalachian Mountains. Lodged between two more celebrated neighbors, Stokes can sometimes get overlooked. With 25 named trails, that should never happen for canine hikers. Before you start, stop in the office and pick up the best trail guide in New Jersey.

Any type of canine hike is possible here - you could fill up a day just walking on beginner-to-moderate type trails that explore attractive streams, visit old mine sites or just disappear with your dog in a remote patch of woods land. But most visitors will point their dogs in the direction of Kittatinny Ridge and 1,653-foot Sunrise Mountain. Four trails lead to the *Appalachian Trail* atop the ridge in the vicinity of Sunrise Mountain enabling you to create hiking loops of between four and ten miles, depending on how long you want to walk on the ridge soaking in the views. This is absolutely a workout for your dog and the terrain can be rocky - take care especially coming down across large slabs of stone.

To cap off your dog's day at Stokes Forest head to Tillman Ravine for easy walking through a dark, shady evergreen forest of eastern hemlock. The Tillman Brook that carves this moist ravine is one of the prettiest in the state. Unfortunately, dogs are not permitted in the campgrounds so that will be the end of your dog's day at Stoke Forest. Until you come back tomorrow.

Branchville, New Jersey
(973) 948-3820
www.state.nj.us/dep/parksandforests/parks/stokes.html

DESTINATION
IDEA #7: DOGGIN AMERICA'S LARGEST PARK

Adirondack Park was established in 1885 to protect water resources but is now a favorite for lovers of all aspects of the land; trails are under the guidance of the Department of Environmental Conservation. Adirondack Park is the largest park in the lower forty-eight states. Blending public and private lands across its six million acres, the park dwarfs several American states.

Dogs have a long history in the Aidrondacks. 6,000 years ago the Archaic peoples who roamed what would become New York State cherished their dogs enough to bury them with honors—and with humans. Their descendants, the Iroquois, believed that one could share in some of a dog's special powers by loving a dog. They valued the tracking and guarding abilities of their canine companions.

When Europeans moved into the area to live, dogs were depended on to help settlers survive in the oft-time harsh environment. Dogs hunted, herded livestock, guarded homesteads, pulled sleds and even powered unwieldy wooden butter churns on treadmills. It is said the term "vacation" was invented in the Adirondacks in the 1800s when rich New Yorkers "vacated" the heat of the city for the crisp mountain air. When they came they brought their hunting dogs to the grand lodges with them.

Today, it is hard to find an unhappy dog in Adirondack Park. Does your dog love to swim? There are 3,000 ponds and lakes in the region. Does he prefer a walk in the woods? America's largest and most elaborate hiking system featuring more than 2,000 miles of trails allows dogs without restriction, save in the Adirondack Mountain Reserve and in the Ausable Lakes Region. Is your dog not satisfied with a day's outing unless she's looked down from a mountaintop? Try one of the forty-six 4,000-footers in the park. Or launch a canoe, camp under the stars, hike to the remains of an historic lodge, enjoy one of the many dog-friendly outdoor cafes in the Adirondacks...

(518) 523-9258
http://www.visitadirondacks.com/

2

DOGGIN' AMERICA'S WATERS

DOGGIN' AMERICA'S BEACHES

DESTINATION
IDEA #8: 50 GREAT OCEAN BEACHES TO TAKE YOUR DOG

Have you ever noticed how many TV commercials and magazine ads show happy people walking down a beach with their dog? Fast forward to real life. Yes, it is hard to imagine any place a dog is happier than at a beach. Whether running around on the sand, jumping in the water or just lying in the sun, every dog deserves a day at the beach. But all too often dog owners stopping at a sandy stretch of beach are met with signs designed to make hearts - human and canine alike - droop: NO DOGS ON BEACH.

The reality is that about half of the beaches in America never allow dogs on the sand. Most of the rest only allow dogs in the off-season. Whenever you see a lifeguard stand you can assume your dog will not be welcome. But all is not lost. Here, running clockwise from the Northeast around the country, are 50 great places where you can get that dream vacation at the ocean with your dog...

1. Old Orchard Beach, Maine

Maine is known for its rocky coastline, especially in the northern stretches, but the many coves offer small sandy beaches in places. Old Orchard Beach is a classic resort beach with plenty of white sand and a long fishing pier. No dogs allowed on the beach midday during the summer but you don't have to get off the beach until 10:00 a.m.
(207) 934-2500
www.oldorchardbeachmaine.com/

2. Wells, Maine

Wells is a dog-friendly place with several beaches. Drakes Island Beach is a wonderful, secluded choice. In the summer, dogs are allowed only before 8:00 a.m. and after 6:00 p.m. so use that time to explore Maine's famous rocky coast.
(207) 646-5114
www.wellstown.org/

3. York, Maine

At York Harbor Beach you'll find a big, convenient parking lot next to a wide sand beach in a sheltered cove. You have to arrive early or come late in the summer but your dog can play here under voice control.

(207) 363-1000
www.yorkmaine.org/

4. Good Harbor Beach, Massachusetts

The old fishing and shipbuilding towns - Salem, Essex, Marblehead et al - are more famous for their maritime heritage than their beautiful beaches but all your dog will see is sand and water. At Good Harbor Beach in Gloucester the water is shallow and the surf calm - just begging for a thrown stick. She won't see it in the summer, however, no dogs on the beach from Memorial Day to Labor Day around here.

(800) 649-6839
www.ci.gloucester.ma.us/

5. Duxbury Beach, Massachusetts

In the less crowded areas of Duxbury Beach, dogs are allowed on leashes. Stop by Town Hall -- it's on the way to the beach -- with your dog license and get a permit. You'll snag the best nonresident parking by approaching the beach through Marshfield and parking in the lot near the snack shack.

(781) 934-1100
www.town.duxbury.ma.us/

6. Watch Hill Beach, Rhode Island

In the westernmost part of the westernmost town of Rhode Island is a small beach that is always worth a stop. Parking at the beach is for Watch Hill residents only so you may need to park out by the main road and walk down the hill to the sand. As long as you have your dog in walking mode head out for a coastal walk to Napatree Point where you can enjoy a private beach feel much of the year.

www.visitwatchhill.com/

7. Fire Island National Seashore, New York

Fire Island has attracted settlers for centuries, drawn by its bountiful stores of seafood and waterfowl. But by 1964 Fire Island was the only developed barrier island in the United States without any roads and the national seashore was established to keep it that way. Dogs are permitted anywhere on the wide, dune-backed sands between Labor Day and mid-March when driving is also allowed here. If you have a private boat or take a dog-friendly ferry to the interior of 32-mile Fire Island during the summer, dogs are allowed on any non-ocean, non-lifeguarded patch of sand. If the pounding Atlantic surf is too intimidating for your dog, you can also find some sandy access along the Great South Bay.

(631) 687-4750
www.nps.gov/fiis/

8. East Hampton Main Beach, New York

There are five beaches in East Hampton (only three are life-guarded) and Main Beach on Ocean Avenue is perennially ranked among the best beaches in America. Dogs are permitted on the beach before 9:00 am and and after 6:00 p.m. daily from the second Sunday in May through September 30. After that your dog is welcome any time. Access can be problematic - and pricey - for non-residents in any of the Hampton towns in the summer anyway but the deserted sands spread far and wide for your dog in the off-season.

(631) 324-4140
www.town.east-hampton.ny.us/

9. Ditch Plains Beach

This remote beach backed by high bluffs can be reached by hiking through undeveloped Shadmoor State Park or from township parks from Ditch Plains Road off the Montauk Highway. Although there are large cobbles on the beach, this is the last big stretch of Atlantic Ocean sands on the eastern tip of Long Island.

(631) 668-3781
nysparks.state.ny.us/parks/info.asp?parkID=83

10. Asbury Park Beach, New Jersey

Asbury Park was once a seaside resort to rival its southern counterpart Atlantic City. Both fell on hard times; casinos helped revitalize Atlantic City but even Bruce Springsteen couldn't repopulate the deserted streets of Asbury Park. The upshot is that dogs can't go to Atlantic City but they are welcome on this wide, boardwalk-backed beach anytime in the off-season and at select points in-season.

(732) 775-2100
www.cityofasburypark.com/

11. Corson's Inlet State Park, New Jersey

Corson's Inlet was established in 1969 before every last inch of Jersey shorefront became developed. There aren't many places in the Garden State where the public can explore ocean dunes and a maritime forest but Corson's Inlet is one. Even rarer still is to find a dune system that permits dogs but this is the place - from September 16 through March 31 anyway. If your dog finds the excitement of the Atlantic surf too intimidating, walk around the corner and enjoy the expansive crescent beach along the inlet with its calm, inviting waters.

(609) 861-2404
www.state.nj.us/dep/parksandforests/parks/corsons.html

12. Fowler Beach, Delaware

The sand is a little rockier and the beach a little narrower but if you are looking to spend undisturbed days on the beach with your dog come to the small towns of the Delaware Bay. Fowler Beach is one of the best. With no development and backed by dunes, this is the Delaware Bay beach that most resembles an ocean beach. The sloping coastline promotes excellent wave action and you can walk your dog for several solitary hours.

13. Delaware Seashore State Park, Delaware.

Stay away from the swimming beaches and you can bring your dog to this six-mile stretch of undeveloped beach right through the year. Those concrete towers you see on the beach were used during World War II to track German U-boat activity. You can also access the gentle waters of Rehoboth Bay where your dog can walk out a half-mile and scarcely get his tummy wet.

(302) 227-2800
www.destateparks.com/park/delaware-seashore/

14. Assateague Island National Seashore, Maryland.

Miles and miles of undeveloped beach march south out of the campground on this lovely barrier island. Entrance fees are good for one week and your dog is always allowed in the Atlantic Ocean here. When you drive onto the island make sure to turn right - straight ahead is the state park that doesn't even allow dogs out of the car.

(410) 641-1441
www.nps.gov/asis/

15. Virginia Beach, Virginia

You can get your dog on all of Virginia Beach's clean, white sand at some point during the year; after Halloween every grain is open to dogs from Cape Henry to the North Carolina border. In the summer, while you wait for "The Strip" to open for your dog, head around the corner to First Landing State Park where your dog can enjoy the wide sand beach at the mouth of the Chesapeake Bay. Just move your dog down away from the bathhouse.

(800) VA-BEACH
www.vbfun.com/

16. Duck, North Carolina

This could well be the best place in America to rent a vacation beach house with your dog. Arriving onto the Outer Banks most people follow Route 12 south but when others go right you'll turn left to the towns of Duck and Corolla. In Duck your dog can go on the beach year-round under voice control. If it's a long walk you are after, head north.

(252) 255-1234
www.townofduck.com/

17. Crystal Coast, North Carolina

Most towns on Crystal Coast permit dogs on the beach year-round; Emerald Isle has the most parking. At the far eastern end is Fort Macon State Park where the pentagonal coastal defense fort still stands. Your dog can walk through the massive masonry fort and enjoy the best dune-backed beach on the Crystal Coast.
(877) 206-0929
www.crystalcoastnc.org/

18. Topsail Beach, North Carolina

Dog owners will not be disappointed with a vacation rental on this chunk of Cape Fear. Dogs are allowed year-round on the beach and when the summer ends can romp on the sand under voice control. (If you are starting to get the idea that North Carolina just might be the place for a summer vacation at the beach with your dog, you would be right...)
(910) 328-5841
www.topsailbeach.org/

19. Brunswick Islands, North Carolina

When vacationing in these towns just north of the South Carolina border your beach choices for your dog will be limited in the middle of the day but your dog is welcome at either end of the day. After 6:00 p.m. bring your dog to the residential beach of Sunset Beach for a stroll into the setting sun behind the dunes.
(910) 755-5517
www.ncbrunswick.com/

20. Grand Strand, South Carolina

Your dog isn't allowed in Myrtle Beach proper - 34 blocks worth - but you didn't think she would be did you? Just south of town you'll find two state parks your dog will love. At Myrtle Beach State Park, South Carolina's oldest, there is over one mile of dune-backed sand where your dog can relax and a 100-acre maritime forest for trail time. A bit further down Route 17 some of the money from the original Transcontinental Railroad dribbled down to the magnificent surfside estate built here in the early 20th century. Today, head for the northern section of Huntington Beach State Park for long walks on the beach with your dog.

(843) 626-7444
www.VisitMyrtleBeach.com

21. Edisto Beach, South Carolina

The fame of Edisto Island cotton spread far and wide. It is stated that at one time the Vatican insisted that the Pope's garments be made only from "Sea Island Cotton." The Boll Weevil and the Civil War tag-teamed the destruction of the cotton fields and after that development slowed to a crawl. So today the Edisto Beach State Park maintains 1.5 miles of Atlantic Ocean beachfront, backed by some of the Palmetto State's tallest trademark trees. The beach is wide with plenty of room for your dog to stretch out for a hike. And if that isn't enough sand time, the park adjoins Edisto Beach that has remained a residential beach so your dog can just keep going.

(843)869-2756
www.edistobeach.com/

22. Fernandina Beach, Florida

Florida ranks among the most dog-unfriendly of states. Entire counties and regions ban dogs from the beach. So if you are driving south to vacation in Florida you will want to get your dog onto the sand as soon as possible. This residential/vacation beach will fill the bill nicely. It will get dreary for dogs along the Atlantic Ocean soon enough.

(904) 261-2440
www.ameliaisland.com/

23. Sombrero Beach, Florida

A vacation in the Florida Keys is a mixed bag for dog owners. The dog beach in Key West can scarcely fit a pair of Golden Retrievers onto its meager sands. Unlike the mainland Florida coast the Keys are not mile after mile of sandy beach. The coastline instead is pockmarked by mangrove swamps and rocky reefs. Not that you can't find a pretty stretch of sand beach - one of the best is Sombrero Beach in Marathon, on the Atlantic Ocean side at Mile Marker 50 near the Seven-Mile Bridge. The wide beach is framed by palm trees whose only downside is that they don't drop any branches for your dog to fetch in the clear emerald waters. The soft sands extend far into the water so you can join your dog in the gentle surf. Even the beach sand is special. Pick up a handful. Looking closely, you'll see it comes in many shapes. Some grains look like bits of oatmeal, other like miniature deer antlers. Fashioned by special algae which thrive in Marathon's warm waters, these specks contribute much of the sea bottom and beaches surrounding the Keys.

(305) 292-4560
thefloridakeys.com/parks/sombrero.htm

24. Fort DeSoto Park, Florida

Fort DeSoto was named "America's Best Beach" by Dr. Beach in 2005. Your dog can't actually go on that champion Gulf of Mexico beach but around the corner there is an enormous dog park and paw-friendly groomed sand on Tampa Bay. There are even doggie showers to spruce up a bit before you head home.

(727) 582-2267
www.pinellascounty.org/park/05_Ft_Desoto.htm

25. Bonita Beach, Florida

Dog lovers vacationing on Florida's Suncoast will want to stitch directions to Bonita Beach into their dog's collar. A short walk through the trees leads to a long beach and shallow, gentle water on the Gulf of Mexico - and it is just for dogs. look for the well-marked turn-off for the dog beach off the main drag.

(239) 992-5011
bonitasprings.com/beaches/bonita_beach/

26. Brohard Park, Florida

Slowly - but surely - some Florida communities are coming to realize that opening just a few grains of sand to dogs is not the onset of the Apocalypse. Sarasota County is at the forefront of the movement with four tail-friendly beaches> "paw Beach" at Brohard Park is the most popular with a grassy area, shade, water bowls, dog washing stations, and a fenced run for small dogs.

(941) 861-5000
www.scgov.net/

27. Honeymoon Island State Park, Florida

Pioneers called this place "Hog Island" but a New York developer built 50 palm-thatched bungalows in 1939 and somehow persuaded honeymooners to come down despite the unfortunate monicker. Your dog is likely to fall in love as well with the sun-drenched Gulf of Mexico Pet Beach inside the state park.

(727) 469-5942
www.floridastateparks.org/honeymoonisland/

28. St. George Island State Park, Florida

With foresight the State of Florida began buying up land on the eastern tip of St. George Island before the Patton Bridge brought recreation seekers from the mainland in 1965. You can find spots among the salt marshes and dunes covered in sea oats along St. George Sound where water does not equal the beach and dogs are allowed.

(850) 927-2111
www.floridastateparks.org/stgeorgeisland

29. St. Joseph Peninsula State Park

This lengthy sand spit extending out from Cape San Bias is one of America's truly great white sand beaches, but your dog will never see it. Not allowed in the campground or wilderness preserve either. But there is still plenty of room for your dog to stretch out on the white sand trails along St. Joseph Bay where she can find a swim in the water.

(850) 227-1327
www.floridastateparks.org/stjoseph

29. St. Andrew's State Park

Another award-winning beach your dog can't enjoy. But bring your dog anyway. Only when you pull into the park, turn left when everyone else goes straight for the beach parking lot. Your destination is the mostly ignored Grand Lagoon side of the park you and your dog can enjoy a narrow strip of sand and leisurely swimming in the shallow, gentle waters. The Grand Lagoon is reached by the *Heron Pond Trail*, a rolling exploration of the scrubby dunes. In the town of

nearby Panama City your dog can dip a toe into the Gulf of Mexico at the Pier Park dog beach.
www.floridastateparks.org/StAndrews/

31. Dauphin Island, Alabama

Dauphin Island is your go-to beach destination with your dog between Florida and Texas. The beaches start to the west of Highway 193 on the island and it is mere seconds from parking lot to wide expanses of white sand. Walking east along the shore you will soon enough find low-lying dunes and the calm waters of a back bay where your dog will be sharing the water with windsurfers. If the city beach gets too crowded try the scruffy gray sands of the beach behind Fort Gaines at the eastern tip of the island. The only beach that bans dogs on Dauphin Island is all the way at the West End where folks have to pay for the disappointment of not bring their dogs.
(251) 861-3607
www.dauphinisland.org/

32. Hancock County, Mississippi

This is the highest point along the Gulf Coast but at 12 feet the beaches were no match for the 30-foot storm surge of Hurricane Katrina that made its final landfall here in 2005 and obliterated the towns of Bay St. Louis and Waveland. Recovery is measured in years but the miles of paw-friendly beach are still there, backed by a concrete sidewalk that runs along the shore.
(228) 463-9222
www.mswestcoast.org/

33. Grand Isle State Park, Louisiana

People don't seek out Louisiana for its sandy beaches, most of the coastline is made up of bayous. Grand Isle has a beach but it is not the manicured sand that attracts sunbathers - which means it is ideal for dogs. Bring plenty of bug spray for the squadrons of mosquitoes - and don't forget to spray your best traveling companion as well.
(985) 787-2559
www.crt.state.la.us/Parks/igrdisle.aspx

34. Bolivar Peninsula, Texas

On the 27 miles of Bolivar Peninsula plenty of open beach await your dog; check in at the towns of Bolivar and Crystal Beach if you require civilization. Unfortunately that will not be as easy as before 2008 when Hurricane Ike roared ashore across the peninsula. In the good times these hard-packed sands are open to vehicles as well as dogs so with a permit you can just set up camp right on the beach.

(409) 684-4929
www.bolivarpeninsula.com/

35. Galveston Island, Texas

In the eclectic town of Galveston your dog is also welcome on the beach. The sand in front of the breakwater is not the prettiest but your dog certainly won't mind. Since the surf is gentle most of the time it is hard to imagine this was the site of America's worst natural disaster when more than 6,000 people died in the aftermath of a storm on September 8-9, 1900. The oldest part of the 10-mile seawall built to protect the city is still visible from 6th Street to 39th Street and dates to 1902. Don't expect any open dunes here - the island is almost completely developed. On the north end your dog can visit Stewart Beach Park and to the south there is beach access through the rental houses, especially at the three "pocket parks."

(888) 425-4753
www.galveston.com/

36. Mustang Island, Texas

Everything that Galveston Island is not, Mustang Island is - one of the few undeveloped barrier islands on the entire Texas Gulf Coast. Five miles of sandy beach are backed by dunes as high as thirty feet. There is no driving allowed on the hard sand here so this is one of the best places for beach-combing with your dog in Texas. The namesake wild horses have been gone from the island since the late 1800s but plenty of other critters make their homes here. If you don't catch a glimpse of the coyotes, jackrabbits or one of the 400 bird species that have been recorded here, look for tracks in the sand.

(361) 749-5246
www.tpwd.state.tx.us/spdest/findadest/parks/mustang_island/

37. Padre Island National Seashore

Padre Island is America's longest barrier island and the world's largest undeveloped barrier island. For most of the time here the only inhabitants were range animals.- There is plenty of room for dogs to roam on its 113 miles of sand; with 4-wheel drive you can access the 60 northern miles. The only place your dog can't go is directly around the Malaquite Visitor Center. Certainly one of the best places to vacation with a dog anywhere, and absolutely the destination of choice when you want to camp directly on the Gulf of Mexico; stays are limited to 14 consecutive days.

(361) 949-8068
www.nps.gov/pais/

38. San Diego Dog Beach (North Ocean Beach), California

Southern California is not the place to vacation with a beach-loving dog (remember that "rule" about people beaches equaling "no dogs"). When you are practically the only beach within a short drive of 20 million people that allows dogs you can expect to be busy and city officials estimate that as many as 10,000 dogs visit each week. With 38 acres at the north end of Ocean Beach, Dog Beach is the second largest leash-free beach for dogs in America.

www.oceanbeach.com/

39. Huntington Dog Beach, California

Less than an hour south of Los Angeles and only 10 miles from Disneyland in Anaheim, Dog Beach is located on Pacific Coast Highway between 21st Street and Seapoint Street. One mile of golden sands and Pacific Ocean waves have been set aside for Dog Beach, a rare chance for your dog to frolic in the SoCal saltwater.

www.dogbeach.org/

40. Pismo Beach, California

A good, hassle-free beach to bring your dog on the Central Coast. When you see trucks lining up to drive on the beach, you can assume no one is going to much mind about your dog. Convenient parking in town as well.

(805) 773-4657
www.pismobeach.org/

41. Pfeiffer Beach, California

The Big Sur coastline south of the Monterey Peninsula is a must-see for any
traveler. A string of state parks provides the best access to seascapes that Robert
Louis Stevenson described famously as "the greatest meeting of land and sea in
the world." Your dog, sadly, will not be able to confirm that since the Big Sur
state parks ban dogs for the most part. But Big Sur is not a complete washout for
dog lovers. A short, sandy trail leads to Pfeiffer Beach, one of the most beautiful
public beaches in California. The sand is wrapped in spectacular rock formations
making this a very secluded beach indeed. The rocks are sprinkled in the surf
as well, forming coves and making for exciting play in the waves for dogs. The
turn-off from Highway 1 is obscured and easy to miss on the crest of a hill so be
diligent when seeking out Pfeiffer Beach.

(831) 667-2100
www.bigsurcalifornia.org/beaches.html

42. Carmel-by-the-Sea, California

You will never find a more dog-friendly beach than Carmel Beach where dogs
and people mingle freely on soft white sand. This is the biggest beach among the
craggy headlands of Monterey Peninsula. Dogs are also welcome on Carmel River
State Beach at the east end of town. Along famous 17-Mile Drive your dog can
enjoy small cove-like sand at Fanshell Beach and Sand Beach.

(831) 620-2000
www.carmelcalifornia.com/

43. Point Reyes National Seashore, California

You just can't hit the beach with your dog at the national seashore - there are
restrictions for the snowy plover at certain times and elephant seal mating at other
times but there is also plenty of open sand and interesting terrain around the
peninsula for your dog.

(415) 464-5100
www.nps.gov/pore/

44. Crescent Beach, California

Dogs aren't allowed to poke around popular Redwoods National Park too much but they are allowed on this wide semi-circle of sand. The waves in the broad cove usually lap softly onto the shore but this was the site of a tsunami that wrecked Crescent City in 1964. A century earlier, the side-wheeler Brother Jonathan struck a submerged rock spire known as the "Dragon's Teeth." Lifeboats were deployed but only one made it to shore with 19 survivors. The loss of 215 lives remains the worst maritime disaster in California history.

(707) 464-7483
www.crescentcity.org/

45. Gold Beach, Oregon

The wild and scenic Rogue River is on the radar for every outdoorsman. Gold Beach, where the Rogue reaches the Pacific Ocean is noted for its clean sands. Your dog can help with the beach-combing in the state recreation area.

(800) 525-2334
www.goldbeach.org/

46. Sunset Bay State Park, Oregon

Dog's choice here: swimming from beautiful sandy beaches under rugged sandstone cliffs or scenic walks through pristine coastal forests atop the headlands.

(541) 888-4902
www.oregonstateparks.org/park_100.php

47. Jessie M. Honeyman Memorial State Park, Oregon

There are two miles of sand dunes between the park and the ocean; if you come in March look for whales out in the Pacific from the ridgetops. Your dog can also enjoy two natural lakes in the park that sports the second largest campground in Oregon.

(541) 997-3641
www.oregonstateparks.org/park_134.php

48. Long Beach Peninsula, Washington

The uncrowded Pacific Coast beaches of Washington are some of the dog-
friendliest in America for a vacation - even Olympic National Park, which bans
dogs from almost all of its 632,324 acres, opens some of its remote coastal beaches
to dogs. On Long Beach Peninsula you will find miles of wide open sand and
county officials who promise not to enforce leash laws on the beach providing
your dog is well-behaved. Now that is a deal all dog owners can live with!
(360) 642-2400
www.funbeach.com/

49. Grayland Beach, Washington

No resorts, no bustling beach towns here - just about a mile-and-a-half of
uncrowded, impossibly wide sand beaches. The sand is so wide the exhausted
waves give up long before breaking on shore so any level of canine swimmer will
find fun here. You can settle into the state park campground (no dogs in the
swimming beach) or park near one of the public beaches on the surrounding
Cranberry Coast and walk west.
(800) 473-6018
http://www.cranberrycoastcoc.com/

50. Kalaloch Beaches, Washington

You shouldn't have to go to the corners of the country just to vacation on the
beach with your dog but you'll want to come to the northwest coast of the
Olympic Peninsula. The Kalaloch Beaches and Ruby Beach on US 101 are the
most accessible but you may want to seek out even more remote beaches for your
dog in the Olympic Wilderness. Some consist of deep, soft sand; others of the
more pebbly variety. Keep an eye out from giant driftwood logs the surf can bring
in. Great for whale watching, beach-combing, dog walking and sunsets. After
coming all this way, you won't want to leave in a hurry - and you won't have to.
Dogs are allowed to stay in the cabins at Kalaloch Lodge.
(800) 443-6757
www.forkswa.com/5day/hohforest.html

DESTINATION
IDEA #9: 10 GREAT GREAT LAKES BEACHES TO TAKE YOUR DOG

Your dog might not agree they are "great lakes" when she discovers that dogs are not allowed on Michigan state beaches and most county and town beaches. In-season, the jurisdictions of Indiana, Illinois, Ohio and Wisconsin are even more restrictive. But all is not lost for the outdoor canine adventurer when visiting the Great Lakes. Here are the 10 best places to take your dog when vacationing around these inland seas, moving east to west...

1. Point Gratiot Park   (Lake Erie, New York)

Although its shores are the most densely populated of any of the Great Lakes, there is plenty of opportunity for a dog to explore Lake Erie. The smallest of the five lakes, Lake Erie waters average only about 62 feet in depth and warm rapidly in the summer for happy dog paddling.

The headlands here contain Dunkirk Beach, a U.S. Coast Guard Naval Reserve Station and an historic lighthouse. Around the west side of the headlands are low bluffs fronted by a wide, sandy beach. Dogs are welcome, there is plenty of easy parking - and it's free.

(716) 366-5050
www.dunkirklighthouse.com/Point_Gratiot.htm

2. Presque Isle State Park   (Lake Erie, Pennsylvania)

Pennsylvania's most popular state park is believed to have formed 11,000 years ago from the deposits of sand carried by wind and water across Lake Erie. This "flying spit" of sand is the largest in the Great Lakes region and the only one in Pennsylvania. Presque Isle State Park is estimated to be moving eastward at the rate of one-half mile per century. Although Presque Isle is French for "almost an island," the area has often been completely surrounded by water. One such breech in the sand peninsula, designated a National Natural Landmark, lasted 32 years.

During the War of 1812 Commodore Oliver Hazard Perry used a harbor on the east side of Presque Isle as a base of operations for the critical Battle of Lake Erie on September 10, 1813. After the clash with the British fleet, Perry returned to Presque Isle for the winter, using a shallow pond to bury American dead. The harbor was named Misery Bay in light of the hardships suffered that winter. Today the Perry monument on Crystal Point remembers the American exploits here.

Dogs are welcome on all trails but ticks are heavy so avoid the trail fringes. Dogs are not allowed on the swimming beaches but you can hike a little ways up the peninsula past the supervised beaches where dogs can freely enjoy the frisky waves of Lake Erie.

(814) 833-7424
www.dcnr.state.pa.us/stateparks/parks/presqueisle.aspx

3. Lakeshore Reservation   (Lake Erie, Ohio)

Of Ohio's 262 miles of Lake Erie shoreline it is estimated that only about 40 are open for access by the public - and a lot fewer than that are open to your dog so that makes this a very special place indeed for dog owners. The highlight in the 84-acre park for your dog is the driftwood-littered sandy beach that can be hiked between staircases that drop you off the bluffs. Strong swimming dogs will love the challenge of Lake Erie waves crashing onto shore.

Back on top of the bluffs the short, groomed trails in Lakeshore Reservation have a garden-like feel. The principal private landowner, Charles Irish, was a pioneering arborist who spotted non-native ornamental trees and shrubs around his home amidst the typical Ohio beeches and maples. The park is oriented east-west and each side contains its own loop that mirror each other. The beach stroll can be used to create a canine hiking loop from side to side.

www.lakemetroparks.com/select-park/lakeshore.shtml

4. Indiana Dunes National Lakeshore   (Lake Michigan, Indiana)

The Indiana Dunes National Lakeshore is a park of striking contrasts. More than 1,400 plant species have been identified within park boundaries, ranking it 7th among national parks in native plant diversity. Growing zones clash here at the southern base of Lake Michigan so southern dogwood mixes with arctic bearberry and northern conifer forests thrive alongside cacti. The park itself stands in stark relief from the industrial surroundings of Gary, Indiana and Chicago. The national lakeshore was designated in 1966 and preserves 25 miles of Lake Michigan shoreline.

Canine hikers will also find the dog-friendly trails, with dips and climbs, to be of a different style than the generally flat northern Indiana area. The high point on the dunes is 123-foot Mt. Baldy at the extreme eastern point of the park. Dogs are allowed across the park and fantastic doggie dips await in Lake Michigan.

Dogs are not allowed on the *Ly-Co-Ki-We Trail* but can spend the night in the Dunewood Campground. More superb canine hiking can be found in Indiana Dunes State Park, entombed by the national lakeshore. There are many numbered trails - some quite challenging - that ascend high vista points such as Mt. Tom. The best trails on the lake's edge can be found in the state park.

(219) 926-7561
www.nps.gov/indu/

5. Sleeping Bear Dunes National Lakeshore   (Lake Michigan, Michigan)

Long ago, according to Ojibway Indian legend, a forest fire ravaged the Wisconsin shoreline driving a mother bear and her two cubs into the waters of Lake Michigan. The three bears swam for safety across the entire lake but the two cubs tired in the crossing. The mother bear continued to the shore and climbed a high bluff to wait for her cubs who couldn't make it and drowned within sight of shore. The Great Spirit Manitou created two islands to mark the spot where the cubs disappeared and then created a solitary dune to represent the faithful mother bear. The national lakeshore, established in 1970, protects 35 miles of dunes - the highest 480 feet above the lake - that are the product of several glacial advances and retreats that ended 11,000 years ago.

Your dog isn't allowed to make the *Dune Climb* up a mountain of sand but she may thank you for that. Otherwise dogs are welcome on Sleeping Bear Dunes National Lakeshore trails. The best canine hike is the *Cottonwood Trail* off the popular Pierce Stocking Scenic Drive. The loop leads out into dunes speckled with the bleached remains of overwhelmed trees and the hardy survivors adapting to their sandy world. The rollicking trail, open May to October, is completely on thick sand that, while soft to the paw, can tire an unfit dog.

In the north section of the park the *Good Harbor Bay Trail* is a flat, wooded walk. Most of the starch has been taken out of the Lake Michigan waves here for gentle canine swimming. More adventurous dog paddlers will want to test the frisky waves in the southernmost Platte Plains section. You have your choice of trails here to choose how much you want to hike before reaching the surf. The 13 mid-length trails throughout the park are all hiker-only. Dogs are not allowed on North or South Manitou Island, both floating just offshore.

(231) 326-5134
www.nps.gov/slbe/

6. Old Mission Peninsula　　　(Lake Michigan, Michigan)

Old Mission Peninsula is an 18-mile appendage that splits Lake Michigan's Traverse Bay neatly in half. Presbyterian Minister Peter Dougherty arrived in 1838 to establish the missionary for which the peninsula would be named. As settlers arrived they discovered ideal growing conditions on the narrow land moderated by the surrounding waters of Lake Michigan. Getting the crops to market was not so easy as growing them, however, thanks to a series of rocky shoals around the tip of the peninsula. Today Old Mission is still renowned for its cherry harvest.

Congress authorized funds for the building of a lighthouse here in 1859 but the Civil War prevented construction until 1870. The Mission Point Light remains the focal point of the park that was created by the state of Michigan after World War II. The lighthouse sits directly on the 45th parallel - halfway between the equator and the North Pole.

The trail system stitches several paths into a loop of a couple miles around the tip of the peninsula that works through woodlands and along the shore of Lake Michigan. This is easy hiking for your dog on mostly level terrain with plenty of opportunity for your dog to visit the waters of the lake.
www.oldmission.com/

7. Lake Michigan Sand Dunes　　　(Lake Michigan, Michigan)

The year 2007 marked the 50th anniversary of the opening of the Mackinac Bridge that connects the lightly populated Upper Peninsula of Michigan to lower Michigan. Traditionally the bridge has attracted hunters and other woods-loving types but that list should also include beach-loving dog owners.

Just across the bridge on the Upper Peninsula head west on Route 2 out of St. Ignace and eight miles past the town of Brevort you will come to an unnamed, unsigned stretch of dune-backed, sandy white beach. You are actually in the East Side Section of the Hiawatha National Forest. Pull off the water-side of the road and park your car. There are miles of beach and not much traffic so there will be plenty of room for your dog to romp in the Lake Michigan waves. If you need facilites, travel a bit further west to the Lake Michigan Picnic Area.
(906) 786-4062
http://www.fs.fed.us/r9/forests/hiawatha/

8. Pictured Rocks National Lakeshore   (Lake Superior, Michigan)

Possessing the largest surface area of any freshwater lake in the world, there is enough water in Lake Superior to easily fill the other four Great Lakes combined to overflowing. Lake Superior is known for its cold water and rugged shoreline but there are some sandy beaches scattered across its 300 or so miles of southern shores. Other beaches are more of the cobble variety. Most of the shoreline is sparsely populated which bodes well for finding a dog-friendly beach.

The "pictured rocks" on the south shore of Lake Superior were painted by mineral stains on exposed sandstone cliffs scoured by glaciers. The colorful streaks on the cliffs - as high as 200 feet above the water - result from groundwater that seeps out of cracks in the rock. The oozing water contains iron, limonite, copper, and other minerals that brush the cliff face with colors as they trickle down. In 1966, the Pictured Rocks were preserved as America's first national lakeshore. The park stretches along Lake Superior for 40 miles.

Dogs are not allowed to trot everywhere in Pictured Rocks National Lakeshore's 72,000 acres (a detailed pet area map is available) but there is plenty of superb canine hiking on tap here. Day hikes lead to clifftops and cobble beaches through hardwood forests and windswept dunes. The best beach for dogs is at the western end of the park where dogs are allowed on Sand Point until the trail begins to climb the cliffs.

(906) 387-2607
www.nps.gov/piro/

9. Apostle Islands National Seashore   (Lake Superior, Wisconsin)

Twenty-one jeweled islands in Lake Superior have been rounded up by the National Park Service and herded into Apostle Islands National Seashore. Dogs are not permitted on any of the park service shuttles from the mainland so the emerald forests and pristine beaches of the islands are restricted to travelers on private boats. The National Lakeshore, however, includes 12 miles of Lake Superior frontage on the mainland.

Dog owners will want to steer towards Meyers Beach at the western end of the park. Here your dog will find a lengthy beach of thick sand and frisky waves of crystal clear Lake Superior waters. Driftwood is in abundance for your favorite fetcher.

The one hiking trail on the mainland departs from Meyers Beach and pushes east over three miles to a pack-in campground. Unless you're spending the night, your hike on the Lakeshore Trail will likely end about two miles in at the top of cliffs above sea caves that have been carved into the sandstone bluffs. Be careful when you arrive with your dog to peer into the caves. If you don't have a boat or kayak another way to explore these magnificent foundations is to visit in February when Meyers Beach is usually covered in thick ice and snow. You can then hike with your dog right along the shore to reach the caves at lake level.

(715) 779-3397
www.nps.gov/apis/

10. Whitefish Dunes State Park   (Lake Michigan, Wisconsin)

Door County is a magnet for Lake Michigan recreation. For dog owners it is hit and miss among the parks and forests but one place your dog can enjoy the sandy lake beaches is Whitefish Dunes State Park. Long considered the best sand dunes on the western shore of Lake Michigan, this wilderness was the target of conservationist before World War II. Finally in 1967 the state park was established. Parts of the beach are open for your dog to swim in Lake Michigan.

(920) 823-2400
www.dnr.state.wi.us/Org/land/parks/specific/whitefish/

DESTINATION
IDEA #10: THE BEST BEACH TRIP YOU CAN TAKE WITH YOUR DOG

In 1929 Samuel Boardman, 55 years removed from his childhood in Massachusetts, was assigned the new post of Parks Engineer for the Oregon Highway Department. The Great Depression was just beginning to sweep across the land and local governments everywhere were slashing budgets and squirreling away funds. Boardman saw the financial crisis differently. The Oregon coast had yet to see much development and he knew land prices there would never be so cheap again. he proposed the issuance of $500,000 of state bonds to acquire coastal land.

Boardman received little political support but the zeal with which he spread his conservationist vision inspired an outpouring of private donations and eventually public funding. The State of Oregon had 4,070 acres scattered in 46 small parks when Sam Boardman began his career. When he retired in 1950, the number of parks had increased to 181 and the acreage to 57,195. And every grain of sand along Oregon's 363 miles of coastline was open to you - and your dog.

Ambitious canine hikers with about a month to spare can experience all of Oregon's sandy beaches and spruce-shrouded headlands up close on the Oregon Coast Trail that begins at the mouth of the Columbia River in Fort Stevens State Park and concludes at the California state line. Most travelers, however, will choose to sample the craggy Pacific shoreline with their dogs from numerous waysides, picnic areas and parks sprinkled along the spectacular US 101 coast highway. You can stop just about anywhere and and find a solitary beach walk with your dog but here are some of the standouts, from north to south...

Oregon's North Coast is dominated by dramatic cliffs and the resort town of Seaside. **Seaside** (www.seasideor.com/) is near the site where Lewis and Clark's Corps of Discovery joyously reached the beach in 1805 after two years of crossing the continent and not too many decades later Oregon's first seashore resort began taking shape. Today you can take a long hike with your dog on the wide sandy beach or use the famous 1.5-mile Promenade that fronts the beach behind a concrete balustrade. Originally platted on boards in the 19th century, the wide, strolling path was redone in pebbly concrete in 1920.

Just down the road is your first must-see park along the Oregon Coast. **Ecola State Park** (www.oregonstateparks.org/park_188.php) boasts conifer-speckled cliffs with many trails leading to the water. An easy 3-mile round trip hike at the park's Indian Beach takes your dog to a scenic bluff 150 feet above the sea and panoramic views of the Pacific Ocean. If you arrive in winter and spring keep a look-out for migrating gray whales.

Next door is **Cannon Beach** (www.cannonbeach.org/), an artists' colony-turned-upscale resort that got its name when the naval vessel USS Shark ran aground and split in half. The part of the deck with a cannon attached washed ashore. You will want to bring your dog to the town beach for a sitting with Oregon's most-photographed landmark - the 235-foot Haystack Rock that looms only a few yards offshore. The monolith is one of the largest free-standing rocks in the world. South of Cannon Beach, water-loving dogs will howl for a stop at the **Hug Point Recreation Site** (www.oregonstateparks.org/park_191.php) where frisky waves bang up against a rocky cove.

Moving south, your next target is the **Three Capes Scenic Route** (www.pacificcity.org/3capes/drive.html), a 30-mile alternative to US 101 that links a trio of breathtaking headlands. Before you exit the main road, however, treat your dog to the tallest waterfall in the Coast Range in the rustic **Munson Creek Falls State Natural Site** (www.oregonstateparks.org/park_245.php), six miles south of Tillamook.

The first of three scenic destination capes is **Cape Meares** (www.oregon stateparks.org/park_181.php) where parallel trails lead to the 38-foot Cape Meares Lighthouse tucked on a bluff, one of seven Oregon coast lighthouses you can visit with your dog. Next up is **Cape Lookout State Park** (www. oregon stateparks.org/park_186.php) where your dog can romp on expansive sand beaches. Waves crash around a sandstone bluff at **Cape Kiwanda** (www. oregonstateparks.org/park_180.php) - this is a surfer's hangout and the turbulent waters will test the mettle of any dog looking for a swim here.

Back on US 101, the next state park you come to is **Devil's Punch Bowl** (www.oregonstateparks.org/park_217.php), site of a collapsed sea cave. The circular beach thwarts most of the big waves, making this a good choice for an inexperienced sea-swimming dog. Your next must-stop highlight lurks just down the road.

Perched more than 800 feet above the waves, **Cape Perpetua Scenic Area** (www.fs.fed.us/r6/siuslaw/recreation/tripplanning/capeperpetua/) is the highest viewpoint you can access by car on the Oregon Coast. In 1966 almost 3,000 acres were set aside here by the federal government where the temperate spruce rainforest transitions to the sea. The *St. Perpetua Trail* switches back and forth here up 700 feet in over a mile to reach the "Best View on the Oregon Coast."

When your dog tires of the 75 miles of coastline visible in either direction you can sample Cape Perpetua's other 26 miles of foot trails. Many slip quietly through old growth forests, including the mile-long, mostly level *Giant Spruce Trail* that leads to a 500-year old Sitka spruce. Others lead down to the rocky coves where your dog can explore tide pools and dodge the sea spray from the Devil's Churn.

Situated roughly at the coastal mid-point is the Super Bowl for canine play - 40 miles of tail-friendly beach in the **Oregon Dunes National Recreation Area** (www.fs.fed.us/r6/siuslaw/recreation/tripplanning/oregondunes/). These mountains of sand extend inland for 2.5 miles and are the tallest dunes in North America. The star canine hike in this vast alien landscape is at the Tahkanitch Area where a five-mile loop crosses the open oblique dunes, explores the inter-dune forest and reaches the Pacific Ocean where you can enjoy an isolated beach for as far as your dog's eye can see. For a quicker way to experience the dunesland consider the *John Dellenback Dunes Trail* south of Reedsport that deposits your dog amid towering sand piles and island of trees.

Oregon's South Coast is the stronghold of working fishing boats, classic bridges spanning exhausted rivers spilling into the Pacific Ocean and pocket beaches embraced by rocky alcoves. **Bullards Beach State Park** (www.oregon stateparks.org/park_71.php), near Bandon, is one of the best places here for long walks on a dune-backed beach here. **Port Orford Heads State Park** (www. oregon stateparks.org/park_61.php) preserves the site of one of Oregon's most famous life-saving stations where crews operated from 1934 to 1970. The station at Port Orford retains the Cape Cod and Craftsman features, with its cedar shingles, typical of the Pacific coast architecture. Later stations were built in a starker, military model. The park also features mossy, wooded trails out to scenic overlooks on Port Orford Head.

The coarse sand at **Ophir Beach** is another good choice for canine travelers. Swimming dogs will enjoy a pit stop at Merchant Beach on the south end of twisty Seven Devils Road. Pay tribute to the architect of Oregon's coastline parks at **Samuel H. Boardman State Scenic Corridor** (www.oregonstateparks.org/park_77.php), only without a time schedule - you will need to pry your dog from the pulsing waters of Whales-head Beach.

Your last chance to enjoy the Oregon beaches with your dog comes at **Harris Beach** (www.oregonstateparks.org/park_79.php), named after Scottish pioneer rancher George Harris, north of Brookings. The Pacific surf here is squeezed by offshore rock formations so there is good fetching to be had. Look around the massive driftwood on the constricted beach - you'll know your Oregon beach journey has ended at redwood country and the forests of Northern California.

𝒟ℰ𝒮𝒯ℐ𝒩𝒜𝒯ℐ𝒪𝒩
IDEA #11: DOGGIN' CAPE COD

For generations of New Englanders, a vacation has meant just one thing - "the Cape." It wasn't always so. Shortly after the Pilgrims landed in Provincetown in 1620 farming began and it wasn't long before every tree on Cape Cod was cleared for cropland. The dune grasses that left behind were picked clean by by grazing cattle and Merino sheep. By the mid-nineteenth century there wasn't much left on the land to support anyone.

With improved rail transportation, wealthy Bostonians began coming to

Cape Cod for rest and relaxation around 1900. By 1950 there were almost as much forestland back on the cape as there was 300 years previously. In 1961 Cape Cod denizen John F. Kennedy squelched housing development plans by creating the **Cape Cod National Seashore** (www.nps.gov/caco/) that encompasses most of the wide, sandy beaches of the cape's east-facing Atlantic seaboard.

There is no need to call the kennel when planning a vacation to Cape Cod. The beckoning finger of land features 559 miles of shoreline and some 60 public beaches, many operated by the small towns that are the backbone of Cape Cod life. Many have restrictions against dogs only in the summer and then only where people are swimming.

At Cape Cod National Seashore, with 40 miles of coastline, dogs are permitted on the beach year-round, except on swimming beaches and where closures may occur to protect nesting shorebirds. Walking the beaches at Cape Cod is a special experience due to limited sight distance caused by the curvature of the coastline. The effect can be that of moving from one private beach to another as you travel from beach alcove to beach alcove backed by impressive highlands.

In addition to Atlantic Ocean beaches, the park extends across the cape in places to include bayside beaches with gentler waves for doggie swims. Exploring Cape Cod with your dog becomes more problematic the further you move from the shore, however. Dogs at the national seashore are not allowed on most of the nature trails - and certainly not on the prime destinations such as Fort Hill, but are confined to a horse trail or bike path for the most part. Other popular trails, such as those at Wellfleet Bay, are under the auspices of the Massachusetts Audubon Society and also off-limits to your dog.

If your dog is hankering for trail time in the dunes try **Sandy Neck**, a six-mile long barrier beach on Cape Cod Bay near the town of Barnstable (www.town. barnstable.ma.us/SandyNeck/default.asp). The complete circuit loop that travels past protected marshland and along 100-foot dunes fronting the open waters of the bay covers 13 miles but several cross-overs can shorten your dog's explorations here to as little as 1.6 miles. It doesn't take much for the *Marsh Trail* to go underwater so check tide charts before planning a full day's adventure with your dog on Sandy Neck.

DESTINATION
IDEA #12: DOGGIN' THE JERSEY SHORE

Approximately 30 million people live within a two-hour drive of the Jersey Shore. If the summer is hot and dry, the wide, white sand beaches can receive seven or eight million visitors between Memorial Day and Labor Day. Even with 127 miles of beach, that's a lot of people. No wonder Jersey shore towns don't roll out the red carpet for dogs in the summer.

Come to New Jersey in the off-season, however, and you won't need a guidebook. The deserted beaches open wide to dogs, most are public and parking is a snap. But enjoying summer at the Jersey shore with your dog is not out of the question, you just need to work a bit harder to find that special spot, like these...

Cattus Island County Park

Much of the New Jersey coastline is comprised of barrier islands, behind which calm bays and marshes beckon outdoor adventurers. During the Revolutionary War, patriots used this peninsula jutting into Barnegat Bay to off-load cargo from captured British frigates. In quieter times farmers harvested salt hay from the marshes. Private owners bought Cattus Island in 1961 but before it could be developed the New Jersey Wetlands Act of 1970 saved it for open space.

A paved and unpaved road runs for one mile down the spine of the 500-acre Cattus Island peninsula. Two main trails loop across the road and a smaller loop radiates off it near the end for a total of five miles of walking paths. Come here for relaxed canine hiking on level paths through the maritime forests and salt marshes.

Cattus Island is one of the best places in New Jersey to take your dog for a swim. The *Island Loop* touches briefly on the frisky waves of Mosquito Cove from a small sand beach and a longer stretch of sand on the open waters of the Silver Bay at the end of the unpaved road will excite any dog. If your dog prefers a more peaceful body of water try the namesake patch of sand on the Barnegat Bay from the *Hidden Beach Loop*.

Toms River, New Jersey
(732) 270-6960
www.ocean.nj.us/parks/cattus.html

Higbee Beach/Sunset Beach

Cape May has more Victorian buildings than any similar-sized town in America and apparently town officials are concerned that dogs will mess up all that fancy gingerbread trim. Dogs are never allowed on the boardwalk, in parks or on the beach. I'm not sure what happens if you try to drive through town with a dog in the car - I'm scared to try it. But if you plan a vacation along the southern Jersey shore you can go to the tip of Cape May and cross over to Higbee Beach, where strict regulations melt away (this used to be an unofficial nudist beach).

Higbee Beach is around the corner from the Atlantic Ocean on the Delaware Bay which is why your dog is allowed here year-round. With its wide sand and easy wave action your dog won't know the difference. You can also hike through the last remaining dune forest on the Delaware Bay. The beach next door to Higbee is the similarly dog-friendly Sunset Beach, famous for its Cape May Diamonds. The "diamonds" are actually pieces of quartz crystals that have been eroded from the Upper Delaware River and been polished by a 200-mile journey of churning and jostling that can last a millennium or two.

The stones, that can be cut and faceted to do a passable imitation of a diamond, are found in abundance here because the tidal flow bounces off a unique concrete ship that rests offshore. The *Atlantus* was built to transport soldiers during steel-short World War I. The reinforced-concrete ship worked but the recovery of post-war steel supplies made her obsolete and as she was being towed to Cape May to serve as a ferry slip an accident dumped her on a sand bar where she remains today.

Cape May, New Jersey
609-628-2103
www.state.nj.us/dep/fgw/ensp/higbee.htm

Island Beach State Park

The best place to take your dog to the Jersey shore in the summer is this ten-mile, undeveloped barrier island smack in the middle of the coastline. Henry Phipps, compatriot with Andrew Carnegie in U.S. Steel, purchased the island in 1926 with visions of a grand shore resort. But the stock market crash halted his assault on these natural dunes after erecting only a handful of rambling houses. The Phipps estate sold the property to New Jersey in 1953 and the park opened to the public in 1959.

There are a series of short nature trails (less than one mile) as you drive down the main park road to its end at Barnegat Inlet but once your dog gets that whiff of salt air in her nose, she may not be in any mood to tarry. Get to the beach! From the last parking lot to the southern tip of the island is a hike of over one mile on the piles of white sand. Parking is limited, however, and if you don't arrive early enough in the summer you will be shut out.

Seaside Park, New Jersey
(732) 793-0506
www.state.nj.us/dep/parksandforests/parks/island.html

North Brigantine Natural Area

In the shadow of the neon of Atlantic City is a Jersey shore rarity - more than two miles of undeveloped beach. After a losing day at the blackjack tables turn north and when the town of Brigantine ends, park and let your dog onto the beach year-round. Other refugees from the swimming beaches, four-wheel drive vehicles and surf fishermen, also favor North Brigantine. Your dog's hike on the beach continues all the way to the inlet; if your dog has been intimidated by the crashing Atlantic Ocean waves, the gentle bayside waters await around the corner.

Brigantine, New Jersey
www.njaudubon.org/Tools2.Net/IBBA/SiteDetails.aspx?sk=3144

DESTINATION
IDEA #13: DOGGIN' THE OUTER BANKS

North Carolina's Outer Banks serve up more than 130 miles of the dog-friendliest beaches travelers are likely to find. But pulling onto the barrier islands from Route 158 don't dive right into its conventional charms just yet. Instead, head north for a bit and check out the unhurried towns of Duck and Corolla. Your dog can romp on these residential beaches under voice control. A perfect prelude to your dog's vacation on the Outer Banks.

Moving south, your first major attraction is Kitty Hawk where flight enthusiasts make the pilgrimage from around the world to celebrate the birth of powered manned flight. While famous for flight, the skies over Kitty Hawk are quiet now. Not so just south of the Wright Brothers Memorial at **Jockey Ridge State Park** (www.jockeysridgestatepark.com/). Flamboyant kites, model planes and hang gliders frequently fill the skies here. On the ground, Jockey's Ridge is one giant sandbox for a playful dog. The deep sands, steep dunes and brisk breezes can make for invigorating canine hiking at Jockey's Ridge. Your dog can play anywhere on these dunes - some of the highest on the Atlantic Ocean - or for those who like their walking on the structured side there are two interpretive nature trails marked by posts across the sand.

While you are in Kitty Hawk remembering famous firsts, travel a bit further south to Roanoke Island and the **Fort Raleigh National Historic Site** (www.nps. gov/fora/). Here an expeditionary force in the 1580s established the first English settlement in America. The group was well represented by scientists, merchants and other gentlemen of prominent social standing but conspicuously missing, however, were farmers and craftsmen whose skills might have made the colony work.

When a supply ship returned to the settlement on Roanoke Island there was no trace of the "lost colony." Your dog can explore the mystery with you, including the recreated earthworks of Fort Raleigh and the birth site of Virginia Dare, the first English-speaking baby born in the New World. The *Thomas Hariot Nature Trail*, named for a scientist on that first voyage, is a rollicking ramble through a maritime forest that emphasizes the natural riches on the island that the doomed English settlers hoped to exploit for riches rather than adapt for survival. The sandy trail pops out onto peaceful Roanoke Sound for some superb dog-paddling.

All this to do with your dog on the Outer Banks and you haven't even traveled the two blocks east to one of the great ocean beaches of the world yet - **Cape Hatteras National Seashore** (http://www.nps.gov/caha/). Dogs are allowed year-round on the non-swimming beaches. With only four such beaches in more than 70 miles that leaves little for your dog to whine about here.

Cape Hatteras National Seashore, designated America's first such beach in 1953, is actually comprised of three islands connected by a free bridge and a free ferry. Unlike many other national seashores, Cape Hatteras permits dogs on its nature trails. There is a short 3/4-mile nature trail on each of the three islands. These interpretive paths emphasize the harshness of the saltwater environment and the struggle of the plants and animals that colonize the dunes. These rolling, wooded walks on soft sand are a shady treat for dogs after a day of sun and surf. Dogs are not allowed on the trails in the Pea Island National Wildlife Refuge on the northern end of Hatteras Island.

For centuries storms, shifting sands and war have visited the turbulent waters off the coast of the Outer Banks. More than 600 ships have wrecked in the seas offshore that have earned Cape Hatteras recognition as "the Graveyard of the Atlantic." Each of the three islands sports its own historic lighthouse to help steer ships safely. The queen of the trio is the 208-foot Cape Hatteras Light, the tallest brick lighthouse in America. The Ocracoke Lighthouse, a squat 75-foot tower tucked into a residential neighborhood, has been in service since 1823 and is the oldest operating lighthouse in North Carolina. The least known of the Hatteras lighthouses is the Bodie Island Lighthouse, the northernmost. Located away from shore behind a freshwater marsh and partially ringed by pine trees, the Bodie Light's beam reaches 19 miles out to sea from its 156-foot crown. You can hike with your dog on the grounds of all three historic lights.

After driving the length of Cape Hatteras National Seashore you may not feel the need to take the free ferry across to Ocracoke Island but you would be depriving your dog of one of our best year-round tail-friendly beaches. There is a big campground so you can stay awhile (although it is closed in the off-season) and a trail through a maritime forest across the road. Take your dog through the historical village at the southern end of the island - notorious English pirate Edward Teach, better known as Blackbeard, used to hang out here.

Cape Hatteras looks much different today than in the days when Blackbeard cruised these shores. Hundreds of dunes have been built along the beach to protect the Cape. And with so much for your dog to do here, you will want to return again and again to monitor the future changes.

DESTINATION
IDEA #14: DOGGIN' THE GOLDEN ISLES

The Georgia mainland is completely protected by a chain of barrier islands that march down the coastline. So the mainland is comprised of salt marshes and the beaches are on the barrier islands. Several of the islands are wildlife refuges. The northernmost, Tybee Island, is the playground for Savannah and dogs aren't allowed there. The southernmost, Cumberland Island, is a national seashore reached only by passenger ferry. No dogs allowed there either.

For dog owners that leaves only one target in the Peach State - the Golden Isles (http://www.bgivb.com/).

The Golden Isles are four barrier islands centered around the historic port town of Brunswick. They are easily differentiated for the visiting dog owner. There is no land access to Little St. Simons Island. Sea Island is private and also has no access. St. Simon Island is heavily residential with a sandy beach that swings around its southern tip. The beach is backed by small dunes, beach houses and high rises. Dogs are allowed to trot the beach anytime except during the high season from Memorial Day to Labor Day. In the summer you can hike the beach before 9:00 am and after 6:00 p.m.

The first structure to illuminate this coastal Georgia island began on St. Simon Island in 1807 and was built of tabby, a common Southern coastal building material of lime and crushed oyster shells. The original octagonal tower was steadily improved but destroyed by Confederate troops during the Civil War to prevent its use by Union troops. A 104-foot replacement rose in 1872 and is still in use today. The lighthouse and adjoining Victorian keeper's house (the light was automated in 1954) are now a museum. The sandy beach in front of the St. Simons Light, hard by the downtown area, welcomes dogs and the easy waves of the sound make it a fine place for a doggie dip.

Most dog lovers visiting the Golden Isles will want to head straight for the fourth barrier isle, Jekyll Island, billed as "Georgia's jewel." First developed in the late 1800s as a hunting club for America's riches families, today the entire island, including 11 miles of Atlantic Ocean beach, is a state park. Dogs are allowed on all the beaches anytime.

The beaches around Jekyll Point at the south end are undeveloped and you can hike with your dog for hours beside natural wind-sculpted dunes. At the north end is Driftwood Beach where the forests come right down to the beach. Here the sands are harder and the surf gentler; a great beach for strolling with your dog.

Away from the beaches there is no trail hiking for your dog in the Golden Isles, unless you like to travel on paved bike paths. On Jekyll Island you can walk your dog through the 240-acre historic district anchored by the opulent Jeykll Island Club. You will wander on carriage roads around fantastic cottages built by the Vanderbilts, Morgans, Rockefellers, Goodyears, Pulitzers - enough titans of industry that it was once estimated that one-sixth of all the world's wealth was represented on Jekyll Island.

DOGGIN' AMERICA'S BAYS

DESTINATION
IDEA #15: DOGGIN' THE CHESAPEAKE BAY

The Chesapeake Bay is one of our great recreation destinations. More than 1 in every 15 Americans live within a short drive of the nation's largest estuary and millions come each year for the sailing, the lighthouses, the Atlantic Blue Crabs... What about for your dog? Some of the best Maryland state parks on the Bay don't allow dogs (Calvert Cliffs, Sandy Point) but there are some fine beaches to take your dog to nonetheless. Here are the 14 best, counter-clockwise from the mouth of Chesapeake Bay...

1. First Landing State Park

One of the finest state parks you'll find anywhere features an ocean-type beach at the mouth of the Chesapeake. You can easily hike with your dog for over an hour on the beach with views of the Chesapeake Bay Bridge Tunnel and ocean-going vessels in view the entire time.

Virginia Beach, Virginia
(757) 412-2300
www.dcr.virginia.gov/state_parks/fir.shtml

2. Kiptopeke State Park

Features more than a half-mile of wide sandy beaches, backed by dunes. Off-shore nine concrete World War I surplus ships have been sunk as a breakwater, leaving gentle waves for your dog to play in. Also an easy 1.5-mile *Baywoods Trail* when your dog wants to dry out from the water. Dogs are welcome in the campground.

Cape Charles, Virginia
(757) 331-2267
www.dcr.virginia.gov/state_parks/kip.shtml

3. Wye Island Natural Resources Management Area

The *Ferry Landing Trail* was once the only access road to the island, lined with Osage orange trees imported from a small region of Texas, Oklahoma and Arkansas to serve as a natural fence. This mile-long path ends at a small, sandy beach.

Queenstown, Maryland
(410) 827-7577
www.dnr.state.md.us/publiclands/eastern/wyeisland.html

4. Eastern Neck National Wildlife Refuge

Technically the secluded sandy beach at the end of the Boxes Point Trail is on the Chester River and not the Chesapeake Bay but your dog won't quibble when she tests these fun waves. Good fetching sticks are never in short supply on this driftwood-laden beach.

Rock Hall, Maryland
(410) 639-7056
www.fws.gov/northeast/easternneck/

5. Matapeake Park

This small park on the Chesapeake Bay features a pleasant one-mile wood-chip trail through a pine forest but the reason to come here is a stretch of sandy beach where your dog is welcome off-leash. The beach is a bit too industrial for sunbathers which makes it the perfect place for dogs to romp. Matapeake Park is just south of the Bay Bridge with splendid views of the bay and bridge.

Stevensville, Maryland
www.parksnrec.org/

6. Terrapin Nature Park

Terrapin Park has over 4,000 feet of beach frontage at the tip of Kent Island. Frisky waves and canine swimming in the north shadow of the Bay Bridge. The trail to the beach takes you across oyster chaff.

Stevensville, Maryland
www.byways.org/explore/byways/2261/places/37805/

7. Elk Neck State Park

The park is situated on 100-foot bluffs above the Chesapeake Bay where the Elk and Northeast rivers converge. Narrow, informal trails lead down to the water's edge where gaps in the stone breakwater produce little sandy beaches just for your dog. Atop the bluff an easy walking trail climaxes at Turkey Point lighthouse and long looks over the bay.

Northeast, Maryland
(410) 287-5333
www.dnr.state.md.us/publiclands/central/elkneck.html

8. North Point State Park

Although only 20 acres in size, the Bay Shore Amusement Park was considered one of the finest amusement parks ever built along the Chesapeake Bay. Opened in 1906, the park featured an Edwardian-style dance hall, bowling alley and restaurant set in among gardens and curving pathways. There were rides such as a water toboggan and Sea Swing. Visitors would travel to the shore from Baltimore on a trolley line. Your dog can explore the remains and dive in the Chesapeake at a small wading beach at the Visitor Center.

Edgemere, Maryland
(410) 329-0757
www.dnr.state.md.us/publiclands/central/northpoint.html

9. Downs Memorial Park

Looking for a dog-friendly park? At Downs Memorial Park there is a "pet parking" stall outside the information center. A dog drinking bowl is chained to a human water fountain. Best of all is Dog Beach, an isolated, scruffy 40-yard stretch of sand where you can let the dog off leash for canine aquatics in the Chesapeake Bay. The wave action is just right for dogs and there is enough sand for digging. Need we say more?

Pasadena, Maryland
(410) 222-6238
www.aacounty.org/RecParks/parks/downs/index.cfm

10. Flag Ponds Nature Park

Thick woods and an isolated sandy beach backed by wild grasses but don't come too early - the park doesn't open until 9:00 a.m and is only open Memorial Day to Labor Day and week-ends all year round.

Lusby, Maryland
www.calvertparks.org/Parks/FlagPonds/FPhome.htm

11. Point Lookout State Park

A Civil War prison to hold Confederate soldiers was built here at the mouth of the Potomac River and is the main attraction of the park but dogs aren't allowed there. Before crossing the causeway to the island, however, is a small, sandy dog beach with excellent wave action.

Scotland, Maryland
(301) 872-5688
www.dnr.state.md.us/publiclands/southern/pointlookout.html

12. Hughlett Point Natural Area

You will start your exploration with your dog here on a wide, soft and exceedingly agreeable path through a fragrant loblolly forest. Soon you will pop out on the beach of the Chesapeake Bay where you will be excused for thinking you have just landed on Tom Hanks' deserted island in Cast Away. Ghost trees and fallen trunks pepper the enchanted shoreline - ineffective guardians against the relentless Chesapeake wave action.

Kilmarnock, Virginia
www.dcr.virginia.gov/natural_heritage/natural_area_preserves/hughlett.shtml

13. Gloucester Point Park

Here in the shadow of America's longest double-swing bridge your dog will find a smooth sand beach and swimming in the light waves of the bay. There is also a small grassy area for your dog to roll around in.

Gloucester Point, Virginia
(804) 642-9474
www.gloucesterva.info/pr/parks/gpb.htm

14. Grandview Nature Preserve

You bring your dog to Grandview to hike on its two miles of white sand beach - and that is the only place your dog is permitted - and then only between September 15 and May 15. But that is plenty for dogs to think highly of this bay front beach.

Hampton, Virignia
www.hampton.gov/PARKS/waterfront_and_feature_parks.html

DESTINATION
IDEA #16: DOGGIN' SAN FRANCISCO BAY

In 1972 a menagerie of government properties around the San Francisco Bay that included forts, a prison, an airfield, beaches and forests came together as the **Golden Gate National Recreation Area** (www.nps.gov/goga/), becoming one of the world's largest urban national parks. In the park are such popular destinations as Alcatraz, the Presidio and the Cliff House at Lands End. Today the park administers 75,388 acres of land - including 28 miles of shoreline - on more than 20 separate parcels.

You will not be wanting for things to do with your dog in the Golden Gate National Recreation Area. One of the best places for dog owners to head is Fort Funston on the Pacific Ocean at the southern extreme of the park in the city (off Skyline Boulevard - Route 35). There are trails to romp along among the cliffs and plenty of unrestricted access to the beach. Look for hang gliders soaring above the cliffs. Except for areas of bird nesting and small China Beach, dogs are permitted on the sand in the city of San Francisco all the way north from Fort Funston to the San Francisco Bay.

Your dog will be no less happy as you begin fanning out from the Golden Gate as you travel south, counterclockwise around San Francisco Bay. At **Candlestick Point** (www.parks.ca.gov/default.asp?page_id=519), so named because the burning of nearby abandoned ships in the bay caused the flaming masts to resemble lighted candlesticks, 170 acres of landfill intended for a U.S. Navy shipyard that was never built have been converted from a garbage dump into a bayside park by the State of California. Experienced travelers with dogs know that when they hear the words "converted garbage dump" that this will be a place for dogs. In addition to spectacular bay view from its open trails your dog can play off-leash in the dirt areas that are used for parking during sporting events at nearby Candlestick Park.

Traveling south from San Francisco on Highway 101 past the San Francisco
International Airport skip Coyote Point natural area (no dogs allowed) and make
tracks for **Don Edwards San Francisco Bay National Wildlife Refuge** (www.
fws.gov/desfbay/), America's first urban National Wildlife Refuge. Some 30,000
acres of open bay and salt marsh mudflats host millions of migrating shorebirds.
The refuge is not an escape from its urban setting - you are hard by the roaring
highway and industry intrudes on your pretty picture-taking - but your dog will
love the open spaces and easy trotting over wide path/roads. Try the three-mile
perimeter loop around Bair Island where cattle once grazed and salt was harvested
or any of the several shorter trails at the Refuge Visitor Center. If the gates are
locked feel free to park and walk in anytime during daylight hours.

Before crossing over to the East Bay make a stop at San Mateo's **Bayfront
Park**, another garbage reclamation project. A maze of unmarked dirt ribbons dart
across the little hills of the small park, now covered in unfettered grasslands.

After crossing the Dumbarton Bridge you can head north and begin your
dog's exploration of the East Bay. At **Crown Beach** in Alameda (www.ebparks.
org/parks/crown_beach) you are likely to marvel at nature's handiwork as you
hike with your dog along the bicycle trail flanked by rolling sand dunes. But
you would be wrong, partly at least. This was historically the largest beach on
San Francisco Bay and renowned as an amusement center but wind and water
conspired to erode much of it away until restoration began in 1982. Sand is being
regularly pumped ashore by pipeline from a barge. Keep your dog on the paved
path unless she wants to roll in the grassy lawns - no dogs on the beach.

The views for your dog are so spectacular in Berkeley's **Cesar Chavez Park**
(www.ci.berkeley.ca.us/ContentDisplay.aspx?id=12102) - three bay bridges and
the San Francisco skyline - you will forget you are standing on yet another landfill.
And with hardly any vegetation higher than mown grass in the park even your
dachshund can enjoy the views. Not that your dog will be interested - the 17 acres
at the tip of 90-acre Cesar Chavez Park are one big off-leash dog play area.

Pulling out of the parking lot your dog is probably thinking it couldn't get
much better around San Francisco Bay. She would be incorrect. In Richmond the
Point Isabel Regional Shoreline (www.ebparks.org/parks/pt_isabel) is billed
as the "largest public off-leash dog park in the nation" with 23 landscaped acres.
The park logs more than 500,000 dog visits annually. The easy-going trails wind
around the shoreline serving up constant views of the Golden Gate and the Marin

Headlands. Your dog can even spruce up with a do-it-yourself dog wash before you leave.

Around the bay there is first-rate canine hiking back in Golden Gate Recreation Area in the Marin Headlands and the Oakwood Valley on designated trails. Elevations in the wooded hills climb to over 1000 feet. Dogs are not permitted in the Muir Woods or the Tennessee Valley, the two most significant and regrettable prohibitions against dogs in the Golden Gate National Recreation Area.

Oh yes, before your dog's tour is through you can walk him across the famous Golden Gate Bridge. The familiar orange bridge is maybe the most photographed man-made structure in the world. The crossing is more than 1.5 miles one-way and an estimated 3,800 people make the walk each weekday with foot traffic doubling on the weekends. This is not a hike for a skittery dog - you are only feet from speeding traffic, it is noisy and the bridge does sway.

You will pass under the world's two highest bridge towers, 220 feet above the water. Views from the bridge on a clear day can extend 20 miles out to sea, although the pedestrian walk-way is on the east (city) side. Now, that's a canine hike with a view.

DESTINATION
IDEA #17: DOGGIN' GREEN BAY

Rather than tour the shores of a great bay like Chesapeake or San Francisco this vacation tour is a loop of the peninsula that forms Green Bay in Lake Michigan. This Door County Peninsula is home to over 30 county and local parks and five state parks, most of which are located on the county's more than 300 miles of shoreline.

Your dog's tour of Door County begins in earnest once you cross Sturgeon Bay, an arm of Green Bay that slices ten miles into the peninsula. A ship canal finishes the job of severing most of Door County from the mainland. Before crossing, however, make a point to stop at **Potawatomi State Park** (www.dnr. state.wi.us/org/LAND/parks/specific/Potawatomi/), which was considered as a national park in the 1920s. Its spot on the shores of Sturgeon Bay was considered strategic in the event of war with Canada so the War Department controlled it for over a century. A 75-foot wooden tower with wide, dog-friendly steps and landings was built in 1932 and still peeks out over the treetops for your dog to scout upcoming Door County and Green Bay.

Traveling up the east side of the peninsula your first Lake Michigan destination is Wisconsin's busiest day-use park - **Whitefish Dunes State Park** (www.dnr.state.wi.us/Org/land/parks/specific/whitefish/). In spite of the crowds, dogs are welcome on the southern end of the extensive sandy beach, long considered the best dunes on the western shore of Lake Michigan. This is the only swimming beach your dog will be welcome in Door County's state parks. From here on in, when you want to give your dog a sandy romp in Lake Michigan steer towards one of the many town beaches like Anclam Park or Baileys Harbor that are generally pet-friendly.

If you didn't take the opportunity to hike up to **Cave Point County Park** (www.uwm.edu/People/carriel/index.html) pull into the small parking lot before heading back to Route 57. The shoreline rocks have been fending off waves for eons creating unusual formations and caves in this beautiful 19-acre park. Keep your dog leashed as you approach the unfenced ledges - some of the breakers can spray water 20 feet or more into the air.

You will have to pass the popular Ridges Sanctuary near Baileys Harbor (no dogs allowed) and angle away from the eastern shore to head for **Newport State Park** (www.dnr.state.wi.us/org/land/parks/specific/newport/), Wisconsin's only designated wilderness park. Sporting 38 miles of trails, many of which hug 11 miles of sweeping shoreline, this park is a favorite of backpacking campers and day hikers - and likely your dog as well. If your dog enjoyed these uncrowded trails there is more at hand by continuing north by ferry to Washington Island and Rock Island.

Begin your tour back down the Green Bay side of the peninsula, part of the same geology that created Niagara Falls, at **Ellison Bluff Park** (www.dnr. state. wi.us/Org/land/er/sna/sna378.htm). The limestone-capped escarpment on view here formed from sediment from ancient inland seas and extends from New York to Wisconsin. The softer rock under the tough limestone surface eroded away leaving bluffs that rise 200 feet above the water.

Again, you'll have to skip the charming Ephraim Preserve but your dog's consolation is next door in one of the jewels of the Wisconsin state park system, **Peninsula State Park** (www.dnr.state.wi.us/org/land/parks/specific/peninsula/). Established 100 years ago in 1909, the park mixes passive and active recreation across almost 4,000 acres, including seven miles of cobblestone and natural sand beaches. The 20 miles of paw-friendly trails are the best-groomed on the peninsula. The star in the park is the *Eagle Trail* that picks its way along water's edge past haunting sea caves, up over rocky bluffs and around woodland springs. The loop is only two miles but budget two hours to complete the challenge.

One way to anchor your dog's tour of Door County Peninsula is by visiting the lighthouses that ring the rocky shores of the peninsula. There are 10 of them - more lights than any other county in America. Most of the beacons went into operation shortly after the peninsula was settled in the mid-1800s. The four most accessible Door County lighthouses are: **Cana Island Lighthouse** (www.dcmm. org/canaisland.html), Canal Station Lighthouse, Baileys Harbor Range Lights and **Eagle Bluff Lighthouse** (www.eagleblufflighthouse.org/).

DOGGIN' AMERICA'S LAKES

DESTINATION
IDEA #18: DOGGIN' LAKE CHAMPLAIN

The year 2009 marks 400 years since explorer Samuel de Champlain sailed onto the lake that bears his name and claimed the area for France. It was no small claim. Lake Champlain is America's sixth largest freshwater lake in the Lower 48 - and the largest not tagged a "Great Lake." It stretches for over 100 miles to form a natural boundary between Vermont and New York State.

Lake Champlain is over 400 feet deep in places - deep enough to spawn legends of its own sea monster. The Iroquois people who lived here for centuries called the creature Tatoskok. Hundreds of documented sightings later, he is known as "Champ." Champ is described as being thick of body with a longish neck and elongated tail and anywhere from 15 to 50 feet long.

Unfortunately, when visiting Lake Champlain with your dog you are as likely to see Champ as a beach that allows dogs. Your dog is almost universally banned from public beaches in New York and Vermont. So it will require a bit of imagination to enjoy Lake Champlain with your dog - but travelers with dogs are used to that. Here's a clockwise look at a sampling of parks for your dog, starting on the southern shores...

Crown Point State Historic Site - New York

With an occasional portage, the most important being a two-mile land link between the southern tip of Lake Champlain and Lake George, it is possible to travel from Montreal to New York City by canoe. Control that portage and you own the vital highway through the heart of Colonial America. The French built the first fort here in 1758 and dealt the British Army one of its worst defeats ever in North America to defend it. The British returned a year later to overwhelm what they called Fort Ticonderoga. During the American Revolution the British and Americans tussled over Ticonderoga even as its stone walls were being plundered for local building material.

Your dog is also not allowed on Fort Ticonderoga grounds today but a bit further north she can explore the Crown Point State Historic Site where the lake narrows to only 400 yards. Both the British and French constructed forts here. Ruins of both forts remain as they always have been. There is plenty of grass for your dog to romp on and an interpretive footpath of almost three miles leads around the forts and into the interior of two magnificent remains of Georgian-style stone barracks.

Crown Point, New York
(518) 597-4666
www.nysparks.com/sites/info.asp?siteID=8

Coon Mountain Preserve - New York

Coon Mountain, with a handful of small rocky summits, has been a local landmark on the western shore of Lake Champlain since settlers arrived. The first colonizer of the towns of Willsboro, Essex and Westport, William Gilliland, perished on the mountaintop in February 1796 after becoming disoriented in the snow. Local lore tells of the Coon Mountain panther that cried like a damsel in distress, luring men into the deep woods where it would spring on its victim. Many dogs were lost to the panther in attempts to hunt it. When the ornery cat was finally shot in mid-pounce it fell into one of the small pocket ponds on the summit and was never found.

Local teenage volunteers carved a one-mile nature trail to the top of Coon Mountain. This is a relatively easy purchase of spectacular views of Lake Champlain and the surrounding valley. Limited parking increases the odds you will be enjoying those views only with your dog.

Westport, New York
(518) 576-2082
www.nature.org/wherewework/northamerica/states/newyork/preserves/

Ethan Allen Homestead - Vermont

Ethan Allen strode across the early Vermont landscape like the folk hero he has become: settling the frontier, helping found the state, executing daring exploits in the battle for American Independence. He spent his final years on this quiet homestead outside of Burlington on the Winooski River.

There are some four miles of hiking for your dog in fields and light woods around the park, much of it within barking distance of the river. Access to the easy-flowing water is possible for a refreshing doggie dip.

Burlington, Vermont
(802) 865-4556
www.ethanallenhomestead.org/

Waterfront Park - Vermont

Burlington is the largest town on Lake Champlain and one of the prettiest anywhere. Waterfront Park isn't large - about three blocks long and less than a block wide but there are grassy lawns for a game of fetch and it is a great place to enjoy a sunset with your dog.

Burlington, Vermont
(802) 865-7247
www.enjoyburlington.com/Parks/WaterfrontPark.cfm

Snake Mountain Wildlife Management Area - Vermont

Snake Mountain is a prominent feature of the Champlain Valley, looming above the surrounding level countryside from an elevation of 1,287 feet. A resort hotel operated on the summit in the 1800s, promoting the panoramic views of Lake Champlain and the Adirondack Mountains. The hotel closed in 1925 and later burned to the ground.

Now owned mostly by the Vermont Fish & Wildlife Department, a three-mile trail along an abandoned carriage road takes visitors to the summit of Snake Mountain. This is a very hike-friendly route for any dog, passing through mixed hardwoods and a rare bog covered with sphagnum moss.

Snake%20Mountain%20WMA.pdf

Mount Independence State Historic Site - Vermont

After the Americans overran a lightly manned Fort Ticonderoga on May 10, 1775, they quickly moved to defend Ticonderoga's weak northern exposure. Across Lake Champlain - only 1,300 yards at this point - General Philip Schuyler ordered the clearing of timber and the construction of a sister fort. The horseshoe-shaped battery, protected by steep cliffs, was named Mount Independence following the arrival of a copy of the Declaration of Independence on July 18, 1776. A floating bridge connected the fortified complex.

During 1777, Mount Independence was even better fortified than famous Ticonderoga. But even together the forts were no match for British invaders. On July 5 both posts were evacuated. British and German forces remained at Mount Independence until November, when they burned and destroyed the site after the British surrender at Saratoga.

Mount Independence remains an archaeological site with four interpretive trails winding through 400 acres of foundations and ruins. Among the ruins are a general hospital, barracks and a blockhouse. Your dog is welcome to explore this striking promontory on the shore of Lake Champlain.

Orwell, Vermont
(802) 759-2412
www.historicvermont.org/mountindependence/

DESTINATION
IDEA #19: DOGGIN' LAKE GEORGE

Lake George, gateway to New York's fabled North Country is a family-oriented tourist mecca, bursting with motels, shops, amusement parks and even the requisite wax museum on its southern end. Outdoor adventurers will want to shuffle past all this traffic and take your dog up Lakeshore Drive to the hiking trails to see the beauty of the island-speckled lake that led America's wealthiest men to build summer retreats here a century ago.

The most spectacular - and grueling - hike in the Lake George region is the *Tongue Mountain Range Loop*. The range is a five-mile peninsula that thrusts down the middle of the lake. The loop tags the summit of five named mountains and several unnamed knobs on the eastern side of the peninsula before returning along lake level on the western edge. The mountains never reach 2,000 feet in height but the ascents and descents make it seem like climbing across the back of a stegosaurus. There are steep, rocky drops - nothing that a dog can't handle - but canine hikers are best served by taking the loop clockwise.

Views from the lightly forested ridges are splendid up and down the lake, including memorable looks at some of Lake George's 365 islands, many clustered in the Narrows caused by the peninsula. Your destination is the very Tip of the Tongue, where the mountain range dips into Lake George. Here, wide rock perches make ideal diving boards for a well deserved doggie dip. In the background across Northwest Bay will be the venerable Sagamore Hotel on Green Island in the heart of Millionaires Row. The loop is closed with a 4.8-mile return trip along the sometimes-steep shoreline. The total distance for this invigorating exploration is about 13 miles. Bring plenty of water for the dog as there is none aside from the lake.

The tallest mountains surrounding Lake George are on the eastern shore. Trails to Buck Mountain (2,330 feet), Black Mountain (the highest at 2,646 feet) and others make good use of old bridle paths and logging roads and are technically easy for a dog to climb. Fires have visited most of the bare rock summits clearing views from the spruce and oak-beech forests. Mossy hemlocks proliferate on the damper lower slopes. The *Black Mountain Loop*, best tackled by canine hikers in a counter-clockwise direction so a tricky pick-your-way trail is encountered moving downhill, is enlivened by a series of valley ponds and beaver marshes.

Lake George, New York
www.visitlakegeorge.com/

DESTINATION
IDEA #20: DOGGIN' LAKE TAHOE

The Washoe Indians named the lake, with 72 miles of shoreline, "big water." Native legend maintained that the Great Spirit gave a young man a branch of leaves to help him elude the pursuing Evil Spirit. Each time the man dropped a leaf from the branch it would create a pool of water the Evil Spirit would be forced to race around. In the heat of the chase, however, the young man became frightened and dropped the entire branch in one spot - creating Lake Tahoe.

At its deepest point the floor of Lake Tahoe is 1,645 feet beneath the surface, making it America's third deepest lake. At 6,229 feet above sea level, Tahoe is one of the world's largest alpine lakes. The glacial water is so clear - 97% pure - that if you dropped a meatbone over the edge of a boat your dog could watch it drop for 70 feet.

It is possible to fill a vacation with your dog by examining the beauty of Lake Tahoe from every angle. The *Tahoe Rim Trail*, a footpath completely around Lake Tahoe, was the inspiration of United States Forest Service officer Glenn Hampton. He built a coalition of support that would attract more than 10,000 volunteers working 200,000 hours before the 165-mile trail was completed in 2001. The *Tahoe Rim Trail* visits two states, six counties, three national forests, state parkland and three wilderness areas. It stands as one of the largest volunteer projects ever completed in the United States.

The lowest point of the ridge-running route is 6,300 feet at Tahoe City and the trail reaches its apex at Relay Peak where the summit is tagged at 10,333 feet. Dogs are welcome to enjoy hiking on the *Tahoe Rim Trail*; the going is often on soft, sandy terrain as you pass through lush forests and playful meadows. If you hike the entire trail you become eligible for the "165-Mile Club." These long-distance hikers receive a patch from the Tahoe Rim Trail Association but no word yet on laurels for your dog's completing the trail. Fortunately for vacationers on a time budget, a cornucopia of shorter trails reveal Lake Tahoe's magnificent scenery in bite-size chunks...

EAST SHORE TRAILS

Winnemucca Lake: This trail goes through Carson Pass, pioneered by hunter and trapper Christopher "Kit" Carson. When his team made the first successful winter crossing of the Sierras in 1844, the gap at 8,754 feet was called simply "The Pass." Gold-seekers who came several years later started calling this passageway "Carson Pass." The hike through Carson Pass tags a string of jeweled alpine lakes, the most popular being emerald green Winnemucca Lake. The trail is a delight for humans and dogs alike - wide and sandy with no severe climbs for more than a mile. This is the Lake Tahoe hike to take for wildflower lovers in summer - Lupine, Mules Ear and Indian Paintbrush color the ground. Canine hikers in search of a more spirited walk can continue past Winnemucca Lake. Another mile down the trail - and 400 feet higher - is Round Top Lake and behind it Round Top Mountain is waiting to be climbed. The scenery is some of the best in the Northern High Sierra.

Prey Meadows/Skunk Harbor: Part of this easy-going canine hike reveals an old railroad grade built in the 1870s to supply lumber to the Virginia City building boom. The path forks but is short enough that canine hikers will want to take both routes. The left fork takes you into Prey Meadows with waves of springtime wildflowers; to the right is Skunk Harbor, a twinkling cove on the Tahoe shore. Along the way come glimpses of Lake Tahoe through thick pine and fir trees. If the meadows and mountains look familiar it is because this is where Ben, Adam, Hoss and Little Joe Cartwright rode for years on *Bonanza*.

SOUTH SHORE TRAILS

Tallac Historic Site: The southwest shore of Lake Tahoe was a favorite playground to the wealthy and the Tallac Historic Site features three separate rustic estates built from the 1890s through the 1920s. One belonged to Lucky Baldwin, a California real estate investor who operated "the greatest casino in America" here at his Tallac Resort. The Forest Service acquired the area between 1969 and 1971, and has been restoring and renovating ever since. Pine-scented paths meander around the three estates and poke out to Kiva Beach on the lake, a free beach. Your dog is welcome to trot easily through charming buildings and gardens, man-made ponds and an arboretum. The Tallac Historic Site is linked by a short trail to the Lake Tahoe Visitor Center where dogs are welcome to enjoy a variety of short nature trails. The *Rainbow Trail* is the feature trail, an interpretive 1/2-mile loop that illuminates the importance of marshes and meadows to the unrivaled clarity of Lake Tahoe. The *Forest Tree Trail* focuses on the life cycle of the Jeffrey Pine, the dominant tree in the Lake Tahoe basin. Across the road is the *Trail of the Washoe*, dedicated to life of Tahoe's original settlers.

Mt. Tallac Trail: Mt. Tallac is the monarch of the Lake Tahoe shoreline, rising over 3,000 feet above the water. Many trails lead to its summit and the *Mt. Tallac Trail* is one of the best day hikes at Tahoe. The first half of the 5-mile climb is moderately paced until you reach smallish Cathedral Lake, ideal for a doggie dip. Then the going gets rougher as you grind your way up the front face of the 9,735-foot peak. Once on top there won't be much that escapes your view. Lake Tahoe, Fallen Leaf Lake, the Desolation Wilderness and even the casinos across the state line in Nevada all reveal themselves on Mt. Tallac. Mt. Tallac is in the Desolation Wilderness that requires access by permit. Permits for day hikers can be obtained at the trailhead.

WEST SHORE TRAILS

Cascade Falls Trail: This is a short out-and-back trail of less than one mile that leads to memorable views of 200-foot Cascade Falls. The trail gains scarcely 100 feet of elevation and can get crowded so you will need to keep your dog under close control. The trail itself picks its way among rocks and Jeffrey pines as it clings to the mountain slope.

Cascade Lake below and Lake Tahoe in the distance are in almost constant view. The final steps as you near the falls are across open granite slopes that can be slippery under paw. Across the road from the campground is Inspiration Point, with views of Emerald Bay that have been called the most photographed in America. Below on the shore at the head of the bay is the estate of Vikingsholm. A trail leads down to the Viking castle on the beach but you will have to take it without your dog. All the trails around Emerald Bay, including the short but demanding Eagle Falls hike, are extremely popular and recommended only for well-behaved dogs.

NORTH SHORE TRAILS

Mount Rose Wilderness: Mount Rose is the most heavily used of the three wilderness areas around Lake Tahoe. The centerpiece trail is a 6-mile, 2,000-foot ascent to the summit of Mount Rose. This trip is for experienced canine hikers since the paw-friendly hard-packed sand trail gives way in the last two miles to rough shale that can give sharp, uncertain footing to a dog. From the top of 10,776-foot Mount Rose there are long vistas of Lake Tahoe, the Truckee Meadows and, on clear days, Pyramid Lake beyond Reno. Other trails exploring the canyons and ridges of the high country of the Carson Range are at Mount Rose. The *Jones/Whites Creek Loop Trail* covers 8 miles and the 2-mile *Hunter Creek Trail* explores the northern section of the wilderness. The 3-mile *Thomas Creek Trail* leads canine hikers to small lakes and lively meadows in the interior of the park. A pleasant leg-stretcher for canine hikers at Mount Rose is the 1.3-mile *Mount Rose Meadows Interpretive Trail*. The easy loop is paved for full access but bikes and horses are not allowed. It trips through rushing streams and rough granite boulders along the way to the alpine meadow that is awash in wildflowers after the snowmelt.

Lake Tahoe, California/Nevada
www.visitinglaketahoe.com/

DESTINATION
IDEA #21: DOGGIN' LAKE BONNEVILLE

Lake Bonneville isn't there anymore - at least the water. The prehistoric lake dried up about 17,000 years ago when the climate changed. Until then, however, Lake Bonneville was as large as Lake Michigan is today, and much deeper. What it left behind, however, will be of interest to canine adventurers...

Antelope Island State Park

The most conspicuous remnant of Lake Bonneville is the Great Salt Lake, shallow and eight times saltier than sea water. So salty is the water that only two things live in the lake - brine shrimp and algae the shrimp feed on. Only the Dead Sea holds saltier water than the Great Salt Lake, the biggest lake in the American West.

Antelope Island is the largest of the Great Salt Lake's 10 islands. The ancestral antelopes for which John Fremont and Kit Carson named the island in 1843 disappeared but were reintroduced to the 28,022-acre park in 1993. The animal stars of the park instead are the bison, first shipped here in 1893 and now 600 strong. Sheep also grazed here for decades, supporting the busiest sheering operation west of the Mississippi River. The first state lands on the island were purchased in 1969 and the entire island became a state park in 1987.

At the heart of the 20-mile hiking system on Antelope Island is the *White Rock Bay Loop*, over 9 miles of long ascents and descents from the shoreline. Like most of the canine hiking in the park, the landscape is exposed all the way and gets hot in the summer. There is no fresh water available so bring plenty to keep your dog refreshed. The trail is often paw-friendly sand.

A quicker way to see the island is the *Buffalo Trail*, a one-mile round trip that features benches to stop and gaze around the native vegetation of the Great Basin. For extended views get on the *Mountain View Trail* that provides hours of easy canine hiking. A popular hike on Antelope Island is to the summit of 6,596-foot Frary Peak, named for George and Alice who homesteaded here. The entire Wasatch Front Range comes into view at the top but your dog will never see it. No dogs are allowed on Frary.

Every dog will want to include a quarter-mile trail to Beacon Knob on the day-hiking agenda. This trail high point serves up panoramas of the Wasatch Front Range across the water. To get close to the Great Salt Lake the *Lakeside Trail* is a 3-mile out-and-back shadow on the shore.

Visiting the Great Salt Lake, you can be overwhelmed by the stench of the air -the result of billions of decaying organisms that have died after being washed from freshwater streams into the briny water. The smell is confined mostly to the eastern shore (where the micro-biotic slaughter occurs), however, and, canine hikers can usually expect fresh, salty air on Antelope Island.

Syracuse, Utah
(801) 652-2043
www.utah.com/stateparks/antelope_island.htm

Uinta-Wasatch-Cache National Forest

The majestic peaks and rugged backcountry of the Uinta-Wasatch-Cache National Forest loom over the eastern shore of the Great Salt Lake. The Forest gobbles up more than two million acres and includes seven wilderness areas. One of the most popular destinations for dog owners is Mill Creek Canyon and its many forested trails. Your dog's choice will, naturally, be scenic Dog Lake, named not for the many dogs who swim here (it is the only lake in Mill Creek Canyon were dogs are permitted to enjoy a doggie dip) but for its salamanders that are also known as "dog fish." Dog Lake is located at an elevation of about 8,745 feet, and you gain about 1,440 feet as you hike but the elevation gain is spread out over three miles and so your dog won't be left panting by the side of the trail.

Of the many mountains overlooking the Great Salt Lake, Mount Olympus, with its two summits is the dominant peak in the Wasatch Front. The climbing trail on Mount Olympus stalks the south face of the mountain with the South Summit as its destination. Many canine hikers opt to conclude the journey at the overlook but those seeking to tag the 9,026-foot summit face a steady - but manageable - haul of almost four miles.

If your dog conquers Mount Olympus with fine fettle, Grandeur Peak will be the proverbial walk in the park. This 8,299-foot summit on the east side of the Salt Lake Valley is one of Utah's easier mountains to summit. At the top you get extensive views over the Great Salt Lake, and also of neighboring peaks.

Salt Lake City, Utah
(801) 236-3400
www.fs.fed.us/r4/uwc/

Bonneville Salt Flats

Just to the west of the Great Salt Lake is another one-of-a-kind natural phenomenon: the 30,000 acres of the Bonneville Salt Flats. The salt flats are a world famous destination for lovers of speed but not so much for dog owners. There are no facilities or services on the flats unless you visit during a racing day. The best place for your dog to sample the Bonneville Salt Flats is from a rest stop on westbound Interstate-80. Here you can hike as you like on the barren, featureless ancient lake bed.

(801) 977-4300
www.utah.com/playgrounds/bonneville_salt.htm

TOUR

IDEA #22: DOGGIN' AMERICA'S DAMS

Few sites symbolize the might and can-do spirit of America like a massive concrete dam and the artificial lake behind it. That won't matter any to your dog; dams will mean only one thing to him: watery fun...

Bonneville Dam (Oregon)

Doggin' the Army Corps of Engineers while traveling often yields an adventure of the first rank for your dog. Many dam sites built and operated by the Army have well-developed - and mostly unknown - recreation areas. Bonneville Dam has one of the largest public viewing facilities in the Corps. Named for Army Captain Benjamin Bonneville, an early explorer credited with charting much of the Oregon Trail, the dam and lock complex was built in 1938 to tame the wild Columbia River. The original navigation lock was the largest single-lift lock in the world when it opened.

The Recreation Area at Bonneville Dam is along the Oregon side of the Columbia River. It is favored mostly by fishermen and picnickers but is a good place to get out with your dog to walk around and appreciate the majesty of the Columbia Gorge around you.

Cascade Locks, Oregon
(541) 374-8820
www.nwp.usace.army.mil/op/b/home.asp

Conemaugh Dam (Pennsylvania)

The greatest dam failure in American history took place on the Little Conemaugh River when several days of rain in 1889 collapsed an earthen dam. Downstream the flood waters slammed into the steel city of Johnstown, triggering a firestorm in the accumulated debris. Four square miles of the town were destroyed and 2,209 lives were lost in the Johnstown Flood. In the aftermath several stories of dramatic rescues emerged, including a number that involved heroics by horses and dogs. Most notable was the saga of Romey, a Newfoundland-like dog who plunged into the floodwaters to save three members of his family who slipped off the roof of their submerged home.

Since its construction by the U.S. Army Corps of Engineers in 1952 it is estimated that the Conemaugh Dam has prevented over $2 billion in flood damage. The 137-foot high dam created a lake over seven miles long and as deep as 125 feet. Canine hiking at Conemaugh River Lake commences at the dam that has plugged the valley. The narrow *Woodchuck Nature Trail* begins atop a sandstone cliff overlooking the turquoise waters behind the concrete dam and twists pleasingly up the hillside for about one mile.

This is also an access point for the *West Penn Trail*, a 17-mile network of pathways that generally follow the route of the Pennsylvania Main Line Canal and Portage Railroad that operated from 1830 to 1864 between Pittsburgh and Harrisburg. The highlights of the 3.5-mile stretch behind the Conemaugh Dam are four multi-arch stone bridges that date to 1907. This is easy going for your dog but if you head towards Bow Ridge prepare for a slow, gradual switch-backing trail up the face of the ridge. How intimidating is Bow Ridge? To avoid going over it, the third tunnel in the United States was constructed here.

Loyalhanna, Pennsylvania
(724) 639-3785
www.lrp.usace.army.mil/rec/lakes/conemaug.htm

Grand Coulee Dam (Washington)

The angled, mile-wide Grand Coulee Dam, the largest concrete structure ever built in the United States, was conceived and constructed by the Bureau of Reclamation, an agency of the Department of the Interior responsible for managing water resources in the the West. It is the first of eleven dams blocking the Columbia River after the river flows into America from Canada and irrigates a a half-million acres of dusty land parched dry by the Pacific Cascade Mountains to the west.

Grand Coulee Dam backs up the Columbia for 130 miles into the slender Franklin D. Roosevelt Lake that is a magnet for boaters, fishermen and campers. Dogs are allowed everywhere in the Lake Roosevelt National Recreation Area except at picnic tables and on one of the ten designated swim beaches. Formal trails are scarce, limited essentially to a handful of short interpretive trails, none of which provide a view of Grand Coulee Dam.

The best way to see the dam with your dog is from the parks and overlooks downstream in the town of Grand Coulee. The steel truss Grand Coulee Bridge that crosses the Columbia River displays historic photographs from the dam's ten-year construction from 1932 to 1941 and is anchored by a park with statues of Woody Guthrie who was commissioned by the United States government to chronicle the Columbia River dams in folk song.

Coulee Dam, Washington
(509) 633-9441
www.nps.gov/laro/

Hoover Dam (Nevada)

One of the man-made wonders of the world, the Hoover Dam remains high on the list of America's greatest engineering triumphs 75 years after it was into operation. Many of the techniques employed in its construction had never been tried before and 112 men lost their lives to plug the Colorado River in the Black Canyon. The 726-foot high Hoover Dam is still the second highest dam in America (only the Oroville Dam in California is higher and it is earth fill) and the river backs up 110 miles behind it to fill Lake Mead, the country's largest man-made reservoir.

Millions of people come to vacation in the Lake Mead National Recreation Area above and below the dam, a water playground smack in the middle of an unforgiving desert. Your dog is welcome to join the fun-seekers on the water and in the campgrounds. The vast majority of acreage in the park is not under water, however, A rewarding trip plan at Lake Mead to experience the eastern fringes of the Mojave Desert is to drive to the various short hikes that have been created by the park service around the lake.

Experienced canine hikers will want to explore the canyons and washes of the designated wilderness areas of the desert, backcountry where dogs are not often permitted. This is rough steep terrain and during the summer temperatures can reach 120 degrees so the best time to log this on your dog's trip planner is between November and March.

Boulder City, Nevada
(702) 293-8990
www.nps.gov/lame/

Norris Dam (Tennessee)

The Tennessee Valley Authority (TVA), created by Franklin Roosevelt in 1933 to provide navigation, flood control and electricity to a region particularly ravaged by the Great Depression, remains one of America's grandest public works programs. The TVA roster would come to include, not without controversy, 11 fossil-powered plants, 29 hydroelectric dams, three nuclear power plants and six combustion turbine plants serving customers in parts of seven states.

Norris Dam was the first to be built, completed in 1936. It still has the largest flood control storage of any TVA dam on a tributary of the Tennessee River - Norris Reservoir extends 73 miles up the Clinch River and 56 miles up the Powell River. Including islands, the shoreline covers more than 800 miles. The TVA established several demonstration public parks on Norris Reservoir in the 1930s that became the nucleus of Tennessee's state park system. In addition to the trio of state parks, Tennessee administers two large game management areas and 59 public access sites. There are also three county parks. Think your dog can find an outdoor adventure here?

The stop at Norris Dam itself features three hiking trails. The *River Bluff Trail* is the longest at 3.1 miles and offers rich pockets of wildflowers; the others are pleasing nature strolls in the shadow of the 265-foot high dam. At pet-friendly Loyston Point Campground you take your dog on the *Hemlock Bluff National Recreation Trail*, possibly the definitive Norris Reservoir experience. The seven-mile loop trips through a rich pocket of hemlock forest along the steep lakeshore ridges and bluffs.

Andersonville, Tennessee
(856) 632-2101
www.tennessee.gov/environment/parks/NorrisDam/

Shasta Dam (California)

When construction across the Sacramento River began in 1938, the Shasta Dam was one of the most ambitious construction projects ever conceived. Completed in 1945, the water spilling over the Shasta Dam created the largest artificial waterfall ever seen - three times higher than the drop at Niagara Falls. Shasta Lake, fed by three rivers, is the largest lake in California.

The Shasta-Trinity National Recreation Area features more than 30 miles of paw-friendly dirt trails in three arms of the lake. Most are located in the McCloud Arm, including several less than one mile for canine hikers who like to bag many trails in an outing. The *Bailey Cove Trail* is a stand-out here as it loops for 2.9 miles around a peninsula in the lake. A longer scenic hike around a peninsula is the 7-mile *Clikapudi Trail*. This popular trail is shared with equestrians, joggers and mountain bikers.

Redding, California
(530) 226-2500
www.fs.fed.us/r5/shastatrinity/recreation/nra/shasta/index.shtml

DOGGIN' AMERICA'S WATERFALLS

DESTINATION
IDEA #23: DOGGIN' NIAGARA FALLS

Of all the crown jewels in America's natural tiara - Yellowstone, the Grand Canyon, Yosemite - none is as dog-friendly as Niagara Falls. Save for special guided tours, your dog can walk anywhere you walk to view the world-famous falls in both New York's **Niagara Falls State Park** and Ontario's **Queen Victoria Park**. And even with 12 million visitors a year, give or take a few heads, there is room for your dog.

It is hard to imagine these days but Niagara Falls, one of the world's most visited tourist destinations, was originally looked upon as a key military post and industrial site. One of the first Europeans to see the falls was 51-year old French priest Father Louis Hennepin in 1678. Hennepin is reported to have dropped to his knees in prayer and muttered, "the universe does not afford its parallel."

The French military, while perhaps appreciating the romantic sentiment, was more interested in building a fort to defend the natural trade route between Lake Erie and Lake Ontario. Travelers did not begin to arrive in western New York in great numbers until the opening of the Erie Canal in 1825 and the coming of the railroads in the 1830s. Many enjoyed the same reaction as Father Hennepin.

The tradition of honeymooners coming to Niagara where "the love of those who honeymoon here will last as long as the falls themselves" dates to the early 1800s when members of the French ruling Bonaparte family came on wedding trips. By the middle of the century the area around the Falls was a confused hodgepodge of water-powered mills and private resorts. Following the Civil War, a small group of visionaries began to look for a way to heal the scars to Niagara's natural beauty.

The "Free Niagara" crusade led to the creation of the Niagara Reservation, America's first state park in 1885. Frederick Law Olmsted, designer of New York City's Central Park and one of the leaders of the movement, laid out the park's network of wooded footpaths along the banks of the Niagara River. Olmsted's belief in retaining natural beauty while providing public access - for human and dog - endures at Niagara Falls to this day.

Niagara Falls reigns as one of the world's premier sightseeing destinations and your dog is welcome along. Due to the crush of visitors around the edge of the Falls it is best to begin your explorations of Niagara Falls State Park with the dog in the early morning hours when it is easier to maneuver around to the various vantage points. Even in the busiest times there are grass fields and shady promenades for the dog to romp. Begin your tour on the paved paths of Goat Island in the middle of the Niagara River, flanked by ferocious rapids on all sides. Pedestrian bridges lead to the Three Sisters Islands and Green Island for close-up looks of the wild river as it approaches the Falls.

Descend a flight of stairs to Luna Island, nestled in between the American Falls and the Bridal Veil Falls, before crossing back across Goat Island to the precipice of the Horseshoe Falls on the Canadian side. You and the dog can stand at the edge of all three falls and drink in the spray of water before the droplets fall 18 stories over the crest into the gorge. Forty million gallons of water spill over Niagara Falls every minute.

From these vantage points you can stand and contemplate the first recorded person to jump into the Falls. That was Sam Patch in October 1829, who leaped twice from a platform 110 feet high. He survived both jumps. The first person to successfully ride over the falls in a barrel was a woman, Annie Taylor, who survived the stunt on October 24, 1901. Of the 16 known attempts to ride the falls in a barrel or similar capsule - a stunt that is now illegal - 10 survived.

And dogs going over Niagara Falls? Sadly, there is one recorded account of just such an event. In December of 1874 some local hotel owners purchased an old Great Lakes schooner and planned to send it over the Falls to lure visitors to Niagara. To add drama to the spectacle the organizers loaded the ship with a buffalo, three bears, two foxes, a raccoon, a dog, a cat and four geese and cut their "Reverse Noah's Ark" loose in the rapids. The animals were observed scampering around the deck as the schooner slipped over the edge of the falls and smashed into hundreds of pieces on the rocks below. Only two geese were believed to survive the stunt.

For panoramic views of all three falls you will need to cross the gorge into Canada where you can take the dog for a stroll among the flower gardens of Queen Victoria Park. The park, managed by the Niagara Parks Commission, actually predates Niagara Falls State Park. Landscaping of the area with the sublime views of the rushing cataracts began in 1837 and it became a park in 1882. Both parks are free to visit, as are the nightly light shows illuminating the falls.

Niagara Falls has loads in store for the serious canine adventurer as well. The thrills of the Niagara River are not completely spent when the water crashes 170 feet down the falls into the gorge. The river, one of the shortest in the world, rumbles another turbulent 7 miles before disgorging its contents into Lake Ontario. The rapids in the river are among the wildest and fiercest in the world, rated a 6 on the navigable scale of 1-6. The dangerous Niagara River has historically had as strong a hold on daredevils as the falls themselves. Matthew Webb, the first man to swim the English Channel, perished in an attempt to swim across the Niagara River in 1883. Today, whirlpool jet boats ply the tamer of the rapids for thrill-seeking tourists.

The flat, paved *Niagara Gorge Rim Trail* runs six miles from the American Falls at Prospect Point along the canyon, linking a necklace of New York state parks along the way. Several sets of 300+ steps descend into the gorge in the parks to reach connecting trails along the river's edge. Much of the trail below the rim follows the roadbed of the historic Great Gorge Railway. The railway operated until September 17, 1935 when 5000 tons of rock slid down the cliffs and buried the tracks. Part of the trail crosses this rubble and involves considerable rock-hopping for an athletic dog.

These periodic rock falls - seldom of this magnitude - are more common in the winter and early spring and hiking in the gorge is recommended only between mid-May and November 1. The trail leads to the edge of the waves where the 35-foot deep river can reach speeds of 22 miles per hour. While the views of the water churning through Devil's Hole Rapids and Whirlpool Rapids can be mesmerizing, don't forget to look up now and then and perhaps spot the occasional bald eagle circling about, no doubt looking for an easy meal of dazed and battered fish.

The northern-most park along the Niagara Gorge is the **Earl W. Brydges Artpark** in Lewiston, where the cocktail was reportedly invented by a local tavern owner. She mixed gin and herb wine in a tankard and stirred her concoction with the tail feather of a handy stuffed cock pheasant. More traditional artists and crafts folk display their creations on the grounds of the 200-acre park. The river has calmed down enough by this point to permit a cautious swim for the dog.

The cliffs of the gorge at Lewiston are where Niagara Falls began some 12,000 years ago at the end of the Ice Age. Torrents of water from melting glacial ice poured over the edge of the Niagara Escarpment, as the cliff is known. The sheer force of the water has slowly worn away the rock and moved the falls to their present position seven miles upstream. Today, the falls are eroding at the rate of an inch per year. You can trace the travels of the falls in the rocks that line the gorge.

The *Niagara Gorge Trail System* ends at the imposing concrete dam of the Robert Moses Power Plant, completing a journey from the beauty of Niagara Falls to the hard reality of its practicality. Power plants on the American and Canadian sides of the Falls use water diverted from the Falls to generate enough electricity to light 2,500,000 100-watt light bulbs.

As impressive as the Falls are today, they are only a fraction as mighty as our ancestors saw - as much as half of the Niagara River's flow is diverted for hydroelectric production. Some day in the next 3,000 years Niagara Falls will wear away entirely and the power will dry up as water flows placidly between Lake Erie and Lake Ontario. Until that day, however, there is ample opportunity to take the dog and marvel at the power of Niagara.

Niagara Falls, New York
(905) 356-6061
www.niagarafallstourism.com/

DESTINATION
IDEA #24: DOGGIN' ITHACA

"Ithaca is Gorges." The college town's (Cornell University, Ithaca College) ubiquitous slogan was appropriately coined by a local professor in the 1970s who gave anyone the right to use it for free. The town on the southern end of Cayuga Lake comes by its moniker honestly - there are said to be 150 waterfalls within ten miles of town.

The namesake **Ithaca Falls** is the closest to lake, right in town in a small park with an oft-time muddy and slippery trail to its base. Fall Creek finishes its run from Beebe Lake to Cayuga Lake, dropping 400 feet along the way, with this final 75-foot plunge. Strap on your dog's hiking boots and take off on a two-mile round-trip on the *Cayuga Trail* and you'll pass Forest Falls, Foaming Falls, Rocky Falls and finally Triphammer Falls on the campus of Cornell University. There are vigorous climbs to many steep cliff tops and unprotected views down to the water. Keep a close rein on an exuberant dog. Fall Creek is spanned by a number of pedestrian bridges, including two suspension bridges.

Three creekbeds actually race through Ithaca, spilling dozens of waterfalls in their wake. South of Fall Creek is Cascadilla Creek where a short hike in the gorge will be rewarded with a view of nine waterfalls. The star is 50-foot **Cascadilla Falls**.

The City of Ithaca pulls four million gallons of drinking water daily from Six Mile Creek but there is still plenty for looking at. Unlike the area's other gorges that required an army of workers to construct stone paths along the water, the trails along Six Mile Creek evolved more naturally. It is a tamer walk and although you are close to downtown Ithaca your dog will find the wooded creekside quiet and leafy. From the **Mulholland Wildflower Preserve** there are several miles of streamside hiking along Six Mile Creek.

Another nearby town defined by its waterfall is **Ludlowville**. Here a wide creek bed crosses a thick erosion-resistant limestone caprock that lead to a combination plunge and bouncing cascade. The softer rock beneath the capstone has been scooped out by the pulsating water to form a cavern behind the curtain of water and interesting rock formations. In the small town park boot-carved trails lead to the top and bottom of the falls.

Ithaca is ringed by waterfall-themed state parks. To the south is **Buttermilk Creek** that storms 600 feet down two separate glens in the Cayuga Valley. It culminates in a wide curtain of water and public swimming pool that your dog can enjoy out of season.

Close by Buttermilk Falls is the "Lost Gorge" of Lick Brook and a trio of impressive waterfalls. The trails to the bottom of the 500-foot gorge could pass for a state park but it is in fact the **Sweedler Preserve** of the Finger Lakes Land Trust (www.fllt.org/protected_lands/protected_lands1.php?id=29). The conservation group hungered to preserve this spectacular property for years and finally obtained it when owner Moss Sweedler - who was going to deed it after his death to the Trust anyway - swapped his land on Lick Brook for a lesser piece of property with a pond where his dogs could swim.

To the southwest, about eight miles out of town, is **Enfield Glen**, arguably the most impressive of the Finger Lakes gorges. Robert Treman, an outstanding baseball pitcher at Cornell in the 1870s and later Deputy Governor of the Federal Reserve Bank of New York, donated 387 acres in Enfield Glen to the State. The marquee plunge in Robert H. Treman State Park is 120-foot Lucifer Falls; the Civilian Conservation Corps during the Great Depression did some of its most impressive stonework along Enfield Creek to make the gorge accessible to your dog.

Eight miles north of Ithaca, directly on Route 89, **Taughannock Falls** (nysparks.state.ny.us/parks/info.asp?parkId=93) drops to the west side of Cayuga Lake. That fall would be a single drop of 215 feet - 33 feet higher than Niagara and higher than all but one cataract east of the Rocky Mountains. A hiking loop can be created with climbs up both sides of the falls or your dog can just admire the falls after a flat hike from the lakeside state park.

Ithaca, New York
607-272-1313
www.visitithaca.com/

DESTINATION
IDEA #25: DOGGIN' THE ENDLESS MOUNTAINS

When the first European settlers grew restless on the shores of New England and began to migrate westward they encountered strings of north-south mountain ranges with few breaks or passes. It is no wonder that frustrated travelers hung the name "Endless Mountains" on these northeast Pennsylvania uber-hills.

A good waterfall trail might yield three, maybe four waterfalls. How about a trail that goes past 23 named waterfalls? That's what your dog will find on the always magical *Falls Trail* in **Ricketts Glen State Park** (www.dcnr.state.pa.us/ stateparks/parks/rickettsglen.aspx), a Y-shaped exploration along two branches of the Kitchen Creek. One of the most uniquely scenic areas in the Northeast, Ricketts Glen was slated to become a national park in the 1930s but World War II shelved plans for this development. Instead, it opened as a state park in 1944. Gradually the Commonwealth of Pennsylvania continued purchasing blocks of land from the descendants of Robert Bruce Ricketts until the park spread across more than 13,000 acres.

The remoteness of the land in the 19th century kept the waterfalls, ranging as high as the 94-foot Ganoga Falls, undiscovered until 1865. Colonel Ricketts hired a crew to build a trail along and across the plunging water and the project took 28 years. Today the *Falls Trail* remains a maintenance challenge and its steep grades can be muddy and slippery and your dog's four-wheel traction will be most welcome.

Kitchen Creek slices through the Ganoga Glen to the left and Glen Leigh to the right before uniting at Waters Meet. The two prongs of the trail connect at the top of the twin falls via the 1.2-mile *Highland Trail*. The complete falls experience encompasses almost seven miles. The stem of the trail flows through Ricketts Glen, among towering hemlocks and oaks, before tumbling over three cascades at Adams Falls near the trailhead.

Twenty miles to the west an arresting landscape awaits in **Worlds End State Park**(www.dcnr.state.pa.us/stateparks/parks/worldsend/). So named because the first road built here atop steep ridges left travelers feeling as if they were at the end of the world, these hiking trails wind to panoramic views of the Loyalsock Creek Gorge. The heart-stopping *High Rock Trail* is one of the most challenging short trails in Pennsylvania and features life-threatening drop-offs that mandate a tight leash on the dog. Your reward for these tough miles, are visits to High Rock Falls and a series of plunges along Double Run.

A third state park gracing the Endless Mountains, **Salt Springs** (www. dcnr.state.pa.us/stateparks/parks/saltsprings.aspx), serves up an enchanting run of cascades on the *Falls Brook Trail* with three signature waterfalls on one of Pennsylvania's most spectacular footpaths. The trail unwinds underneath a forest of Eastern hemlocks, some of which are estimated to be over 500 years old.

Endless Mountains, Pennsylvania
(570) 836-5431
www.endlessmountains.org/

DESTINATION
IDEA #26: DOGGIN' TRANSYLVANIA COUNTY

Transylvania County, in the mountains of western North Carolina, calls itself the "Land of Waterfalls" and backs up its claim with some 250 hydro-displays. Canine waterfall chasers will concentrate on three public areas: the Pisgah National Forest, DuPont State Forest and Gorges State Park.

But before diving into the heart of this bounty of tumbling water, head for **Nantahala National Forest** (www.cs.unca.edu/nfsnc/) on the North Carolina-South Carolina border for a look at Whitewater Falls. Upper Whitewater Falls is the highest waterfall east of the Rockies with an amazing plunge of 411 feet. South Carolina's Lower Whitewater Falls drops another 400 feet. The rugged setting does not afford easy access so your dog won't be playing in the falls here - just a short walk and some picture taking.

Up the road is **Gorges State Park**, a new public space where an elevation that rises 2,000 feet in only four miles and a rainfall in excess of 80 inches per year conspire to create a a superb collection of waterfalls. Your dog can reach splashdowns from conveniently located parking spots inside the park.

The **DuPont State Forest** in the southeastern slab of Transylvania county is home to three of the more impressive and accessible waterfalls in the North Carolina mountains. High Falls is the tallest of the Little River falls, hugging a granite slope for 150 feet as it charges down a mountain. Downstream the Little River darts right and left, breaking into three separate waterfalls. Triple Falls is easily reached on a wide, graded dirt path. Bridal Veil Falls requires a bit longer hike but the pay-off comes in a unique hydrospectacular where the Little River drops off an overhanging ledge and then spreads across a long, shallow inclined plane of granite before dumping into a pool at the bottom. There is water play aplenty for your dog in the Little River here.

The **Pisgah National Forest** is sprinkled with waterfalls, some that highlight sporty hikes with your dogs and others that wait just off forest roads. The most popular is Looking Glass Falls off US 276, where a stairway and observation deck afford access to the 65-foot curtain of water.

Moore Cove Falls is reached by a shortish, twisting trail that ends when the trail leads behind a 50-foot waterfall spilling over a rock lip. At ultra-popular Sliding Rock swimmers indeed slide down a sloping rock face propelled by 11,000 gallons of cold mountain water per minute. Your dog can't join the fun on the slide but can enjoy the pools downstream.

Transylvania County, North Carolina
www.transylvaniacounty.org/

DESTINATION
IDEA #27: DOGGIN' THE SIPSEY WILDERNESS

With nearly 25,000 acres under protection, this is the third largest wilderness area in the country east of the Mississippi River. Wild-flowing creeks in northwestern Alabama converge to become the Sipsey River, 61 miles of which has been designated Wild and Scenic. Enough water tumbles over cracks in limestone foundations that Sipsey, a part of the Bankhead National Forest, has been hailed as the "Land of 1,000 Waterfalls."

Unlike the waterfall hunting in other regions you do not drive from one hydrospectacular to another in the Sipsey Wilderness. Instead, you plant yourself in a camp and explore the region with your dog on foot. Six established trails can be combined to form hiking loops of many hours duration into the heart of Sipsey. Many of the waterfalls can't be reached by trail regardless - when you hear falling water start bushwhacking through the forest to find the source, often drips over wide, moss-covered rock ledges.

One of the most reliable and easiest to reach water spouts is **Fall Creek Falls** that is directly on *Trail 209*, less than one mile from its eastern junction with *Trail 200*, a major north-south passage through the forest. Traveling south from the Borden Creek Bridge trailhead the journey is less than three miles and as lovely a hike as you can take with your dog to a waterfall but involves a water crossing on a sandy creek bed and a memorable 100-foot passage for your dog through a narrow cave (remember, this is a wilderness).

Bankhead National Forest, Alabama
(205) 489-5111
www.fs.fed.us/r8/alabama/

DESTINATION
IDEA #28: DOGGIN' THE UPPER PENINSULA

Sooner or later all serious waterfall hunters make their way to Michigan's Upper Peninsula. The Wolverine State claims some 200 named waterfalls and all but one lie in the Upper Peninsula. In this remote land much of the plunging water is easier for your dog to hike to than for you to drive to but aim your car down Route 28 and you will hit most of Michigan's watery highlights.

Traveling east to west after crossing the Mackinac Bridge your first stop is your most dramatic. The 200-foot wide Tahquamenon River reaches a 50-foot escarpment and dumps more than 50,000 gallons of amber-tinged water per   second over its edge. A narrow trail leads your dog away from the typical crowds and meanders four miles downstream to the eclectic Lower Falls in **Tahquamenon Falls State Park** where the river tumbles around an island across a wide panorama (www.michigan.gov/dnr/).

The Upper Peninsula's prime attraction, the **Pictured Rocks National Lakeshore**, looms to the west. Blessed with a half-dozen waterfalls, it is nonetheless not an earmarked destination for the traveling dog owner. Dogs are not permitted on the trail to Sable Falls and the spectacular Spray Falls, that pours directly into Lake Superior, is best viewed by boat. Still, Miners Falls and Munising Falls are impressive and easy for your dog to reach.

Back on Route 28 heading west, a short sidetrack lands you at **Wagner Falls** where your dog is welcome on a short trail that leads up to a viewing platform. Due west of Munising is the **Laughing Whitefish Scenic Site** (www.michigandnr. com/parksandtrails/Details.aspx?id=422&type=SPRK) where the river slides delicately down a 100-foot rock face. A well-trod trail leads to the top of one of Michigan's highest waterfalls and stairs lead to the bottom where your dog can play in the river. In drier weather the flow becomes thin enough to negate a visit.

After slipping into Ontonagon County you reach two more state scenic sites at **Agate Falls** and **Bond Falls**. Just off the road across the Ontonagon River Agate Falls drops 40 feet with a crest twice that high. To the south, down U.S. 45 and east of Paulding, is a full-fledged member of the pantheon of Michigan waterfalls: Bond Falls. A boardwalk takes your dog to the base of this 100-foot wide hydrospectacular.

Just before leaving Michigan, pick up the Black River Scenic Byway north of Bessemer. The Black River produces a series of plunges on its journey to Lake Superior. The two most accessible and picturesque are the neighboring Potawatomi and Gorge Falls. Nearby is **Porcupine Mountains State Park** (www. porcupinemountains.com/) where the Presque Isle River's final sprint to Lake Superior is characterized by a series of wide drops over bare rock. Your dog can hike on both sides of the river to reach these falls and trot over a suspension bridge to Presque Isle.

Upper Peninsula, Michigan
906-774-5480
www.uptravel.com/

DESTINATION

IDEA #29: DOGGIN' IRON COUNTY

The north woods of Wisconsin are laced with waterfalls and are a worthy destination for any connoisseur. But dog owners beware - many of the Dairy State's most popular cataracts are in state parks (Brownstone Falls and Copper Falls in Ashland County, for example) and are reached via designated nature trails. And dogs are not allowed on Wisconsin state park nature trails.

Iron County, south of Lake Superior, has the state's most displays of tumbling water -15 - and three are among the state's six highest. Since most of these hydrospectaculars are off the beaten path your dog will be welcome if you make the effort to seek them out. The most beautiful of Iron County's falls is on the **Potato River** southwest of tiny Gurney. A 131-step descent leads your dog to the brink of the powerful Upper Falls as they maneuver around old volcanic rock. The impressive Lower Falls can be explored by adventurous canine hikers on steep, informal trails that lead into the river gorge.

Your dog will likely relish the scrambling to the plunge pool of 35-foot **Peterson Falls** on the Montreal River north of Hurley. The short footpath leads to the lip of the falls but further on you can slide down a conifer-anchored bank and pick your way back to the cascade where your dog can score a refreshing swim.

Further downstream, near its mouth on Lake Superior, the Montreal River makes its last gasp in Wisconsin as it falls 90 feet at **Superior Falls**. From a power company recreation area in Michigan a short trail winds down to Lake Superior before turning and heading to the plunge basin framed by rocky gorge walls.

Waterfall seekers may also want to head east to Marinette County which bills itself as "Wisconsin's Waterfall Capital." The water here is heading not to Lake Superior but is part of the Lake Michigan watershed. The county's nine waterfalls are not so much dramatic plunges as rapids on steroids. The best is **Long Slide Falls** that powers 50 scenic feet down the shale and sandstone of the North Branch of the Pemebonwon River. A sprightly trail in a county park leads to a ledge overlooking Long Slide. You can take your dog down a steep embankment to the water and onto a 1.5-mile trail upstream to **Smalley Falls** through a classic Wisconsin woodland.

Iron County, Wisconsin
www.wisconline.com/attractions/waterfalls.html

DESTINATION
IDEA #30: DOGGIN' LAKE SUPERIOR'S NORTH SHORE

The westernmost edge of Lake Superior is characterized by craggy headlands blanketed in thick coatings of pine and birch. Along the coast dozens of fast-flowing streams are cascading down small mountains to mingle with the waters of Lake Superior. Hardy canine hikers can take in the entire north shore on Minnesota's Superior Hiking Trail that winds through 200 miles of wilderness but most visitors will choose to explore these waterfalls via the North Shore Scenic Drive on Highway 61, immortalized by Bob Dylan in 1960s music lore.

Pulling out of Duluth, your first destination is **Gooseberry Falls** (www.dnr. state.mn.us/state_parks/gooseberry_falls/), located past the Port of Two Harbors where the 3M Company had its beginnings more than a century ago producing sandpaper. Twinned with a highway rest stop, you and your dog will likely be sharing the intertwining trails around a pair of 30-foot Gooseberry River cascades with plenty of casual waterfall hunters.

Next up for your water-loving dog is **Tettegouche State Park** (www. dnr. state.mn.us/state_parks/tettegouche/) where a mile of trails lead to hydrospectaculars on the Baptism River. At High Falls your dog can work down to a dip in the plunge pool but this requires a crossing of the river on an open grate bridge that may stop an overly cautious dog. Downstream, a long wooden staircase takes your dog to water's edge and a swim in front of 2 Step Falls.

Wayside parking areas serve up your dog's next gateway to adventure along Lake Superior. At the sign for "Caribou" pull off to the parking lot on the west side of the road. Here the *Superior Hiking Trail* hugs the **Caribou River** for a half-mile until you reach a spot where a cataract of water is pinched through a gap in the granite and plunges powerfully down 60 feet. Further along, near the village of Schroeder, the Cross River Falls can be viewed from the paved wayside. Next a series of rocky gorges and waterfalls on the Temperance River can be accessed from the wayside parking lot. If your dog is feeling frisky a six-mile round trip hike to Carlton Peak here leads to panoramic views of Lake Superior.

The "cascades" of the **Cascade River** can be absorbed with a canine hike of less than an hour to view them rushing into Lake Superior. There is plenty of swim time for your water-loving dog along the many trails in this state park. In **Judge Magney State Park** a hike along the rugged mile-long footpath to the Brule River is rewarded with the beauty of Devil's Kettle waterfall.

The northern bookend of your dog's North Shore waterfall tour comes in **Grand Portage State Park** (www.dnr.state.mn.us/state_parks/grand_portage/) where the Pigeon River forms the border between the United States and Canada. Here the river rushes over a 120-foot drop in a series of torrents that forms the highest waterfall in Minnesota and the second highest around the entirety of Lake Superior. A well-traveled one-mile trail and boardwalk take your dog to the high falls area.

Superior North Shore, Minnesota
www.northshoreguide.com/

DESTINATION
IDEA #31: DOGGIN' THE COLUMBIA GORGE

In 1986 the Columbia River Gorge between Oregon and Washington was designated America's first National Scenic Area. Created by a cataclysmic blast of glacial lake water 15,000 years ago, the Columbia river flows through one of the few east-west canyons in the world. Some 77 waterfalls tumble off ridges and sheer walls that soar 2,000 feet above the river. Included in this hydrospectacular bounty is the largest concentration of high waterfalls in North America.

The best way to explore these falls is along a remnant stretch of the Historic Columbia River Highway that was carved out of the cliffs in 1916. The two-lane passageway, punctuated by intricate stonework and artful bridges, serves up a series of trailheads between Exits 35 and 28 of I-84. From the trailheads you will find a pleasing array of canine hiking choices ranging from gentle paved pathways at feature falls to steep, day-long backpacking scrambles into the interior of the Gorge.

The centerpiece of the Columbia Gorge waterfall collection is **Multnomah Falls**, America's second-highest year-round plunge at 620 feet in two sheer drops. The trails surrounding Multnomah can be linked to form energizing hiking loops to neighboring falls. The five-mile round trip westward leads to 242-foot **Wahkeena Falls** that squeezes through a basaltic cliff, passes drape-like Fairy Falls and skirts several waterfalls on Multnomah Creek. A short downhill spur leads your dog right to the lip of Multnomah Falls.

To the east a shorter loop tags falls in the Oneonta Gorge chasm, the twisting **Horsetail Falls** (176 feet) and its picturesque cousin further upstream, **Ponytail Falls**. After trotting behind this 80-foot cataract down a curving basalt alcove your dog can play in the plunge pool. The plunge pool below Horseshoe Falls is also easy for your dog to walk in and take a swim.

As you travel east through the Columbia Gorge the average yearly rainfall drops about an inch a mile and the temperature rises. Just east of the Columbia River Highway at the Bonneville Dam Exit of I-84 is the scenic loop along Tanner Creek to powerful **Wahclella Falls**. The east side of this mile-long trail travels through cedar glades and stately Douglas firs while the west side of the gorge resembles a western desert.

At the next exit (#41), still traveling east on I-84, you bring your dog to *Eagle Creek Trail*, the most popular hike in the Columbia Gorge. The footpath in places has been blasted directly into the basalt cliffs as it traces Eagle Creek through impossibly green forests. The resulting surface has been left jagged and rough which will challenge the paw pads of your dog in these short crossings.

Although the trail continues further, the destination for most ambitious canine hikers is six miles out at **Tunnel Falls** where the trail passes behind a shower of falling water. Less determined dog adventurers can content themselves with a two-mile jaunt to **Punch Bowl Falls** where the waters pound into a blue-green pool set in a large grotto. This is easy going just about the entire way but sheer drop-offs from the unguarded cliffs make Eagle Creek a trail only for well-behaved dogs.

Columbia River Gorge, Oregon
(541) 308-1700
www.fs.fed.us/r6/columbia/forest/

DESTINATION
IDEA #32: DOGGIN' AMERICA'S HIGHEST WATERFALL

Yosemite Falls plunges a total of 2,425 feet in three drops making it by far the highest waterfall in the United States and one of the ten highest in the world. The falls are fed mostly be snowmelt so if you show up late in the summer with your dog Yosemite Falls may be totally dry. And yes, your dog can stand at the bottom of Yosemite Falls.

Dogs are not allowed on trails or in the backcountry of **Yosemite National Park**. This prohibition includes ski trails in winter. Dogs are, however, allowed to walk anywhere on the Yosemite Valley floor between the Happy Isles Nature Center or Mirror Lake parking lot and the Pohono bridge. Yosemite Falls are visible from several spots around the Yosemite Valley. Other falls that you can take your dog to on the paved surfaces are Bridalveil Falls (620 feet) that you see on the south side of Yosemite Falls as you enter the valley and its neighbor Ribbon Falls that spills 1,612 feet over a bare rock cliff. These hyrdospectaculars are even more tenuous that Yosemite Falls - arrive in May to observe peak flow for these falls.

Yosemite is generous to dogs in its campgrounds - four campgrounds, located in each of the major sections of the park, allow dogs throughout and another four have sections of the campground set aside for dog owners.

Yosemite, California
(209) 372-0200
www.nps.gov/yose/

DOGGIN' AMERICA'S COASTAL ISLANDS

Who doesn't want to get away to an off-shore island with the dog? Let's do a quick round-up of America's off-shore islands accessible for your dog only by passenger ferry or private boat...

DESTINATION
IDEA #33: DOGGIN' MONHEGAN ISLAND

It was artists who first popularized this tiny island (.7 of a mile wide and 1.7 miles long) about ten miles off the Maine coast in the late 1800s. They came to capture the light dancing off the highest cliffs on the New England shore, the epitome of the famous rocky Maine coast. Artists today will see much the same images - the island still has no electricity, save for private generators, and no automobiles.

About half of the island's 650 acres have been protected by the Monhegan Associates. Some 17 miles of foot paths connect scenic headlands with marshy lowlands. Novice canine hikers may wish to confine their explorations to Lobster Cove Road, the island's sole road and *Whitehead Trail #7* that rolls past an 1824 lighthouse and out to the 160-foot high cliffs of White Head overlooking the Atlantic Ocean. Another good choice is Cathedral Woods, an area of dark spruce trees. More adventurous trail dogs will find challenging fare along the sea with steep climbs and rugged going.

This is likely to be a day trip with your dog, rather than a vacation. There are only five places to stay on the island unless you know someone with a cottage or rent your own.

(island transportation: foot traffic for visitors and golf carts for residents)
Monhegan, Maine
www.monheganassociates.org/

DESTINATION
IDEA #34: DOGGIN' NANTUCKET ISLAND

Thirty miles off the coast you can reach Nantucket with your dog by ferry (dogs go free) or commuter plane (about $10 for your dog). Upon disembarking in the Nantucket Sound you are looking at a hike of between two and six miles to reach the various ocean beaches across the island. You can use paved bike paths if you have to but dogs are allowed on the island shuttles (free again for dogs). Much of the coastline is in private hands so access to the shore is a privilege when granted.

Strong canine swimmers who enjoy riding big breakers will want to cross the island to test the Atlantic surf spanking the South Shore. The convenient town beaches of the North Shore are of a gentler nature, suitable for any dog to dip a paw into.

For a long beach stroll with your dog head for the Eastern Shore and aim north towards the secluded Great Point. Seven miles away is the whitewashed, solar-powered Great Point Lighthouse that is a replica of an 1818 tower washed away in a "noreaster" that blew across the island in 1984.

For tamer pursuits, your dog can enjoy a romp at Tuppency Links, where a basket of tennis balls is kept at the ready. And there is no reason to run off the island after your day is done - many Nantucket lodges are pet-friendly. One, The Woof Hotel, a 12-room inn at Harbor Village offers special doggie beds, a fenced bark park and a Yappy Hour.

(island transportation: limited vehicular)
Nantucket Island, Massachusetts
nantucket.net/

DESTINATION

IDEA #35: DOGGIN' MARTHA'S VINEYARD

Human habitation is thought to have begun on Martha's Vineyard before it was an island in the time before melting glaciers raised the level of the Atlantic Ocean. Some are convinced that the Norsemen visited here around 1000 A.D. and in 1524 Verrazzano is known to have sailed by and named the island Indians called Noepe, "Louisa." Other explorers gave the island a name but its enduring moniker came in 1602 from Bartholomew Gosnold, who immortalized one of his young daughters and the wild grapes that grew in abundance.

Just off the southern coast of Cape Cod, Martha's Vineyard is an extremely dog-friendly resort destination. For canine hikers, the Sheriff's Meadow Foundation has conserved over 2,100 acres of land on Martha's Vineyard in more than 100 separate parcels. From these protected lands the Foundation has created eight sanctuaries open to the public, including dogwalkers. The largest trail system is at Cedar Tree Neck Sanctuary where two miles of paw-friendly trails visit hilly woodlands, secluded ponds and a small sandy beach.

Colonial Martha's Vineyard was a vibrant place with butter churning from its inland farms and its ports a constant whirl of activity. However, British raiders during the American Revolution torched the towns and stole 10,000 sheep and 300 head of cattle from Patriot farms. The island economy was crippled until a small congregation of Methodists staged a religious camp meeting in 1835. Within 20 years the yearly retreat was drawing more than 10,000 attendees and Martha's Vineyard was reborn as a resort destination. The tents from the camp meeting gave way to wooden cottages in Wesleyan Grove. Today more than 300 of these eclectic Victorian cottages remain clustered on the circular paths behind the main streets of Oak Bluffs. You and your dog can wander through the campground, placed on the National Register of Historic Places in 1979 on the Centennial of the historic Tabernacle, that served as the centerpiece of the camp meetings.

(*island transportation: vehicular*)
Martha's Vineyard, Massachusetts
(508) 696-7400
www.mvol.com/

DESTINATION
IDEA #36: DOGGIN' BLOCK ISLAND

There are 17 miles of public beaches on Block Island, resting an hour ferry ride off the Rhode Island mainland, so your dog is sure to get an ocean swim here. Most day-tripping dog owners arrive without a car and queue up with their dogs ready for some spirited walking on the island. The ferry rate per person is less than $20 round trip and dogs ride free.

Crescent Beach, a few pawprints from the ferry landing, is the most convenient but crowded in-season. One beach that is too small for sun worshippers but ideal for dogs is just south of Old Harbor along Spring Street - as you reach the crest of a hill drop down to the sand in front of a guardrail for great canine swimming along a breakwater in frisky waves.

Once on the island there are two famous beach bluffs within walking distance: to the north is Clay Head, the one you see on the ferry, and to the south are the Mohegan Bluffs. To do both in one day on foot is quite an undertaking so without transportation you will be forced to decide on a destination. This is not a win-lose proposition by any means - especially since you'll probably vow to return to Block Island again.

If you head for Mohegan Bluffs, you will be using *The Greenway*, a system of about 12 miles of footpaths crisscrossing the southern half of Block Island in the tradition of walking the English countryside. What is your dog interested in? Open fields? Sporty hills? Long vistas? A romp on the beach? A swim in a pond? Unique woodlands? The Greenway has them all.

Turning north there is only one road to take and setting out for a couple of miles on Corn Neck Road. You will eventually reach a trail system known as "The Maze." These grassy trails are unmarked but well-maintained and a delight for your dog. You can pop out at a stone wall or one of the best views on the East Coast. The *Clay Head Nature Trail* runs for about one mile along the top of the 70-foot bluffs. It is easy going but will be one of the longest miles you've ever taken with your dog when you factor in the frequent stops for watching the crashing waves or charting the progress of a passing vessel.

(*island transportation: limited vehicular*)
Block Island, Rhode Island
(800) 383-BIRI
www.blockislandchamber.com/

DESTINATION
IDEA #37: MACKINAC ISLAND

At first blush, tourist mecca Mackinac Island in Lake Huron would seem to be a horrible place to bring a dog - teeming with crowds and literally thousands of bikes in the narrow streets. But do not despair. No one is coming to Mackinac to hike so once you walk your dog a half-mile from the landing dock, past the neatly kept shops and beyond the historic fort, you reach a Mackinac Island that existed long before any settlers arrived. You are likely to go for an hour or more and never see anyone.

Mackinac Island is about three miles long and two miles wide. A bike path - heavily used by wheelers and walkers - circles the island for 8.3 miles at shore level. The water's edge is alternately muddy and rocky and not conducive for doggie dips in Lake Huron so after sampling the coast awhile your dog will gladly trade dodging the whizzing rental bikes for the peaceful footpaths of the island's interior. These wooded highlands reach heights over 300 feet - enough elevation change to support a lively hike and provide inspired Great Lakes views but not enough to tire a vacationing dog.

The trails are a pleasing mix of natural footpaths and wide cartpaths laid down for Victorian guests to the island a century ago. The island's unique location and elevation changes support an enchanting mix of North Woods conifers and southern hardwoods. There is no hurry to hustle your dog back to the mainland after a day on Mackinac Island. Several lodges and resorts allow dogs.

(*island transportation: foot and bicycle only*)
Mackinac Island , Michigan
http://www.mackinac.com/

DESTINATION
IDEA #38: GRAND ISLAND

The largest island in south Lake Superior is only a five-minute ride across the perpetual 48-degree waters. But forget the high speed, fully loaded catamarans that whisk you to tourist islands like neighboring Mackinaw Island. The small boat to Grand Island, part of the Hiawatha National Forest and designated a National Recreation Area, holds about a half-dozen people and dogs.

The ferry makes only a handful of trips a day so you can expect hiking with your dog along wide dirt roads to be a private affair. At four miles long by two miles wide a full day of hiking will take your dog around the entire forested island on well-marked routes. As you work deeper into Grand Island you climb atop 300-foot bluffs. Destinations include deserted sand beaches and overlooks of Lake Superior coves. If your dog can't be enticed to leave the excellent swimming in the shallow, crystalline waters of the beach at Trout Bay, come prepared and camp overnight.

(*island transportation: foot and mountain bike only*)
Grand Island , Michigan
www.grandislandmi.com

DESTINATION
IDEA #39: CATALINA ISLAND

More than one million people a year cross the channel to rocky Catalina Island, about 22 miles off the southern California coast. It's a big island - 22 miles long and 8 miles across at its widest. The natural parts of the island are controlled by the Catalina Island Conservancy that allows dogs on its extensive trail system. A free daily hiking permit is required before setting out on the network of old ranching roads and footpaths.

(*island transportation: limited vehicular, mostly bicycle and golf cart*)
Catalina Island, California
(310) 510-1520
www.catalinachamber.com/

DESTINATION
IDEA #40: SAN JUAN ISLANDS

This cluster of hundreds of islands (60 are populated) spans the United States-Canadian border, with the most popular being San Juan Island. It is best to arrive with a car where you can set out to visit the many parks and preserves that will welcome your dog. Most feature small, scenic trail systems that require less than one hour. Many of the roads and paths are remnants of old sheep trails. Two of the must-see parks are **Lime Kiln Point State Park**, the only park in the world dedicated to whale watching (especially killer whales) and the **San Juan Island National Historic Park** where dogs can accompany you on guided tours. The trailheads at this dog-friendly park feature mutt mitts. For a top beach, head for Grandma's Cove at American Camp.

Orcas Island is the largest of the San Juans with over 50 square miles. The centerpiece for outdoor recreation is 5,000-acre Moran State Park that serves up old-growth forest, a handful of lakes and 30 miles of trails. The summit of half-mile high Mount Constitution with 360-degree views can be purchased by car or paw power. Ellsworth Storey, one of Seattle's most popular architects from the first half of the 20th century, designed the 52-foot lookout atop Mount Constitution to resemble a medieval watchtower. Built by Depression-era Civilian Conservation Corps workers, the sandstone blocks were quarried on the island.

(island transportation: vehicular)
San Juan Islands, Washington
(888) 468-3701

3

ROAD TRIPPIN' WITH YOUR DOG

GOING THE DISTANCE

TOUR

IDEA #41: DOGGIN' THE BLUE RIDGE PARKWAY

Begun as a Depression-era public works project, the Blue Ridge Parkway was America's first rural parkway. When ultimately completed it was also the nation's longest - 469 miles of uninterrupted mountain roads linking Shenandoah National Park in the north to the Great Smoky Mountains National Park in the south. The Blue Ridge Parkway is far and away the most popular destination in the National Park System - more than 19 million recreation visits per year. One of the explanations for its enduring popularity could be that the Blue Ridge is also one of America's most dog-friendly destinations.

Designed for leisurely motoring, the speed limit never exceeds 45 mph on the Parkway and roadside parking is permitted on the shoulders the entire way. In many places the beautiful road is lined by low stone walls. You will never see a billboard and scarcely any development. Parks and recreation areas - several spanning thousands of acres - appear roughly every 30 miles, although most are located in the Blue Ridge Mountains, the 355 miles that comprise the northern part of the route. The lower 114 miles wind through the powerful Black Mountains, named for the dark green spruce that cover the massive slopes, and they offer more limited leg-stretching opportunities for your dog.

There is no reason for your dog to enjoy the Blue Ridge solely with his head hanging out the car window. Dogs are allowed on the more than 100 varied trails throughout the Blue Ridge Parkway, ranging from easy valley strolls to demanding mountain summit hikes. Travelers and canine hikers can spend a week motoring on the Parkway and barely sample all its treasures. And it is no trouble to slow down and take as much time as you like on the trails - all the nine first come, first served campgrounds on the Parkway welcome dogs. You will find many of the inns and restaurants in the small towns that flank the Parkway to be dog-friendly as well.

Tracing the route from the north, an early highlight comes within the first ten miles at the **Humpback Rocks** (Milepost 5 to 9.3) where the *Greenstone*

Nature Trail leads to the unusually shaped boulders. A strenuous climb accesses the *Appalachian Trail* in another two miles. Canine hikers will look forward to the **Peaks of Otter**, in the vicinity of the highest mountains on the Virginia section of the Parkway, beginning around the 75-mile mark. Three mountains - Sharp Top (3,875 feet), Flat Top (4,004 feet), and Harkening Hill (3,364 feet) comprise the Peaks of Otter (Milepost 84 to 87), a popular hiking destination since Colonial days when Thomas Jefferson was an enthusiastic visitor. The 4.4-mile trail to the Flat Top summit is graded most of the way until jumbled rocks provide athletic dogs a tail-wagging workout.

Also in the Peaks of Otter is a quick loop hike threading through rhododendron and mountain laurel on Onion Mountain and the 1.6-mile loop of the *Fallingwater Cascades National Scenic Trail* (Milepost 83.4). Both offer splendid views in exchange for moderate effort. At the 167-mile mark comes **Rocky Knob** (Milepost 167 to 174), with 15 miles of trails across 4,800 acres. The marquee walk here is the rugged 10.8-mile *Rock Castle Gorge National Recreation Trail*. Just down the road is picturesque **Mabry Mill** (Milepost 176.1) with an easy, self-guiding trail spiced with interpretive exhibits and in-season demonstrations on rural Appalachian life. Water-powered Mabry Mill is the most photographed landmark on the Blue Ridge Parkway.

The first canine hiking after the Parkway crosses the Virginia state line into North Carolina comes on **Cumberland Knob** (Milepost 217.5). A quick 15-minute loop here leads to the knob and a more challenging 2-mile loop traces Gully Creek. Next up is 7,000-acre **Doughton Park** (Milepost 238.5 to 244.7), the largest recreation area on the Blue Ridge Parkway. More than 30 miles of trail and a dog-friendly campground are the prime attractions here.

The **Moses H. Cone Memorial Park** (Milepost 292 to 295) is a popular stopping point for relaxing or exploring. Many miles of horse and carriage trails jump off from the Historic Cone Manor House and many more trails crisscross neighboring **Julian Price Memorial Park** (Milepost 295.1 to 298), which includes Price Lake, one of the few lakes along the Parkway. Even if hiking isn't on your itinerary when you reach this spot, you will want to stop and sit on the Manor House lawn with your dog and take in the views. In another 10 miles you cross the **Linn Cove Viaduct** (Milepost 304.4), an engineering marvel skirting the side of Grandfather Mountain. Ground was broken on the Blue Ridge Parkway on September 11, 1935 at Cumberland Knob on the North Carolina-Virginia border, near the mid-point of the proposed route. By 1967 all but seven and one-half of its 469 miles were complete. The final section, around the rocky slopes of Grandfather Mountain, one of the world's oldest mountains, would not be finished until 1987.

Finishing the Parkway without massive cuts and fills on the fragile mountainside called for the most complicated concrete bridge ever built - the serpentine Linn Viaduct. The 12 bridges of the Viaduct were constructed from the top down at an elevation of 4,100 feet to eliminate the need for a pioneer road. In fact, the only trees cut down during the entire project were those directly beneath the roadbed. The only construction on the ground was the drilling of seven permanent piers upon which the Viaduct rests. Exposed rock was even covered to present staining from the concrete epoxy binding the precast sections. To further minimize the intrusion on the mountain, concrete mixes were tinted with iron oxide to blend with existing outcroppings. Trails lead to views underneath this engineering marvel and access the 13.5-mile *Tanawha Trail* from Beacon Heights to Julian Price Park. You and your dog can wander along an interpretive trail to close-up views of the Viaduct.

You can leave the Parkway for less than a mile and let your dog explore **Grandfather Mountain** (Milepost 305) that you have been driving around. For its abundance of rare and endangered plant species, Grandfather Mountain (www.grandfather.com/) has been designated one of the world's few International Biosphere Reserves. Most of the preserve is privately owned and your dog is welcome, even to cross the Mile-High Swinging Bridge. Well-behaved dogs can hike the extensive trail system with you off-leash, although extended rambles up the mountain are limited by ladder climbs on some Crest trails. Your best bet for a day hike with your dog is a one-mile rock-studded string along the *Black Rock Nature Trail* that trips past rock formations to a set of boulders with views across the Blue Ridge Mountains (note: a pull up a rope is necessary to access the views which your dog may not be able to share)

A most-anticipated highlight of the Blue Ridge Parkway will be the upcoming **Linville Gorge** (Milepost 316.3), one of the most remote locations in the Appalachians. Unblazed trails lead deep into the wilderness but most canine hikers will stick to the two main hiking trails surrounding Linville Falls. *Erwins View Trail* is a sporty walk that takes in four distinct overlooks of the plunging waters in its .8-mile journey. More challenging is the hike on the opposite side of the water into the gorge that descends through a virgin hemlock forest via a switchback to the water's edge beneath the Falls. Enjoy a superb doggie dip.

South of Linville Falls the elevations climb and the canine hiking opportunities fade away. **Craggy Pinnacle Trail** (Milepost 364.4) is a narrow ridge trail that tunnels through purple rhododendron to a hilltop opening in a veritable sea of trees. A second moderate trail here is the Craggy Gardens nature trail. Nearby, a spur road leads up **Mount Mitchell** (Milepost 355.4). Your dog can make the final paved ascent to the 6684-foot summit and stand on the highest point of ground east of the Mississippi River. The mountain was named for Dr. Elisha Mitchell, who fell to his death when trying to prove the actual height of the peak.

At Milepost 395, turn off the Parkway and turn into the **North Carolina Arboretum**. Your dog can't tour the exhibition gardens but those are a small part of the presentation. Move straight to the trail system that flows from the Exhibit Center down the wooded hillside to Bent Creek. The flat, serpentine dirt Bent Creek Road is the main travelway through the Arboretum but if the cyclists are a nuisance ump onto the narrow footpath that parallels Bent Creek. Use this corridor to craft hiking loops with the other park trails, some of which are padded in paw-friendly wood chips.

The last major recreation area on the Parkway comes south of Asheville at **Mount Pisgah** (Milepost 408.6), once part of the 125,000-acre Biltmore Estate owned by George W. Vanderbilt. Vanderbilt directed trail building efforts across his vast property to provide access for hunting and horseback riding. It was the first large tract of managed forest land in America. The trail to summit views of Mt. Pisgah (5,721 feet) is a hardy 1.26-mile climb.

The final gasps for canine hiking on the Blue Ridge Parkway before entering **Great Smoky Mountain National Park** - where dogs are not allowed on the trails - occur at Milepost 431 where Richard Balsam's self-guiding trail wanders through the remnants of a spruce-fir forest on the highest point on the Parkway (6,047 feet) and at **Waterrock Knob** at Milepost 451.2. Here a mountain trail leads to the knob and its panoramic, 4-state views of the Great Smokies.

Allow yourself three to five days to explore the Blue Ridge Parkway with your dog - a distance that could be covered in six hours of driving on the Interstate. Even that may not be enough time. Don't be surprised if you find yourself wanting to turn around and do it all again.

Blue Ridge Parkway, Virginia/North Carolina
www.blueridgeparkway.org/

TOUR
IDEA #42: DOGGIN' THE NATCHEZ TRACE PARKWAY

Long used by the Natchez, Chickasaw and Choctaw Indians as a hunting path from the Mississippi River to the Tennessee River, the Trace became an important trade route with the arrival of European settlers. The French mapped the trail as early as 1733 and enough travelers tramped down the crude path that became the most-heavily used road of the Old Southwest. The route was dotted with roadhouses and familiar to traders in the Ohio Valley who floated goods down the Mississippi River, sold their flatboats for lumber and rode or walked home on the 400+ miles of the Natchez Trace. The importance of the Trace waned in the early 1800s with the arrival of the steamboat and it gradually quieted to the feel of a country lane.

In the 1930s a 444-mile Natchez Trace Parkway between Nashville, Tennessee and Natchez, Mississippi was begun, by which time much of the original Trace had been destroyed by development. Today, modern-day travelers with dogs can enjoy an unhurried trip through the Old South that mimics the route of the original trace...

Just six miles from the Northern terminus below Nashville comes an engineering highlight in the construction of the Parkway - the innovative **Double Arch Bridge** (Milepost 438) that rises 155 feet above the valley. Another dozen miles down the road your dog can sample the **Old Trace** (Milepost 426.3) for the first time on a section cleared by the U.S. Army back in 1801. These chances for leisurely excursions on the historic pathway come at regular intervals, seldom longer than a quarter mile.

In fact, most your outings with your dog along the Parkway will be of the laid-back, strolling variety. Your first campground/picnic area comes a bit more than an hour into your journey at the **Meriwether Lewis Site** (Milepost 385.9). There are foot trails here for your dog along the Little Swan Creek and a re-creation of the rough hewn Grinder's Inn where the co-captain of the Lewis & Clark Corps of Discovery and one-time governor of the Louisiana Territory died of unexplained gunshot wounds in 1809.

In another 15 minutes a turn-off takes you along a narrow 2.5-mile road that follows the original trace route. In another hour the Parkway briefly visits the State of Alabama. Your dog's highlight in his short time in the Yellowhammer state will probably be at **Colbert Ferry** (Milepost 327.3) where he can enjoy a swim in the Tennessee River. The story goes that George Colbert charged Andrew

Jackson $75,000 to ferry his army across the river here during the War of 1812. At **Freedom Hills Overlook** (Milepost 317) a steep quarter-mile trail leads to Alabama's highest point on the Parkway, 800 feet.

Crossing into Mississippi, the Parkway begins its final 300 miles by crossing through the largest state park on the route. **Tishomingo State Park** (Milepost 304.5), named for a Chickasaw medicine man and warrior, offers plenty of outdoor recreation for your dog. Up ahead is the first city of any note, Tupelo, that was known as Harrisburg in the heyday of the Natchez Trace. You can exit for several attractions here, none too time-consuming. A small one-acre site on West Main Street marks the **Tupelo National Battlefield** (Milepost 259.7) where Confederate General Nathan Bedford Forrest and withering Delta heat were able to halt a Union advance during the Civil War on April 14, 1864. Civil War buffs can detour from the Parkway for more significant battle sites at Shiloh National Military Park in Tennessee and Brices Cross Roads National Battlefield Site and Vicksburg National Military Park in Mississippi. Your dog can also spend a few minutes wandering around the boyhood home of Elvis Presley while in Tupelo.

The next 150 miles of the Parkway, until you reach a break in the road, is mostly a driving stretch punctuated by bits and pieces of the original Trace. Highlights include the **Jeff Busby Site** (Milepost 193.1), named for Thomas Jefferson Busby, a Congressman from Mississippi who introduced the bill in 1934 to create the Parkway. The *Little Mountain Trail* crawls about a mile to an overlook from a height of 603 feet, one of the highest on the road. Another must-stop comes at Milepost 122 for a one-mile loop hike through a water tupelo-cypress swamp.

After taking a break from the unfinished Parkway to get around the capital city of Jackson, rejoin the two-lane ribbon for your final 80-mile stretch to the Mississippi River. Short trails lead through mixed pine forests, to nearby waterfalls and old town sites. Pull off to walk you dog through **Port Gibson** (Milepost 39.2), a town Ulysses S. Grant declared "too beautiful to burn" during the Civil War. If you haven't stopped to take your dog through one of the deeply eroded "Sunken Traces" of the original wilderness road yet, your last chance comes at Milepost 41.5.

One of the first inns along the Trace, **Mount Locust,** has been restored at Milepost 15.5. All along the ancient passageway their have been scattered mounds built by prehistoric people for ceremonies and village sites. The final one to explore comes at Milepost 10.3, the **Emerald Mound.** Built around the year 1400, this is America's second-largest ceremonial mound. It covers nearly eight acres and you can take your dog on the trail right to the top. And catch one last look at the original Trace presents itself just before the Parkway ends and the antebellum river town of Natchez awaits.

Natchez Trace Parkway, Tennessee/Mississippi
www.nps.gov/natr/

TOUR
IDEA #43: DOGGIN' I-95

When road-tripping daydreams page languidly through our minds, I-95 seldom intrudes. The brute stretches from the Canadian border to Miami and is America's highway for more than 110 million people. What it lacks in beauty, it makes up for in traffic. Of its 1,917 miles more than 1,000 are classified as "under heavy congestion." Each day 13,000,000 vehicles steer onto an I-95 on-ramp an on special days that total can easily exceed 50 million.

That doesn't sound like a road-tripper's paradise but there is plenty on the I-95 corridor to set a travelin' dog's tail to wagging. Aside from its convenience to so many dog owners it is easy to find pet-friendly lodging along the interstate. And there are a surprising wealth of canine adventures just a fetch away from an upcoming exit. Let's take a state-by-state look...

Coming south from the northern terminus of I-95 at Houlton you will have driven through the **Maine** woods for hours and chances are your dog will be itching for a look at the Atlantic Ocean. Leave the highway at Exit 182 south of Bangor and follow Route 1 for 43 miles to **Camden Hills State Park** (www.state. me.us/cgi-bin/doc/parks/find_one_name.pl?park_id=14) on the shores of West Penobscott Bay. The park encompasses 5,700 acres, including ten named mountain peaks. The trail system features 20 short trails - most less than two miles - that visit all ten peaks, including Mount Megnticook, the highest mainland mountain on the entire Atlantic coast. Of the paths to 1,300-foot Ocean Lookout, the *Megunticook Trail* is the one to take for its extended sea views on the return route down the *Tablelands Trail*.

Making your way back to I-95 the highway begins to hug the famous Maine coast, peppered with dog-friendly beaches. Two of the best can be experienced at **Old Orchard Beach** (Exit 36) and **York Beach** (Exit 7). For a quiet enchantment with your dog stop at the **Rachel Carson National Wildlife Refuge** (Exit 25, rachelcarson.fws.gov/), named in honor of the pioneering conservationist and author whose seminal work *Silent Spring* introduced Americans to the dangers inherent in widespread use of chemical pesticides in 1962. The refuge is scattered along 50 miles of rocky Maine coast. The *Rachel Carson Trail* in Wells is the only place dogs are permitted. It is a one-mile loop located at refuge headquarters that meanders through pine woods and offers views of rippling tidal salt marshes, a very easy leg-stretcher for your dog.

Coastal **New Hampshire** doesn't hold many delights for your dog so it is best to keep motoring into **Massachusetts**. Eight miles south of Boston and just a short trot off the interstate at Exit 12 is **Blue Hills Reservation** (www. mass.gov/ dcr/parks/metroboston/blue.htm). The Metropolitan Parks Commission made the Blue Hills one of their first purchases for land set aside for recreation back in 1893 and today there are more than 7,000 acres of hills, meadows, forests and even a rare Atlantic white cedar bog waiting for your dog in Boston's backyard. Great Blue Hill, rising 635 feet above the Neponsett Valley, is the highest of the 22 hills in the Blue Hills chain. Most of the 125 miles of trails are marked but a trail map is a wise purchase for dog day hikes.

Moving into **Rhode Island**, after you pass Providence the Ocean State becomes a sea of trees. By Exit 5 you will be in the middle of **Arcadia Management Area** (www.riparks.com/arcadia.htm), the largest in the state with almost 14,000 acres kept in a natural state "more or less," as the brochure says. The sheer variety and quality of these shady trails conspire to make Arcadia the best place in Rhode Island for a day of hiking with your dog. For an exceedingly peaceful hike take the *Ben Utter Trail* north of Route 165 to visit Stepstone Falls. The soft dirt path traces the lively Wood River under giant pines that escaped logging due to their awkward location by the stream and passes foundations of old mills. If your dog is after views and sniffing in every direction, include the *Mt. Tom Trail* on your agenda. This pleasant trail skirts Parris Brook and climbs quickly but easily to the 430-foot summit - not the highest point in the park but blessed with 360-degree views of miles of treetops from the rocky ledges.

The Long Island shoreline that I-95 traces through **Connecticut** is notoriously dog-unfriendly, and not that welcoming to human visitors either. Just south of the interstate at Exit 88 in Groton, **Bluff Point Coastal Reserve** (www. ct.gov/dep/cwp/view.asp?a=2716&q=325178&depnav_gid=1650) is the last remaining undeveloped public land of any size along the Connecticut coastline. That is an irony since it was one of the first to be developed when Governor John Winthrop (1698-1707), grandson of the founding governor of the Massachusetts

Bay Colony, made his home on the peninsula and subsequent generations farmed the land for more than a century.

Over the years more than 100 vacation homes were built around the headlands of Bluff Point. Each and every cottage was destroyed during the Hurricane of 1938 and none was rebuilt which is why you bring your dog here today. Most of your dog's trotting around Bluff Point will take place on a wide, level cart road that serviced the long-gone agricultural fields. The trip from the parking lot to Bluff Point in the Long Island Sound is 1.6 miles through alternating maritime forest and open shore land. Easy grades take you up to your ultimate destination atop the pink granite rocks of the bluff. A short detour leads to a one-mile wide sand spit that connects to the small Bushy Point Beach where your dog can romp between October 15 and April 15.

For the best hiking with your dog in the Nutmeg State take Exit 47 up I-91 to New Haven and **Sleeping Giant State Park** (www.sgpa.org/). The "giant" is an east-west running basaltic ridge that resembles a man resting on his back. Just about any kind of canine hiking fare is on the menu in this cherished park. There are more than 30 miles of trails running from the feet to the head of the Giant, the first trails in Connecticut to be designated a National Recreation Trail. Most are rocky and tricky but even the novice trail dog can tackle the gently ascending road that makes up the 1.6-mile *Tower Path*. Your destination on top of 739-foot Mount Carmel is a hulking four-story stone observation tower that would not be out of place in King Arthur's time.

Most of I-95's 23 miles in **New York** traverse the bedroom communities of Westchester County but before crossing the George Washington Bridge and exiting the state why not get off in Manhattan and visit **Central Park** (Exit 1)? Everyone knows Central Park (www.centralpark.com/) but if you have never walked through its 843 acres chances are your image of what it looks like is wrong. Are you picturing rock outcroppings? Rolling hills? Waterfalls in dense woodlands? It's all part of Central Park.

The park covers 6% of the entire island of Manhattan. It would take the better part of a week to cover all 58 miles of footpaths with your dog, taking you past 9,000 benches and across 36 individually designed bridges. The park is studded with 26,000 trees and a good part of its acreage is under the water of 14 lakes and ponds. And the genius of Central Park is that every inch of it was crafted not by nature but the hand of man. This naturalistic appearance is the design of architects Frederick Law Olmsted and Calvert Vaux 150 years ago.

As improbable as it may seem, even with a typical 70,000 visitors in a day it is possible to fin relative solitude with your dog in Central Park. The two best places to disappear with your dog are The Rambles in the center of the park where many twisting paths intersect under a tangle of trees and hillocks and in the rugged northern end around Great Hill and the Ravine. Although your dog is not allowed to swim in any of the lakes, ponds or fountains here you can find some doggie splashing on a hot day, including a waterfall in the stream.

Your dog will be trotting on surfaces that range from asphalt to wood chip to dirt and even a bit of paw-friendly grass in the Wildflower Meadow. Dogs are also allowed to share the bridle paths in the park. Best yet, dogs can hike with you off-leash between the hours of 9:00 p.m. and 9:00 a.m. During the day you will find groups of dog owners congregating with dogs romping off-leash in places like the Great Lawn and elsewhere. Keep a leash in hand in case you are asked to tether your dog.

New Jersey may be America's most densely populated state but lying due east of the New Jersey Turnpike that doubles as I-95 in the Garden State is more than a million acres of scrub pine and sand so remote that they have spawned tales of the legendary winged creature known as the "Jersey Devil." So far there have been no documented captures of the creature with the head of a horse supported by a four-foot serpentine body. Perhaps your dog can sniff one out.

The **Pinelands** is our country's first National Reserve and a U.S. Biosphere Reserve of the Man and the Biosphere Program. This internationally important ecological region is 1.1 million acres in size and occupies 22% of New Jersey's land area. It is the largest body of open space on the Atlantic seaboard between Richmond and Boston and is underlain by aquifers containing 17 trillion gallons of some of the purest water in the land.

Your best way to explore this vast tapestry of impenetrable scrub pine, swamps and bogs is through the **Wharton State Forest** (Exit 3, www.state. nj.us/ dep/parksandforests/parks/wharton.html), most of which is the former 100,000-acre estate of Philadelphia financier Joseph Wharton. You can hike with your dog for months on the maze of unmarked sand roads through the Pinelands. For formal routes the star here is the *Batona Trail*, a wilderness path that begins at Ongs Hat to the north and ends at Lake Absegami in **Bass River State Forest**. The original 30 miles of the *Batona Trail* were routed and cleared through white cedar and pitch pine forests by volunteers in 1961.

Today the total length of the trail with the distinctive pink blazes is 50.2

miles with many road crossings that make different lengths of canine hikes possible. This is easy walking on paw-friendly sand for most of its length. Despite the overwhelming flatness of the surrounding countryside, there are undulating elevation changes on the trail itself. Any dog could walk end to end with no problem, if that was the goal.

The high point on the *Batona Trail* is **Apple Pie Hill**, soaring a whole 209 feet above sea level (there is a fire tower you can scale - the steps are too open for dogs - and literally scan the east-to-west entirety of New Jersey from Atlantic City to Philadelphia). A superb canine hike is the four-mile walk here from the Carranza Memorial, where immortal Mexican aviator Emilio Carranza perished in a plane crash in 1928. For the most part, however, there are no vistas beyond what you see around you - cedar swamps and millions of pine trees. In season wild blueberries and huckleberries can be gobbled along the trail.

I-95 splits from the New Jersey Turnpike to cross the Delaware River into **Pennsylvania** and follow the tidal flow for 50 miles through Philadelphia. Take Exit 22 and cross the city on the Vine Street Expressway to **Fairmount Park** (www.fairmountpark.org/), the largest contiguous landscaped municipal park in the world. Begun with just five acres in 1812 it now covers 9,000 acres and is the bucolic home to an estimated 2,500,000 trees. The backbone of the park is the Forbidden Drive, so named when it was closed to automobiles in the 1920s. The 7-mile paved trail travels along the Wissahickon Creek to the Schuylkill River; canine hikes can be shortened by several bridges across the Wissahickon. In addition, there are many blazed single-track trails climbing steeply out of the Wissahickon Gorge. Oh, and before you leave, take your dog for a run up the steps of the Philadelphia Museum of Art - just like Rocky. The world class museum overlooks the Schuylkill River in the park.

Your short hop through **Delaware** passes directly over **Wilmington State Parks** (Exit 7B, www.destateparks.com/wilmsp/wilmsp.htm). You can hike with your dog under that award-winning bridge through **Brandywine Park** that was the final link in I-95 between Boston and Washington when finished in 1967. The park, The First State's first when created in 1885 by Central Park designer Frederick Law Olmsted, is listed on the National Historic Register. It connects to two other parks: **Rockford Park**, with its signature Italian Renaissance tower, and **Alapocas Woods**, where the dramatic granite cliffs are high enough to claim the state's only natural waterfall and plentiful enough for the Brandywine Granite Company to have quarried over 600,000 tons of Wilmington "Blue Rocks" from this site between 1883 and 1888. All told, your dog can explore the Brandywine River here for roughly 10 minutes for every minute he will spend in the car getting through Delaware on I-95.

In **Maryland** I-95 crosses the Susquehanna River just about at the spot where the longest river on the East Coast ends its exhausting 444-mile journey before dumping into the Chesapeake Bay. Also at this point the highway skirts **Susquehanna State Park**, a winning combination of history, scenery and wildlife (www.dnr.state.md.us/publiclands/central/susquehanna.html). Take Exit 89 to visit the 2,500-acre park with your dog. The well-maintained trails are short enough to complete and challenging without being exhausting. The abundance of large rocks in the Susquehanna River enables you to sit out in the water while your dog splashes around you.

If using the green-blazed *Deer Creek Trail* be on the look-out for a magnificent spreading white oak in the middle of the walk. The *Lower Susquehanna Heritage Greenways Trail*, which connects the park at Deer Creek with the Conowingo Dam, America's longest concrete slab dam, is as pleasant a hike as you can take with your dog. Tracing the route of the 160-year old Susquehanna and Tidewater Canal towpath, the wide dirt path stretches 2.2 shaded miles along the water. Below the dam you can chance to spot bald eagles diving to pluck stunned and splattered fish from the spillways. The great piscivorous birds favor massive nests in the 100-foot treetops along the banks of the Susquehanna River.

South of Baltimore, and just east of I-95 at Exit 38, is reputedly the largest patch of undeveloped green space that can be seen from the air on the East Coast between Boston and Raleigh. A scrawl of the pen by Franklin Roosevelt in 1936 established the **Patuxent Research Refuge** (patuxent.fws.gov/) as America's only refuge to support wildlife research. The original 2,670 acres swelled to its current size of 12,750 acres with the addition of 8,100 acres formerly belonging to adjacent Fort Meade (visitors must sign a waiver regarding possible live ammunition encountered on the grounds - don't let your dog dig in strange holes!). There are some 20 miles of trails in the North Tract, including the paved 8-mile Wildlife Loop access road which is lightly traveled. The best hiking for your dog is on the *Forest Habitat Trail*, opposite the visitor center. The wide, soft trail contours pleasantly as it circles for 2.5 miles through mature forest with limited understory. Two other hiker-only trails of less then a mile are available: the *Little Patuxent River Trail* which loops through the moist ground by the river and the sandy *Pine Trail*.

After circling the nation's capital, I-95 plunges south again into **Virginia** and shortly slices through Prince William Forest Park (Exit 150, www.nps.gov/prwi/), the largest protected swath of land in the Washington DC metropolitan area at over 15,000 acres. This was some of the earliest European-settled land in the country. Early tobacco farming drained the land of much of its nutrients and for centuries only a few farms survived around the creeks flowing into the Potomac River. During the Depression of the 1930s this was one of 46 locations of marginal farm land selected to be developed for recreation. **Prince William Forest** became a part of the National Park System in 1940 when work camps from the Civilian Conservation Corps were established to build roads and trails and bridges.

Although just south of the nation's densely populated capital, the trails in the forest are refreshingly uncrowded - always an attraction for canine hikers. As you motor around the Scenic Drive loop the dozen or so parking lots at trailheads scarcely have space for ten vehicles each. That makes these 37 miles of trails a prime destination for a lively dog. The canine hiking here is through the only preserved Eastern Piedmont forest in the National Park Service. You will be working up and down and around the many slopes in the Quantico Creek watershed - often with long views through the forest that features little understory.

If you head off on the *North Valley Trail* and continue about one mile down the *Pyrite Mine Trail* along the North Branch of the Quantico Creek you will reach the remains of the Cabin Branch Pyrite Mine. The mine opened in 1889, pulling nugget-like rocks known as "fool's gold" for their appearance to the precious metal. In fact pyrite is loaded with sulfur that kept the operation profitable into the 1920s, including an important stretch during World War I when as many as 300 men worked the mine. Many acres of historic underground workings, pilings and foundations have been reclaimed and are remembered today.

The 182 miles of I-95 through **North Carolina** cut an invisible line between the coastal plain and the rolling Piedmont hills, passing through no major public recreation areas. So this is a good time to immerse your dog in a bit of American military history. Dogs are almost universally allowed on our preserved battlegrounds and you can explore both our Civil War and American Revolution heritage in the Tarheel State.

South of Exit 90 the last full-scale Confederate offensive of the Civil War took place on March 19-21, 1865. Some 25,000 weary Confederate troops under General Joseph Johnson opposed 60,000 marauding Union soldiers under the command of William Tecumseh Sherman at **Bentonville Battlefield** (www. nchistoricsites.org/Bentonvi/Bentonvi.HTM). After an initial burst the Confederates withdrew from the field and the war's end was only two weeks off. The 6,000-acre battlefield is now a state historic site with well-preserved earthworks. Harper House, which houses the Visitor Center, served as a Union hospital during the battle; there were more than 4,000 casualties on both sides during North Carolina's largest Civil War battle.

Leaving the interstate at Exit 20, travel east for 46 miles to **Moores Creek National Military Park** (www.nps.gov/mocr/). Here on February 20, 1776 General Donald MacDonald, marching to the sea with 1,600 Loyalists to join the regular British Army were tricked into funneling across Moores Creek - a dark, sluggish stream - at a narrow ford in front of hastily erected American earthworks. Planks on the Moores Creek bridge were removed and the Highlanders had to pick their way through the fog across the creek. Reaching the opposite bank they were met with withering fire at the earthworks.

What Patriot musketry didn't take care of, a swivel gun and artillery did. The Loyalists lost 30 killed and 40 wounded. Only one Patriot died. The victory demonstrated surprising American strength, discouraging the growth of Loyalist sentiment in the Carolinas and convincing the British there would be no quick crushing of the rebellion. In fact, a little more than one month later North Carolina instructed its delegation to the Continental Congress in Philadelphia to vote for independence, the first American colony to do so. Big consequences emanated from a small battle in the swamps of North Carolina.

Moores Creek is a landscaped park masquerading as an historical site. The one-mile interpretive history trail rolls across a well-groomed landscape of pine trees, open space and a winding creek. The reconstructed bridge and preserved earthworks, rehabilitated in the 1930s, vividly tell the tale of the trap set by the Patriots and the unwelcome terrain the Loyalists had to fight through. There is more convivial canine hiking around the picnic area and on the *Tarheel Trail*. This interpretive path ducks into the forests to interpret the production of naval stores (tar, pitch and turpentine) that were the region's chief economic resource during the Revolution.

Rolling into **South Carolina**, cross Lake Marion, the Palmetto State's largest lake and make the first exit west (Exit 90). Up the road is the **Congaree National Park** (www.nps.gov/cosw/) that protects the largest contiguous area of old-growth bottomland hardwood forest remaining in the United States. More than 52 million acres of floodplain forests have been decimated in the southeastern United States in the past century making Congaree's 2,000 acres of virgin forest special indeed.

The marquee trail under the 150-foot canopy of pine, tupelo and bald cypress is a two-mile boardwalk loop that lifts hikers above the flooding of the Congaree River that occurs an average of ten times a year. The park's forests harbor 20 state or national champion trees including loblolly pines, hickories and bald cypress.

Dogs are not allowed on the boardwalk but a *Dog Trail* has been created to take your best hiking partner through the swamp. Dogs are permitted on all other park trails, unimproved roads and primitive campgrounds. This is all flat, easy going for any dog on uncrowded trails - and a marked canoe trail explores the meandering Cedar Creek.

Back on I-95 the highway angles back to the Atlantic Ocean and the first major city in 430 miles since Richmond, Savannah, **Georgia** (Exit 99). Savannah is about as pet-friendly a city as you will find along I-95. Your dog can join you for refreshment at one of the many outdoor cafes that line the Spanish mossdraped streets. And if you ask, your dog might be able to join you on one of the trolley tours that haunt Savannah's 22 historic squares laid out by city founder James Oglethorpe in 1732. Don't make the trip out to Savannah's Atlantic Ocean beach, Tybee Island, however. Dogs are not allowed on the beach any time during the year.

Instead, head back for I-95 and travel an hour south to Exit 29 where the highway gets the closest it has been to the Atlantic Ocean since Maine. The destination is **Jekyll Island** (www.jekyllisland.com/), one of the best places you can bring your dog anywhere in the country. Dogs have a long history on Jekyll Island, back to its founding as a hunting club in 1886. Today dogs are welcome on all ten miles of Jekyll Island's Atlantic Ocean beaches from the dunes of St. Andrews Beach in the south to the jungle-backed Driftwood Beach in the north. Poop bags are provided at beach access points.

For all intents and purposes your dog's tour of I-95 ends here, even though **Florida's** 382 miles of interstate still lie ahead. You can tiptoe over the state line to Exit 373 and take your dog to the beaches on Amelia Island but after that you find mostly restrictions and prohibitions against your dog in coastal parks and ocean beaches. But your dog should agree that it has been quite a trip.

I-95 Exit Services from Maine to Florida
www.i95exitguide.com/index.php

TOUR
IDEA #44: DOGGIN' ROUTE 66

Sooner or later all road-tripping dogs will make their make their way to Route 66. Dubbed the "Mother Road," this 2,400-mile, dog bowl-shaped highway from Chicago to Los Angeles inspired popular songs, movies and an iconic television show that lured millions of travelers to it two lanes of concrete. Route 66 was done in by the interstate system - some of which was laid on top of the old road - and doesn't appear on modern maps anymore but lives forever in the imaginations of any dog with a hint of wanderlust...

Route 66 was never a static road, especially as paving was introduced. The original plan in the 1920s was to connect the main streets of rural and urban communities and over time the route shifted to eliminate sharp turns, bypass some smaller communities, eliminate railroad crossings, and to shift routings in major metropolitan areas to avoid traffic congestion. Nowhere is this more apparent than at its very start (if you're heading west) in Chicago. Originally, Route 66 kicked off on Jackson Boulevard at Michigan Avenue and later moved to Jackson at Lake Shore Drive. Wherever you begin to follow the essence of Historic Route 66, look for the brown markers and get your dog's odyssey rolling through **Illinois**.

Your dog's first great chance to get out and run is southwest of Chicago at the former Joliet Arsenal, where the government once manufactured ordnance from World War II through the Vietnam War. In 1996 more than 7,000 acres of the old ammo plant were converted by the United States Forest Service into America's first national tallgrass prairie. In addition to propagating and restoring native grasses, **Midewin National Tallgrass Prairie** (www.fs.fed.us/mntp/) offers more than 20 miles of multi-use and hiker-only trails. Your dog is welcome on all. So are hunters so stick to the marked trails. Along the *Twin Oaks Trail* you can see a remnant of the former Joliet Arsenal by taking your dog to a World War II-era ammunition bunker.

Route 66 tackled the Mississippi River in two places, one went directly into

St. Louis and the other slid around the northern edge of the city. This Route 66 Bypass crossed on the **Chain of Rocks Bridge** (www.trailnet.org/trail_main.php), a private toll bridge built in 1929 at the cost of $3,000,000. The "chain of rocks" were a dangerous set of rocky shoals that were eliminated by dams and canals in the mid-20th century. The bridge itself was notable for a sharp 22-degree bend that slowed traffic and fostered pile-ups. For that reason the bridge was not used by the Interstate Highway System and was eventually closed in 1967. It sat decaying for 30 years, spared from demolition only be a crash in the market for scrap metal. A local trails group raised over four million dollars for renovations and re-opened the mile-long bridge for pedestrian and bicycle use. The Chain of Rocks Bridge has been decorated as a Route 66 memorial with vintage cars, signs and gas pumps. This is the most scenic walk you can take with your dog across the Mississippi River; the Gateway Arch in St. Louis is visible downstream.

In **Missouri**, "America's Main Street," ran through the wooded bluffs of the Meramec River valley. The resort community of Times Beach once welcomed visitors here. The town was abandoned in 1980 after waste oil sprayed on the streets to keep dust down proved to be toxic. When the cleanup was complete the 409-acre **Route 66 State Park** (www.mostateparks.com/route66.htm) was created in 1999 to showcase the beauty of the valley and preserve some of the history of the Mother Road. The canine hiking is light and easy on the seven-plus miles of trails that circle the park. You can even walk the dog along a stretch of historic Route 66 that remains in the park.

Just ahead are the Meramec Caverns (www.americascave.com/), one of the most famous destinations along old Route 66 and the birthplace of the bumper sticker. These roomy limestone caves were first used to mine saltpeter to manufacture gunpowder and are still a popular tourist attraction today. Your dog can't tour the cave but can stay in the campground.

Route 66 was born in **Oklahoma**. Cyrus Avery, a Tulsa businessman and Oklahoma's first highway commissioner, spearheaded the national committee that created the U.S. Highway System in 1926. He championed the Chicago-to-Los Angeles route (making sure it dropped south to his home state before turning west) and picked the now famous double sixes as the new road's official number.

Oklahoma has about 400 miles of Route 66 and more drivable miles of the old highway than any other state, although in a pastiche of new route numbers that requires its own guidebook. This should make you happy when traveling with your dog - and that's a good thing since it is a law on the Oklahoma books that if you make an ugly face at a dog, you could be fined or jailed.

Historic Route 66 through Oklahoma is studded with the small towns and kitschy roadside buildings that came to define the Mother Road. There are a string of places to get out and poke around with your dog; one that is a short jog off the highway in Foyil that is certainly worth a stop is **Totem Pole Park**. Spanish-American War veteran and retired school teacher Ed Galloway settled here in 1937 and began building a totem pole on the back of an outsized turtle. After 11 years he had built a 60-foot totem pole of concrete over a scrap metal and sandstone rock skeleton. Billed as the "World's Largest Totem Pole," Galloway's creation was considered to be a monument to the tribes that lived here when Oklahoma was reserved as Indian Territory but the sculptor himself always said he built it simply to have something to do. He built other structures on the property including a house supported by 25 concrete totem poles. Galloway's handiwork was disintegrating for decades after his death in 1962 when they were preserved in the 1990s for this park and placed on the National Register of Historic Places.

One of the most recognizable natural features in the Route 66 corridor is Inscription Rock, a 200-foot high sandstone mesa in the **New Mexico** desert that has served as a beacon for travelers for hundreds of years. More than 2,000 stopped to inscribe their signatures dating back to the Spanish conquistadores and the petroglyphs of ancestral Puebloans. There are more than a few of the "I was here" variety as well mixed into the historic graffiti. To protect the mesa and help sort out the significant from the silly, Inscription Rock is now **El Morro National Monument** (www.nps.gov/elmo/). Your dog is welcome to take the short trail out to one of America's greatest guest books done up in soft yellow stone. The trail continues 250 feet up to the top of a windswept bluff with views of a box canyon and two large American Indian ruins.

East of Inscription Rock via Route 53 is another national monument, **El Malpais** (www.nps.gov/elma/). Spanish for "badlands," the jagged volcanic terrain easily earns it name. The last of many eruptions between 2,000 and 3,000 years ago has littered thousands of acres with shiny black lava flows, cones and tubes. Your dog is welcome here, too , but walking on the lava can easily puncture paw pads so plan accordingly.

In **Arizona**, east of Flagstaff at Exit 204 of I-40 that is blanketing Historic Route 66 through much of the state, **Walnut Canyon National Monument** (www.nps.gov/waca/) was established in 1915, four years before the Grand

Canyon. Many of the great prehistoric cliff dwellings around America are off-limits to dogs but here your dog can peer into the homes of peoples who lived deep within these canyon walls 700 years ago. The *Island Trail* descends 185 feet (on steps) to provide access to 25 cliff dwelling rooms; the *Rim Trail* is an easier journey suitable for any dog that ambles through a Ponderosa pine forest to a pair of spectacular canyon overlooks. This is about as good a two hours as you are likely to spend with your dog in any park.

Entering **California**, the end of your journey on old Route 66 is in sight. The old road survives intact for most of its 315 miles through the state. Across the Mojave Desert, through the San Bernadino Mountains and... you arrive at the Pacific Ocean in Santa Monica, one of the most densely populated urban areas in the United States - one in every 17 Americans live within an hour's drive of the Santa Monica Mountains.

The expansive **Santa Monica Mountains National Recreation Area** (www.nps.gov/samo/) is an amalgamation of 150,000 private, city, county, state and federal acres knitted into a single entity in 1978. The park stretches 46 miles from east to west with a Mediterranean climate - hot, dry summers mixing with mild, wet winters in a coastal location - that is the rarest in the world. Only four other areas in the world enjoy the same climate, the fewest acres of any ecosystem.

The national recreation area is a paradise for canine hikers but not an unfettered one. Dogs are not allowed on state park trails so you will need to limit your explorations to national and city park lands. An easy introduction to the park near the Visitor Center in Thousand Oaks is at Rancho Sierra Vista (Satwiwa) where a loop trail slips 1.5 miles through grasslands and chaparral-covered hillsides. The loop begins and ends at the Satwiwa Native American Indian Culture Center.

Athletic dogs will want to test the many canyon trails at Zuma Canyon, Solstice Canyon, Franklin Canyon and more. Expect extended ocean views and scenic looks where the land has been folded into peaks and canyons by shifts along the San Andreas Fault. Some of the sportiest canine hiking in the Santa Monica Mountains is at Circle K Ranch where trails ascend to Sandstone Peak, the highest point in the park at 3,111 feet. One, the *Backbone Trail*, will one day stretch 65 miles across the entire national recreation area. Dog owners may want to skip the downhill hiking on the Grotto Trail. After going two miles, dogs are not allowed on the final 1/8 mile to The Grotto.

The park features more than 50 miles of shoreline on the Pacific Ocean but the prime swimming beaches are off-limits for dogs. Several rockier beaches in the western end - County Line Beach, Thornhill Broome and the beach at Leo Carillo State Park - are open to dog paddling. And if you want to really to cap off your dog's Route 66 adventure take a stroll down the world famous Santa Monica Pier (dogs can't go into Pacific Park or on the beaches) that celebrates its centennial anniversary in 1909.

Historic Route 66
www.historic66.com/

TOUR
IDEA #45: DOGGIN' THE SANTA FE TRAIL

In 1821 the western frontier of the United States was the state of Missouri. The only reason to leave the country and push further west into Mexico across harsh, arid lands and the territory of hostile Indians was money problems and that is what motivated War of 1812 veteran William Becknell to organize a trading party to Santa Fe, New Mexico. Bankrupt and facing jail for his debts, he brought home a profit with his venture. The following year he led his first wagon train beyond our borders and by 1825 he was helping grade America's first intercontinental trade highway, the Santa Fe Trail.

The Santa Fe Trail remained the major trade route into the territories of the Southwest until 1880 when the railroad arrived. Over the years gold prospectors, fur trappers, the military and just plain adventurers trod these 900 miles. Thanks to the Santa Fe National Historic Trail organized by the federal government you and your dog can replicate the remarkable overland journey this must have been...

Following the route of the pioneers, traveling west, one of your first points of interest for your dog in eastern **Kansas** is the **Tallgrass Prairie National Preserve** (www.nps.gov/tapr). When wagons first rolled down the Santa Fe Trail tallgrass prairie covered 140 million acres of North America. Today less than 4% remains, mostly in the Kansas Flint Hills. The preserve protects a nationally significant remnant of the once vast tallgrass prairie. Your dog is limited to two trails in the park but one is the *Southwind Nature Trail* where big bluestem grows abundantly. A single blade of big bluestem might have a root system descending over 8 feet underground - deep enough so the plant will emerge in the spring even without rainfall.

A succession of military forts became the lifeline for protection and communication between Missouri and Santa Fe. Of these, **Fort Larned National**

Historic Site (www.nps.gov/fols/) in central Kansas is one of the best preserved of all frontier forts with nine restored original sandstone buildings. Although your dog isn't allowed in fort buildings, she can trot the grounds.

Continuing west, you can examine the longest continuous stretch of clearly defined Santa Fe Trail rut remains in Kansas, nine miles west of Dodge City on U.S. 50. The **Santa Fe Trail Remains**, a National Historic Landmark, forms a two-mile arc, 300-400 feet wide in places.

Before exiting Kansas on Route 27 the **Cimarron National Grassland** (www.fs.fed.us/r2/psicc/cim/) contains the longest stretch of the Santa Fe Trail in the country, 23 miles. The *Companion Trail*, north of Elkhart, closely follows the existing remnants of the Santa Fe Trail across the prairie. Sagebrush and cacti have been removed to make the trail sufficiently evident to the hiker without noticeably altering the prairie vistas.

The Santa Fe Trail split at this point with the Mountain Branch tracing the Arkansas River north into Colorado and the Cimarron Cutoff, easier but more arid, slicing across the corner of Oklahoma before reaching **New Mexico**. The two rejoined six miles south of Fort Union that was once the largest outpost on the Southwestern frontier. Between 1851, when it was established, and 1891, it was the chief quartermaster for more than 50 forts in the region and primary station for troops in charge of protecting settlers along the Santa Fe Trail. The largest visible network of Santa Fe Trail ruts can be seen here when you wander with your dog amidst the adobe ruins and foundations of **Fort Union National Monument** (www.nps.gov/foun) along a mile-and-a-half long interpretive trail.

Before reaching the end of the trail in Santa Fe, stop in at **Pecos National Historic Park** (www.nps.gov/peco). Your dog is permitted on all the trails here and throughout the developed area of the park. In addition to Santa Fe Trail sites the park preserves 12,000 years of history in the ancient pueblo of Pecos and a famous 20th century ranch. Also administered by the park, but not regularly open to the public, is the Glorietta Battlefield where outnumbered Colorado volunteers fought Confederate invaders to a draw and ended the Southerners' dream of invading the West during the Civil War forever.

Santa Fe National Historic Trail
www.nps.gov/safe/

TOUR
IDEA #46: DOGGIN' THE MIGHTY MISSISSIPPI

Back in the 1930s the governors of the 10 Mississippi River states banded together to promote tourism along the river. Rather than build a costly continuous parkway they decided to create the Great River Road by welding existing rural roads meandering back and forth across the river into a historic north-south transcontinental byway. Some states have been more enthusiastic than others in promoting the route but you can pile your dog in the car, aim for the green Pilot's Wheel road signs and follow America's greatest river from Minnesota to the Gulf of Mexico...

In 1832, Anishinabe Indian guide Ozawindib led explorer Henry Rowe Schoolcraft to the source of the Mississippi River at Lake Itasca, ending a years-long search for the true headwaters of America's mightiest river. Or was it? Finally in the late 1800s, Jacob V. Brower, historian, anthropologist and land surveyor, came to the region to settle the dispute of the actual location of the Mississippi Headwaters. Brower 's work not only definitively established the source but his tireless efforts to preserve the area led to the creation of **Minnesota's** first state park on April 20, 1891.

The trail to the source of the Mississippi River from the Visitor Center is really just a few easy bounds for your dog. Once there your dog can prance across the river without getting her tummy wet as it sneaks out of the back of the lake to begin its 2,320-mile journey; in New Orleans the river will be 200 feet deep. At this point the river is 20 feet wide; it would be more than two miles across before extensive locks and dams were built along the river. Here the elevation is 1,475 feet; when the Mississippi River reaches the Gulf of Mexico the elevation will be 0. A raindrop falling in Lake Itasca will arrive in New Orleans in about 90 days.

After the novelty of stepping across the great river and crowds have worn thin, step away and take your dog down the North Arm of Lake Itasca on the mile-long *Schoolcraft Trail*. The most substantive canine hiking in the park is south of the lake where a multitude of trails skirt sparkling lakes and trip through piney woodlands. One way to craft your dog's hiking day at **Lake Itasca State Park** (www.dnr.state.mn.us/state_parks/itasca/index.html) is to drive the 10-mile Wilderness Drive and hike the numerous nature and interpretive trails.

Two hundred miles downstream the Mississippi reaches its first big city, Minneapolis. The Dakota Indians considered the spot at the confluence of the Minnesota and Mississippi rivers the center of the world; European visitors recognized its strategic importance for trade and defense. On September 21, 1805 Zebulon Pike picked up 100,000 acres here in exchange for $200 of trinkets, a keg of whiskey and the promise of a trading post. Colonel Josiah Snelling shaped the post into a military fort when he arrived in 1820 and it operated as such through World War II. Fort Snelling was spared destruction when it was named as the first National Historic Landmark in Minnesota in 1960 and the park - now the state's most visited - opened two years later to conserve open space in the heart of the Twin Cities.

Fort Snelling State Park (www.dnr.state.mn.us/state_parks/fort_snelling/) is packed with canine hiking opportunities - 18 miles of foot trails, 18 miles of cross-country trails and 5 miles of multi-use trails. This is easy, shady hiking in mature woodlands. A good place to start is the 3.2-mile hiking-only trail that circles Pike Island, site of the treaties that allowed establishment of the first European settlement in Minnesota. Fort Snelling is part of the diverse **Mississippi National River and Recreation Area** (www.nps.gov/miss/) that includes dozens of parks and Mississippi River heritage sites. Most are open to your dog and a handful feature off-leash dog parks.

Minnesota is the only state the river flows through - it will form a boundary for the next nine states you visit. Crossing into **Wisconsin**, Highway 35 takes the Great River Road through a land of sandstone bluffs and native grasslands called goat prairies. Several state parks along the route offer shortish trails to scrumptious overlooks of the Mississippi River valley. **Perrot State Park** (www. dnr.state.wi.us/org/land/parks/specific/perrot/), at the confluence of the Trempealeau and Mississippi, has a menu of options to climb to Brady's Bluff that rises 460 feet above the river. Brady's Bluff Prairie, a designated state natural area, contains over 100 species of native Wisconsin plants. The Riverview Trail follows the Mississippi for more than two miles and gives your dog easy-going close-up views of the river.

The highlight along **Iowa's** 326 miles of Great River Road comes early, just after crossing the Mississippi from Priarie du Chien. **Effigy Mounds National Monument** (www.nps.gov/efmo/) preserves 206 mounds built by American Indian tribes over 1,000 years ago. The mounds are considered sacred - no one knows what they were built for or why mound-building ceased - and no vehicular traffic is allowed inside the monument. You can explore the 14 miles of self-guiding trail that weave among the mounds, 31 of which are in the shape of animals such as bears and birds. Some of this hiking can be challenging as the

2,526-acre park preserves wetlands and high limestone bluffs alongside the Mississippi River.

Up ahead is the most famous of all Mississippi River towns - Mark Twain's Hannibal. You can walk your dog through the streets of Samuel Clemens' youth in the historic district fronting the river although he probably won't get much from the Huck Finn impersonators and Tom Sawyer dioramas. Twain's whitewashed boyhood home is on North Main Street. Your dog will be more interested in getting to **Riverview Park** (www.greatriverroad.com/hannibal/riverview.htm) in the north end of town where landscape designer Ossian Cole Simonds laid out a system of winding carriage roads across a forested bluff overlooking the river. Open in 1909 and planted with with oaks, maples and flowering shrubs, Riverview Park is on the National Register of Historic Places. Look for statues of Samuel Clemens and **Missouri** lumber magnate Wilson Boyd Pettibone, who donated the space to the town, in the park. Crossing the Mark Twain Bridge, your dog can swim in the Mississippi at the recreation area directly across from Hannibal.

It is the Illinois River, not the Mississippi that is the star at **Pere Marquette State Park** (dnr.state.il.us/lands/Landmgt/PARKS/R4/Peremarq.htm). The first European explorers, led by Louis Joliet, a cartographer, and missionary Father Jacques Marquette, paddled down the Mississippi River in search of the Pacific Ocean in 1673. When they learned from Illini tribal scouts that the river headed south and not west they turned back, heading up the Illinois River and stopping here, just past the mouth.

The park is noted for its brilliant fall color displays across 8,000 acres of hardwoods. A bundle of shortish but sporty and well-marked trails lead to nine scenic overlooks on the towering bluffs of the Illinois River. The lush forests support a thriving population of poison ivy - your dog isn't affected by poison ivy but can give it to you.

At the southern tip of Illinois you will want to drive through the town of Cairo and out to **Fort Defiance Park**. The park looks like many a town park with a few scattered trees and large swaths of mown grass. What isn't typical is the view: your dog will be rolling in the grass at the very point of confluence of the powerful Ohio and Mississippi Rivers, one of the world's great natural highways that allows travel between Pittsburgh and New Orleans.

In the winter of 1811-12, the central Mississippi Valley was struck by three of the most powerful earthquakes in United States history. The force of these seismic seizures, the first ever reported in the country, was said to have caused chimneys to topple in Maine, bells to ring in Boston churches and plaster to crack in Washington D.C. These stories may be apocryphal but one thing the quake did for certain was create new lakes around the Mississippi River, most notably Reelfoot Lake in **Tennessee.**

Today the 15,000 acre lake is considered to be one of the greatest hunting and fishing preserves in the nation. In addition to swimming for your dog, **Reelfoot Lake State Park** (www.state.tn.us/environment/parks/ReelfootLake/) also has three hiking trails of interest and an auto tour that circles the lake. The *Airpark Trail* is a 45-minute walk through old cypress forest and second growth vegetation. The *Keystone Trail* winds along the shoreline of Reelfoot Lake for 1.5 miles and is the only lakeshore foorpath. The *Black Bayou Trail* goes along the old bayou for approximately two miles and is an excellent bird watching and wildlife observation walk. Oh, and you may want to walk fast - even today, this region has more earthquakes than any other part of the United States east of the Rocky Mountains. Scientists estimate a 7 to 10 percent chance, in the next 50 years, of a repeat of a major earthquake like those that occurred in 1811-1812.

Below Memphis the Mississippi River flattens out and the roads stray from its banks. At the end of a dusty road 12 miles west of Port Gibson, **Mississippi** in a field of eerie quiet, stand 23 towering Corinthian columns. These are the **Ruins of Windsor.** They are all that remain of the largest ante-bellum mansion ever built in Mississippi. The lofty cupola atop Windsor was used as a Confederate observation point to scan the Mississippi River during the Civil War and Union troops appropriated the building as a war hospital after the Battle of Port Gibson. The pleas of its mistress saved the house from destruction on at least three separate occasions and Windsor survived the Civil War but it burned to the ground in 1890 - the victim of careless smoking.

With that haunting introduction to the antebellum South you will soon reach **Louisiana** and Plantation Alley. The **Houmas House Plantation** (www.houmashouse.com/) was already producing cotton before Thomas Jefferson bought this land from Napoleon in 1803. The "Crown Jewel of Louisiana's River Road," as it came to be known, would eventually increase its land holdings to 300,000 acres, becoming the largest sugar plantation in Louisiana. By the late 1800s the plantation was producing 20 million pounds of sugar each year - the largest output in America.

The Mississippi River ended it all in 1927, the year it roared out of its banks in "The Great Flood." The house survived but the sugar fields could not be rebuilt in the wake of the Great Depression. Over the years the mansion was restyled and Hollywood showed up to make movies here, including the Bette Davis-fueled *Hush, Hush Sweet Charlotte* in 1963. Today your dog will have to skip the house tour but can take in the lush 38 acres of gardens and native plantings.

You can't drive to the mouth of the Mississippi River below New Orleans so this is as fine a place to quit the Great River Road as any. It's been a long trip, your dog must be exhausted.

www.experiencemississippiriver.com/

TOUR
IDEA #47: DOGGIN' AMERICA'S CANALS

Canals are great places to take your dog. From earliest Colonial times, ambitious entrepreneurs dreamed of connecting America's waterways to ease travel and promote commerce. George Washington was one of the first. He chartered the Patowmack Company in 1784 to construct a series of five canals along the Potomac River to reach into the virgin territory of the Ohio Valley.

The American Canal Age lasted approximately from 1790 until 1855. Many of the great projects were still under construction when the rise of the railroads made them obsolete and unprofitable. Most canals were privately funded and limped along financially until the early 1900s.

Some abandoned canals were filled in; others drained and returned to nature. Old canals were naturals to be converted into parks and are great places to take your dog for a hike. Towpaths are often left in their natural state or covered with gravel - not paved over like most abandoned railroads. The hiking is always easy on wide, flat towpaths once trod by horses and mules and there is usually plenty of swimming for your dog. When you're out traveling, look for a canal park to enjoy with your dog. Here are a few to consider...

Chesapeake & Ohio Canal (Maryland)

A canal that could connect the Potomac River to the Ohio River in Pittsburgh would provide a continuous water link from New Orleans to the Chesapeake Bay. That canal, dubbed the "Great National Project" by President John Quincy Adams, was finally started on July 4, 1828. It would take 22 years to complete - actually construction just stopped since the canal route never made it out of Maryland with only 184.5 of the planned 460 miles dug. The Chesapeake & Ohio Canal lasted for 75 years floating cargo from Cumberland, Maryland to Georgetown. The ditch survived filling in through the efforts of Supreme Court Justice William O. Douglas who championed the canal as "a long stretch of quiet and peace."

At Great Falls Tavern dogs are denied the extraordinary views of the powerful Great Falls of the Potomac and Mather Gorge - they are banned from the boardwalk trails on the Olmsted Island Bridges and the rock scrambling on the *Billy Goat "A" Trail* around Bear Island. But canine hikers are welcome everywhere else and park staff even maintains a watering bowl for pets at the Visitor Center drinking fountain.

The packed sand and paw-friendly towpath is one of the most scenic of its ilk - the canal section around the Great Falls opens wide and the boulder-edged water calls to mind the Canadian Rockies rather than suburban Washington. Away from the Potomac a trail system penetrates the wooded hills above the river. These wide dirt trails make for easy dog walking through an airy, mature forest.

The key route is the *Gold Mine Loop* that pushes out from behind the Visitor Center. Various short spur trails, some marked and some not, radiate off the 3.2-mile loop. During the Civil War, a Union private camped at Great Falls discovered gold-bearing quartz while tending to his chores. After the war he returned to Great Falls and began mining operations that triggered a mini-gold rush to the area. Although the Maryland Mine was active from 1867 until 1939, it yielded less than $200,000 of precious metal. The Falls Road Spur takes you to the ruins of the mine and diggings can be seen at several places on the trails.

The *River Trail* above the Washington Aqueduct Dam takes canine hikers along river's edge for about one mile. Even though the water can seem placid at this point, beware of unpredictable currents in the river if your dog wants a swim - the Potomac River has claimed scores of lives over the years.

The prime attraction for canine hikers at the western end of the canal route is Paw Paw Tunnel at Mile 155. Bring a flashlight for the 15-minute dogwalk on the towpath through the 3,118-foot tunnel. It took 14 years and six million bricks to bypass the six mile stretch of the Potomac River known as Paw Paw Bends. The return trip can come via the orange-blazed *Tunnel Hill Trail*, a strenuous two-mile haul to a ridge 362 feet above the tunnel.

Chesapeake & Ohio Canal, Maryland
(301) 739-4200
www.nps.gov/choh/

Delaware Canal (Pennsylvania)

The 60-mile Delaware Canal is the only remaining continuously intact canal of the great towpath canal building era of the early and mid-19th century. The last paying canal boat completed its journey through the Delaware Canal on October 17, 1931. Today, the canal retains almost all of its features as they existed during its century of commercial operation.

The towpath runs from Easton to Bristol and is a National Recreation Trail. Together, the Delaware Canal State Park and the Delaware and Raritan Canal State Park have formed a series of looping trails connecting Pennsylvania and New Jersey, using five bridges across the Delaware River. Loop trail connection bridges are in the Pennsylvania towns of Uhlerstown, Lumberville, Center Bridge, Washington Crossing and Morrisville.

Delaware Canal State Park, Pennsylvania
(610) 982-5560
www.dcnr.state.pa.us/stateparks/parks/delawarecanal.aspx

Delaware & Raritan Canal (New Jersey)

When canal building fever swept America in the early 1800s it didn't take much imagination to dream of a water route between New York and Philadelphia across central New Jersey. Ships could navigate up the Delaware River to Bordentown and to New Brunswick in the east so all that was required was to dig a ditch between the two villages.

Construction began in 1830 and by 1834 the canal was open. The main artery - 75 feet wide and seven feet deep and all hand dug - stretched 44 miles and another feeder line ran down the Delaware River to Trenton for 22 miles. The Delaware & Raritan was one of America's busiest canals and staved off competition from the railroads at a profit until almost 1900. It remained open until 1932 until the last coal barge was grounded. The State of New Jersey took over the property as a water supply system and today the canal remains virtually intact. The state park is a 70-mile linear park connecting fields and forests along its route.

Canine hiking along the old towpath uses natural and crushed gravel surfaces. Several mill buildings, wooden bridges and canal structures are reminders of the bustling times that were once routine here. The canal still brims with activity today - almost any time you can count on sharing the trail with

153

joggers, fishermen, cyclists, horseback riders - and other dogs. Hike back to another century with your dog along the canal route as you encounter wooden bridges and 19th century bridge tender houses, remnants of locks, cobblestone spillways and hand-built stone-arched culverts.

Delaware & Raritan Canal State Park, New Jersey
(609) 397-2000
www.dandrcanal.com/

Erie Canal (New York)

As early as 1809 DeWitt Clinton had been appointed one of seven commissioners to examine and survey a route for a canal from the Hudson River to the Great Lakes. Months after he was elected Governor in 1817, on July 4, Clinton turned the first shovelful of dirt for the Erie Canal, of which he was its greatest champion.

Eight years later, hand dug by farmers and immigrant workers, the 363-mile long waterway linking the Atlantic seaboard and the American interior. The Erie Canal, the county's first heroic engineering marvel, quickly became the world's most successful and famous canal.

The original canal was gradually expanded to 70 feet wide and seven feet deep but its usefulness in the railroad age was waning. By 1922 the canal here was dry and abandoned. In 1972 the township purchased a seven-mile stretch from New York State and volunteers began an energetic campaign of cleaning the canal bed, building infrastructure and filling the canal once again.

Land on either side of the canal has been cleared to provide hiking trails along a four-mile stretch of the enlarged Erie Canal route in Camillus. The park is centrally located so you can hike an approximately four-mile loop with your dog on either side of Devoe Road. Most canine hikers will opt for the East Side trails that end impressively at the imposing piers and abutments of the Old Erie Canal Aqueduct that carried water in a wooden trough over the Nine Mile Creek. It took three years to build the aqueduct in 1839 and it is being restored today. The Nine-Mile Creek, by the way, is an excellent canoe trail to paddle with your dog.

This is all easy trotting for your dog with plenty of shade. There are also a couple of side trails to extend your hiking day around the Erie Canal. John Sims operated a provisions store on Warners Road where it crosses the canal in 1856. He did well enough to eventually sell out and move his family of seven children to Belle Isle. The original building stood until it burned in a fire in 1963. Volunteers built a replica of the Sims Store to serve as park headquarters on Devoe Road. The first floor retains the feel of a 19th century general store and the upstairs rooms serve as a museum of canal history. Behind the Sims Store the *Clinton Ditch Trail* runs along portions of the original Erie Canal.

Erie Canal Park - Camillus, New York
(315) 488-3409
www.eriecanalcamillus.com/

Ohio & Erie Canal (Ohio)

The Cuyahoga River south of Cleveland takes 90 miles of twists and turns bumping into resistant rock to cover 30 miles as the proverbial crow flies. The American Indians who lived in the valley as long as 12,000 years ago called it Ka-ih-ogh-ha, the "crooked river." There are 1,000 miles of canals in Ohio and a navigable water link between Lake Erie and the Ohio River was the first priority. In 1832 the Ohio & Erie Canal became a reality. The main trail to hike with your dog through the park is the nearly 20 miles of the *Towpath Trail* along the route of the historic canal. Ten trailheads make it easy to hike the crushed limestone path in biscuit-size chunks. The trail is a mix of meadows and forests and the remnants of locks and villages.

One of the river's severe turns creates a peninsula from which a 19th century village took its name. When the Ohio & Erie Canal opened in 1827 Peninsula became a booming port town overnight. Fourteen bars and five hotels sprung up to service the flow of traffic on the canal. The canal era lasted a few scant decades before railroads drained their customers.

Peninsula is an ideal starting point to experience the *Ohio & Erie Canal Towpath Trail* with your dog. Boston Store is an easy 2.5-miles to the north for a car shuttle or an out-and-back canine hike. A short distance to the south is Deep Lock Quarry with a 1.2-mile loop trail up the valley hills to the old excavation site, now liberally covered in trees. Along the way you pass Lock 28, the deepest lock on the canal, dropping the water level 17 feet, a critical linchpin in the entire waterway.

Ohio & Erie Canalway, Ohio
www.ohioanderiecanalway.com/

Schuylkill Canal (Pennsylvania)

Pennsylvania's first canal system was cobbled together in 1815 using 120 locks to stretch 108 miles from the coal fields of Schuylkill County to Philadelphia. Railroads began chewing away at canal business in the 1860s and the last coal barges floated down the Schuylkill River in the 1920s. Today, the only sections of the canal in existence are at Manayunk and Lock 60, built by area name donor Thomas Oakes, at the Schuylkill Canal Park.

In 1985 the Schuylkill Canal Association formed to keep the canal flowing and maintain the lock and towpath. In 1988, the area was added to the National Register of Historic Places. After years of fundraising and handiwork volunteers have rebuilt Lock 60 and it is now in operating condition. You can see it work during Canal Days in June.

In Schuylkill Canal Park your dog can either enjoy the flattest walk in the area or the steepest. The peaceful canal towpath covers 2 1/2 miles from the Lock House, built in 1836, to the eastern end of Port Providence. Across the canal are houses and town buildings looking much as they did throughout the canal era. Upstream from Lock 60 are the *Ravine Trail*, with three ascents to the 100-foot high rock bluffs overlooking the Schuylkill River, and the *Valley View Trail*, which deadends - for dog-walking - at the Upper Schuylkill Valley Park. No dogs are allowed in that park.

Mont Clare, Pennsylvania
(610) 917-0021
www.schuylkillcanal.com/

HEAD FOR THE HILLS

America's "hills" were the first vacation destinations with names like the Catskills and Poconos. Whether you come to hike up a mountain with your dog or just look at them, you can't go wrong with a vacation with your dog in one of our country's miniature mountain ranges...

DESTINATION
IDEA #48: DOGGIN' THE NORTHEAST KINGDOM

The rolling hills of Vermont's Northeast Kingdom offer the canine traveler more than one million acres to step back in time when being outdoors was not a goal but a way of life. Four out of every five of those acres are covered by forests and the terrain is dominated by rolling hills that top out on Jay Peak at 3,858 feet. Don't be surprised if much of your vacation with your dog in the Northeast Kingdom is spent walking down country lanes...

BEST PLACE TO HIKE ALL DAY WITH YOUR DOG: **Kingdom Trails**. The natural beauty of northern Vermont spreads before you on mile after mile of winding trails and long-forgotten cart roads. Privately owned, these trails are superbly maintained, mapped and marked.
East Burke, Vermont
(802) 626-0737
www.kingdomtrails.com

MOST HISTORIC HIKE WITH YOUR DOG: **Bayley-Hazen Military Road**. You will find bits and pieces of this dirt-and-corduroy log road built between 1760 and 1779. General Benedict Arnold used the road in his assault on Canada during the American Revolution but the road never reached the border. Explore its northern terminus in Hazen's Notch, the steep-walled gap between Sugarloaf and Haystack Mountains.
Westfield, Vermont

BEST HIKE TO A VIEW WITH YOUR DOG: **Mount Pisgah.** The South Trail at Lake Willoughby makes a moderate ascent up Mount Pisgah and within an hour your dog will be standing on a rock overhang 650 feet above the lovely fjord-like lake that is squeezed between two mountains.

Willoughby State Forest
(802) 748-6887
www.vtfpr.org/

BEST HIKE THROUGH MEADOWS WITH YOUR DOG: **High Meadow Trail.** This trail uses a restored woods road to traverse meadows and pastureland planted with apple trees in the 1950s. Along the way enjoy majestic views of Jay Mountain and Burnt Mountain.

Hazen's Notch, Vermont
(802) 326-4799

BEST ONE-HOUR WORKOUT FOR YOUR DOG: **Burke Mountain.** Twenty years before ski lifts they were racing down 2,000-foot drops on Burke Mountain thanks to trails cut through the alpine forest in the 1930s by Civilian Conservation Corps workers. You can still drive to the summit today on their Toll Road and explore on gentle trails or work your way up the demanding *West Peak Trail.*

East Burke, Vermont

YOUR DOG-FRIENDLIEST HIKE: **Dog Mountain.** After surviving a coma in 1994 sculptor/artist Stephen Huneck was struck by a vision to build a dog chapel on his property outside St. Johnsbury. The white-steepled New England-style chapel is festooned with dog sculptures, hand-carved dog pews and the interior is lit through dog-themed stain glass windows. Your dog is welcome, of course, in the dog chapel but she will likely be eyeing the series of trails that are cut though meadows up the side of Dog Mountain. Also on the 400-acre property are ponds that are perfect for a doggie swim and an agility course for your dog to try.

St. Johnsbury, Vermont
(802) 748-3075
www.dogmt.com/

BEST HIKE TO A WATERFALL WITH YOUR DOG: **Willoughby Falls**. A short walk reaches a spot where the Willoughby River slams down a corridor of dark, jagged bedrock in a series of cascades. These falls are especially worth a visit in the spring during the spawning run of rainbow trout that skip up the falls.
Orleans, Vermont

DESTINATION

IDEA #49: DOGGIN' THE BERKSHIRES

The natural splendor of the Berkshire Hills in western Pennsylvania has inspired artists and writers for generations, among them Henry David Thoreau, Nathaniel Hawthorne and James Taylor. The parks and forests in the Berkshires are as pet-friendly as you are likely to find when traveling with your dog...

BEST PLACE TO HIKE ALL DAY WITH YOUR DOG: **Greylock Reservation**. More than 45 miles of trails meander across the park, including the *Appalachian Trail*. If there is one must-do major canine hike in the Berkshires it is probably The Hopper. Surrounded on three sides by steep slopes, this unique U-shaped valley covered in old-growth red spruce has been designated a National Natural Landmark. An 11-mile loop includes the *Hopper Trail*, the *Mt. Prospect Trail* and the *Money Brook Trail* and tags the summits of Mt. Prospect, Mt. Williams and Greylock.
Lanesborough, Massachusetts
(413) 499-4262
www.mass.gov/dcr/parks/mtGreylock/

BEST HALF-HOUR HIKE WITH YOUR DOG: **Stockbridge Trails**. Your dog won't leave many footprints picking his way through Ice Glen; the route may be only a quarter-mile long but it plays bigger with boulders littering the ravine floor. Your dog will relish the cool shade of some of New England's largest pines and hemlock trees.
Stockbridge, Massachusetts

BEST DOGGIE SWIMMING HOLE: **Waconah Falls State Park**. Your dog will find plenty of superb swimming, both in the plunge pool and further downstream.

Dalton, Massachusetts
(413) 442-8992
www.mass.gov/dcr/parks/western/wahf.htm

BEST HIKE TO A WATERFALL: **Bash Bish Falls**. Bash Bish Falls is the highest waterfall in Massachusetts and one of the prettiest anywhere as it splits across a diamond-shaped rock. The entire area is studded with hemlocks and can be penetrated down a serpentine trail.

Mt. Washington, Massachusetts
(413) 528-0330
www.mass.gov/dcr/parks/western/bash.htm

BEST ONE-HOUR WORKOUT FOR YOUR DOG: **Tyringham Cobble**. After hiking the two-mile loop up to the Appalachian Trail through a blend of active pastures and woodland your dog will be asleep on the ride home.

Tyringham, Massachusetts
(413) 298-3239
www.thetrustees.org/pages/370_tyringham_cobble.cfm

PRETTIEST HIKE WITH YOUR DOG: **Stevens Glen**. There are no traces of its time as a recreation destination, only airy hemlock and mixed hardwood forest where your dog will enjoy sweeping ups and downs and energetic streams.

West Stockbridge, Massachusetts

BEST HIKE TO A VIEW WITH YOUR DOG: **Mount Washington State Forest**. The 2.8-mile trek up Alander Mountain starts with as many drops as climbs but eventually your dog will be rewarded with 270-degree views.

Mt. Washington, Massachusetts
(413) 528-0330
www.mass.gov/dcr/parks/western/mwas.htm

MOST HISTORIC HIKE WITH YOUR DOG: **Monument Mountain.** You can take your dog on the same hike that took place on August 5, 1850 when two giants of American literature, Herman Melville and Nathaniel Hawthorne, met for the first time during an outing on Monument Mountain.
Great Barrington, Massachusetts
(413) 298-3239
www.thetrustees.org/pages/325_monument_mountain.cfm

BEST HIKE THROUGH MEADOWS WITH YOUR DOG: **Field Farm.** The star trails at Field Farm are the trips through airy pastures with views of the Taconic Range to the west and Mount Greylock to the east.
Williamstown, Massachusetts
(413) 298-3239
www.thetrustees.org/pages/303_field_farm.cfm

BEST PLACE TO CIRCLE A LAKE WITH YOUR DOG: **Beartown State Forest.** When your dog takes the 1.5-mile Benedict Pond loop the calm waters are in sight almost the entire way.
Monterey, Massachusetts
(413) 528-0904
www.mass.gov/dcr/parks/western/bear.htm

DESTINATION
IDEA #50: DOGGIN' THE CATSKILLS

The Catskill Mountains were introduced to the world by the Hudson River School of landscape painters in the mid-1800s, the first major art movement in the United States. Shortly thereafter the first great resorts in the country began to be developed for wealthy New York vacationers. The fabulous retreats went into decline but the natural wonders of the Catskills are still there for your dog to explore...

BEST DOGGIE SWIMMING HOLE: **North-South Lake.** First developed as a recreational destination during the Depression, a sliver of earthen dam between North and South lakes was removed in the 1980s to create today's large, island-speckled lake.
Haines Falls, New York
(518) 357-2234
www.dec.ny.gov/outdoor/24487.html

BEST HIKE TO A WATERFALL WITH YOUR DOG: **Kaaterskill Falls**. A sometimes rugged .7-mile trail through a hemlock-filled gorge ends splendidly at the two-tiered Kaaterskill Falls, New York state's highest waterfall. The upper ribbon of water drops a full 175 feet - the same as Niagara Falls - and the lower falls tumble another 75 feet into a rocky basin.

Hunter, New York

BEST ONE-HOUR WORKOUT OR YOUR DOG: **Hunter's Mountain**. Four routes lead to a firetower atop Hunter Mountain, at 4,040 feet the second highest peak in the Catskills. The route on Devil's Path rises to the summit from Stoney Clove notch, a climb of 2,040 feet in just over two miles. Although it is the steepest climb on the trail, the route up the mountainside is technically easy for a dog, using old service roads. There is scarcely a downhill step on the long, steady pull up Hunter Mountain.

Catskill Forest Preserve, New York
(518) 473-9518
www.dec.ny.gov/lands/5265.html

BEST HIKE TO VIEWS WITH YOUR DOG: **Escarpment Trail**. Where the elevation rises abruptly from 540 feet at the base of its cliffs to 2,500 feet this path scampers north for 24 miles with an almost continuous series of overlooks. You don't need to tackle the entire track for the Catskill views that have long inspired artists - the overlook from the Site of the Catskill Mountain House is easily reached from the North-South Lake campground. On a clear day five states spread before you.

Haines Falls, New York
(518) 357-2234
www.dec.ny.gov/outdoor/24487.html

PRETTIEST HIKE WITH YOUR DOG: **Curtis-Ormsbee Trail**. This route down Slide Mountain plunges steeply through birches and hemlocks and bounds over boulders and rock formations so save this alternate route for athletic dogs.

Catskill Forest Preserve, New York
(518) 473-9518
www.dec.ny.gov/lands/5265.html

MOST HISTORIC HIKE WITH YOUR DOG: **Slide Mountain**. Just east of the Slide Mountain summit - the highest in the Catskills at 4,180 feet - is a small cliff overhang in a clearing, where John Burroughs, the "Father of the American Nature Essay," spent many a night garnering inspiration for his influential ideas in the 1870s.

Catskill Forest Preserve, New York
(518) 473-9518
www.dec.ny.gov/lands/5265.html

BEST PLACE TO HIKE ALL DAY WITH YOUR DOG: **Devil's Path**. So-called for the rugged terrain it follows, this 27-mile east-west journey slices through the heart of the Catskill Mountains, tagging seven mountain peaks. From start to finish, the Devil's Path features an elevation gain of 18,000 feet - more than three miles of climbing.

Catskill Forest Preserve, New York
(518) 473-9518
www.dec.ny.gov/lands/5265.html

DESTINATION
IDEA #51: DOGGIN' THE POCONOS

Lying within a two-hour drive of both New York City and Philadelphia the Pocono Mountains have long been a favorite vacation destination, especially for honeymooners. Thanks to its many resorts, the Poconos are synonymous with the heart-shaped bed. When you come with your dog, however, you won't want to spend time inside, thanks to the wonders outside...

BEST SWIMMING HOLE FOR YOUR DOG: **Rock Creek, Loyalsock State Forest**. Along the Old Loggers Trail you'll find many a crystal clear pool for your dog to paddle but the rock amphitheater where the Yellow Dog Run spills into a ten-foot pool will delay your journey for hours.

Dushore, Pennsylvania
(570) 946-4049
www.dcnr.state.pa.us/Forestry/stateforests/loyalsock.aspx

BEST HIKE TO A WATERFALL WITH YOUR DOG: **Pocono Environmental Education Center**. The Tumbling Waters Trail stretches for three miles past two scenic ponds, through a pine-and-hemlock forest, up the ominously named Killer

Hill to reach a switch-backing path down to a series of powerful cataracts tearing down the mountainside.

Dingmans Ferry, Pennsylvania
(570 828-2319
www.peec.org/

BEST PLACE TO CIRCLE A LAKE WITH YOUR DOG: **Delaware State Forest.** Bruce Lake is one of six glacial lakes in the forest; the route combines wide, paw-pleasing logging roads and the usual rocky Pocono paths as it rolls along.

Swiftwater, Pennsylvania
(570) 895-4000
www.dcnr.state.pa.us/FORESTRY/stateforests/delaware.aspx

BEST ONE-HOUR WORKOUT FOR YOUR DOG: **Lehigh Gorge State Park.** The Glen Onoko Run tumbles 900 feet down seven waterfalls in less than one mile and your dog can hike to the top, moving almost straight up at times, hopping across the stream and picking his way at others.

Jim Thorpe, Pennsylvania
(570) 443-0400
www.dcnr.state.pa.us/stateparks/parks/lehighgorge.aspx

BEST HALF-HOUR HIKE WITH YOUR DOG: **Woodbourne Forest & Wildlife Preserve.** The *Yellow "Swamp Loop" Trail* trips down a short hill through open fields and descends into the largest remaining stand of virgin, unlumbered forest in northeastern Pennsylvania where some of the giant eastern hemlocks are estimated to be 400 years old.

Dimorck, Pennsylvania
www.woodbourneforest.org

PRETTIEST HIKE WITH YOUR DOG: **Frances Slocum State Park.** The *Lakeside Trail* traipses around a boot-shaped peninsula surrounded by Frances Slocum Lake, traveling under groves of hemlocks and past natural rock shelters

Wyoming, Pennsylvania
(570) 696-3525
www.dcnr.state.pa.us/stateParks/parks/francesslocum.aspx

BEST HIKE TO VIEWS WITH YOUR DOG: **Delaware Water Gap National Recreation Area.** The hike up 1,463-foot Mount Minsi is a tough rewarding climb either on an old fire road or the twisting *Appalachian Trail* to views of the famous gap.

East Stroudsburg, Pennsylvania
(570) 588-2451
www.nps.gov/dewa

MOST HISTORIC HIKE WITH YOUR DOG: **MAUCH CHUNK LAKE PARK.**
The *Switchback Trail* travels on the roadbed of one of America's earliest railroads. After it closed the gravity railroad spent time as one of America's first rollercoasters and a popular destination for thrill seekers.

Jim Thorpe, Pennsylvania
(570) 325-3669
www.carboncounty.com/park/

BEST PLACE TO HIKE ALL DAY WITH YOUR DOG: **Hickory Run State Park.** More than 20 trails across 40 miles in three natural areas await your dog; don't miss the Boulder Field, an Ice Age relic of bowling ball-sized rocks that is a National Natural Landmark.

White Haven, Pennsylvania
(570) 443-0400
www.dcnr.state.pa.us/stateparks/parks/hickoryrun.aspx

DESTINATION
IDEA #52: DOGGIN' THE LAUREL HIGHLANDS

The southern Allegheny Mountains, cloaked in rugged, forested slopes, are one of America's premiere outdoor vacation destinations. The *Laurel Highlands Trail* extends for 70 miles from the 1,000-foot deep Conemaugh Gorge near Johnstown across the ridgeline to Youghiogheny River Gorge. But you don't need to set off on a week-long hike with your dog to enjoy this spectacular region - it supports 10 Pennsylvania state parks and forests and 11 state game lands...

PRETTIEST HIKE TO TAKE WITH YOUR DOG: **Ferncliff Trail.** The signature canine hike in one of America's best state parks is luckily the easiest and most centrally located - the three miles of trails that sweep around and across the Ferncliff Peninsula. Hugging the water for most of its 1.7 miles, the hemlock-draped footpath leads to detours through mature hardwoods, carpets of ferns and past hotel ruins.

Ohiopyle State Park, Pennsylvania
(724) 329-8591
www.dcnr.state.pa.us/stateparks/Parks/ohiopyle.aspx

MOST HISTORIC HIKE WITH YOUR DOG: **Fish Run Trail**. This hike mimics the route of the Pittsburgh, Westmoreland and Somerset (PW&S) Railroad. The line began in 1899 to haul logs off Laurel Hill and evolved to also tote passengers to the summit. Grades were as steep as 12% and locomotive brakes needed to be replaced once a week. The trail uses part of the PW&S route that was abandoned in 1916.

Laurel Summit State Park, Pennsylvania
(724) 238-6623
www.dcnr.state.pa.us/stateparks/parks/laurelsummit.aspx

BEST HIKE WITH YOUR DOG TO A WATERFALL: **Meadow Run**. The famous Lower Yough begins after the Ohiopyle Falls and flows seven miles downstream to the Bruner Run Take-out. This is the busiest section of whitewater east of the Mississippi River, studded with Class III and Class IV rapids. Your dog can only watch the action but can enjoy of the country's best waterslides at Meadow Run.

Ohiopyle State Park
(724) 329-8591
www.dcnr.state.pa.us/stateparks/Parks/ohiopyle.aspx

BEST HIKE TO VIEWS WITH YOUR DOG: **Wolf Rocks**. The Wolf Rocks are a jumble of sandstone boulders that provide a 180-acre view of the Linn Run Valley. They are reached on a two-hour loop hike through airy, second-growth woods that were last timbered in 1908.

Laurel Summit State Park, Pennsylvania
(724) 238-6623
www.dcnr.state.pa.us/stateparks/parks/laurelsummit.aspx

BEST HIKE TO CIRCLE A LAKE WITH YOUR DOG: **Lakeside Trail**. This two-mile loop around Keystone Lake on park roads and walkways circles a water supply originally built to wash bituminous coal and douse the coke from ovens of the Keystone Coal & Coke Company.

Keystone State Park
(724) 668-2939
www.dcnr.state.pa.us/stateparks/parks/keystone.aspx

BEST DOGGIE SWIMMING HOLE: **Blue Hole Run.** An unusually deep pool in an otherwise shallow stream makes the water appear a translucent blue deep in Forbes State Forest. In addition to dog paddling there is a submerged rock ledge for diving dogs to make an artful entrance. Blue Hole Run can be accessed by a dirt road in the forest.

Forbes State Forest, Pennsylvania
(724) 238-1200
www.dcnr.state.pa.us/forestry/stateforests/maps/ForbesBlueHole.pdf

BEST PLACE TO HIKE ALL DAY WITH YOUR DOG: **Quebec Run Wild Area.** A "wild area" means no amenities and no developments, including access roads. Quebec Run is the best of the bunch in the Laurel Highlands and one of the best hikes your dog will take anywhere. The hemlock and Rhododendron-shaded waters of Quebec Run that split the forest are a prime destination for most visitors.

Forbes State Forest, Pennsylvania
(724) 238-1200
www.dcnr.state.pa.us/forestry/stateforests/maps/ForbesQuebecRun.pdf

BEST HALF-HOUR HIKE WITH YOUR DOG: **Flat Rock Trail.** The out-and-back footpath is level, wide and paw-friendly. The trail is decorated by hemlocks and Rhododendron. Although the adjacent Linn Run is racing downhill your dog will find pools in which to cool off.

Linn Run State Park
(724) 238-6623
www.dcnr.state.pa.us/stateparks/parks/linnrun.aspx

BEST HIKE THROUGH MEADOWS WITH YOUR DOG: **Friendship Hill National Historic Site.** The nine miles of trails at Friendship Hill, wilderness estate of influential Secretary of the Treasury Albert Gallatin in the early 1800s, serve up the best combination of woods and meadow hiking in southwest Pennsylvania.

New Geneva, Pennsylvania
(724) 725-9190
www.nps.gov/frhi/

DESTINATION

IDEA #53: DOGGIN' THE OZARKS

The Ozarks were formed by volcanic eruptions more than a billion years ago, some of the oldest mountains on earth. They are so old and so eroded that today none of the "peaks" that cover 50,000 square miles in four states (mostly Arkansas and Missouri) reach 3,000 feet. Instead of soaring mountaintops the Ozarks are characterized by crystal clear streams fed by underground springs and more caves than any region in the United States...

BEST HIKE ON THE ROOF OF THE OZARKS WITH YOUR DOG: **White Rock Mountain.** Somehow the Civilian Conservation Corps found their way to this remote mountaintop in the 1930s and constructed a handful of rustic cabins and a bunkhouse lodge. They also laid out a two-mile trail loop around the rim of White Rock Mountain that is one long continuous 360-degree view for your dog. The native stone shelters perched on the bluffs are particularly beautiful; watch for sheer drop-offs - they continue on forever as well.

Ozark National Forest, Arkansas
(479) 964-7200
www.fs.fed.us/oonf/ozark/

BEST HIKE TO A WATERFALL WITH YOUR DOG: **Mina Sauk Falls.** Your dog can score a two-fer here: the highest point in Missouri and the highest waterfall. The trek to the summit of Taum Sauk Mountain is an easy one, things get a bit rougher as the three-mile trail continues to seasonal Mina Sauk Falls. When the water is cascading over the series of rock ledges the 132-foot drop is the tallest in the Show Me State.

Taum Sauk Mountain State Park, Missouri
(573) 546-2450
www.mostateparks.com/taumsauk.htm

BEST RIVER TO CANOE WITH YOUR DOG: **Current River and Jacks Fork River.** These two adjoining rivers provide more than 134 miles of spring-fed waters, typically flowing at an easy-going Class II level. If you don't have your own canoe there are 19 concessionaires along the rivers to provide canoe rentals and shuttle service.

Ozark National Scenic Riverways, Missouri
(573) 323-4236
www.nps.gov/ozar

BEST HIKE TO A CAVE WITH YOUR DOG: **Devil's Den State Park**. Packed with unusual natural rock formations, this was one of the first sites chosen for a state park in Arkansas in the 1930s. The signature *Devil's Den Trail* covers 1.5 miles with less than a 100-foot elevation gain and leads to Devil's Den Cave, Devil's Ice Box and trailside crevices. The caves are safe to explore so bring a flashlight to help your dog poke around. Across the creek the *Yellow Rock Trail* is less crowded and wanders past more of the Devil's "possessions" in old-growth woodlands.

Devil's Den State Park
(479) 761-3325
www.arkansasstateparks.com/devilsden/

BEST HIKE TO CIRCLE A LAKE WITH YOUR DOG: **Crane Lake**. This double-loop National Recreation Trail around clear blue 100-acre Crane Lake is lightly used which means two things, one good and one bad. There is lots of room for your dog to roam and the leaf-littered footpath through the dense white oak forest (primarily on the east side) can be hard to follow. The northern loop covers three miles and circumnavigates the lake with the water in view most of the time, especially from the fire road on the west side. The southern loop is a two-miler below the dam passing through a series of glades and rocky areas, the traverse of which can be tricky for overly cautious dogs.

Mark Twain National Forest, Missouri
(573) 364-4621
www.fs.fed.us/r9/forests/marktwain/

BEST HIKE TO VIEWS WITH YOUR DOG: **Pedestal Rocks**. You will seldom have to spend such little effort to purchase such exhilarating views as here in Ozark National Forest. A modestly rolling 2.2-mile loop leads through the forest to the Pedestal Rocks, ancient columns of weathered limestone that have broken along the bluff line. Careful with your dog along these unprotected cliffs that sweep around the hillside. You should have plenty of energy remaining to take the neighboring 1.7-mile neighboring loop to King's Bluff, a massive slab of rock that serves up a waterfall and more views across the valley.

Ozark National Forest, Arkansas
(479) 964-7200
www.fs.fed.us/oonf/ozark/

BEST SWIMMING HOLE FOR YOUR DOG: **Blue Spring Trail.** There are two Blue Springs of note in Mark Twain National Forest; the better known is the 90-million gallon per day spring that feeds the Current River and is the state's deepest and bluest spring. This environmentally sensitive area forbids swimming. The better choice for your water-loving dog is the Blue Spring on the North Fork White River, 16 miles west of West Plains. A scenic half-mile loop from the campground leads to the oval natural spring nestled in a dramatic rock amphitheater. It averages a flow of seven million gallons per day of cold clear water. If your dog is feeling frisky after a dip in the 57-degree water he can tackle the *Devil's Backbone Trail* in this wilderness area.

Mark Twain National Forest, Missouri
(573) 364-4621
www.fs.fed.us/r9/forests/marktwain/

MOST HISTORIC HIKE WITH YOUR DOG: **Prairie Grove Battlefield.** Civil War battles in the Ozarks in 1862 determined the destiny of the state of Missouri to remain in the Union. Pea Ridge, northeast of Rogers, Arkansas, was the biggest battlefield west of the Mississippi River. The fate of Arkansas was less certain and it was tussled over east of the town of Prairie Grove on December 7, 1862. Both sides claimed victory as more than 2,500 troops fell during the fighting. Now a state park, you can walk your dog around 130 acres of one of America's best-preserved battlefields, including the historic Borden House, the scene of the most deadly fire fights that day.

Prairie Grove Battlefield State Park, Arkansas
(479) 846-2990
www.arkansasstateparks.com/prairiegrovebattlefield/

BEST ONE-HOUR WORKOUT FOR YOUR DOG: **Robinson Point Trail.** You don't have to search too hard for a good workout for your dog in the Ozarks - you are in the mountains after all. What sets this one apart is Norfork Lake, which this National Recreation Trail skips beside. One of the many offerings from the U.S. Army Corps of Engineers in the Ozark Mountains, this 1.5-miler gives your dog a chance for a refreshing swim on the way out to Robinson Point, a high bluff overlooking the heart of Lake Norfork, and on the way back home.

Mountain Home, Arkansas
870-425-2700
www.swl.usace.army.mil/index.html

BEST TOWN TO STAY TO HIKE A VARIETY OF SHORT TRAILS WITH
YOUR DOG: **Eminence**. Two miles to the north the Missouri Department of
Conservation maintains a one-mile, stacked loop journey through a Missouri
hollow on the *Lick Log Trail*. Five miles to the west is postcard pretty Alley Mill
where your dog can enjoy a leisurely stroll around Alley Spring and an energetic
climb on the 1.5-mile *Alley Overlook Trail* that tops off with an overlook directly
over the spring and mill. To the east, trails hard by the Current River lead to Blue
Spring Natural Area, one of America's deepest blue springs and a spur road takes
your dog to the delightful plunge pool of Rocky Falls. A bit further away, to the
southeast, is Big Spring, where 276 million gallons of water per day pour out from
under a hillside. The overlook trail at this spring has been unmaintained of late
and doesn't look over the spring but the stone path is easy to follow and a good
outing for your dog.

Ozark National Scenic Riverways, Missouri
573-323-4236
www.nps.gov/ozar

PARK YOU MOST WANT OPEN TO YOUR DOG THAT ISN'T: **Buffalo National
River**. Originating in the Boston Mountains and edged by dramatic bluffs that
reach as high as 500 feet, the Buffalo was America's first national river. Dogs aren't
allowed in the park. Maybe someday.

DESTINATION
IDEA #54: DOGGIN' TEXAS HILL COUNTRY

Only 3% of the land in America's second largest state is publicly owned but
luckily a strong percentage of Texas parks are located in what is known as Hill
Country, a verdant stretch of rolling land between Austin and San Antonio.
Mountaintops and dramatic views are not the attraction of this vacation mecca,
however - it is water. Over 800 fresh water springs percolate to the surface in
crystalline rivers and lakes that make the Texas Hill Country famous...

MOST HISTORIC HIKE WITH YOUR DOG: **Lyndon B. Johnson State
Historical Park**. Texas Hill Country was the birthplace and life-long home of the
36th President of the United States. Several sites around Johnson City, including
Johnson Settlement and the LBJ Ranch are open to the public but the only place
your dog is allowed is this park located across the Pedernales River from LBJ

Ranch. There is a nature trail, living history farm and plenty of grassy open space for a game of fetch in the 700-acre park.

Lyndon B. Johnson State Historical Park, Texas
(830) 644-2252
www.tpwd.state.tx.us/spdest/findadest/parks/lyndon_b_johnson/

PRETTIEST HIKE WITH YOUR DOG: **Guadalupe River State Park**. The park features four miles of river frontage and the stretch by the day-use area carves its way through limestone bluffs where its banks are dotted with huge bald cypress trees.

Guadalupe River State Park, Texas
(830) 438-2656
www.tpwd.state.tx.us/spdest/findadest/parks/guadalupe_river/

BEST HIKE TO A WATERFALL WITH YOUR DOG: **Pedernales Falls**. The flow varies widely in the Pedernales River as it meanders through the park but on an average day the falls pick their way down 50 feet of limestone ledges in a wide canyon. Near the campground, tranquil blue-green waters make a picturesque double drop in a secluded glen before reaching the river.

Pedernales Falls State Park, Texas
(830) 868-7304
www.tpwd.state.tx.us/spdest/findadest/parks/pedernales_falls/

BEST HIKE TO VIEWS WITH YOUR DOG: **Enchanted Rock**. This massive dome of pink granite is considered a batholith - an underground rock formation uncovered by erosion. It is one of the largest batholiths in America. The climb to the top of the 425-foot Enchanted Rock is mostly up bare rock and waiting on top for you an your dog are panoramic 360-degree views of the surrounding Texas Hill Country. Come early on weekends - the popular park can fill up before noon.

Enchanted Rock State Natural Area
(830) 685-3636
www.tpwd.state.tx.us/spdest/findadest/parks/enchanted_rock/

BEST SWIMMING HOLE FOR YOUR DOG: **Devil's Waterhole At Inks Lake.** If your dog likes to dive in the water she can join in the fun popping into the water from the rocks surrounding this tip of Inks Lake.

**Inks Lake State Park, Texas
(512) 793-2223
www.tpwd.state.tx.us/spdest/findadest/parks/inks/**

BEST ONE-HOUR WORKOUT FOR YOUR DOG: **Lost Maples State Natural Area.** A pair of four-mile loops climb through steep limestone canyons onto plateau grasslands. Each features one big, rock-infested climb before leveling off at the top. The *East Trail* spends more time on the Sabinal River and visits the namesake stand of Uvalde bigtooth maples that are relics from the last Ice Age when Texas was wetter.

**Lost Maples State Natural Area, Texas
(830) 966-3413
www.tpwd.state.tx.us/spdest/findadest/parks/lost_maples/**

BEST PLACE TO SPOT WILDLIFE WITH YOUR DOG: **South Llano River State Park.** This is the largest concentration of Rio Grande Turkeys to be found in the American Southwest. The gregarious birds winter in large flocks around cottonwood riparian areas like the South Llano River, which numbers between 600 and 800 birds. Turkeys can be spotted year-round, especially along the scrubby brush and open grasslands of the *Fawn Trail* that loops up open slopes for three miles.

**South Llano River State Park, Texas
(325) 446-3994
www.tpwd.state.tx.us/spdest/findadest/parks/south_llano_river/**

BEST PLACE TO HIKE ALL DAY WITH YOUR DOG: **Hill Country State Natural Area.** The bulk of these more than 5,000 acres were a donation from the Merrick Bar-O-Ranch with the stipulation that it "be kept far removed and untouched by modern civilization." There are more than 40 miles of primitive trails running through grassy valleys and up limestone hills. A good sampler is the four-mile loop around the Comanche Bluff Camp Area across from the park office.

**Hill Country State Natural Area, Texas
(830) 796-4413
www.tpwd.state.tx.us/spdest/findadest/parks/hill_country/**

DESTINATION
IDEA #55: DOGGIN' THE BLACK HILLS

The Black Hills of South Dakota describe a small, isolated mountain range that are home to the tallest peaks east of the Rocky Mountains. It is not the mountains themselves that are "black" but the sea of trees that cover the hills. Gold was discovered in the Black Hills in 1874 that led to the area's first incursion of visitors but that rush pales to today's invasion by outdoor enthusiasts...

BEST HIKE TO A WATERFALL WITH YOUR DOG: **Spearfish Canyon**. The waterfalls in Spearfish Canyon are some of the most beautiful in all of the Black Hills; the trails to Little Spearfish and Roughlock Falls are manageable for any trail dog.

Black Hills National Forest, South Dakota
(605) 673-9227
www.fs.fed.us/bhnf/

BEST HIKE TO VIEWS WITH YOUR DOG: **Harney Peak**. Harney Peak, at 7,242 feet, is the highest point in America east of the Rocky Mountains. The most traveled route to the summit is on *Trail 9*, a 6-mile round trip. There is some rock scrambling near the top but your dog can make it all the way and even go up the steps into the observation tower.

Custer State Park, South Dakota
(605) 255-4515
www.sdgfp.info/Parks/Regions/Custer/

BEST HALF-HOUR HIKE WITH YOUR DOG: **Badger Hole Trails**. For a short woodlands walk, take your dog to Badger Hole, home to Badger Clark, South Dakota's first poet-laureate. Clark planned part of this footpath behind his four-room cabin that picks its way along rocky hillsides through a mixed pine and hardwood forest.

Custer State Park, South Dakota
(605) 255-4515
www.sdgfp.info/Parks/Regions/Custer/

MOST HISTORIC HIKE WITH YOUR DOG: **Flume Trail.** This National Recreation Trail follows the actual flume bed that carried water 20 miles from Spring Creek to the placer diggings of Rockerville that enabled miners to take over $20 million in gold out of the Black Hills.

Black Hills National Forest, South Dakota
(605) 673-9227
www.fs.fed.us/r2/blackhills/recreation/trails/brochures/flume_trail_50.pdf

BEST PLACE TO CIRCLE A LAKE WITH YOUR DOG: **Sylvan Lake.** Sylvan Lake, a calendar-worthy pool of water flanked by giant granite boulders was formed when Theodore Reder dammed Sunday Gulch in 1921. A pleasant one-mile loop circumnavigates the lake and offers plenty of dog-paddling along the way.

Custer State Park, South Dakota
(605) 255-4515
www.sdgfp.info/Parks/Regions/Custer/

BEST RAIL-TRAIL TO HIKE WITH YOUR DOG: **Mickelson Trail.** To level off the roller-coaster terrain of the Black Hills railroad builders constructed more than 100 wooden trestles on the right of way that became the *Mickelson Trail.* The largest was the Sheep Canyon Trestle, 126 feet high and 700 feet long; the rickety trestle was considered so dangerous engineers and brakemen would walk over the bridge instead of riding in the train.

www.mickelsontrail.com/

BEST PLACE TO HIKE ALL DAY WITH YOUR DOG: **Carson Draw and Sundance Trail System.** There is something for all level of canine hiker on the 17 footpaths that cover 47 miles here. Some of the routes that dip into densely forested canyons and explore scenic ridgetops will test even the most energetic of trail dogs.

Black Hills National Forest, South Dakota
(605) 673-9227
www.fs.fed.us/r2/blackhills/recr

MAKE YOUR DOG A TOP DOG

Highpointers are folks who seek to stand atop the highest point in each of the 50 states. The first person known to have tagged the summits of the 48 contiguous states was a fellow named Arthur Marshall back in 1936. After Hawaii and Alaska were added to the union in the 1950s, Vin Hoeman became the person to reach the top of all 50 states. To date fewer than 200 people have been documented to have climbed - as the case may be - all 50 highpoints.

Your dog can be a Highpointer too. She can't complete all the peaks - there are places she can't go legally (the spectacular Mount Katahdin at the northern terminus of the *Appalachian Trail* in Maine, for instance), mountains she can't climb physically (the vertical rock climbs at the top of Gannett Peak in Montana), or both (Mount McKinley, the highest of American peaks at over 20,000 feet). But that leaves plenty of state summits for your dog to experience...

DESTINATION
IDEA #56: THE HIGHEST POINT YOUR DOG CAN HIKE TO IN THE UNITED STATES

The highest mountain in America's Lower 48 is California's Mount Whitney at 14,505 feet. But the hike to the top is not arduous and so popular permits are rationed out to get on the trail. You can hike with your dog to the shadow of the summit but the final steps will be yours alone as you leave the dog-friendly Inyo National Forest and travel into Sequoia National Park, where dogs are banned from the trails.

The highest spot in America where your dog is allowed to go is Mount Elbert in Colorado, only 65 feet lower than Whitney. Located in the Sawatch Range of the San Isabel National Forest, Mt. Elbert was named for Samuel Elbert who was a controversial territorial governor of Colorado in 1873. The first recorded summit of the peak was by H.W. Stuckle of the Haydon Survey in 1874. Before that, the more famous Pikes Peak was assumed to be the highest point in Colorado.

Mount Elbert is still not well known, despite its lofty position as the highest peak in the Rocky Mountains. Some members of the 14ers, the group of outdoor enthusiasts who tackle all 53 of Colorado's 14,000-foot mountains, look at Mount Elbert with a degree of scorn because it is so "easy" to summit. There were even people who piled rocks on neighboring Mount Massive to give it the extra twenty feet it would need to surpass Mount Elbert. The summit has been reached by jeep and there have been proposals over the years to build a road to the top of Mount Elbert.

Of course, "easy" is relative and all prudent precautions for being on a 14,440-foot mountain must be taken. But any trail dog accustomed to a ten-mile hike can scale Mount Elbert. There are five routes to the top, the most popular being the *North Mount Elbert Trail*. From the trailhead to the summit is 4.5 miles, the first two climbing through alpine forests. After the trail bursts above the treeline the route switches back twice before pulling straight to the summit. There is no rock scrambling or "mountain climbing" necessary. Views along the way are outstanding and unforgettable when you reach the top roof of the Rocky Mountains.

Mount Elbert
(719) 553-1400
www.fs.fed.us/r2/psicc/

DESTINATION
IDEA #57: DOGGIN' AMERICA'S MOST POPULAR MOUNTAIN

It's not the highest peak in Colorado - there are actually 29 higher - but Pikes Peak is the most visited mountain in the United States. A half-million people make their way to the summit every year, most in their cars. When it opened in the Fall of 1888, the 14-foot wide Pikes Peak Carriage Road was billed as the highest road in the world. The first automobile chugged to the summit in 1901 - today the climb is 6,710 feet over 19 miles on the toll road.

Pikes Peak, with its height and position in the Front Range, was the first landmark seen by settlers heading west. Explorer Lieutenant Zebulon Pike, on assignment by Thomas Jefferson, first saw the mountain in 1806. He was thwarted by a blizzard in his attempt to scale the "Great Peak." The first recorded successful ascent was made by a scientist named Edwin James in 1820. In 1858 Julia Archibald Holmes - sporting bloomers - became the first woman to tag the summit and spent two days on top. The footpath up the eastern face was re-worked and built by Fred Barr between 1914 and 1918. It was pick-and-shovel duty, with an occasional dash of black powder for moving rocks and trees.

Dogs are welcome to tackle the *Barr National Recreation Trail* all the way to the summit. Near the top there are rock steps that most dogs can negotiate. The 13-mile pull to the 14,110-foot summit of Pikes Peak begins in Manitou Springs at an elevation of 6,300 feet. It is the biggest elevation gain of any trail in Colorado, with an average grade of 11%. Serious canine hiking indeed. Barr Camp, where Fred ran a burro concession, is at the halfway point and makes a handy turn-around point for those not prepared to make the assault on the summit. There are three miles of hiking above the treeline and the peak gets afternoon storms nearly daily so come prepared. The *Barr Trail* is well-trod and well-marked. It gets extremely hot in the mid-summer and there is no natural water for your dog on Pikes Peak.

There is no shame for your dog in riding to the top - there is still first class hiking to be had at Pikes Peak at a more moderate pace. At the base of the mountain is a one hour out-and-back ramble through the aspen groves, pine forests and impressive boulders of Crowe Gulch. This land was opened to homesteading in 1862 but farming was difficult in a place where snow could come in July. The Crowe family was one that tried but abandoned their 160-acre parcel before the five years of residency required for ownership. If you come to Pikes Peak just for this tranquil ramble there is no charge; just tell the folks at the toll booth that you don't want to drive to the top, just hike in Crowe Gulch.

Pikes Peak, Colorado
(800) 318-9505
www.pikespeakcolorado.com/

TOUR

IDEA #58: TAGGING NEW ENGLAND'S HIGHPOINTS

New England is the ideal place to introduce your dog to highpointing, where your dog can easily tag five proximate state rooftops in a short vacation...

Mount Washington (New Hampshire)

Mount Washington, at 6,288 feet, is the highest and most famous mountain in the Northeast. Darby Field, a British colonist from Exeter, made the first recorded ascent of what would later be called Mount Washington in 1642. In 1819 Ethan Allen Crawford and father Abel built the first trail to the summit and it is the oldest continuously used mountain trail in the United States. Not long afterwards a bridle path was carved up the mountain and a hotel opened on the summit in 1852 (built by workers who had to hike 2 miles up Mount Washington each day to meet material hauled nine miles by horses over rough trails). In 1861 the 8-mile long Mt. Washington Auto Road opened for carriages. Mt. Washington Cog Railway, using the first rack-and-pinion mountain climbing system, later would haul passengers up one of the steepest railway tracks in the world.

The weather on Mount Washington is considered the worst in the world. The highest wind velocity ever measured - 231 miles per hour - was clocked on the summit on April 12, 1934. Winds average 35 mph every day with a hurricane force wind (75 mph) registered one day in three. Dense fog and clouds envelop the summit 315 days a year which makes your chances of enjoying the 130-mile views to New York, Quebec and even the Atlantic Ocean about 1 in 10.

At least 15 long, rugged hiking trails wind to the top of popular Mount Washington. The most traveled, and one of the most scenic, climbs the eastern slope on the *Tuckerman Ravine Trail* from Pinkham Notch. On the western face the *Ammonoosuc Ravine Trail* and *Jewell Trail* combine for an invigorating loop. Go up the *Ravine* and down the *Jewell* as the latter affords long exposed views as it works along cliffs; the *Ravine Trail* is thickly wooded and follows the plunging river all the way up. From the Appalachian Mountain Club Hut the original *Crawford Trail* climbs 1.4 open miles and nearly 2000 feet to the busy top. Much of the way is boulder hopping but your dog can make it without too much difficulty. Be careful of some crevasses along the ridge, however.

Mount Washington, White Mountain National Forest, New Hamsphire
(603) 466-2713
www.fs.fed.us/wildflowers/regions/eastern/MountWashington/index.shtml

Mount Mansfield (Vermont)

Mount Mansfield (the name seems to have drifted up from Connecticut landowners) is Vermont's highest peak, noted primarily for its skiing and the resemblance of the ridgeline to an elongated human face. The geographic features of the mountain have subsequently been given corresponding human facial feature names. Underhill State Park is a gateway with several trails, including a paved road, to ascend busy Mount Mansfield, site of the Stowe Mountain Resort. *Laura Cowles Trail* (2.7 miles), *Sunset Ridge* (3.0 miles), and *Halfway House* (2.5 miles) are all moderate length climbs to the summit.

From the end of the Mount Mansfield Toll Road the relatively easy scramble to the summit is totally across bare rocks (the surrounding vegetation area, one of only two places in Vermont you can find true alpine tundra is, in fact, off limits). Once on the "Chin" of Mount Mansfield your dog can soak in extensive 360-degree views. You'll know if it is a clear day if you can see Mount Royal and the skyscrapers of Montreal.

Mount Mansfield, Underhill State Park, Vermont
(802) 899-3022
www.vtstateparks.com/htm/underhill.cfm

Mount Greylock (Massachusetts)

Long before Mt. Greylock became the first Massachusetts state park in 1898, it had attracted New Englanders with its inspiring five-state views. Great American writers such as Edith Wharton, Nathaniel Hawthorne, Herman Melville and Henry David Thoreau regularly trekked up the trails to Mt. Greylock's 3,491-foot summit.

Threatened by logging and industrial development in the late 1800s, a group of Berkshire County businessmen formed a private land conservation association and purchased 400 acres at the summit to preserve Mt. Greylock. The Massachusetts Legislature purchased Greylock as a State Reservation in 1898 and over the next century the park grew to encompass some 12,500 acres.

For serious canine hikers there are several long-distance options to tag the summit. One of the wildest but most scenic routes on the mountain is the *Thunderbolt Trail* that picks up 2,175 feet in elevation in less than two miles. The steep, twisting route was constructed by the Civilian Conservation Corps as a championship ski trail in 1934 and named after a famous roller coaster at Revere Beach in Boston because both gave such an unforgettable ride. Today your dog can hike where many a past major downhill race was contested, including the 1938 and 1940 United States Eastern Ski Association Championships.

Dogs are permitted on all the trails and in the 35-site campground in the Reservation. A 100-foot tall stone War Memorial Tower commands the views at the summit of Mt. Greylock. Although your dog can't scale the tower the same sweeping views of the Hoosic River Valley are available from the stone wall and benches on the edge of the ridge.

Mount Greylock, Mount Greylock State Reservation, Massachusetts
(413) 499-4262
www.mass.gov/dcr/parks/mtGreylock/

Mount Frissell (Connecticut)

The Commonwealth of Massachusetts and the State of Connecticut squabbled over their common border for more than 150 years. When the dust settled in 1806 and the agreed-upon boundary was drawn, the summit of Mount Frissell wound up jusssssssssssssst that little bit into Massachusetts. But the side of the mountain residing in Connecticut happened to be higher than any other place in the Nutmeg State. And so Connecticut is the only one of the 50 states whose highpoint is not a summit.

There are several options for your dog to stand at the roof of Connecticut. The most direct is from the trailhead on East Street that takes you up and over Round Mountain and onto Mount Frissell in a little over a mile. The climbs are steady but won't overwhelm a healthy trail dog. A little ways past the highpoint marker and 80 feet higher is the open, grassy summit that has been heretofore obscured by the thick trees.

If your goal is simply to tag the highest point in the state, turn around and head back. But as long as you're up here... The marquee canine hike in Mount Washington State Forest (where you are) is the trek to 2,239-foot Alander Mountain and expansive 270-degree views that are the best in western Massachusetts. After passing the Tri-State Marker you can head north on the lightly traveled *Ashley Hill Trail* through lush forests and head back up to Alander Mountain.

Until the campground about halfway back to the summit the going is on a wide jeep road and there will be plenty of unbridged stream crossings that your dog will happily bound through. When your dog gets his fill of mountaintop views of the Hudson Valley and the Catskills continue across to the *South Taconic Trail* to close your loop. If you plan to make the big loop you can also start your day in the forest headquarters and just take a jog down the *Mount Frissell Trail*, rather than cross Round Mountain. The loop over Alander Mountain will cover about eleven miles.

For your dog to actually stand on the highest SUMMIT in the Nutmeg State go over a few mountaintops and scale Bear Mountain. Long thought to be the Connecticut highpoint, the most popular route up Bear Mountain is via the blue-blazed *Undermountain Trail* to the *Appalachian Trail*, tagging the peak in just under three miles. Bear Mountain is an honest mountain - there is scarcely a downhill pawfall on the ascent to the top - no depressing drops into saddles and ravines that set tails to drooping when you know you should be headed up. You are gaining over 1,500 feet in elevation on this canine hike but the serious panting does not begin until the final half-mile.

Mount Frissell, Mount Washington State Forest, Connecticut
(413) 528-0330
www.mass.gov/dcr/parks/western/mwas.htm

Mount Marcy (New York)

Mount Marcy is the highest peak in the Adirondack Mountains and in New York, soaring 5,344 feet above sea level. It is the monarch of the 46 mountains that comprise the High Peaks of the Adirondacks.

Working for the New York State Geological Survey, Professor Ebenezer Emmons organized and led the first recorded ascent of Mount Marcy on August 5, 1837, naming the peak for New York Governor William Learned Marcy. The mountain was also known as Tahawus, an Indian name meaning "Cloud Splitter."

Today the Mount Marcy summit can be reached on well-marked trails from four directions around the mountain. All are long hikes for your dog but none are technically difficult. The shortest, and most popular, route comes in from the north on the *Van Hoevenberg Trail*. It is still seven miles one way, with an elevation gain of 3,224 feet. About two miles in the trail crosses Marcy Lake - a perfect refresher for your dog on the way up and on the way back.

The views are scant along the way as you work moderately through a dense spruce forest. Nearing the summit, Mount Marcy is covered in dense stands of scrubby balsam fir and the trail narrows considerably and a bit of rock climbing is introduced. A few hundred feet below the summit the treeline fades away and your dog is left with a scramble to the top. Views in every direction of the High Peaks await.

Mount Marcy, Adirondack Park, New York
(518) 582-2000
www.adkvic.org/

TOUR
IDEA #59: TAGGING THE MID-ATLANTIC HIGHPOINTS

Another good place to bag a pawful of highpoints in a short trip is the Middle Atlantic states where you can almost throw an old dog blanket across the ceilings of Pennsylvania, West Virginia and Maryland...

Mount Davis (Pennsylvania)

As tagging Eastern highpoints goes, Mt. Davis is unique. Scaling mountain peaks does not spring to mind. Assuming you don't drive to the summit and take the short, flat walk to the highpoint, your dog's approach to the top of Pennsylvania will be a hike of nearly a mile from the Mt. Davis Picnic Area on the High Point Trail. This sliver of path is essentially a straight shot through an area recovering from a destructive 1951 fire. After a gentle ascent your dog will reach the highest natural point in Pennsylvania - a rock.

How long has Mt. Davis been the highest point in Pennsylvania? Well, always, of course. But it wasn't recognized as such until 1921 when the U. S. Geological Survey established the fact that the crest of Negro Mountain is 3,213 feet above sea level. This survey officially snatched the honor of "Pennsylvania's Roof" away from Bedford County's Blue Knob.

The slight rise in the 30-mile plateau of Negro Mountain was named for the long-time 19th century owner of the land, John Nelson Davis, rather than recognizing the heroic exploits of the unidentified black man who fought heroically during the French and Indian War and was buried on the mountain. Davis, himself a Civil War veteran, was a naturalist said to be able to identify all the shrubs, wildflowers and plants growing in the area.

Mount Davis, Forbes State Forest, Pennsylvania
(724) 238-1200
www.dcnr.state.pa.us/forestry/stateforests/forbes.aspx

Spruce Knob (West Virginia)

Spruce Mountain is the tallest mountain in the Alleghenies, although even at 4,863 feet it doesn't stand out in the Monongahela National Forest. There are over 75 miles of hiking trails around the mountain but the route to the Spruce Knob summit comes on a half-mile *Whispering Spruce Trail* that starts after a drive to the top of the mountain.

This is a supremely easy trot for your dog on a lightly graveled path. The knob gets its name honestly, loaded with dense spruce forests that drape the summit in an alpine feel. After enjoying several panoramic views along the way you reach a stone and steel observation tower that is easily climbed by your dog for 360-degree views.

Spruce Knob, Monongahela National Forest, West Virginia
(304) 257-4488
www.fs.fed.us/r9/mnf/sp/spruce_knob.html

Backbone Mountain (Maryland)

At 3,360 feet above sea level Backbone Mountain, a long slab of rock in the Allegheny range, is the highest point in Maryland, the 32nd highest "highpoint" in the United States. When you reach the summit you and your dog will actually be standing on the point of Hoye-Crest, named for Captain Charles Hoye, a prominent chronicler of Maryland lore and founder of the Garrett County Historical Society.

Backbone Mountain is the Eastern Continental Divide - rain that falls on the eastern slope drains into the Atlantic Ocean via the Potomac River and water on the western side eventually finds it way to the Gulf of Mexico.

The highest point in Maryland is less than two football fields from West Virginia and the easiest way to get to Hoye-Crest is to start across the state line in the Monongahela National Forest. You will use an old logging road to reach the ridge of Backbone Mountain; it is steep enough to get your dog panting but not so arduous you will need to pull over and rest. Once you reach the ridge it is a short ways to the high point. It is less a summit than a lookout from the woods.

Once your dog is through soaking in the experience of being on the roof of Maryland the way down is the same as the way up - a two-mile round trip. There are plenty more trails to explore across Backbone Mountain but there won't be any wayfinding aids at the trailhead. Your dog can go off leash in Potomac State Forest.

Backbone Mountain, Monongahela National Forest, Maryland
(304) 636-1800
www.fs.fed.us/r9/mnf/

Mount Rogers (Virginia)

If these relatively tame summits have left your dog wanting more you can steer down I-81 to tackle Virginia's highpoint - Mount Rogers. At 5,729 feet, Mount Rogers is the highest of the state highpoints east of South Dakota that lacks a road to the summit.

The summit is assaulted from three directions, each route covering about 4.5 miles one way. The most popular approach leaves from Grayson Highlands State Park and traverses open pastures (expect to encounter free-ranging wild ponies) and hardwood forests to reach the *Appalachian Trail* where a half-mile spur leads to the top of Mount Rogers. There are no views on the spruce-enclosed summit so take time to soak in the panoramic vistas along the trail; you can spot Mount Rogers on the ascent and the stand-out peak to the west is 5,520-foot Whitetop Mountain.

You can also start directly on the *Appalachian Trail* from Elk Garden to the west. Here you can return on the *Virginia Highlands Horse Trail* to complete a 4-5 hour hiking loop. All of your dog's canine hiking takes place on Mount Rogers and can be handled by even beginning trail dogs. Expect a generous helping of rocky terrain under paw, especially on the horse trail.

Mount Rogers, Mount Rogers National Recreation Area, Virginia
(540) 265-5100
www.fs.fed.us/r8/gwj/mr/

DESTINATION
IDEA #60: DOGGIN' AMERICA'S TOP SKI RESORTS

No, we're not talking about schussing down a mountain slope side-by-side with your dog. And dogs and tightly groomed cross-country trails don't mix. But if you are seeking a first-class destination for your trail dog come summer you can do a lot worse than considering some of America's top ski resorts. Here are some ideas to get you started...

Lake Placid (New York)

In the United States, Lake Placid is synonymous with winter sports. Lake Placid is one of only three cities to host two Winter Olympic games, in 1932 and 1980 and today the permanent facilities are part of the official U.S. Winter Olympic Training Center.

Melville Dewey, the genius behind the Dewey Decimal System of library book classification, established Lake Placid as a resort community when he built the Lake Placid Club in the onetime iron-making town. Today, although its winter heritage is much in abundance, outdoor adventurers seek out Lake Placid year-round.

Lake Placid is the destination of choice for canine hikers in search of spectacular views of the High Peaks in the Adirondacks. The premier area trail is the *Wilmington Trail*, a long, straight climb up and over Marble Mountain and across a rocky ridge to the summit of 4,867-foot Whiteface Mountain. The going can be wet and muddy on the well-worn path and views won't kick in until reaching the rocky glacial deposits but the 360-degree views at the top are unforgettable. After all the hard work from you and your dog on the 5.2-mile linear trail you will be sharing the summit with many others who have driven cars up the Whiteface Mountain Memorial Highway.

More outstanding views can be found on Haystack Mountain (of the High Peaks and the Saranac Lakes chain to the west); Mt. Van Hoevenberg (of the High Peaks and Mount Marcy to the south); and Mt. Jo (open vistas of the High Peaks Wilderness in three directions). All these hikes feature similar moderate woodlands walks before steep final climbs to exposed rocky ledges. Mt. Van Hoevenberg can be approached from the north or south - the northern approach tours the Olympic bobsled and luge runs. Mt. Jo is the only loop in the bunch (2.3 miles) and nearby is the trail to Rocky Falls, a series of tumbling cascades with a canine swimming hole.

When you want to take a break from scaling the Adirondack Mountain slopes you can relax on the *Brewster Peninsula Nature Trails*, a spiderweb of pleasant wooded trails on the shore of Lake Placid.

Lake Placid, New York
(800) 447-5224
www.lakeplacid.com/

Notchview (Massachusetts)

With more than 40 kilometers of cross-country trails spread across 3,000 acres Notchview is one of the premier nordic ski destinations in the Northeast. They average more than 80 days a year of trail skiing and you can even ski on one trail with your dog - a 2-kilometer loop south of Route 9. The rest of the year Notchview is one of the best places in Massachusetts for active dog owners.

The earliest inhabitants of this land were the Mohican Indians who were run off their land in Albany, New York and relocated to Stockbridge in 1664. It would be another century before English settlers filtering out of eastern Massachusetts would force the Mohicans off this land as well. Remnants of the tribe today can be found in Wisconsin.

By the end of the 19th century the land that would become Notchview supported 20 disjointed homesteads. In 1920, Lieutenant Colonel Arthur Budd, who earned The Distinguished Service Cross for extraordinary heroism in France in World War I, met the widowed Helen Bly in London. Mrs. Bly lived in a 250-acre estate she called Helenscourt. The two married and returned to the Berkshires where they set about consolidating the local farms and building the 3,000-acre estate Notchview. After considering leaving the property to the Commonwealth or the Episcopal Church, Colonel Budd decided to bequeath his farm to The Trustees of Reservations. He died in 1965 and the park opened to the public in 1969. Colonel Budd was seldom seen on the farm without his beloved dogs - they are welcome at Notchview still.

Whatever you have in mind for hiking with your dog is on the menu here. There are more than 15 miles of paw-friendly hiking trails available. First time visitors can sample Notchview on the *Circuit Trail* that loops back through the middle of the property, ducks out of the trees for a quick view and finishes back at the Visitor Center. The 1.8-mile trip travels just about the entire way on a pebbly farm road that is kind to the paw. Although the land has long supported farming most of the open spaces have been reforested in red spruce and northern hardwoods.

After this easy ramble you can decide how much of the large park to chew off with your dog. The highest point at Notchview is the 2,297-foot Judges Hill but the reserve averages more than 2,000 feet so your dog can keep his four-wheel drive in reserve for most of the day. Across Route 9 is an excellent leg stretcher - the *Hume Brook Forest Interpretive Trail*. This route was created in the 1970s to educate the public about multiple use management and demonstrate the basic principles of modern forestry.

Notchview, Massachusetts
(413) 684-0148
www.thetrustees.org/pages/1401_ski_notchview_.cfm

Steamboat Springs (Colorado)

James Crawford is the father of Steamboat Springs, having settled in a cabin on Soda Creek in 1874. Instead of becoming "Crawfordville" legend has it the town was named for the rhythmic chugging of a hot spring that disgorged mineral water 15 feet into the air. The medicinal springs brought the first settlers to the valley and later the town became an international ski jumping mecca with the arrival of Norwegian champion Carl Howelsen in 1913. Today outdoor enthusiasts don't wait for the snow to fall to make their way to "Ski Town USA."

In town, the *Yampa River Trail* system links Steamboat Springs with the surrounding mountain area. The trails provide easy dog walking along the Yampa River and through city parks. The *Hot Springs Walking Tour* visits seven of the more than 150 historic springs that gurgle around town, including Heart Springs. The origin and history of each spring is detailed on interpretive signs.

To get out of town head for the *Spring Creek Trail*, an 8-mile round-trip that begins at the corner of Amethyst Drive and East Spring Street. The route is an easy canine hike on a well-graded trail that meanders up to the Spring Creek Reservoir and Dry Lake Campground. Just north of town is Fish Creek Falls, a 283-foot plunging waterfall that is the town's leading visitor attraction. Canine hikers will know it as the starting point for the *Fish Creek National Recreation Trail*. Long, wooded inclines at the beginning of the trail give way to a steep, rocky climb before leveling off in alpine meadows on the 5-mile journey to Long Lake. Continuing past Long Lake, you shortly reach the Continental Divide. The elevation gain on this out-and-back trail, *Forest Service Trail #1102*, rises from 7,400 to more than 10,000 feet and and patches of snow in shady spots will delight your dog even into the summer.

Steamboat Springs, Colorado
(970) 879-2060
steamboatsprings.net/

Stowe (Vermont)

The first settlers in what would one day become world-famous ski resort Stowe arrived, appropriately enough, in 1793 pulling a sled. In 1807 Thomas Jefferson signed an embargo act forbidding trade with Great Britain and its North American colony, Canada. Not about to be cut off from their most lucrative market in Montreal, northern Vermonters began driving cattle north of town through a sliver of trail between the thousand-foot cliffs of Spruce Peak and Mount Mansfield, Vermont's highest peak at 4,395 feet. Thus was born Smuggler's Notch. Later, fugitive slaves used the notch as an escape route and in the 1920s illegal liquor flowed from Canada down through the famed crack. Today, Smuggler's Notch State Park is the keystone of Mt. Mansfield State Forest, Vermont's largest public woods with 37,242 acres and Smuggler's Notch Resort.

Across Smuggler's Notch is a rollicking hike on the *Elephant's Head Trail* to a small clearing at the top of a 1,000-foot cliff. The trail climbs stone steps from the roadway to Sterling Pond, the highest life-sustaining alpine pond in New England (trout are stocked by helicopter). The trail drops to the shoreline where canine hikers will meet a single impassable rock climb for most dogs. A bushwhacking detour through thick spruce will probably be in order. From this point the way is seldom level with plenty of hopping from root to rock. Keep an eye out for many species of plants found nowhere else in Vermont that reside happily among these moist, cold cliffs.

The views from Elephant's Head sweep up and down the rugged notch and directly across to hulking Mount Mansfield, scarred by a 1983 landslide. The return trip can be over the same route or continue down the hillside switch-backing across rocks and roots. This loop, completed only by walking the dog along the narrow, winding Route 108 through the notch, is closed from February to mid-July to protect peregrine falcons.

In the T-shaped village of Stowe the popular *Stowe Recreation Path* begins behind the Community Church on Main Street with various connecting places along the Mountain Road. This is an easy canine five-miler though farm fields, meadows and woodlands with ample opportunity for a splash for your dog in the adjacent meandering Little River.

Stowe, Vermont
(802) 253-7321
www.gostowe.com/

Sun Valley (Idaho)

In 1879 a tall, wiry prospector named David Ketchum built a small shelter along the Trail Creek to use as his base of operations in the area. He did not stay long. By 1880, when mining operations began to be permanently established, Ketchum was long gone, rumored to be in Arizona, or perhaps dead in a saloon standoff. The new town called itself Leadville but the United States Post Office turned down the name because Leadvilles were as common as dashed dreams in the West by that time. The settlers decided to name their town after pioneering David Ketchum, whose rudimentary shelter still stood down by Trail Creek.

For more than a decade Ketchum boomed but the collapse of the silver market in 1894 opened a gash in the town's economy that drained 90 percent of its population. The town recovered some with an infusion of sheep ranching but by the 1930s there were fewer than 300 people living in Ketchum. In 1935 Austrian Count Felix Schaffgotsch was hired by Union Pacific Railroad Chairman W. Averell Harriman to scout the American West for the best site to build a destination ski resort like the tony resorts in the European Alps. Schaffgotsch scoured the mountain regions of the West and rejected such places as Aspen, Jackson Hole and Yosemite. He was prepared to return to New York and report his failure when a railroad representative from Idaho asked him to check out Ketchum. Within three days, the Count wired Harriman: "Among the many attractive spots I have visited, this combines more delightful features of any place I have seen in the United States, Switzerland, or Austria for a winter sports resort." Eleven months later Sun Valley Resort opened to international acclaim and Ketchum's future viability was assured.

Ketchum features over 40 miles of trails located within a 5-mile radius of town. The marquee walk is the 5-mile *Bald Mountain Trail*, at the end of 3d Avenue at River Run Plaza on the edge of town. The trail crosses numerous ski trails up 3,400 feet to an elevation above the tree line at 9,151 feet. Not only are dogs allowed on Bald Mountain, but halfway up the mountain, in a glade of giant fir trees, is a drinking fountain with a perpetually-filled dog drinking bowl built right into the trail. About the only place dogs are not allowed is on the ski lifts.

Other trails around Ketchum include hikes around Corral Creek in the Sun Valley resort and additional alpine walks north of town on Highway 75 at Fox Creek and Adams Gulch. These dirt and grass trails are afire with wildflowers through the summer months. Further up Highway 75, just seven miles from Ketchum is the Sawtooth National Recreation Area, with 756,000 acres of public land. A highlight in the Sawtooth Mountains, with more than 40 peaks higher than 10,000 feet, are more than 300 high mountain lakes. Several of the lakes, including Baker Lake and the Norton Lakes are within two miles of a trailhead.

The *Harriman Trail* is a 31-kilometer corridor in three segments that is open to hiking and biking in the summer and cross-country-skiing and snowshoeing in the winter starting at the Sawtooth National Forest headquarters. The trail climaxes in Galena, overlooking the headwaters of the Salmon River.

Ernest Hemingway spent his final years in Ketchum and he is remembered with a memorial on a shaded bank of Trail Creek in Sun Valley. Nearby, in the Ketchum Cemetery on the northern edge of town on Route 75, is Hemingway's unadorned grave. Guarded by a sentry of trees, the marker is flush with the ground and offers no more than a name and dates for the life of America's most celebrated writer of the 20th century. Hemingway's four dogs - Black, Negrita, Neron, and Linda - are buried in a neat patio at his home in Cuba.

Sawtooth National Forest, Idaho
(208) 737-3200

DOGGIN' AMERICA'S PANHANDLES

When you pull out a map of the United States one of the first things you notice are these strange appendages sticking out of some states. There are square states and oddly shaped states whose borders are defined by rivers and these states with panhandles. What's up with those? Maybe its time to pack your dog's traveling bag and find out...

DESTINATION
IDEA #61: DOGGIN' THE FLORIDA PANHANDLE

Looking at a map, it appears the Florida Panhandle exists only out of spite to keep Alabama from reaching to the sea. In fact, before Florida was a state, the people of the Panhandle voted to join the State of Alabama. But before the annexation could be carried out, a financial scandal in the Alabama legislature scuttled the plan. Shortly after the Civil War Florida considered ceding the state's western arm to Alabama for a million dollars. Alabama didn't want it and called the Panhandle "a sand bank and gopher region."

The first thing vacationers with dogs will want to know is, "Where can I take my dog to the beach?" Florida's Gulf Coast beaches are world famous for their sparkling sugar sands but dogs, save for a sliver of sand in Panama City, aren't allowed on any of these. But, with the salt air tickling their nostrils, dogs are allowed to explore the dunes trails at many spectacular Florida beachside parks...

Camp Helen State Park

It is easy to blow past Camp Helen, developed as a resort for vacationing textile workers after World War II, when traveling along US 98 and that would be a loss for your trail-loving dog. There is only one trail in the park, covering a bit over one mile, but it is sure to be one of your dog's favorites. After exploring the lodge and cottages of Camp Helen the trail drops to the shores of Lake Powell, one of Florida's largest examples of a rare coastal dune lake. At several spots your dog can slip into the water for a cooling dip. Moving on you soon traverse a salt marsh before bursting onto the wide, sugary sands of the Gulf of Mexico. Although your dog can't continue all the way to the Inlet Beach proper, this is one of the few places on the Panhandle he can trot the sands, see the waves and at least feel like it's a day at the beach.

Before your dog can get too giddy, however, the trail turns up into the dunes and shortly you reach a dense maritime hammock and the shade of moss-draped live oaks and tall pines. The wide, sandy path swings past Duck Pond before finishing back among the camp buildings of the old resort. All in all, quite a bit to pique your dog's interest here.

Panama City Beach, Florida
(850) 233-5059
www.floridastateparks.org/camphelen

Grayton Beach State Park

The star hike for your dog at Grayton Beach, a park of 2,000 acres, is the nature trail that is squeezed in the wild dunesland between the Gulf of Mexico and Western Lake. You will find this double loop at the very end of the paved parking lot.

Your dog will be ushered into the *Barrier Dunes Trail* through a tunnel of scrub oak twisted by the Gulf breezes and salt spray. Although separated from the sunbathers enjoying one of America's perennially top-rated beaches by only a few yards, you are a world away.

The sand trail emerges on the shores of Western Lake where it joins the *Pine Woods Loop* and a totally different natural community on the backside of the dunes. Sand gives way to a wooden boardwalk for part of the trip. The tall, slender pines afford a measure of shade on the shifting sands. Western Lake is a coastal dune, a unique ecosystem so rare that there are only 17 in the entire world - three in the park and the others in remote portions of Africa and Australia.

Santa Rosa Beach, Florida
(850) 231-4210
www.floridastateparks.org/graytonbeach

Gulf Islands National Seashore - Naval Live Oaks

Live oak trees, prized for their rot-resistant and incredibly dense wood, have long been the lumber of choice for building durable sailing ships. Sixth President John Quincy Adams considered the United States Navy, which he called "our wooden walls," to be of critical importance in defending America from foreign invasion and in 1828 he started the country's first tree farm here for the single purpose of growing live oaks for shipbuilding. Now a unit of the Gulf Islands National Seashore, the Naval Live Oaks area preserves 1,400 acres of forested terrain between Santa Rosa Sound and Pensacola Bay.

There are more than seven miles of hiking trails in these historic forests. The *Brackenridge Nature Trail* is a good place to start your dog where exhibits identify plants and describe how live oaks were used in shipbuilding. Laid out in a figure-eight, this lush, narrow pathway runs along a bluff above the Santa Rosa Sound. You can also leave behind the casual strollers and continue down the 1.2-mile *Fishing Trail* through the thin strip of live oak forest.

Across the highway, your dog can stretch out on the sandy and wide *Andrew Jackson Trail*, a two-miler that runs the entire length of the Naval Live Oaks property. This time-worn path is a remnant of the Pensacola-St. Augustine Road, the first road connecting East Florida to West Florida. Congress ponied up $20,000 of 1824-money to build the road when Florida was still a territory.

Gulf Breeze, Florida
(850) 934-2600
www.nps.gov/guis

Topsail Hill Preserve State Park

Topsail Hill is the most intact coastal ecosystem in all of Florida. The state moved to protect this unique natural area by purchasing 1,637 acres here in 1992. There are 14 identifiable ecosystems, including freshwater coastal dune lakes, wet prairies, scrub, pine flatwoods, marshes, cypress domes, seepage slopes and 3.2 miles white sand beaches - the remnants of quartz washed down from the Appalachian Mountains. Topsail Hill gets its name from the landmark 25-foot high dune that resembles a ship's topsail.

Topsail Hill is the best place that you can take your dog for an extended hike along the Gulf of Mexico. The trail of choice is the *Morris Lake Nature Trail*, a 2.5-mile balloon route laid out through ancient coastal dunes. The dunes trail is wide open and exposed to the elements so bring plenty of water for your dog on a hot day and since every step of the way is across glistening soft white sand, your dog will get a workout any time of the year. In fact, look for iron tracks laid down during World War II that allowed heavy trucks to travel across the thick sand when these dunes were used as a bombing range. The trail climbs briefly into a Florida shrub community where your dog can find some shade among the sand pines and shrubby oaks before finishing along the Gulf of Mexico beach.

Santa Rosa Beach, Florida
(850) 267-0299
www.floridastateparks.org/topsailhill

Torreya State Park

Hardy Bryan Croom, a planter and naturalist of some renown, began amassing land in northern Florida in the 1820s and in 1833 purchased 640 acres of the Lafayette Land Grant for what would become Goodwood Plantation. While exploring from his cotton plantation, Croom discovered one of the rarest conifers in the world along the banks of the Apalachicola River. He named the small evergreen "torreya" after the botanist Dr. John Torrey. It would turn out the torreya was native to only five other spots in the world - one in California, four in Japan and China, and on the bluffs of the Apalachicola. Croom's own botanical career would be cut short in 1837 when he perished with 89 others aboard the *S.S. Home* off the coast of Cape Hatteras in the Racer's Storm, one of the most destructive hurricanes of the 19th century.

On the way to nowhere, your dog will thank you for making the special trip to Torreya State Park, developed during the Great Depression. This is the best traditional woodland hiking your dog can get on the Florida Panhandle, stalking terrain more familiar in Appalachian foothills. Indeed, the mix of hardwoods thriving at the various elevations in the park conspire to whip up Florida's best display of autumn colors.

There are two hiking loops at Torreya, each about seven miles around. Along the Apalachicola River the *Rock Bluff Trail* dips and rolls through ravines with some climbs that may set your dog to panting. Several park roads and connecting trails can be used to dissect this loop into manageable chunks. That is not the case with the Torreya Challenge in the eastern section of the park. Once you cross the stone bridge your dog you won't see the trailhead again for several hours. She will think she has left Florida on this scenic ramble.

Rock Bluff, Florida
(850) 643-2674
www.floridastateparks.org/torreya

DESTINATION
IDEA #62: DOGGIN' THE IDAHO PANHANDLE

The Idaho Panhandle was created when the Montana Territory was cleaved from it in 1864. The wildest of America's panhandles, more than 80% of these 21,000 square miles are covered with trees and managed by the United States Forest Service. If you are seeking a vacation to disappear in the woods with your dog, northern Idaho is the place to head. But for those with dogs of a more civilized bent there are outdoor adventures awaiting a bit less hard-core...

Heyburn State Park

The 5,744-acre park, embracing the shores of lovely Lake Chatcolet, was the first state park in the Northwest when it was created from the closing of the Coeur d'Alene Indian Reservation in 1908. For decades it was the only state park in Idaho.

Trails wander through centuries-old Ponderosa pines and visit the shores of three lakes. The *Trail of the Coeur d'Alenes*, a 72-mile paved bike trail, rolls through Heyburn State Park on its way north through the Idaho Panhandle. Your dog can trot across the St. Joe River on a 3,100-foot bridge/trestle on the trail.

Plummer, Idaho
(208) 686-1308
parksandrecreation.idaho.gov/parks/heyburn.aspx

Lake Coeur d'Alene

By 1878 enough miners and homesteaders had filtered into the Coeur d'Alene Mountains that the United States government constructed Fort Sherman at the mouth of the Spokane River on Lake Coeur d'Alene. By the time the military outpost shuttered in 1901, tourism was entrenched along the lake. So many vacationers arrived by steamship that Lake Coeur d'Alene was America's busiest inland port west of the Mississippi River. Several times the lake, whose literal translation from French is the meaningless "heart of the awl," has placed highly on lists of the world's most beautiful lakes.

The best place to enjoy the shoreline of Lake Coeur d'Alene are the manicured downtown parks with paved trails, including the 24-mile *North Idaho Centennial Trail*. At the south end of 3rd Street Tubbs Hill Park offers several miles of canine hiking in 120 acres; a 2.2-mile interpretive trail that follows the perimeter of the namesake mini-mountain.

The easiest of several eastern shore trail overlooking Beauty Bay is *USFS Trail #257* at a picnic area off Highway 97. The half-mile loop trail climbs gently through the trees to the most photographed spot on the lake. Hearty canine hikers can access a 15-mile Forest Service Trail here as well, with a 3-mile day hike option. From the campground at *Beauty Bay Creek Caribou Ridge Trail #79* grinds up four switchbacks to the top of Mount Coeur d'Alene. There is an elevation gain of more than 2,300 feet on this 4.6-mile-climb through the timber with glimpses of the lake along the way before reaching extensive views of Beauty Bay from the lookout at the 4,439-foot summit.

Along Caribou Ridge is a good place to hunt for huckleberries, the state fruit of Idaho. Huckleberries are wild blueberries common in coniferous forests, solitary plump, dark fruit dangling from bushes that can grow head-high. Idaho's bluish fruit is the black huckleberry that is most productive at elevations between 4,000 and 6,000 feet. Sweet and ripe in early summer, huckleberries are a favorite of bears.

The must-do hike for dog owners on the shores of Lake Coeur d'Alene is the *Mineral Ridge National Recreation Trail*. Prospecting began on this slope in the 1890s with lead-zinc being the big draw. Construction on the 3.3-mile interpretive trail began in 1963 and two decades later it was designated a National Recreation Trail. The dirt path switches up 660 feet to the 2,800-foot summit through lush stands of Ponderosa pine and Douglas fir and past old mining pit excavations. Views can be had of Wolf Lodge Bay and Beauty Bay and spur trails can add a few miles to your exploration of Mineral Ridge.

Coeur d'Alene, Idaho
(208) 664-3194
www.coeurdalene.org/index.asp?PageId=343

Priest Lake State Park

Priest Lake has long been considered a western beauty, nestled in the folds of the Selkirk Mountains. Noted for its clear water Priest Lake stretches for 19 miles and is connected to the smaller Upper Priest Lake by a no-wake, two-mile long thoroughfare. Day hikes lead to smaller surrounding lakes to keep your water-loving dog saturated. Your dog is welcome on the water and on the trails through dense hemlock-cedar forests but can't go on the sandy beaches.

West of Priest Lake, 14 miles north of Nordman you can hike with your dog among trees estimated to be 2,000 years old in the Roosevelt Grove of Ancient Cedars. A fire in 1926 destroyed most of the original grove and left only two small remains. The Lower Grove, only two acres in size, is easily accessed and has been developed into a small picnic site. An old logging road, more suitable for an energetic dog, climbs to the 20-acre Upper Grove where you can roam under 150-foot giants. This one-mile loop also takes in views of Granite Falls that spills over a sheer rock wall.

Coolin, ID
(208) 443-2200
parksandrecreation.idaho.gov/parks/priestlake.aspx

DESTINATION
IDEA #63: DOGGIN' THE NEBRASKA PANHANDLE

If Nebraska had graduated into statehood without any alterations from its creation as a U.S. Territory in 1854 it would be one of our largest states. But political bargaining by subsequent territories snatched land here and swiped land there and we are left today with the stout, forward-looking panhandle so familiar in the center of the country. For canine adventurers the Nebraska Panhandle is a smorgasbord of prairies, sandhills and wind-sculpted ridgelines...

Chadron State Park

South of Chadron, home of the Museum of the Fur Trade, this park provides the ideal introduction to Nebraska's Pine Ridge, a 20-mile wide swath of broken ridges and sandstone buttes that rudely interrupt the ocean of rolling, grassy swales of the Great Plains. Although it wouldn't be recognizable as a recreation area for fifty years, this was Nebraska's first state park, established in 1921.

The park is a recreation center now, anchored by a modern campground with a swimming pool and a languid lagoon plied by paddleboats. You can even watch demonstrations of fur trading as it took place on the frontier at a simulated trading post. Hiking trails bisect the park, sliding through meadows and dense stands of Ponderosa pines. The well-blazed trails roll out of the park and connect with the expansive *Pine Ridge Trail* system in the Nebraska National Forest.

Chadron, Nebraska
(308) 432-6167
www.ngpc.state.ne.us/parks/guides/parksearch/showpark.asp?Area_No=42

Fort Robinson State Park

With more than 22,000 acres, Fort Robinson is one of Nebraska's largest recreation areas. It is also one of the most historic. Fort Robinson was born as a military post in 1874 and it was here on September 5, 1877 that the great Lakota Sioux chief Crazy Horse, victor at the Battle of Little Bighorn, was killed while in Army custody. Later the post evolved into the world's largest facility for the training of horses and mules for cavalry forces. During World War II the country's K-9 Corps training center was established at Fort Robinson. More than 14,000 dogs were trained for military duty and civilian service here.

Your dog won't recognize Fort Robinson as a military installation - the only fences are strands of barbed wire. Your dog can tour the grounds to inspect the historic buildings and visit the stone pyramid erected at the site of Crazy Horse's death. Trails near the Visitor Center wind around rows of cottonwoods trees along some of the park's numerous waterways. These are just leg-stretchers for the surrounding pine-covered hills, walls of buttes and open prairie where your dog can strike out on 60 miles of trail.

Crawford, Nebraska
(308) 665-2900
www.ngpc.state.ne.us/parks/guides/parksearch/showpark.asp?Area_No=77

Scotts Bluff National Monument

Hiram Scott was one of thousands of anonymous fur traders sent into Indian Territory during the early 1800s to bargain for valuable pelts of muskrat, rabbit and, especially, beaver. That his is the name that survives centuries later on a national monument is by virtue of his premature death - most likely from disease but with every retelling the circumstances became increasingly more dramatic. What is known for certain is that he died near this arid bluff that towers 800 feet above the North Platte Valley. The "hill that was hard to go around" was a path marker for emigrants on the Oregon Trail and with each passing there was mention of the demise of the fur trader at "Scott's Bluff."

When Scotts Bluff National Monument was established in 1919, it was believed to be the highest point in Nebraska (the highest point is actually at a rise in the prairie known as Panorama Point that your dog can visit over in Kimball County near the Colorado state line). It will feel like the highpoint, however, when you lead your dog up the *Saddle Rock Trail*. It is 1.6 miles, paved all the way, to the summit with spectacular views of the surrounding flatlands, Chimney Rock and the panhandle's largest city, Scottsbluff. Less adventurous canine adventurers can drive to the summit and take easy strolls to the overlooks.

Off the bluff, west of the Visitor Center, your dog can walk along a stretch of the actual Oregon Trail, which led 350,000 people into the West on this roadbed between 1841 and 1869. Scotts Bluff is one of the most dog-friendly properties operated by the National Park Service - they even supply courtesy bags at the trailheads.

Gering, Nebraska
(308) 436-9700
www.nps.gov/scbl/

Wildcat Hills State Recreation Area

For pure hiking with your dog in the Nebraska Panhandle, it is hard to top the Wildcat Hills. There are no streams for fishing, no lake for boating, no developed campground. About the only thing to intrude on the purity of the natural experience are a few picnic sites. The Wildcat Hills landscape is a rocky escarpment that rises several hundred feet on the south side of the North Platte River. The plant and animal life is more typical of the Wyoming mountains many miles to the west. Cougars that had been eradicated from the region around 1900 returned to the area in the early 1990s but are seldom seen.

The Wildcat Hills are rippled with steep-walled canyons that are the highlights of the three-mile trail system. The shelters scattered along the trails were built by the Civilian Conservation Corps during the Depression, crafted of native stone quarried nearby. The wood for the footbridges in the canyons came from logs cut in the pine-covered canyons.

Gering, Nebraska
(308) 436-3777
www.ngpc.state.ne.us/parks/guides/parksearch/showpark.asp?Area_No=193

DESTINATION
IDEA #64: DOGGIN' THE TEXAS/OKLAHOMA PANHANDLE

In order to enter the Union as a slave state, Texas surrendered its lands north
of 36°30' latitude above which no slavery was permitted. The 170-mile strip of
land was thus left with no formal territorial ownership. It was officially called the
"Public Land Strip" and was more commonly referred to as "No Man's Land"
and wasn't actually appended to the Oklahoma territory until 1890. Today the
adjoining panhandles of Texas and Oklahoma form a vast, seamless land of sparse
grasslands and persistent winds. Highlights for your dog here are few and far
between but welded together can forge a memorable vacation...

Palo Duro State Park (Texas)

The "Grand Canyon of Texas" is one of the largest in America, yawning for
over 120 miles and reaching depths of 800 feet. This is particularly impressive
since the gaping chasm is invisible as you drive east from the only access town
of Canyon. Early Spanish Explorers are believed to have discovered the area and
dubbed the canyon "Palo Duro" which is Spanish for "hard wood" in reference to
the abundant mesquite and juniper trees. Palo Duro Canyon State Park opened
on July 4, 1934 with over 26,000 acres in the scenic, northern most seven miles of
the canyon.

Dogs are allowed throughout the park and welcome in the campground.
Palo Duro is one of Texas' most visited parks but most folks seem to experience
the canyon by wheeled conveyance so when you get out with your dog to explore
some of the 30 miles of foot trails you will be in for a special treat. The landscape
is painted with red claystone, white gypsum and yellow mudstone. The busiest
trail at Palo Duro is a relatively easy ramble on the *Lighthouse Trail,* three miles
out and three back. The Lighthouse is a dual, 300-foot plump spire of eroded
mudstone. For a desert trail this is easy-going for your dog with few rocks and
mostly paw-friendly sandy dirt. No water along the way, however. Other routes
that will beckon to canine hikers include the easy trotting of the Paseo Del Rio
alongside the Red River and the only route that begins at rim level, *Triassic Trail.*

Canyon, TX 79015
806-488-2227
http://www.palodurocanyon.com/

Lake Meredith National Recreation Area (Texas)

The Canadian River, rising in New Mexico's Sangre de Cristo Mountains and the largest tributary of the Arkansas River, flows across the whole of the Texas Panhandle over a surface as flat as any in the world. Over many eons it cut deep canyons into the High Plains. With the damming of the river in 1965, the resulting Lake Meredith partially filled in these canyons in spectacular fashion with blue water splashing beneath white limestone caprock and reddish-brown coves.

Boating is the main activity with your dog at Lake Meredith, where you can camp for free for up to fourteen days. Off the water you can take your favorite trail companion down a dirt road or explore the open shoreline.

Fritch, TX 79036
(806) 857-3151
http://www.nps.gov.lamr

Black Mesa State Park and Preserve (Oklahoma)

This mesa in the far northwest tip of the Oklahoma Panhandle got its name from the layer of black lava rock that coated the region about 30 million years ago. Black rocks can still be seen scattered about today. The mesa is also the highest point in Oklahoma at 4,973 feet.

The ascent to the roof of Oklahoma covers 4.2 miles and is dead flat almost the entire way, save for a brief switch-backing haul up the back of the mesa. Once on top another level 15-minute hike is required to reach the red granite monument marking the summit. This is an easy go for your dog with a wide, paw-friendly trail except for the rocky slopes of the mesa. There is little shade and no water out on the mesa however, so take the proper precautions.

The Preserve is a lonely 15 miles northwest of the small Black Mesa State Park where you can camp, hike a couple of short nature trails and enjoy Lake Etling if water conditions are right.

Kenton, OK 73946
(580) 426-2222
www.touroklahoma.com/detail.asp?id=1%2B5U%2B3584

Beaver Dunes State Park (Oklahoma)

In such a dry area blasted by relentless winds you might expect to find sand dunes around someplace - and here they are. Debris from the last Ice Age has washed down from the Rocky Mountains and been pushed into massive sandhills by the southerly Oklahoma breezes. Known as the "Playground of the Panhandle," more than half of the 520-acre park is reserved for off-roading adventure in the rolling, shifting sands.

You can take your dog out into the dunes or stick to the interpretive trail near the picnic area. There is also a cozy five-acre lake and campground in the park that was originally created in 1930 as a municipal playground for the City of Beaver. If you arrive after a healthy rain you are liable to find the dunes ablaze in wildflowers.

Beaver, OK 73932
(580) 625-3373
www.touroklahoma.com/detail.asp?id=1+5U+3582

DOGGIN' AMERICA'S HOT ROCKS

When you think about it, a heckuva lot of American vacations boil down to heading out and looking at rocks. Here are some of the best to check out with your dog...

DESTINATION
IDEA #65: DOGGIN NEW HAMPSHIRE'S NOTCHES

Unfortunately, one of America's most famous rocks is no longer there. The Old Man of the Mountain, or Great Stone Face, was a geological oddity some 200 million years in the making. It hovered regally 1,200 feet above the floor of the valley until crumbling in 2003. You can view the Old Man's ghost position from turnouts in the highway or while hiking leisurely with your dog on the 9-mile paved recreational trail that runs the length of the notch. Another natural formation nearby may not be so obvious. Just to the north, a rock formation can be seen suggesting a cannon profile poking from a fortress parapet, hence the name Cannon Mountain.

The Wisconsin Glacier scoured and gouged the granite mountains of
New Hampshire about 15,000 years ago. The retreating ice mass left behind an
embarrassment of natural wonders that began attracting tourists in 1808 with the
discovery of the Flume, a natural 800-foot gorge with perpendicular granite walls
less than 20 feet apart. Stagecoach roads to the area began opening in the middle
of the 19th century when Nathaniel Hawthorne immortalized the Old Man of
the Mountain, five layers of rock sticking out of Profile Mountain. The 40-foot
ancient rock formation emerged from Hawthorne's writings to become the state
symbol of New Hampshire. The greatest of the tourist camps was Profile Inn but
after the hotel burned to the ground in 1923 its owners put their entire holdings
of 6,000 acres up for sale to be cut as timber. A campaign began immediately to
save the notch and the state of New Hampshire matched the $100,000 raised to
create **Franconia Notch State Park** (www.franconianotch.org/) in 1928.

Canine hikers are not allowed down the *Flume Trail*, the most popular walk
in Franconia, but with the abundance of other great hikes it won't even be missed.
Entering the notch from the north, the first doggie delight is *Artist's Bluff Trail*,
where one short, rocky climb bags the 2,368-foot summit and superb views of
beautiful Echo Lake. An easy walk along a lightly wooded ridge with plenty of
filtering light tags Blue Mountain (2,320 feet) to close the loop.

In the heart of Franconia Notch is dog-friendly Lafayette Campground, a
jumping off point for the best walks in the park. From the campground, the *Pemi
Trail* traces the Pemigewasset River to the Basin, a smoothed-out pothole that
has absorbed 25,000 years of pounding from the stream. For an engaging loop,
abandon the level *Pemi Trail* and climb along the boulder-strewn *Cascade Brook
Trail* to Lonesome Lake for views of the Kinsman Range. The mountains plunge
to the alpine waters at 2,743 feet. Close the six-mile loop with a steep, rocky
descent to the campground on *Lonesome Lake Trail*.

Across the parkway from the campground awaits a classic White Mountains
hike for the hardiest of canine hikers - the loop to the *Franconia Ridge Trail*.
Begin on *Falling Waters Trail*, boulder-hopping along and across several
waterfalls. The ascent to the ridge is accomplished on the grueling "45," so named
for the severity of the climb. Once on the ridge you join the *Appalachian Trail*
and walk two shelterless miles above the treeline, crossing Haystack Mountain
(4,840 feet), Lincoln Mountain (5,089 feet) and Lafayette Mountain (5,260
feet). Some of the rock formations can be challenging for a dog but there is
nothing insurmountable on this spectacular hike. Return from the ridge down

Old Bridle Path that features a long, rocky descent across open slopes before dipping into stunted pines. The full loop will cover nine rewarding miles.

Canine hikers come to Crawford Notch not to scale majestic peaks but to look at them. The Crawford family settled in this magnificent mountain pass in 1790 and two years later Abel Crawford and his son Ethan opened the Notch House, ushering in the hotel era in the White Mountains. In 1825 Samuel Willey brought his family to the notch to operate an inn on a farmstead along the Saco River. The next year, after watching a ferocious landslide in the mountains, Willey built a cave-like shelter for his family of seven to escape to in the event of another slide.

He didn't have long to wait. On August 26, 1826 an epic storm shook the White Mountains, raising the river 20 feet and loosening thousands of tons of rock and debris. Rescuers found the house unscathed - apparently because it had been built beneath a ledge - but the family perished seeking safe ground. Today **Crawford Notch State Park** (www.nhstateparks.org/state-parks/alphabetical-order/crawford-notch-state-park/) retains a family feel with many of the trail signs being hand-painted on boards.

Some of the best views of the Presidential Range and Mount Washington can be had from Mt. Willard, an outcropping at 2,804 feet reached from a gradually rising 1.4-mile trail. Similar rewards await on the *Arethusa Falls/ Frankenstein Cliffs Trail*. The exposed outcroppings offer sweeping views down the notch to the south and east. The trail completes a four-mile loop by visiting New Hampshire's highest waterfall - the 200-foot feathery plunge of the Arethusa River. The trail is rocky and rooty and can be slow going at times. Short, easy walks can be taken around the Saco River at the site of the former Willey Farmstead.

DESTINATION
IDEA #66: DOGGIN' NEW YORK'S "GORGE"OUS GORGES

Several times in its history all of New York has been covered completely in glaciers one mile thick. These ice sheets did not melt gently like cubes in your summer lemonade. Instead, the glaciers died an angry death - clawing and scraping and gouging the land as they retreated. Their handiwork can be seen in the Finger Lakes, 11 elongated parallel lakes in the center of the state. Surrounding the lakes are hundred of gullies and gorges, seven of which have been developed as New York state parks. Much of the work building trails and overlooks in these parks was done during the Great Depression of the 1930s by the Civilian Conservation Corps, the "tree army" put to work by President Franklin Roosevelt.

Most of these gorge trails are closed in the winter and often the ice lingers in the cool shadows of the gorge walls into May so plan accordingly. Gorges can be dangerous places to hike (the Ithaca Fire Department has many a sad tale to tell of a gorge rescue) but stay on marked trails and don't cross barriers where trails are closed and you and your dog will be fine.

Let's start this state park orgy with the most famous and least appealing for your dog - **Watkins Glen** (nysparks.state.ny.us/parks/info.asp?parkID=105). Watkins Glen is the only gorge your dog cannot hike through. Dogs are allowed on the *South Rim Trail* and *Indian Trail* above but views are few and far between. Watkins Glen was the first gorge to open when newspaperman Morvalden Ells received permission to charge admission to the series of wooden walkways and bridges built for workers to access a mill in the glen. The grand opening was July 4, 1863. History buffs might recognize that date as one of America's most important. On that day Robert E. Lee's invasion of the North was stopped at Gettysburg, insuring the South would never win the Civil War and at the same time the critical river town of Vicksburg, Mississippi was surrendering to Ulysses S. Grant, winning the West for the Union. Chances are the opening of a private concession in a New York gorge was not front-page news.

Letchworth (nysparks.state.ny.us/parks/info.asp?parkID=12) is the biggest and most popular of the parks, located a bit west of Conesus Lake, the westernmost of the Finger Lakes. The Genesee River attracts plenty of spectators to gawk at its hydrospectaculars in the "Grand Canyon of the East" so, if you can, come early with your dog to hike the *Gorge Trail*. You can certainly escape the crowds behind the museum on the *Mary Jemison Trail* where you'll learn about the woman kidnapped by marauding Seneca Indians as a child who then lived more than 70 years among the Iroquois. In the northern expanse of the park, around the campground, are several isolated trails that lead to gorge views.

Buttermilk Falls (nysparks.state.ny.us/parks/info.asp?parkID=25) is the shortest, narrowest and most intimate of the gorges. You will feel like you are being squeezed through the gorge with the water as you lead your dog into this chasm. There is only one rim trail, on the north side and it climbs steeply to complete your loop. The plunge basin of Buttermilk Falls is a fine place for a doggie swim if the pool is not open.

Robert H. Treman (nysparks.state.ny.us/parks/info.asp?parkId=104) is the biggest canine gorge hike with the *Gorge Trail* and both rim trails clocking in at about two miles. Treman was an early 20th-century New York banker and first Finger Lakes state park commissioner who is most responsible for the preservation of many of the gorges we enjoy today. This was Treman's favorite. From Upper Park take the *Rim Trail* down Enfield Glen, rather than plunging right into the gorge. Delaying your pleasure does two things: one, you will be hiking through the gorge upstream that affords longer views of such cataracts as the 120-foot Lucifer Falls and two, your dog will be going down the amazing Cliff Staircase instead of trudging up it. Your dog is not allowed in the swimming area in Enfield Creek but she can slip in for a refresher from both sides on the *Gorge Trail* and the *Rim Trail*, which gives you an idea of the ups and downs waiting for you on the rim.

Fillmore Glen (nysparks.state.ny.us/parks/info.asp?parkID=35) is named for the 13th President of the United States, Millard Fillmore, who was born in a log cabin about five miles from here. Fillmore was the first unelected President, ascending to office when Zachary Taylor died mid-term. He then served without a Vice-President of his own, the only chief executive to do so. After taking the *Gorge Trail* through this pretty glen, the favored return route is on the *North Rim Trail* that rolls through a rich hemlock forest. The *South Rim Trail* mainly connects picnic areas.

The exact opposite of its gorge park sisters - the *Gorge Trail* at **Taughannock Falls** (nysparks.state.ny.us/parks/info.asp?parkId=93) is the gentle, benign hike. So easy in fact, that it remains open all year long. Only 3/4-mile through a flat, wide opening between 400-foot walls, your destination is 215-foot high Taughannock Falls, the second highest single-drop waterfall in America east of the Rocky Mountains and three stories higher than Niagara Falls. The two rim trails can be combined for a sporty canine hike of about an hour.

Stony Brook (nysparks.state.ny.us/parks/info.asp?parkId=102) glen was de-veloped as a resort in the late 1800s - you can still see the massive concrete supports in the gorge from a high railroad bridge that once brought tourists to a train station where the campground is today. Your dog will be going about one mile into the gorge, passing three major waterfalls along the way.

DESTINATION
IDEA #67: DOGGIN' SHAWANGUNK RIDGE

The Shawangunk Ridge south of the Catskill Mountains is an ultra-hard gumbo of quartz pebbles and sandstone. It resists weathering while the underlying shale erodes relatively easily. The result is a series of dramatic cliffs and talus slopes, particularly noticeable when approaching from the east, which have been sculpted by retreating glaciers. The "Gunks," as they are affectionately called, have been recognized as the best rock-climbing destination in North America. Luckily for your dog, going vertically up a rock face is not the only way to explore the Shawangunk Ridge.

Alfred and Albert Smiley opened the Shawangunk Mountains to the vacationing public after the Civil War when they built the Mohonk Mountain House. Later, a disagreement caused Alfred to move on and build the Cliff House nearby. The last guest checked out in 1979 and the state of New York stepped in to prevent any further development on the Ridge. Today the top of the ridge is mostly public land primarily in Minnewaska State Park Preserve, Mohonk Mountain House, Sam's Point Preserve and Mohonk Preserve. Of this quartet, only the first and last are open to your dog.

Most of your dog's hiking atop Shawangunk Ridge will take place on wide, carefully graded carriageways. After decades of jostling for tourist dollars the Smiley brothers eventually reconciled and began building a network of these graceful roadways between the two hotels. In **Minnewaska State Park Preserve** (nysparks.state.ny.us/parks/info.asp?parkID=78) several long parallel carriageways between Lake Awosting and Lake Minnewaska can be combined for loop hikes of several hours duration. For spectacular views of the Hudson Valley use the *Castle Point Carriageway* to Castle Point, the highest summit in the park. Looks at the Catskill Mountains come quickly on the short, steep *Sunset Path* near the entrance parking lots.

The narrow hiker-only paths, however, are where the adventure begins for canine hikers on the Ridge. These trails are generally moving up and down, leading to treasures deep in the Shawangunks like Stony Kill Falls. The trek to Gertrude's Nose bursts from a dark hemlock forest for extended walking on exposed clifftops. This is not the place for a rambunctious dog (no fencing and long drop-offs) and inexperienced canine hikers may have trouble with the rock scrambles but otherwise is worth every step of the two-mile detour off the *Millbrook Mountain Carriageway*.

One of the best ways to observe the exploits of expert rock climbers is in the **Mohonk Preserve** (www.mohonkpreserve.org/) on the easy-going *Undercliff* and *Overcliff Carriage Roads*. Another popular choice here for your dog is the three-mile round trip across open fields and light woods to Bonticou Crag, a stark-white finger of rock overlooking the valley.

The unique environment on the Shawangunk Mountain ridge is extremely sensitive and access to the park is limited to reduce the impact of human - and canine - intrusion. Capacity in the parks on any given day is limited by the number of parking spaces in the lots. It is not unheard of for the park to be closed before it actually opens - so many cars are lined up for the 9:00 a.m. opening. When one car leaves, another is allowed in. Even with the restrictions the park averages more than 1,000 visitors per day. If you arrive early and get in, however, you will find the trails generally uncrowded, especially on the hiker-only footpaths.

DESTINATION
IDEA #68: DOGGIN' SENECA ROCKS

Legend has it that the spectacular crags of white/gray quartzite that soar 900 feet above the flat valley of the North Fork of the Potomac River were the childhood playground of Snowbird, beautiful daughter of Seneca Indian chief Bald Eagle. To determine the warrior who would win her hand in marriage she staged a contest to see who could scale the magnificent cliff. The first documented roped ascent of the Seneca Rocks, however, didn't take place until 1935. A switch-backing 1.3-mile hard-packed trail ascends the north edge of the Seneca Rocks to a wooden viewing platform. Sure-footed dogs can climb a bit further up bare rock to notches at the very top of the rocks for views of the Allegheny Mountains to the west. The trail is a steady climb but well within the means of even the novice canine hiker. To get back to the flat valley floor you will retrace your pawprints rather than try one of the nearly 400 mapped climbing routes to the rocks.

The Seneca Rocks are the centerpiece of the **Spruce Knob/Seneca Rocks Natural Recreation Area** (www.fs.fed.us/r9/mnf/sp/sksrnra.html), 100,000 acres of unspoiled hillsides and hollows so striking that it was the first such place so designated by the United States Forest Service. Other nearby special places include Smoke Hole Canyon where the South Branch of the Potomac River squeezes between North Mountain and Cave Mountain and you can pitch a tent hard by the river and catch a few trout for your dog's breakfast. In the

Cranberry Glades Botanical Area a boardwalk takes your dog through four acidic wetlands more often found in country hundreds of miles north of West Virginia.

DESTINATION
IDEA #69: DOGGIN' OHIO'S LEDGES

Northeast Ohio is a place that doesn't bubble often to the top of lists of vacation hot spots but if you have an active trail dog, you'll want to consider it. The main attraction are "ledges," limestone that has weathered, eroded and cracked into massive jumbles of SUV-sized blocks. You are actually hiking on the floor of an ancient seabed that once covered Ohio. Millions of years later retreating glaciers covered most of the limestone with scraped soil but some areas were left exposed to the mercy of wind and water that have created fanciful rock formations. While you'll marvel at the scenic wonder of these ledges your dog will love poking in, racing around and romping on top of the rocks. One advantage of visiting ledges in the summer is that these hikes tend to be many degrees cooler than the posted high temperature for the day. Here are some of the best Northeast Ohio parks to experience ledges...

At the small, wooded wonderland known as **Nelson-Kennedy Ledges State Park** (www.ohiodnr.com/parks/nelsonk/tabid/775/Default.aspx) you'll get right into it with your dog. A series of ledges run north-south for about one mile, bracketed by waterfalls at either end. Separate trails run to the top (white-blazed and easy), across the front (blue-blazed and the best way to view the mossy rocks) and down and through the massive, scrambled rocks (red-blazed and difficult). You may chuckle when you see names on the *Red Trail* such as Fat Man's Peril, the Squeeze and the Devil's Icebox but it won't be a laughing matter on the hike when you watch your dog's wagging tail race ahead as you stare at a seemingly impossible passage through the rocks.

Hinckley Reservation (www.clemetparks.com/visit/index.asp?action=rde tails&reservations_id=1011) is famous for the return of buzzards, turkey vultures actually, that arrive from the south every March 15. Two separate sets of ledges and cliffs are open for your dog's exploration, each reached by a trail about one mile long. A short climb to one of the highest points in Northeast Ohio brings you to the base of Whipp's Ledges where your dog can easily scale the 50-foot high rock cliffs. Keep control of your dog as you cross the top of the ledges that feature sheer, unprotected drop-offs. In the the southern end of the reservation are the mossy Wordens Ledges that feature rock carvings of religious symbols.

The highlight of the trail system at Happy Days Visitor Center in **Cuyahoga Valley National Park** (www.nps.gov/cuva/) is a band of 30-foot high ledges that run for the better part of a mile. The *Ledges Trail* circles the rock formations that don't require the crazy passages emblematic of some of its area cousins, making this trail suitable for any level of canine hiker. Spur trails will take your dog to the nooks and crannies and the top of the ledges. Still, there are drop-offs here to be aware of.

The Cuyahoga River Gorge has been luring adventurous hikers since 1882 when it was the site of the High Bridge Glens amusement park. One hundred and twenty five years earlier, 10-year old Mary Campbell was taken from her Pennsylvania frontier home by Delaware Indians and brought to a cave in the gorge, becoming the first white child in America to reach Ohio. The *Gorge Trail* today is a 1.8-mile loop whose highlight comes when your dog has to pick her way through a maze of jumbled rock ledges. Trail signs at **Gorge Metro Park** (www.summit metroparks.org/ParksAndTrails/Gorge.aspx) label this stretch as "difficult" and a bypass is offered but there is nothing here your dog can't handle. In fact, some stone steps have been cut into the most troublesome passages.

The dark forest and sheltered rock outcroppings of the **West Woods** (www.geaugaparkdistrict.org/parks/westwoods.shtml) have long propagated rumors. Runaway slaves were hidden here on the Underground Railroad. Civil War soldiers took refuge under the ledges. Bootleggers operated illegal stills in the hollows. The destination of a 1.5-mile trail in this Geauga County showcase park is Ansel's Cave, named for an early settler from Massachusetts who may have squatted here. This journey is conducted completely under tall, straight hardwoods on wide, paw-friendly compacted stone paths.

The flamboyant Chagrin River that dominates **South Chagrin Reservation** (www.clemetparks.com/visit/index.asp?action=rdetails&reservations_id=1015) was designated a State Scenic River in 1979. On the east side of the river the *Squirrel Loop Trail* slips cautiously above the water under rock ledge sentinels. This is a hike for calm, well-behaved dogs only as steep drop-offs are unfenced. Across the river you can view the rock carvings of Henry Church, a blacksmith and self-taught artist who became celebrated as a primitive folk artist after his death.

DESTINATION
IDEA #70: DOGGIN' KENTUCKY'S ARCHES

The Treaty of Fort Stanwix in 1768 during the French and Indian War triggered a rush to settlement of this wilderness, then part of the great Virginia Colony, that stretched to the Mississippi River. The most prominent pioneer was Daniel Boone from Berks County in Pennsylvania, thanks in part to an autobiographical narrative he published in 1784. After the American Revolution, veterans received land grants for their service and by 1796 nearly a quarter of a million people came into the area on the *Wilderness Trail*, little more than a horse path. Some mined coal, some mined saltpeter necessary to manufacture gunpowder, and some logged but most farmed small plots of cleared land. When the **Daniel Boone National Forest** (www.fs.fed.us/r8/boone/) was established in 1937, 98% of the dwellings were of log and pole construction and the average number of acres on a farm in cultivation was only 17.

There are more than 500 miles of trails in the 700,000-acre national forest that occupies a 140-mile slice of eastern Kentucky. The great variety of trails from flat and easy to steep and twisting help spread out the five million annual visitors. Save for the designated swimming areas, your dog is welcome everywhere in the Daniel Boone National Forest. The *Sheltowee Trace National Recreation Trail* courses through the entire forest for 269 miles. The footpath, blazed in white turtle markers (Sheltowee is the Indian name given Boone when he visited the area meaning "big turtle"), connects the major day-use areas as it visits deep canyons, long ridgetops and craggy rimrock cliffs.

The first destination for many canine hikers in the Daniel Boone National Forest is the **Red River Gorge** (www.fs.fed.us/r8/boone/districts/cumberland/redriver_gorge.shtml) where 300-foot sandstone cliffs and overhangs are decorated with grotesque rock formations. The more than 100 natural stone arches in the area represent the greatest collection east of the Mississippi River. Numerous rock shelters and arches can be found along the driving tour of the Clifty Wilderness in the Cumberland District. Easy explorations include the *Natural Arch Trail* that reaches a bridge of sandstone more than 100 feet across and seven stories high and the *Nathan McClure Trail* along the shores of Cumberland Lake. The lake is graced by towering sandstone cliffs.

TOUR

IDEA #71: DOGGIN' AMERICA'S RED ROCKS

Red Rocks are the iconic symbol of the American West. You can craft an unforgettable vacation with your dog just hunting the twisted pinnacles and monoliths of oxidized sandstone. When you start your planning, don't forget to include these fields of red rocks...

Garden of the Gods (Colorado)

The indigenous Ute Indians referred to this area of protruding, jagged red rocks as "the old red land." The story goes that when the original surveyors of Colorado Springs discovered the sandstone remains of an ancient ocean floor, one referred to it as a great spot for a beer garden. Fellow surveyor Rufus Cable, of a more romantic bent, protested the majestic muted crimson rocks were more suited to be a "garden for the Gods."

Charles Eliott Perkins, president of the Burlington Railroad, bought 240 acres here for a summer home back in the 1800s but never built on the rocks, preferring to leave the formations as the wind and water carved them. Perkins died before formally bequeathing the land to the city for a park but his heirs honored his wishes and gave 480 acres to Colorado Springs in 1909. About to celebrate its Centennial, the park has nearly tripled in size.

Garden of the Gods Park is enormously popular - attracting more than one million visitors every year - so contemplative hikes with your dog can be problematic. A good place to start is on the *Garden Trail* where a paved pathway winds through the heart of some of the most towering formations. The *Chambers/ Bretag/Palmer* trails are a combination of dirt paths that nearly circle the park for three miles with a modest rise of 250 feet, maneuvering through scrub oak just far enough away from the rocks to present sensational skyline views.

For a bit of relief from the crowds try the trails outside the park's main drive that circles the Garden. It will take the better part of a day to fully explore the sculpted rocks, whimsically named for what they resemble: kissing camels, Siamese twins and balanced rock among them. There is one designated area where dogs can run unleashed; south of Gateway Road, West of 30th Street, and east of Rock Ledge Ranch Historic Site.

Garden of the Gods Visitor & Nature Center, Colorado Springs
(719) 634-6666
www.GardenOfGods.com/home/index.cfm

Flaming Gorge National Recreation Area (Wyoming)

Traveling south through Wyoming on Route 191, most likely with a restless dog who was unable to get out in Yellowstone and Grand Teton National Parks, you reach Flaming Gorge National Recreation Area in 250 miles. Legendary 19th century adventurer and naturalist John Wesley Powell named the Flaming Gorge after he saw the sun shining off the red canyon walls on his epic 1869 exploration of the Green and Colorado rivers. Butch Cassidy and other outlaws often used the isolated valleys along the Green River as hideouts. Nearly a century later there were still only primitive roads in the area when construction began on the Flaming Gorge Dam to store water and generate electricity. The 502-foot high dam, backing the Green River up 91 miles, was completed in 1964 and the Flaming Gorge National Recreation Area established four years later.

The best way to see the 1400-foot deep Red Canyon is on the *Canyon Rim Trail*, a multi-use trail accessed at the Red Canyon Visitor Center. In addition to the quiet overlooks at the canyon, this trail, that loops for nearly three miles past the campground, is also a good place to observe moose, elk and deer that graze here. Along the Green River is the *Little Hole National Recreation Trail*, a delightful seven-mile one-way walk below the Flaming Gorge Dam. Your dog may spend more time in the clear green waters than on the level, easy-hiking path. High altitude canine hiking is also available on Dowd Mountain and Ute Mountain while at Spirit Lake Campground a 3-mile loop visits a trio of alpine lakes above 10,000 feet.

Outside the recreation area, just downstream from the *Green River Trail* at Indian Crossing Campground is the John Jarvie Historic Site. In 1880, Scottish immigrant John Jarvie set up shop in the Browns Park area of the Green River. He also later operated a ferry on the river. In 1909, Jarvie was robbed and murdered and his body dumped in a boat and shoved out on the Green River. It floated for eight days before being discovered. The frontier buildings Jarvie used for his enterprises have been preserved by the Bureau of Land Management.

Flaming Gorge National Recreation Area, Wyoming
(435) 789-1181
www.fs.fed.us/r4/ashley/recreation/flaming_gorge/index.shtml

Valley of Fire (Nevada)

When the sun reflects off these red sandstone formations just west of the Lake Mead, which it does just about every day, they can appear to be on fire. Hence, the Valley of Fire. Two thousand years ago the Basket Maker people traveled to this land of great shifting sand dunes and left rock art reminders of their visits that can be seen today. In 1935, the Valley of Fire, now spreading across 34,000 acres fifty-five miles east of Las Vegas, was dedicated as Nevada's first state park.

Dogs are welcome on all nine short interpretive trails in Valley of Fire State Park, each easily accessed from the main park roadways. Trails lead to fanciful rock formations like Elephant Rock, Arch Rock and the Seven Sisters. In many places the canine hiking is over fine red sand trails that are paw-friendly when the sun isn't blazing (temperatures climb over 110 degrees in summer). One route leads to petrified logs that washed into the area from an ancient forest about 225 million years ago.

Some excellent prehistoric Indian petroglyphs can be seen in a small canyon on the trail to Mouse's Tank. The tank is a natural basin in the rock where water collects after a rainfall and is named for a renegade Indian who used the area as a hideout in the 1890s. The feature trail at Valley of Fire is the *White Domes Loop Trail* in the far northern section of the park. The path circles through rock formations and a slot canyon on its one-mile odyssey. Look for the stone ruins of a movie set from *The Professionals* where Lee Marvin led a crew of four hard-edged adventurers on a rescue mission for a kidnapped woman. Many movies have used the Valley of Fire as a backdrop but this is the only set in the park as filmmakers are no longer allowed to abandon their stages. *Star Trek* fans will no doubt recognize some of the scenery in Fire Canyon.

The quick hikes in the Valley of Fire are especially attractive for dogs visiting Las Vegas in the summer but canine hikers visiting in more hospitable weather can also enjoy red rocks on the other side of town (west of Las Vegas on West Charleston Boulevard) in the **Red Rock Canyon National Conservation Area** (www.redrockcanyonlv.org/). A 13-mile scenic drive winds through the iron-tinged sandstone mountains and climbs about 1000 feet. Parking areas are liberally sprinkled along the route that provide access to 19 hiking trails. Many of the routes explore side canyons with only moderate elevation gains of a few hundred feet. Some trails are unimproved and your dog may encounter loose stones and rock scrambles but nearly can be handled by the novice canine hiker. The most difficult of the Red Rock Canyon trails is the climb along the *Turtlehead Peak Trail*. This five-mile round trip is never too punishing as it makes its way to the 6,323-foot summit. Your purchase is sweeping views of the Calico Hills and the city of Las Vegas.

Valley of Fire State Park, Nevada
(702) 397-2088
www.parks.nv.gov/vf.htm

Sedona Red Rock Country (Arizona)

Sooner or later all red rock enthusiasts will wind up in northern Arizona. The best gateway to Sedona Red Rock Country is through the Coconino National Forest where US Highway 89A sashays down the length of Oak Creek Canyon. You can pick and choose the overlooks and swimming pools and hiking trails to share with your dog. Dogs are not allowed in the heritage sites or at Red Rock State Park and can't join in the water fun at Slide Rock State Park but just about anywhere else in the national forest is good to go.

When visiting Coconino National Forest, leave the casual tourists behind and carve out a day to spend with your dog in the lightly visited Sycamore Canyon, the second largest canyon in Arizona. A compressed five-trail network guides your dog through thick forests of Ponderosa Pine and juniper and into a panoply of chaparral. Never far away is another romp in a crystal clear pool courtesy of year-round Sycamore Creek.

Coconino National Forest, Arizona
(928) 527-3600
www.fs.fed.us/r3/coconino/recreation/red_rock/oak-creek-scenic.shtml

Red Rock Canyon State Park (California)

The powerful Sierra Nevada mountains peter out on their southern end in California's Mojave desert, breaking into a spectacular display of colorful desert cliffs and buttes. Nature has unleashed a full palette in painting the park canyons, throwing chocolate brown sandstone and smoothly sculpted clay in with the signature red rock.

This gash in the forbidding Sierra Nevadas has long been a magnet for cross-country travelers. Migrating settlers used the colorful rock formations as a beacon and teamsters steered their 20-mule team freight wagons through this pass. More recently the desert became a haven for off-road vehicles which led to its creation as a state park.

Like many of California's best state parks, dogs can not hike the trails at Red Rock Canyon. But this is not a concern as the wide open spaces are best explored free form. Your dog can poke around hidden canyons and eroded lava beds - and don't be surprised if you see rocks that look familiar. Many television shows and movies, including Jurassic Park, were filmed out in the backdrop of Red Rock Canyon.

Mojave, California
(661) 942-0662
www.parks.ca.gov/default.asp?page_id=631

TOUR
IDEA #72: DOGGIN' AMERICA'S DESERT ROCKS

America's most spectacular rocks, impossibly large and impressively small, are found in the Western deserts where a vacation in places like these with your dog can last days in with nary a tree in sight...

Black Canyon of the Gunnison National Park (Colorado)

Although largely unknown, no other canyon in North America combines the narrow opening, sheer walls, and startling depths offered by the Black Canyon of the Gunnison. The uplifted hard rock is being gouged by an energetic river dropping an average of 96 feet per mile in the park; at its narrowest the canyon walls are a mere 40 feet apart.

Dogs are not welcome on park trails in the canyon or in the wilderness area, as usual in national parks but your best trail companion can trot to the overlooks and several of the nature trails on the rim, including the *Rim Rock Trail*, *Cedar Point Nature Trail*, and *North Rim Chasm View Nature Trail*. Enough to make a visit worthwhile. This canine hiking is flat and, for the most part, unshaded so take precautions with your pet on hot summer scorchers.

Gunnison, Colorado
(970) 641-2337
www.nps.gov/blca/

Glen Canyon National Recreation Area (Arizona)

Next door to the Grand Canyon is Glen Canyon where nature's handiwork has been swapped for man's. A dam was constructed across the southern end of the canyon in 1963 and it took 17 years for Lake Powell to fill completely, becoming the second-largest man-made lake in America - and by far the most scenic. Surrounding the deep clear blue waters are stark sandstone rock formations with practically no vegetation to be seen. Over a million acres of rocks and water have been corralled into the **Glen Canyon National Recreation Area.**

Most of your fun with your dog here is out on the water but he can have a splendid time without a boat as well. Don't worry too much about formal trails - just pull over and walk along the shore or let him jump in the lake. The marquee hike at Glen Canyon is through the breathtaking Cathedral Wash; your dog is welcome to descend into the wash but can't finish the trip when it reaches Grand Canyon National Park in a little over one mile. This is a good place to explore washes and slot canyons but never enter if there is even the hint of rain in the desert.

Page, Arizona
(928) 608-6200
www.nps.gov/glca/

Goblin Valley State Park (Utah)

In Utah your dog won't see some of the country's most fabulous rocks in the five famous national parks in the state. Instead you have to aim for an impossibly remote spot to take your dog - the Goblin Valley.

Those national parks were already drawing visitors before this otherworldly place was even discovered. Word finally leaked out from cowboys searching for lost cattle who were the first to report on the bizarre gnome-like rock formations. You may have already seen the "goblins" yourself if you saw the movie *Galaxy Quest.* The park was used to create the hostile planet Thermia where actors in a televised space drama were recruited to fight a real war.

The goblins are formed by uneven weathering of sandstone rocks of varying hardness. Water erosion and the smoothing action of windblown desert dust conspire to shape the hoodoos and spires in the valley. The State of Utah acquired 3,000 acres to create the park in 1964.

The park does not maintain many formal trails but you are free to drop into the Valley of the Goblins and explore the intricately balanced rock formations with your dog close-up. The valley is flat and any level of canine hiker can enjoy weaving in and out of the goblins. More spirited canine hiking lies just outside the park on the vast lands of the Bureau of Land Management. The *Bell Canyon/ Little Wild Horse Canyon Trails* can be welded to form an eight-mile loop into dry washes and slot canyons. The walls of these canyons constrict to barely the body width of a Golden Retriever at times.

Green River, Utah
www.utah.com/stateparks/goblin_valley.htm

Goosenecks State Park (Utah)

This park is only 10 acres but it will be the most memorable ten-acre park you are likely to ever visit with your dog. The ten acres cover the parking lot and an extended viewpoint. Below you is one of the best examples of an entrenched "meanders" in the world. In the course of one linear mile the turtle-slow San Juan River travels five miles, having cut 1000-foot deep canyons over millions of years. There isn't a hint of vegetation in the serpentine rock ridges.

There are no formal trails at Goosenecks State Park and don't even think about trying to climb into the canyon but you can hike in either direction just about as far as your dog desires. And when you get tired, come back and pitch a tent at the viewpoint and camp for free.

Blandings, Utah
(435) 678-2238
www.utah.com/stateparks/goosenecks.htm

Grand Canyon National Park (Arizona)

The greatest rock sculpture in the world, the Grand Canyon, is not a total loss for dog owners. Dogs are not allowed on trails below the rim but can go on trails throughout the developed areas of the South Rim, including the *Rim Trail* that stretches from the Village Area to Hermit's Rest. There are plenty of canyon views from the partially paved 2.7-mile trail. The less visited North Rim is also less inviting for canine hikers. You can get the dog only on a bridle path between the lodge and the *North Kaibab Trail* for a bit of exercise.

Grand Canyon, Arizona
(928) 638-0534
www.nps.gov/grca/

Petrified Forest National Park (Arizona)

At the Four Corners in Arizona the mineralized remains of an ancient Mesozoic forest were tens of millions of years in the making but the nation's largest field of petrified wood wasn't formally described until 1851. The Atlantic and Pacific Railroad built though this area in the 1880s brought profiteers to the forest. They carried off petrified wood specimens and dynamited the largest logs in search of quartz and purple amethyst crystals.

In 1895 the State of Arizona began petitioning for federal protection and on December 8, 1906 Theodore Roosevelt designated the petrified forest as America's second national monument. In 1962, with the addition of the scenic landscape of the Painted Desert, the Petrified Forest became America's thirty-first national park.

Pets are banned from the 93,533 acres of backcountry and the popular *Painted Desert Rim Trail* near the Visitor Center but there is ample opportunity to experience the petrified forest with your dog. Three paved loops - all less than a mile long - lead into the barren desert amidst remains of the hardened wood. Although short and easy to hike, these interpretive trails are completely without shade so have a supply of water ready on hot days.

The *Crystal Forest Trail* meanders through the remains of obliterated petrified logs, leaving you to only imagine what these crystalized trees once looked like before the pillaging that led to the creation of the Petrified Forest National Monument. Some of those prehistoric trees can be seen on the Long Logs Path. Extinct conifers form the largest concentration of petrified wood left in the park.

The *Agate House Trail* leads up a slight rise to a reconstructed Anasazi Indian Pueblo built entirely of colorful petrified wood sealed with mud. Also available to canine hikers is the one-mile *Blue Mesa Trail*. A sharp drop in the path leads to an amphitheater surrounded by banded badlands of bluish clay called bentontite. Rainwater is the brush that paints streaky patterns in the porous hills.

Petrified Forest, Arizona
(928) 524-6228
www.nps.gov/pefo

Rockhound State Park (New Mexico)

Deep in the Florida Mountains in a remote corner of southwest New Mexico is Rockhound State Park. The dry, unforgiving landscape looks much like the millions of other surrounding acres but what makes this park unusual is that visitors are encouraged to collect and remove samples of rock - up to a 15-pound limit. This includes an abundance of beautiful jasper, a fine-grained quartz that occurs in a variety of colors including red, white, and pink.

There is a fine pet-friendly campground with a one-mile loop trail but you are welcome to roam all through the surrounding land with your dog. Lucky canine hikers may happen upon shiny black perlite or even a thunderegg that can be sliced open to reveal beguiling mineral formations inside but generally you will need a hammer, chisel and spade to work the mineral deposits out of a hillside.

Deming, New Mexico
(575) 546-6182
www.emnrd.state.nm.us/prd/Rockhound.htm

TOUR
IDEA #73: DOGGIN' AMERICA'S INLAND SAND DUNES

If your dog isn't allowed on trails in our national parks, what is the most obvious solution? Take your dog to a park without any trails...

Bruneau Dunes State Park (Idaho)

Unlike its sister dune fields across western America, Bruneau Dunes is the site of the country's highest single-structured sand dune. Sands have accumulated in a natural basin since the Bonneville Flood 15,000 years ago. Prevailing winds blow in opposite directions about equal amounts of time and so, unlike most dunes, these do not drift far. The Bruneau Dunes rise approximately 470 feet.

You are free to climb anywhere on the dunes and vehicles are not allowed which makes for a more enjoyable outing for hikers. The dunes also back a small desert lake waiting to refresh a tired sand-climbing dog. Hardy canine adventurers will want to jump on the *Dunes 5-Mile Hiking Trail* that follows a circular path in semi-wilderness desert terrain, crossing dunesland and marshland.

Mountain Home, Idaho
(208) 366-7919
parksandrecreation.idaho.gov/parks/bruneaudunesstatepark.aspx

Coral Pink Sand Dunes State Park (Utah)

The great national parks of Zion and Bryce and Capitol Reef that are the backbone of Utah's "Color Country" can be seen by your dog only from a parking lot. The same iron oxides and minerals that produce that color are responsible for the coral-colored Navajo sandstone that has eroded and blown into this notch in the mountains over thousands of years. Where the winds are pinched so much they can't sustain enough speed to carry away the grains of sand.

A quick introduction to dune formation comes on a half-mile nature trail at the day-use lot. The *Two Dunes Trail* visits a wind-blown barchan (crescent-shaped dune) and a star-shaped dune caused by winds coming from several directions before returning in less than two miles. Longer canine hikes are possible on the open, windy dunes. Check with the ranger station for latest maps as the shifting sands constantly cover old trails. As with all dune hikes, keep an eye on your dog's paw pads for irritation.

Coral Pink Sand Dunes is a magnet for noisy off-road vehicles so consider early morning hikes here since the onslaught cannot begin until 9:00 a.m. The cooler sands of the morning will be welcome to your dog's paws as well.

Kanab, Utah
(435) 648-2800
www.utah.com/stateparks/coral_pink.htm

Great Sand Dunes National Park and Preserve (Colorado)

The tallest sand dunes in North America formed when sand from ancient dry lake beds got trapped in a low curve of the Sangre de Cristo Mountains. Prevailing winds from the valley floor blow toward the mountains but frequent storm winds blow the dunes back toward the valley. This opposing wind action causes the sand to pile up vertically in the natural pocket.

There are no designated trails in the park sand and your dog is invited to explore the main day use part of the 30-square mile dunefield. When climbing massive dunes use a zig-zag pattern to ascend to the ridgelines. From the main parking lot you'll see the imposing "High Dune" which affords a 360-degree view from its 650-foot summit. To the west is America's highest sand pile, the spectacular 750-foot Star Dune. Your dog's day in this sand box will end when it gets too hot so start early and also consider night hikes. In the heat of the day consider the moist, cool sands of Medano Creek for a canine hike.

Mosca, Colorado
(719) 378-6300
www.nps.gov/grsa/

Imperial Sand Dunes Recreation Area (California)

About 15 miles west of Yuma, Arizona are the Algodones Dunes, the great sand dunes of the lower Colorado River Valley. Stretching for 40 miles and as wide as ten miles, the dune complex, part of the Imperial Sand Dunes Recreation Area, is one of the largest open sand piles in the United States.

The Algodones Dunes have been appearing on movie screens almost since the beginning of Hollywood. The Rudolph Valentino starrer *The Sheik* filmed across the sandy wastelands, which were once crossed by a wooden road (remnants of the Plank Road may be seen at the west end of Grays Well Road, the frontage road south of Interstate 8). Through the years, it has been a good bet that any movie calling for scenes of never-ending sand was staged in the Algodones Dunes that can rise to heights of 300 feet. Such sand-choked classics as *Beau Geste* and *Sahara* were shot here and, more recently George Clooney and Mark Wahlberg came to the dunes to film *Three Kings*.

From 1951 through 1964, portions of the dunes were used as a U.S. Naval Impact Range. While the area has been searched for unexploded ordnance, shifting sands continue to expose dangerous shells, rockets and practice bombs so don't let your dog start digging during your explorations of the more than 100,000 acres open for recreation.

El Centro, California
(760) 337-4400
www.blm.gov/ca/st/en/fo/elcentro/recreation/ohvs/isdra.html

Little Sahara Recreation Area (Utah)

A bit south of the Great Salt Lake, deposits left by a Lake Bonneville feeder stream, the Sevier River, have been whipped around by prevailing winds to create Little Sahara, one of the largest dune fields in the American West. Today there are nearly 60,000 acres of towering sand dunes and sagebush flats that have become known as Utah's greatest sand play area.

The Little Sahara Recreation Area is a paradise for off-highway vehicles who roar in and out of dune bowls and up sand mountains as high as 700 feet. There are no designated trails out in the dunes so there is a chance you can encounter a motorized vehicle just about anywhere you hike, unless you make it across the dunes to Rockwell Natural Area which is a vehicle-free zone. But if you avoid popular holiday weekends there is a good chance to experience a solitary dune hike with your dog somewhere in the 124-square mile system of giant, free-moving sand dunes. If your dog tires of trotting through deep sand there are networks of dirt trails to be had here as well.

Eureka, Utah
(435) 433-5960
www.utah.com/playgrounds/little_sahara.htm

White Sands National Monument (New Mexico)

Dogs have long been welcome on the mystical white sands of southern New Mexico. When America's space age began at White Sands Missile Range with the firing of a Tiny Tim test booster on September 26, 1945, it was important to retrieve small missile parts to analyze success or failure. These searches routinely wasted countless man-hours as ground recovery crews scoured vast expanses of desert for often-buried missile fragments.

That ended in 1961 with the introduction of the Missile Dogs: Dingo, a Weimaraner, and Count, a German Shorthair. For up to a year before firing, important components of a missile were sprayed with squalene, a shark-liver oil that the dogs could smell from hundreds of feet away. After a missile firing, Dingo and Count raced among the sands sniffing out the scent objects. With a 96% recovery rate, the program was so successful that other military and scientific agencies requested the services of the original Missile Dogs of White Sands.

Today you can hike with your dog anywhere in the giant sandbox that is White Sands National Monument. The world's largest gypsum sand dunes form when mineral dissolves in nearby mountains during rainstorms. White Sands offers 6.2 miles of marked dog-friendly trails but there is no need to limit your explorations. Any dune is open to a canine hike. Stay alert for reptiles and rodents scampering on the dunes that have adapted to the white sands and are now a funny bleached white color. During the heat of summer, try a night hike - when the moon is full, the park, located in New Mexico on US 70 between Alamogordo and Las Cruces, stays open until midnight. The desert cools off then and the sands are haunting by moonlight.

Holloman AFB, New Mexico
(575) 679-2599
www.nps.gov/whsa/

TOUR
IDEA #74: DOGGIN' AMERICA'S CAVES

Dogs aren't welcome to explore underground caverns and chambers but there is a surprising amount of adventure awaiting your canine companion when visiting some of America's most famous caves...

Florida Caverns State Park (Florida)

It has only been the blink of an eye, geologically speaking, that Florida has not been under water. During its time undersea, coral, shellfish, and fish skeletons piled up. This created a layer of limestone hundreds of feet thick. When the sea level fell, acidic groundwater gradually dissolved the porous limestone to form cracks and passages. In this part of the Florida panhandle the rock has been pushed up and there are some sizable hills. This area includes numerous caves.

The highly decorated Florida Cavern is as ornate as many of the celebrated tourist caves around the country. Altogether, there are 10 acres of caves here. During the Seminole Wars, they were used as hideouts. In the 1930s, the Civilian Conservation Corp developed the cave for visitors, removing mud, widening passages, and excavating where necessary to provide headroom.

Rocks in northwest Florida? Not an everyday sight but your dog will certainly find some here. The delightful *Visitor Center Trail* is the only walk in the Panhandle that winds through rocky terrain - a fairy garden of whimsical limestone formations. Your dog is not allowed to tour Florida Cavern but he can find his own unique underground adventure on 100 feet of trail in Tunnel Cave.

Towering hardwoods frame the trail as it visits twenty-foot vertical bluffs above the floodplain and descends down to swampland where tupelo gums are anchored in the soggy soil. For longer, albeit more traditional Florida hiking fare, head up to the multi-use *Upper Chipola Trails* that explore the basin of the Chipola River. The waterway collects water from 63 springs, the largest number of any rivershed in Northwest Florida. There are more than six miles of shaded woodland trails across the rolling terrain here.

Marianna, Florida
(850) 482-9598
www.floridastateparks.org/floridacaverns/

Jewel Cave National Monument (South Dakota)

Jewel Cave was first explored around 1900 when prospectors began poking around holes where they heard whistling from the ground. They found jewel-like calcite crystals but no valuable minerals. Efforts to develop a commercial cave failed and in 1908 Jewel Cave was created to protect what was thought to be a small, beautiful cave.

Not so. A half century later Herb and Jan Conn, rock climbers who started caving as a diversion, visited Jewel Cave and fell under its spell. Over a span of two decades the couple made 708 trips totaling more than 6,000 hours into the cave, mapping its secrets. They eventually discovered 65 underground miles of passages. Today 144 miles of large rooms strewn with boulders, tight crawlways and dark fissures have been mapped - with more unknown. Jewel Cave is now the second longest known cave in the world.

Unlike its nearby cousin, Wind Cave, this is a rather compact park with only about 1,200 Ponderosa pine-covered acres. There are two tail-friendly trails at Jewel Cave, one for the more casual canine athlete and the other a sterner test. The *Walk On The Roof Trail* at the Visitor Center is exactly what it advertises, with views of the surrounding forest and canyon around you on this easy half-hour ramble.

The *Canyons Trail* drops into Lithograph Canyon on a gravel path and then follows Hell Canyon to the Historic Area and loops back in 3.5 miles. Your dog will notice the moderately steep inclines, especially on a hot day. A deeper exploration of Hell Canyon can be had on U.S. Forest Service *Hell Canyon Trail*, conducted mostly on a level two-track road after a pitched descent for a half-mile. The full loop covers 5.5 miles.

Custer, South Dakota
(605) 673-8300
nps.gov/jeca/

Leon Sinks Geological Area (Florida)

Leon Sinks is in the heart of the Woodville Karst Plain, a vast area of porous limestone bedrock that stretches 450 square miles from Tallahassee south to the Gulf of Mexico. The terrain is shaped by rain and groundwater that dissolve the limestone formed millions of years ago from ancient coral reefs and shell deposits to form sinkholes, swales and underground caverns.

In 1988 local volunteers undertook the extremely hazardous task of exploring and mapping the underwater cave system lying behind the opening at the front of Hammock Sink. When the divers were finished they had mapped over 41,000 feet of passages from Sullivan Sink to Cheryl Sink and identified six spectacular limestone rooms spacious enough to hold a six-story building. Years later a link between Leon Sinks and Wakulla Springs to the southeast was also discovered. The mapping project confirmed that the Leon Sinks underwater cave system is the largest known in the United States.

Dogs are welcome to hike at Leon Sinks and they keep a plastic water bowl at the trailhead water fountain for a hot, thirsty trail dog. The trail system is a four-mile loop that links the *Sinkhole Trail* and the *Gunswamp Trail* (sinkholes are formed by the underwater aquifer, swamps are created by surface water). A *Crossover Trail* separates the two into a stacked-loop for canine hikers who don't want to experience the entirety of this vibrant community. The *Sinkhole Trail* connects more than a dozen sinkholes, some dry and some filled with water. Boardwalk observation decks provide close-up views. The deepest is the Big Dismal Sink at 130 feet. Keep a close hold on your dog around these sinks - they have steep walls and dogs - and people - have drowned at Leon Sinks.

Except for traffic noise you can't ever quite shake, this is one of the best hikes you can take with your dog in Northwest Florida. From the tupelo gum swamps to the sandy ridges you cannot find a more diverse plant world along a trail. At Big Dismal Sink alone more than 75 different plants cascade down the sink's conical walls. None of the underground limestone penetrates the ground so the trails are paw-friendly sand and a joy for your dog.

Crawfordville, Florida
(850) 926-3561
www.dep.state.fl.us/gwt/guide/regions/panhandleeast/trails/leon_sinks.htm

Mammoth Cave National Park (Kentucky)

Not named for extinct wooly elephants but rather the length of its passageways, Mammoth Cave is by far the longest known cave system in the world. There may be no traces of mammoths in the vast underground world but archeologists have unearthed evidence of human occupation in Mammoth Cave from as far back as 4,000 years ago. In the early days of the country, Mammoth Cave was used commercially to produce saltpeter needed to manufacture gunpowder and in 1941 the cave was protected as a national park. In 1981, Mammoth Cave was named a World Heritage Site.

Your dog won't be able to sniff around the 336 miles of underground passages in Mammoth Cave but there are more than 70 miles of trails above ground to explore in the park. A variety of leg-stretching hikes less than two miles are available around the Visitor Center, including the Green River Bluffs Trail that snakes through thick woods to a promontory above the Green River. For prolonged canine hiking head for the *North Side Trails*. A half-dozen mid-length day hikes launch into the dark hollows and hardwood forests from the *Maple Spring Trailhead* (North Entrance Road). This labyrinth of trails cuts through rugged terrain that has been left in its natural state. In the Big Woods (Little Jordan Road), you can hike the *White Oak Trail* through one of the last remaining old growth forests in Kentucky.

Along Highway 255 (the East Entrance road) is a small parking lot for a short trail to Sand Cave. For several weeks in the 1930s, this remote section of woods was the most famous spot in America. A local cave explorer named Floyd Collins got trapped in the cave and the nation became fixated on the rescue efforts that were meticulously detailed in newspapers and radio reports. Rescuers were ultimately unsuccessful in freeing Collins from a leg-pinning rock. The incident spawned books and a thought-provoking movie starring Kirk Douglas, *Ace In The Hole*. The small entrance of Sand Cave is wired off today and there is little to remind visitors of the drama that once gripped America here.

Mammoth Cave, Kentucky
(270) 758-2180
www.nps.gov/maca

Russell Cave National Monument (Alabama)

While other cave destinations in this section are notable for wondrous geology, Russell Cave is significant for its long and complete archeological record of human habitation. Scientists have carbon-14 dated bone tools, jewelry and pottery fragments unearthed in this limestone rock shelter back 9,000 years.

Like their canine ancestors, dogs are allowed to join their human companions in Russell Cave. A half-mile boardwalk pathway leads to the floor of the upper entrance to the cave. Nearby a short walking trail describes area plants used by the cave dwellers and a 1.2-mile hiking trail - coated in macadam the entire way - snakes up the side of the mountain above the cave. It is a challenge for even the most athletic of dogs.

Bridgeport, Alabama
(256) 495-2672
www.nps.gov/ruca

Wind Cave National Park (South Dakota)

Wind Cave was discovered in 1881 when Jesse Bingham heard a whistling sound in the ground and had his hat blown off by wind from a small hole when he went to investigate. Such winds escaping from caves are the result of changes in atmospheric pressure. Wind Cave was soon protected as America's seventh national park. Subsequent explorations have uncovered more than 100 miles of underground passages making Wind Cave the sixth longest known cave system in the world.

Above ground, the park administers 29,000 acres and more than 30 miles of trails. Canine hiking can be had on only two short trails, each about one mile in length. There is some lemonade to be squeezed from the lemons served up by the National Park Service, however. *Elk Mountain Trail* is a sporty loop around the campground that traverses a beautiful prairie with expansive views. A second option for your dog is the Prairie Vista Nature Trail surrounding the Visitor Center.

Hot Springs, South Dakota
(605) 745-4600
www.nps.gov/wica

DOGGIN' AMERICA'S BIG TREES

When European settlers arrived on these shores virgin forest stretched nearly unbroken to the Mississippi River. Early Americans were extremely adept at clearing land for farms and stripping forests for building materials. By 1900, out of five trees that stood in Colonial days, only one survived. You could travel with your dogs for days and hardly ever see a big tree.

Today, much of the land has been reforested. Most eastern states whose slopes were cut bare in the 1800s now boast of more than 50% forestland. In a land of second- and third-growth woodlands "old growth forests" where trees have stood unmolested since the dawn of the America have become magical places.

Old growth forests conjure up images of huge trees but these ancient forests are best characterized by their diversity. The woods are speckled with large snags that have broken in storms and mammoth trunks of decaying dead trees teeming with life litter the forest floor. A woodland hike through an old growth forest is like no other hike you can take with your dog...

TOUR
IDEA #75: DOGGIN' EASTERN BIG TREES

Cook Forest State Park (Pennsylvania)

Pennsylvania's white pine and Eastern hemlock forests were the nation's most valuable resource in the mid-1800s. The timber built America and the bark tanned leather. Two of the largest sawmills in the world operated in the Pennsylvania woods. So much pine and hemlock were harvested that the mountainsides were stripped bare. The pine and hemlock never came back; the forests that cover northern Pennsylvania today are almost exclusively hardwood forests.

John Cook was the first permanent American settler on the Clarion River. He arrived in 1826 to investigate the feasibility of building a Pennsylvania canal to compete with the new Erie Canal in New York. Instead, he bought 765 acres of land, built a cabin and started operating a water-driven sawmill. the Cook family lumber empire prospered for the next century but the forest cathedral of stately hemlock and white pines lying just outside their back door was so impressive it was never cut. The temptation was great - just four of the giants would provide enough lumber to build a six-room house.

By the 1920s this was one of the last areas of surviving old growth timber stands east of the Mississippi River. The Cook Forest Association raised over $200,000 with the mission that "...this Wood will become a forest monument, like those of the West, known not only in Pennsylvania, but throughout the Country. The East possesses few scenes more impressive than this magnificent area of primeval white pine, surrounded by giant hemlocks and hardwoods." More than 6,000 acres were purchased as a state park and in 1969 Cook Forest was designated a National Natural Landmark.

Nearly 30 miles of trails climb through the ancient forest. Your dog is welcome throughout, including some six tranquil miles under the 300-year old trees of the Forest Cathedral. The star walk is the easy-going 1.2-mile *Longfellow Trail* that visits the heart of the tallest eastern white pinelands in the Northeastern United States. One tops out at 183 feet - the tallest in the Northeast, although it is not marked. Canine hiking loops can be crafted with the rolling *Rhododendron Trail* and the flat *Toms Run Trail* that skirts a picturesque stream. If your cautious dog balks at crossing the swinging bridge connecting the trails, it is an easy scamper through the water.

Hearty canine hikers should head to the Clarion River and begin a one-mile uphill climb to the Seneca Point Fire Tower, passing through a patch of of old growth forest ripped asunder by a 1976 tornado as you travel. A side path near the trailhead leads to a hemlock-draped sulfur spring known as the old Mineral Spring. One hemlock here has been documented as the tallest found in the Northeast. In Victorian days this trail was lighted by natural gas lights. At the top, your dog can climb the open steps of the 80-foot fire tower and scan the treetops along the Clarion River.

A visit to the Swamp Area takes your dog through forests of ancient red and white oaks, red maples and black cherry, some of which surpass 280 years of age. A beloved tradition in Cook Forest are the rental cabins scattered around the hills that are ideals base camps for exploring the big trees. Many welcome your dog.

Cooksburg, Pennsylvania
(814) 226-9500
www.dcnr.state.pa.us/stateparks/parks/cookforest.aspx

Laurel Hill State Park (Pennsylvania)

The Laurel Hill Valley's rugged slopes staved off the lumberman's axe until the 1880s. But the development of 70-ton Shay locomotives that could haul timber up 15% grades with ease ended that. It took logging companies only a few decades to clear-cut the trees from the steep stream valleys of the back-breaking Allegheny Mountains.

In the 1930s the National Park Service targeted five areas for restoration and reforestation, including Laurel Hill. The Civilian Conservation Corps planted trees, built roads and trails and developed recreation facilities. Laurel Hill State Park is a tails-up treat for any dog, featuring a variety of diverse trails with unique highlights. You get a choice of eight, all but one between one and two miles in length.

The marquee attraction of the park is a six-acre stand of virgin hemlock trees that somehow escaped the sawyer's eye. These slow-maturing beauties are more than 300 years old - the record age for an eastern hemlock, designated the Pennsylvania state tree in 1931, is 988 years. An interpretive loop leads your dog through this quiet arboreal shrine, hard by the bank of the rushing Laurel Hill Creek.

Somerset, Pennsylvania
(814) 445-7725
www.dcnr.state.pa.us/stateparks/parks/laurelhill.aspx

Swallow Falls State Park (Maryland)

By 1900 it was highly unusual to see any big tree in Maryland that had escaped a logger's saw, unless it was too costly to reach. That was the case with the grove of white pines and hemlocks at Swallow Falls. The giants are the oldest in Maryland - some trees are estimated to be 360 years old. When philantrhapist Henry Krug acquired this land in Garrett County he refused to allow the trees to be logged - even as they grew in the shadow of a sawmill operating upstream atop Muddy Creek. After a World War I plan to dam the Youghiogheny River fell through their survival was assured.

This is the best single-trail park in Maryland. The *Falls Trail* is easy going for your dog through the river canyon under cool, dark hemlocks. Muddy Creek Falls, Maryland's highest single water plunge at 53 feet, arrives quickly on your canine hike and shortly you reach the confluence of Muddy Creek and the Youghiogheny River. Here you'll travel past several more hydrospectaculars, including the namesake Upper Falls where cliff swallows once nested by the hundreds on a rock pillar, where your dog can play in the water before turning for home. This gorgeous loop covers about one mile.

If your dog is hankering for more trail time there is a 5.5-mile out-and-back trail to Herrington Manor State Park (no dogs allowed in the park - it is the journey, not the destination). You'll get more water views and slip quietly under more giant hemlocks but be advised that this canine hike involves a stream crossing that may not be doable in times of high water.

Dogs are not allowed in the day-use area the Saturday before Memorial Day through Labor Day. Dogs are allowed in the surrounding Potomac-Garrett State Forest. Dogs are also allowed in the campground.

Oakland, Maryland
(301) 387-6938
www.dnr.state.md.us/publiclands/western/swallowfalls.html

TOUR

IDEA #76: DOGGIN' WESTERN BIG TREES

Mt. Baker-Snoqualmie National Forest (Washington)

Connoisseurs of big trees will eventually make their way to the Pacific Northwest. The State of Washington is estimated to have about three million acres of old growth forests and Oregon nearly five million. This does not mean there are endless stretches of virgin forest - here "old growth" is defined as trees not logged for 150 years - but like in Eastern forests, there are pockets of old trees that survived a century of uncontrolled logging. Unlike in the East, many of these arboreal oldsters reside on land managed by the Bureau of Land Management and are still susceptible to logging.

Most of these old growth trees grow in remote areas that can be reached only by long hikes into rugged terrain, if they can be reached by all. Others are on National Park land where your dog is not allowed. But there are also many stands of old growth in Washington and Oregon you can easily enjoy with your dog.

The Mt. Baker-Snoqualmie National Forest abuts the Canadian border and meanders 140 miles down the western slopes of the Cascade Mountains. The best way to penetrate this massive swath of wilderness, about 42% of which has been identified as old growth forest, is by scenic drives that begin off popular I-5. You can reach big trees through long mountain hikes, easy nature trails or just pulling off to the side of the road.

Thirty-three miles east of Bellingham along State Route 542 you will reach the Mount Baker Scenic Byway that leads to Artist's Point below an active 10,778 foot volcano. Mount Baker is half covered in glaciers and this is one of the snowiest places on earth - in 1999 a world record 1,140 inches fell here. Be aware that dogs are not allowed on every trail and not every public space is federally managed. Drive by the *Old Growth Trail* in Canyon Lake Creek Community Forest, for instance. There is nothing for your dog here.

The big tees begin appearing in mass at the 43-mile Post, just after powerful Nooksack Falls. This 1,400-acre stand of virgin timber was protected in 1937 and the road dutifully maneuvers between towering Douglas Fir, Western hemlock and Western red cedar. One of the easiest - and busiest - places to experience the lush forest is on the *Horseshoe Bend Trail* at the Douglas Fir Campground. The route hugs the busy North Fork of the Nooksack River until reaching a turn-around point at a bench one mile in. The path continues roughly after this for another couple of miles along the river before vanishing for extra time with your dog away from the crowds.

The North Cascades Scenic Byway climbs across several passes of the Cascades for 132 miles on State Route 20 from Sedro-Woolley to Winthrop. Stop at Rainy Pass for an easy ramble with your dog that ends at Rainy Lake underneath steep glaciers. The path through dense, mossy woodland is paved the entire way. More traditional canine hiking fare can be had on the frisky *Green Mountain Trail* that climbs modestly through old-growth timber into large meadows after the first mile. Your dog will enjoy a pair of alpine lakes at 2.5 miles and the end at four miles reaches an historic 75-year old lookout with views to Mount Baker and Puget Sound if you catch a clear day.

The Mountain Loop Highway northeast of Seattle is one of the best day trips you can take with your dog to chase old growth timber. You are never far from big trees and many short, easy leg stretchers bring you in close contact with magnificent Douglas Fir, cedar, and hemlock. The *Boulder River Trail* is one of the most popular - a languishing four-mile trot for your dog on an old logging road that gains less than 500 feet along the way.

Everett, Washington
(206) 470-4060
www.fs.fed.us/r6/mbs/

South Whidbey Island State Park (Washington)

Whidbey Island is the largest Island in Washington and the fifth largest island in the contiguous United States. Deception Pass on the north side of the island is the most visited state park in Washington but towards the middle of the island, South Whidbey is a quieter destination, primarily serving as a camping park. Much of the park's 347 acres is covered in old growth of cedar and spruce and hemlock. You can camp with your dog under the dense canopy of these graceful giants.

The 3.5-mile park trail system snakes easily through these woodland oldsters - this is probably the easiest access to low elevation old growth on the Pacific coast. Several short trails encourage a relaxed discovery of the forest. One "Ancient Cedar" corralled behind a rail fence has been pegged at about 500 years old. Other mossy woodland residents have long ago outlived their decaying nurse logs that encourage trees in soggy Northwest forests to grow in straight lines.

South Whidbey also offers nearly a mile of dog-friendly saltwater beach access on the Puget Sound. Storm damage has threatened the viability of the trail but if you can't get your dog in the water here try nearby Double Bluff Park and Joseph Whidbey State Park.

Freeland, Washington
www.parks.wa.gov/parkpage.asp?selectedpark=South+Whidbey

Mount Hood National Forest (Oregon)

Located only 20 miles east of Portland and encompassing more than one million acres, including Oregon's tallest mountain, Mount Hood National Forest is a magnet for big tree hunters. You can find any outing for your dog on the hiking menu here, including some easy journeys into the ancient forests. An ideal jumping off point is the *Old Growth Trail* in the Hood River District that features interpretive signs to sharpen your eye for centuries-old timber.

In the Clackamas River district the *Riverside Trail* negotiates an old growth forest between the Rainbow Campground and the Riverside Campground. Designated a National Recreation Trail, this easy trotting path weaves along the Clackamas River and is well-lubricated by streams and wetlands. The highlight of the Zigzag District is the peaceful canine hike along the 2.6 miles of the *Old Salmon Trail*. Practically flat the entire way, this generous footpath slips quietly beneath 10-foot thick red cedars and towering Douglas firs. Side trails lead to river beaches and deep pools ideal for a doggie dip.

Sandy, Oregon
(503) 668-1700
www.fs.fed.us/r6/mthood/about/

Opal Creek Ancient Forest (Oregon)

When the first settlers arrived in the Opal Creek Valley east of Salem in 1859 it was not the 200-foot trees they were after; it was gold. The mining camps remained in operation until 1992 when the Shiny Rock Mining Company gifted the Friends of Opal Creek 151 acres of land that included woodland with trees estimated to be as old as 700 years. The forest filtered into public ownership and is now enjoyed by 50,000 visitors each year.

Dogs are allowed to hike on the old dirt and gravel mining roads in the hills around the former Jawbone Flats mining camp. In addition to the breathtaking cedar and hemlock oldsters the Little North Fork of the Santiam River and its tributaries serve up a series of cascades and waterfalls. More strenuous hiking options branch into the surrounding mountains that will challenge any trail dog. Pacific Silver Firs, identified by their gray bark, become more abundant at higher elevations.

Nearby is Silver Falls State Park, Oregon's largest state park. Silver Falls boasts its own collection of huge old growth Douglas Fir trees and its marquee *Trail of 10 Falls* is a seven-mile hiking loop that leads your dog to - you guessed it - 10 different waterfalls. South Falls, the highest, plunges 176 feet.

Lyons, Oregon
(503) 892-2782
www.opalcreek.org/

Siuslaw National Forest (Oregon)

This national forest hard by the Pacific Ocean is unique for its ocean-forest interface. One of the dominant species in the woodland is the Sitka Spruce that grows in a narrow four-mile band from the sea. Several outstanding Sitka Spruce individuals can be seen in the Siuslaw.

The old-growth forest ecosystem can be explored on the one-mile *PAWN Trail*, an acronym derived from the four pioneering families in the region beside the North Fork Siuslaw River. This is an easy balloon-style trail for your dog past giant Western hemlocks. A couple of titans have fallen recently enough that they had to be sawed to enable the trail to pass, giving the hike a feel of passing through a canyon pass for your dog.

Coos Bay, Oregon
(541) 750-7000
www.fs.fed.us/r6/siuslaw/

California Redwoods (California)

There are no more magnificent stands of old growth forest on the planet than the redwoods of California's northern coast. Sporting bark impervious to insects and having no known diseases, coastal redwoods can live 2,000 years, grow over 350 feet tall and weigh 500 tons. Your dog, unfortunately, can experience the grandeur of the coastal redwoods only in picnic areas, overlooks and campgrounds. Dogs are not allowed on any trails in Redwood National Park or any of the three California state parks created in the 1920s to protect the redwoods: Jedediah Smith Redwoods State Park, Del Norte Coast Redwoods State Park or Prairie Creek Redwoods State Park. One of the best spots for your dog to get close to monster redwoods is the Templeman Grove along Route 97, hard by the rock-bottomed Smith River.

The closest place to get your dog on the trail under redwoods is the Smith River National Recreation Area, located adjacent to Jedediah Smith Redwoods State Park. Established in 1990, the 305,000-acre park was created around Smith River, the last free-flowing river in California without a dam. Smith River is the largest Wild & Scenic River System in the United States - more than 300 miles have been so designated. The star path is the South Kelsey National Recreation Trail, the remnants of an historic transportation link between the Pacific Ocean and the gold mines in the Klamath River region. A walk of nearly two moderate miles on *Craig's Creek Trail* finds many redwood trees along the South Fork.

Eureka, California
(707) 442-1721
www.fs.fed.us/r5/sixrivers/recreation/smith-river/

Ancient Bristlecone Pine Forest (California)

As long as you are hunting old-growth trees you may as well head for the oldest living trees on earth. Growing at altitudes of more than 10,000 feet, bristlecone pines have been surviving for more than 4,000 years on the harsh slopes of the White mountains, east of Yosemite National Park and north of Death Valley. The cold temperatures, dry soil and short growing season cause the trees, whose dense wood is resistant to invasion by insects, to grow very slowly. The arboreal oldsters have been twisted into tortured shapes by the unforgiving winds and although bleached branches make them appear dead there is often a narrow strip of living tissue connecting the roots to a handful of live branches.

Dogs are welcome in the bristlecone pine forest of the Inyo National Forest and on the trails but don't expect your top trail companion to sniff out the most ancient specimen. The exact location of the oldest living organism on earth, nicknamed "Methuselah" after the longest living person in the Bible, is kept a secret to protect it from vandalism. Core samples taken in 1957 have led researchers to estimate the age of Methuselah to be 4,789 years old.

The world's largest bristlecone pine is located in the Patriarch Grove, a 12-mile drive north of the Visitor Center on a good quality dirt road. The isolated Patriarch Tree measures more than 36 feet in circumference.

Inyo National Forest
(760) 873-2400
www.fs.fed.us/r5/inyo/about/#bristlecone

DOGGIN' HOME & GARDEN

TOUR
IDEA #77: DOGGIN' AMERICA'S CASTLES

Your dog is not welcome to go traipsing through the parlors of America's spectacular Gilded Age mansions of course but the thing about America's castles is that they are usually found in the middle of extensive estates. And when the houses are opened to the public, so are the grounds. And often your dog is allowed to roam outside of those private palaces. So pack your dog's overnight bag to be a welcome house guest...

Biltmore House (North Carolina)

Let's start this tour with America's biggest house, the 250-room French Renaissance-style Biltmore House, designed by Richard Morris Hunt for George Washington Vanderbilt, grandson of shipping and railroad magnate Cornelius Vanderbilt. When Cornelius died in 1877 he was the wealthiest man in America and the richest man ever to die. The Biltmore House would open in 1895 amidst the Blue Ridge Mountains of North Carolina.

Outside the exuberant castle is an 8,000-acre estate that includes a forest, a farm, a winery and gardens designed by Frederick Law Olmsted. Your dog is permitted to explore just about everywhere that isn't a building. The garden paths wind gently down a sloping mountainside from the mansion to the Boat House and Bass Pond, passing through formal gardens, natural woodlands and imaginative meadow plantings. Covering these serpentine trails is likely to whet any dog's hiking appetite but if not you can take off on a paved bike path or bridle trail that wind around the grounds. You can hike for days with your dog at Biltmore and never realize you are in the backyard of America's largest house.

Asheville, North Carolina
(828) 225-1333
www.biltmore.com/

Gillette Castle (Connecticut)

In 1913, when he was 60 years old and world famous as the stage portrayer of Sherlock Holmes, William Gillette sailed down the Connecticut River and past a chain of hills known as the Seven Sisters. He docked at the southernmost hill, clambered up to a viewpoint and knew he had found his retirement spot. The actor and playwright designed his castle and its interior himself and over the next six years a team of laborers crafted Gillette's 24-room vision of native fieldstone in the style of a Norman fortress. Gillette, son of a former United States Senator and direct descendant of Thomas Hooker, the founder of Hartford, would tinker with his masterpiece until his death in 1937. Childless and a widower for half-a-century, Gillette's will protected the property against any "blithering saphead" who might destroy his creation and the State of Connecticut became its steward in 1943.

The pride and joy of William Gillette's 184-acre estate was his three-mile narrow gauge railroad that looped through the woods below the castle. Gillette decorated the route with fanciful bridges, a wooden trestle and an arched tunnel blasted through bedrock. The rails are gone but the bed makes a unique pathway for your dog's travels through the park. The terrain is hilly enough that your dog might wish he could hop a ride on that train but most of the grades work around the hillsides rather than using harsh vertical climbs.

Dogs are not allowed inside the castle walls but the trail does lead to Grand Central Station where you will be able to see Gillette's unique home. If you get a chance to tour the castle pay attention to the forty-seven doors, no two of which are exactly alike. Each door is adorned with an intricate, hand-carved puzzle-latch.

East Haddam, Connecticut
(860) 526-2336
www.ct.gov/DEP/cwp/view.asp?A=2716&Q=325204

Fonthill (Pennsylvania)

Fonthill is the home of Henry Chapman Mercer, noted anthropologist, antiquarian, artist, writer, and tile-maker and a leader in the turn-of-the-century Arts and Crafts movement in America. The mansion, designed by Mercer in 1908 with 44 rooms illuminated by over 200 windows, is an early example of poured-in-place concrete construction. Mercer built in concrete to avoid the fate of an aunt's priceless collection of medieval armor that was destroyed in a fire. Fonthill defies any architectural description and is referred to simply as "the Castle." Mercer also built two other concrete structures in Doylestown; the Moravian Pottery and Tile Works on the same property and the Mercer Museum across town.

Dogs are welcome to roam the park-like grounds that include large swaths of open grass areas and wide dirt trails that crisscross the woodlands. There is about an hour of pleasant dog-walking here. Look for some of Mercer's decorative tiles embedded in the concrete bridges over the estate's streams.

Doylestown, Pennsylvania
(215) 345-0210
www.mercermuseum.org/

Hartwood Acres (Pennsylvania)

William Flinn's family left Manchester, England for Pittsburgh's Sixth Ward in 1852 when he was barely one year old. Young William left the Pittsburgh public schools at the age of nine to work the city streets. His father had been a small contractor but William eyed building on a larger scale. Mixing in Republican politics, Flinn won much of the paving and construction business in Pittsburgh during the exploding industrial times of the late 19th and early 20th centuries. Flinn's daughter Mary used her inheritance to create one of the western Pennsylvania's most magnificent country estates, pivoting around an elegant 16th century Tudor manor house. In 1969, she offered the estate to Allegheny County as a park and just like that the county had a ready-made crown jewel in its park system.

When you bring your dog to Hartwood Acres, you come to walk. There are no recreation or sport facilities on its 629 acres. The manor house, stable and outdoor sculptures are still in place to admire before heading out on the rolling dirt and paved pathways through the wooded countryside. A spiderweb of short and long trails and immaculate bridle paths conspire to provide delightful canine hiking in Hartwood Acres. You can hike with your dog here every day for a month and never take the same route.

For lovers of sunshine begin your dog's day in the Middle Run Lot and enjoy the macadam paths through manicured fields around the Stage, a concert amphitheater. You'll leave most of the trail users (many with a dog in tow) behind if you slip off the main paved paths onto the whimsically named natural trails. The *Heebie Jeebie Trail* utilizes tight switchbacks to climb a short hill. The *Perfectly Good Trail* is just that - a shady circuit in a remote corner of the park through a junkyard of fallen hemlock trees. Hartwood Acres also offers a large, fenced-in grassy off-leash area for your dog.

Pittsburgh, Pennsylvania
(412) 767-9200
www.alleghenycounty.us/parks/hwfac.aspx

Vanderbilt Mansion (New York)

Yet another country estate created for the Vanderbilt family, this one sited on the Hudson River for Frederick William Vanderbilt. Designed in 1898 by America's foremost architects of the Gilded Age, McKim, Mead & White, the

54-room castle is considered a perfect example of the Beaux-Arts architecture style. The Vanderbilt Mansion is maintained today as a National Historic Site by the National Park Service, which doesn't often get entangled in the estates of America's fabulously wealthy. In fact the NPS takes pains to note that the "site was established as a monument to an era rather than a tribute to any one person or family." The connection to the Federal government here is neighbor Franklin D. Roosevelt, whose lifelong home Springwood is also a National Historic Site. Roosevelt encouraged Vanderbilt's niece to donate the property to the National Park Service.

Your dog won't care about all that when she gets a chance to frolic on the manicured Vanderbilt estate grounds which are open free of charge every day of the year from sunrise to sunset. The 211 acres of parkland boast tree plantings back to the 1800s and tail-wagging views of the Hudson River and Catskill Mountains. The *Hyde Park Trail* leads down the river to Springwood, a more modest affair that also includes The Franklin Roosevelt Presidential Library. Roosevelt planted 470,000 trees on his property which your dog can appreciate in boulder-laced Cove Trail Woods.

The *Hyde Park Trail* also leads to a nearby third National Historic Site and the only one dedicated to a First Lady, Eleanor Roosevelt's Val-Kill Cottage retreat. If this outstanding troika is not enough to sate your dog's trail urges, the tiny town of Hyde Park also sports a nature preserve and twin parks behind the village center on both sides of East Market Street.

Hyde Park, New York
(845) 229-9115
www.nps.gov/vama/

Hearst Castle (California)

One shouldn't abandon America's castles without mention of the hilltop palace of newspaper publisher William Randolph Hearst, perhaps the most famous American castle of them all. Dogs are not allowed at Hearst Castle, located midway between Los Angeles and San Francisco. But there plenty of public beaches that allow dogs and several local businesses aware of the ban on pets have sprung up to take care of travelers just like you should you care to visit Heart Castle sans best friend.

San Simeon, California
www.hearstcastle.org/

TOUR
IDEA #78: DOGGIN' SOUTHERN PLANTATIONS

ACE Basin National Wildlife Refuge (South Carolina)

Long the domain of rice plantations and hunting retreats, the ACE Basin represents one of the largest undeveloped wetland ecosystems remaining on the Atlantic Coast. The centerpiece of the refuge is the Grove Plantation that was an original land grant to Robert Fenwick in 1694. The property descended through a parade of owners (one being Owen Winston, a president of Brooks Brothers) until the U.S. Fish & Wildlife Service purchased the Grove Plantation in 1992. Along with another unit on the Combahee River, the ACE Basin National Wildlife Refuge encompasses 11,062 acres and is growing.

For a day of pure hiking with your dog in solitude come to this refuge along the South Edisto River. Come with a mind to explore - these are not groomed trails. When you set out, you will never be sure what you will get. Maybe a rough dirt path. Maybe an old road. Maybe a former railroad grade. Maybe a woodland. Maybe old fields. Maybe a cypress swamp. Maybe a grove of old oaks. There are miles of roads and walking trails crisscrossing the refuge impoundments that will delight any level of canine hiker.

The white-faced Grove Plantation House is one of only three antebellum mansions in the ACE Basin to survive the Civil War. The Federal-style mansion was built around 1828 and is noted for its polygonal rooms and projecting symmetrical bays.

Edisto Beach, South Carolina
(843) 889-3084
www.fws.gov/acebasin/

Butler Greenwood Plantation (Louisiana)

In 1803, after selling more than seven million acres of land to the United States, Spain decided to keep a sliver of land along the Gulf Coast. Unfortunately for the Spanish, the area was settled primarily by English planters who had no taste for Spanish rule. By 1810 the isolated Spanish territory was still not claimed as part of the Louisiana Purchase so a band of planters stormed the fort at Baton Rouge, captured the Spanish governor and set up their own little country they called the Free and Independent Republic of West Florida. This proactive approach finally got the attention of the U.S. government who sent the army to claim the territory two months later.

This pocket of Louisiana around St. Francisville became known as English Plantation Country and was the hub of prosperous cotton and indigo plantations during the antebellum period. Eight such plantations and gardens are open for exploration today. The ideal base of operations for an examination of King Cotton is the Butler-Greenwood Plantation, still run by descendants of the original 1790s owners. Dogs are not only welcome to trot through the gardens that date to the 1840s but are allowed to stay in the Bed & Breakfast cottages as well. The formal garden and grounds spread across 50 acres, ringed by more than 100 ancient live oaks.

St. Francisville, Louisiana
(225) 635-6312
www.butlergreenwood.com/

Chippokes Plantation State Park (Virginia)

A dozen years after the English established a beachhead at Jamestown in 1607, Captain William Powell acquired a grant to this property across the James River. He began clearing land and planting crops but was killed in a raid by Chickahominy Indians in 1623. The farm was then called "Chippokes" after a native chief who befriended the colonists and began producing grain, corn, barley and wheat.

Over the years a succession of prominent Virginians owned the plantation as it expanded to 1,683 acres. The last private owner was Victor Stewart, who took over the plows in 1918. After he died his wife donated the farm to the state in 1967 to be used as a park and maintained as a working farm so visitors could experience day-to-day farm life. And so it remains. Wheat and cotton and corn and peanuts are still grown in the park and the farm is in the running for the title of "Longest Continually Cultivated Farm in America."

In its first 200 years most of the owners of Chippokes had overseers manage or tenants farm the land for them. After Albert Carroll Jones purchased the plantation for $12,000 in 1837 he became one of the first owners to actually live at Chippokes. At first he lived in the River House, built in 1829 and still standing in the park. In 1854 he completed a handsome brick Italianate mansion house for his family. Jones planted vast orchids around the plantation, using the fruit to make alcohol and operate one of the few legal distilleries in Virginia. It is said that

Albert Jones sold his brandies to both sides during the War Between The States and that is why your dog can play in front of the mansion today.

This park is sure to bring out the farm dog in your family pet. No groomed trails here but plenty of chance to trot down farm roads almost four centuries old. Under paw will be some paved paths, some gravel and some dirt. And yes, you will be hiking with your dog past cattle and goats and chickens.

One of the best canine hikes here is down the *James River Trail*. About half of its mile length is around open farm fields and half through light woods. Your destination is the James River and a long beach walk. A gently sloping crescent beach at the James River makes this one of the best places for your dog to swim in Tidewater Virginia.

Surry, Virginia
(757) 294-3625
www.dcr.virginia.gov/state_parks/chi.shtml

Magnolia Plantation & Gardens (South Carolina)

For Thomas Drayton and his son, Thomas, Jr., in 1675 it was Barbados or bust. They boarded the ship Willing Wind and left England only to arrive in what had become the most densely populated colony in the British empire. With all the choice land for a sugar plantation already snapped up the Draytons turned their attention to the new Carolina Colony.

Soon after arriving on the Ashley River young Drayton married Ann Fox and inherited the Magnolia Plantation in 1680. The young couple set about building a plantation house and at the same time planted America's first estate garden, Flowerdale.

Through the Revolution and the Civil War and the end of the age of the gentleman planter the estate was ravaged but the gardens survived intact. In the 1870s, Magnolia Gardens opened to the visitors as one of the country's oldest public gardens. Today the estate remains in the hands of the Drayton family and Flowerdale looks much as it did 300-plus years ago.

How dog-friendly is Magnolia Plantation? Not only are dogs allowed to walk the grounds but they can ride the tour trams and even go in the plantation house (if you carry the dog). And it is quite a treat - you are not likely to have a canine hike like this anywhere else. The prescribed path through the maze of walking paths stops at two dozen points of interest, crosses graceful bridges, looks in on 250 varieties of azaleas, skips through quiet stands of towering bamboo and wanders by 900 types of camellias. More hiking with your dog is available through the 60-acre blackwater cypress and tupelo swamp. Plus there are nature trails on the property and your dog can climb an observation tower to look out over the marshes and rice field.

Charleston, South Carolina
(800) 367-3517
www.magnoliaplantation.com/

Rose Hill Plantation State Historic Site (South Carolina)

In 1860 the State of South Carolina had no official governor's residence so Governor William Henry Gist worked out of his home, a magnificent Federal-style white stucco mansion he called Rose Hill. He rose from modest circumstances as the son of a Charleston merchant, partially on the strength of his skill as a duelist reportedly, to become leader of the Palmetto State. It was from here that Governor Gist, after the election of Abraham Lincoln, issued the orders for South Carolina to be the first state to secede from the Union.

The grounds of the 44-acre plantation are still enclosed by the original wrought iron fence that marked the property when it was built between 1828 and 1832. Your dog is welcome to trot the elegant grounds that feature antique varieties of roses (naturally) and an exceedingly pleasant nature trail down to the Tyger River.

Union, South Carolina
(864) 427-5966
www.southcarolinaparks.com/park-finder/state-park/540.aspx

IDEA #79: DOGGIN' AMERICA'S FORMAL GARDENS

Experienced travelers know there are attractions you drive right by with your dog's nose pressed forlornly against the car window. Formal gardens are typically high on the list of places that do not allow dogs. But not so fast...turn that car around and give these a try...

Boyce Thompson Arboretum (Arizona)

Boyce Thompson was born in Montana, educated in New England, and made his fortune trading mining stocks in New York City but it was the desert landscape of the American southwest that captured his heart. After he purchased the Magma Mine in Superior, midway between Phoenix and Tucson, he moved to Arizona and built his Picket Post house. In the 1920s he established the arboretum to study the plants of desert countries and invited the public to share in the research.

This outdoor museum of desert plants is interspersed amidst two miles of winding paths, which your dog is welcome to enjoy. The arboretum weds plants from the planet's driest regions with enormous examples of native Sonoran Desert vegetation. Where water intrudes on the 320-acre garden in the form of a man-made lake or trickling stream the impact is startling. Shade-giving eucalyptus trees share space with majestic 200-year old saguaro cactus, Chinese pistachio trees are neighbors to spiky palo-verdes and Mediterranean olive trees compete for attention with spiny-branched ocotillo. All told, there are more than 3,200 desert plants on display.

With such a variety, fragrant plants are in bloom practically any time during the year but, of course, your dog will be more comfortable strolling these pebbly paths from October to May.

Superior, Arizona
(520) 689-2811
ag.arizona.edu/bta/

Holden Arboretum (Ohio)

Albert Fairchild Holden was born in 1866, the third of nine children born to Delia Bulkley and Liberty Holden. His mother was instrumental in founding the Cleveland School of Art, which later became the Cleveland Institute of Art. His father made a fortune in the silver mines of Utah and at one time was the owner of Cleveland's major newspaper, *The Plain Dealer*.

After graduating from Harvard with a degree in Mining Engineering in 1888, Holden joined his father in the silver fields of Utah. He later bought his father's mines and organized the United States Mining Company to consolidate his expanding interests. Soon he was smelting more ore than anyone in the country and founded the Island Creek Coal Company in West Virginia to supply his furnaces.

Albert Holden died of cancer in 1913. An avid botanist, he planned to endow the Arnold Arboretum at his alma mater as a memorial to his 12-year old daughter who passed five years earlier but his sister Roberta Holden Bole convinced him that Northeast Ohio deserved a first-class arboretum of its own. Thus was eventually born the Holden Arboretum on 100 acres donated by Mrs. Bole in 1931. Today's "tree museum" has grown into one of the world's largest, with more than 6,000 varieties of plants and trees spread over 3,446 acres.

Most formal arboreta do not welcome dogs so it is a rare treat to be able to bring your dog to these trails. There are more than a dozen here, ranging from garden strolls to meadow romps to mature woodland hikes for your dog. The trails curve pleasingly among the plantings, often visiting the edges of ponds. Energetic dogs will want to push to the park's extremities on the sporty *Pierson Creek Loop* and *Bole Woods Trail* that explore a stunning beech-maple forest, designated a National Natural Landmark. In the southern region the Conifer collection is an embarrassment of evergreen wonder any month of the year. You may be distracted by the beauty of the place and not notice as you hike but your dog can get quite a workout in Holden Arboretum, with several hundred feet of elevation changes. A detailed color map comes with each admission. Did I say detailed? It even tells you how many steps there are on the trail staircases.

The *Layer Rhododendron Garden Trail* was long home to two oaks that were growing before George Washington was born. A gnarly 375-year old white oak can still be seen seen on the edge of Oak Pond but a 275-year old red oak toppled in 2007. Woodcarver Dan Sammon spent five days with chainsaw and torch to create "The Guardians of the Garden" in the base and trunk of the fallen giant.

Kirtland, Ohio
(440) 946-4400
www.holdenarb.org/

Jungle Gardens (Louisiana)

Edmund McIlhenny's world was being torn apart. Approaching Union troops during the Civil War forced the self-made banker of Scotch-Irish descent to flee New Orleans in 1862 for the safety of his wife's ancestral home on Avery Island in the Louisiana bayou. The McIlhennys' refuge was short-lived. The family island yielded mineable rock salt - the nation's first salt mine is there - and salt was needed to preserve meat for feeding troops. The Union army reached Avery Island in 1863 and the Averys and McIlhennys fled to south Texas for the duration of the War.

When they returned, their house was plundered. their plantation in tatters. About the only thing that seemed to survive the Yankee occupation was a patch of hearty Capsicum peppers that thrived in a kitchen garden. From these humble plants would sprout an empire.

Edmund McIlhenny chopped the peppers and blended them with vinegar and Avery Island salt. The fiery potion was left to age in wooden barrels. He portioned off the sauce into discarded cologne bottles and called it "Tabasco" for a river in southern Mexico because he liked the name. The spicy sauce was an immediate hit and McIlhenny sold millions of tiny bottles until his death in 1890.

His son Edward assumed control of the family pepper business in 1898. "Ned" McIlhenny was also an arctic explorer, naturalist and conservationist as well as a pepper sauce king. He expanded the family estate next to the Tabasco factory to more than 250 acres and decorated it with exotic plants from around the world. He took an open sand mining pit and converted it to a Palm Garden. A poor-draining gully became a Sunken Garden. His "jungle gardens" were graced with over 400 varieties of Camelias and thousands of types of iris.

Ned McIlhenny opened Jungle Gardens to the public in 1935. A five-mile driving road snakes through spectacular live oak groves and around man-made lagoons. Most people tour the gardens in their vehicles but get out and walk your dog to truly soak in the sub-tropical atmosphere of the plantings (keep an eye out for alligators). Highlights include an 800-year old Buddha statue and Bird City, a private bird sanctuary started by Ned McIlhenny in 1895 to save the snowy egret that was rapidly being exterminated for its feathers to decorate ladies' hats.

Avery Island, Louisiana
(337) 369-6243
junglegardens.org/

Key West Tropical Forest and Botanical Garden (Florida)

The Key West Botanical Garden began life as a 1930s Depression-era public works project. The equivalent of $10 million was spent to create a 55-acre experimental garden with flagstone walkways, stone walls and an aviary. Plants from all over the world were imported to learn which would survive in this tropical environment.

The early botanical garden was a tourist showplace but it declined during World War II as bits and pieces of the property were appropriated by various government agencies. By 1961 only seven and a half acres and no buildings remained. The neglect was stemmed temporarily when the City of Key West designated the garden as a permanent sanctuary but it would be another two decades before the Key West Botanical Garden Society organized to operate the garden as a family-friendly facility.

Today the Key West Botanical Garden is the only frost-free botanical garden in the United States. Your dog can trot along four self-guided nature trails under the lush leaves of tropical flora. Chief among them are the collection of palms, including saw palmetto and the Florida state tree, the Sabal Palm. Two freshwater ponds in the forest, reached by red arrows, are among the last in the Florida Keys.

Yellow arrows lead your dog along the *Trail of Champion Trees*. The Key West Tropical Forest and Botanical Garden is home to two state champion trees and two national champions: the Wild Dilly and the Locustberry. These trees ordinarily are found in low, shrub-like growth but here they have blossomed as full-blown trees.

Stock Island, Florida
(305) 296-1504
www.keywestbotanicalgarden.org/

Mendocino Coast Botanical Garden (California)

This 47-acre garden, started by a retired nurseryman in 1961, is the only public garden in the continental United States that sits directly on the Pacific Ocean. And dogs are welcome to wander through the diverse plant collections that enjoy their damp, foggy perch above the waves.

The trail system flows from manicured formal gardens (many of the rose varieties were discovered along roadsides and abandoned Mendocino homesteads) through a hardy pine forest out to the Pacific breezes on the edges of a flower-laden coastal prairie. Spurs drop into wetlands and fern-crusted canyons. But don't confine your dog's explorations of the "Garden By The Sea" to the footpaths - step into the grassy areas surrounding the rare collections. The Heather garden, for instance, has been tabbed by the American Public Gardens Association as a Collection of National Significance.

The Mendocino Coast Botanical Garden is known for its spectacular Rhododendrons. Tender species native to the cloud forests of Southeast Asia and the Himalayas thrive in the cool damp climate and are found in this country only in a narrow band along the northern California coast. Hybrid Rhododendrons in reds, purples and pinks dwarf admirers when they burst into flower. Come in spring and winter and you can huddle with your dog in the Cliff House to watch annual whale migrations just off shore.

Fort Bragg, California
(707) 964-4352
www.gardenbythesea.org/

National Arboretum (Washington D.C.)

The United States Department of Agriculture established the National
Arboretum as a research and education facility and living museum in 1927.
Dogs are permitted across the grounds, which include a mix of tree collections
and formal gardens. The major trail system circles Mount Hamilton, at 240 feet
one of the highest points in the nation's capital. A paved road/path winds to the
top where you can peek through the trees to the west and see the U.S. Capitol and
the Washington Monument. On the southern and eastern slopes are over 15,000
hardy azaleas that can still see blooms into November.

Another area with footpaths is the Asian Collection where trees and flowers
from China, Japan and Korea mingle above the Anacostia River. But you need
not limit your explorations with your dog to formal pathways. You can wander on
the grass through the Slow-growing Conifer Collection, the Holly and Magnolia
Collection and the National Boxwood Collections.

Your dog can stroll through gardens devoted to perennials, to herbs and to
energy-producing plants and across a meadow containing twenty-two sandstone
Corinthian columns that once stood at the east portico of the U.S. Capitol.

Washington D.C.
(202) 245-2726
www.usna.usda.gov/

DESTINATION

IDEA #80: TOURIST FARMS & RANCHES

Is there a more natural vacation destination for your dog than a working
farm or ranch? These days farms offering city folk a chance to experience the rural
life can be found just about anywhere in the United States. But do your research
before you pack up your grungiest jeans and old work boots - that "genuine farm
experience" can range from picking a few eggs and touring cropfields to birthing
lambs and branding cattle. It is critical to know what life on the farm you want for
you and your dog before making reservations.

Agritourism is still in its infancy and policies regarding visiting dogs have not
been chiseled in stone at many farms and ranches. Talk with an owner of a farm

you are interested in and discuss the accommodations for your dog. Your dog may have to sleep in the barn, you never know.

TOUR
IDEA #81: BACK TO SCHOOL FOR BOWSER

Maybe it's time to take your dog for a little schoolin'. A college campus is a great place to look for a canine hike when you are traveling. You will find many a campus to be dog-friendly. The best time to visit with your dog is early on a weekend day or when school is not in session. At smaller colleges you can maneuver your dog unobtrusively around campus most any time. These schools will give you an idea of what to expect when your dog goes to college...

Clemson University (South Carolina)

The Simpson Research Center, located seven miles from the main campus, was purchased by Clemson University in the 1960s when most of the 2,236 acres were under the water of Lake Hartwell. It is now dedicated to crop and livestock research.

This spacious farm is a great informal find to hike with your dog. Foot travel is invited and there are lots of different terrains to choose from - woods, ponds, miles of level gravel roads, and huge fields for your dog to run in. On a clear day there are beautiful vistas of the mountains. It's a great, off the leash, unfettered walk with your dog!

Pendleton, South Carolina
virtual.clemson.edu/groups/agsupport/simpson.htm

Cornell University (New York)

According to the arboretum brochure, "The name Plantations was coined by Cornell University professor Liberty Hyde Bailey (1858-1954), who is often called the father of American horticulture. Bailey understood a plantation to be 'a large group of plants, especially trees, under cultivation.'" The Cornell Plantations welcome visitors year-round, are free and open sunrise to sunset. Dogs are allowed.

The trails are divided between cultivated collections and natural areas, spread across rolling terrain. The natural areas include over 3,000 acres of diverse habitats

Falls Creek. Nearby, another four miles of woodland trails beckon in Sapsucker Woods, maintained by the Cornell Ornithology Department, but dogs are not permitted in this sanctuary.

Ithaca, New York
(607) 255-2400
www.plantations.cornell.edu/

Duke University (North Carolina)

College planners began buying up small farms and forestland as a buffer for the Duke campus in the 1920s. The lands have now evolved into the Duke Forest with nearly 8,000 acres spread across six divisions. Much of the canine hiking is easy going in the woods through airy pine trees, including stately loblollies and majestic white pines.

Although there are few footpaths in the Duke Forest there are more than 30 miles of old woodland roads to travel on. There is also a three-mile graded loop used as a cross-county course that winds through the woods around the campus golf course that makes an ideal one-hour canine hike.

Durham, North Carolina
(919) 613-8013
www.dukeforest.duke.edu/

Swarthmore College (Pennsylvania)

The 300-acre Swarthmore campus is developed to be an arboretum, established in 1929 as a living memorial to Arthur Hoyt Scott, Class of 1895. Stop in the office to pick up a tour map to the Scott Arboretum collections that are integrated with the stone buildings of the college that date to 1864.

A dog-friendly campus, you'll find dog water bowls at the drinking fountains as you travel among the 3,000 different kinds of plants. You can finish your tour in Crum Woods where your dog can go under voice control on the rolling dirt paths and even visit Swarthmore's version of Stonehenge.

Swarthmore, Pennsylvania
(610) 328-8025
www.scottarboretum.org/

West Virginia University (West Virginia)

The 91-acre Core Arboretum on the campus of West Virginia University is named for Earl Lemley Core, the Mountain State's leading botanist, one-time mayor of Morgantown and faculty member at WVU for 44 years. Students began coming to the small forest in the early 1900s and the school acquired the property in 1948. Its steep slopes negated development and today visitors (free admission and parking right at the arboretum) can enjoy the old growth forest that covers the hillsides as it sweeps down to the Monongahela River.

There are 3.5 miles of trails for canine hiking that begin in an upper lawn sprinkled with native specimen trees. The trail drops some 200 feet to the river, past trees estimated at 400 years old. Look for specks of black rock that are remnants of an old coal mine that once operated here. The forest changes composition as it nears the floodplain and thirstier species like silver maples begin to dominate the landscape. The *Caperton Trail*, an old rail-to-trail, crosses the park for longer explorations of West Virginia's fifth largest city.

Morgantown, West Virginia
(304) 293-5201
www.as.wvu.edu/biology/facility/arboretum.html

SWALLOWING STATES WHOLE

IDEA #82: THE DOG FRIENDLIEST STATE IN AMERICA

Looking for an off-beat vacation for your dog? Why not consider touring the dog-friendliest state in America. You will have to look long and hard to find a "No Dogs Allowed" sign in Delaware. Maybe in the cabins and yurts in the state parks and on a couple of popular ocean beaches midday in summer but that is about it. This tour of five Delaware state parks will take your dog to fast-flowing streams, lazy ponds, ocean beaches, sporty hills, enchanting forests...

Brandywine Creek State Park

Starting in the north of a state that is less than 100 miles long and never wider than 35 miles, the first Delaware state park you reach, hard by the

Pennsylvania line, is Brandywine Creek, named for the shallow creek that dissects it. Once a du Pont family dairy farm, this spectacular swath of land houses Delaware's first two nature preserves. The stone walls that crisscross the 850-acre park are the legacy of skilled Italian masons who crafted the barriers from locally quarried Brandywine granite - the original "Wilmington Blue Rocks."

There are eight blazed trails totaling 14 miles on both sides of the Brandywine Creek. All are short, all are woodsy and if you can't reach out and touch the water you are moving up or down a hill. The *Hidden Pond Trail* and the Indian Springs Trail each travel along the water, immerse you in the steep valley terrain and traverse the Tulip Tree Woods, where majestic tulip poplar have grown for nearly two centuries. The rugged 1.9-mile *Rocky Run Trail*, winds around the closest thing to a mountain stream in Delaware and nearby, the *Multi-Use Trail* tags Brandywine Creek for the better part of two miles or, on a hot day, walk right down the middle of the stream with your dog.

Wilmington, Delaware
(302) 577-3534
www.destateparks.com/park/brandywine-creek/

White Clay Creek State Park

White Clay serves up the widest menu of canine hiking choices of any park in the First State - almost 40 miles of marked trails. The top choices in the Walter S. Carpenter, Jr. Recreation Area are the hardy 5-mile *Twin Valley Trail* and the sporty 2-mile *Millstone Trail* with its scenic rock outcroppings and two never-finished millstones. A half-mile *Logger's Trail* illuminates the history of lumbering in the area.

The only trail that actually visits the White Clay Creek is the *Penndel Trail*, a superb linear trail for hiking with your dog - flat for its entire length and uniformly wide. Nearby, at the park office on Thompson Station Road, is a trailhead for a rugged hill climb on the homesite of David English, a lease holder of the William Penn family. While you are warming up for hill climbs, visit Possum Hill, where two stacked loop trails fall 150 feet among thick stands of mature beech and oaks that thrive in the moist valleys. The scenery on the 2-mile *Long Loop* is more arresting so save the inner loop for a second go-round.

The fourth - and newest - section of White Clay Creek was acquired in 1998 at the Judge Morris Estate. Along with an elegant 1790s mansion the park annexed one of the finest loop trails in the state. The wooded 3-mile ramble dips and rolls across tumbling terrain and is certain to delight any dog.

Newark, Delawate
(302) 368-6900
www.destateparks.com/park/white-clay-creek/

Killens Pond State Park

The first thing your dog will notice while trotting on the trails at Killens Pond is that it is unusually hilly for central Delaware. Just enough to give the 2.75-mile *Pondside Trail* a nice, sporty feel. Your dog will also approve of the wide, roomy paths and the packed sand and pine straw under paw. The trail circles the entire pond, keeping sight of the water most of the way.

Chances are you will just be getting warmed up with this pleasing ramble and luckily Killens Pond serves up a few more choices. The *Ice Storm Trail* is a loop that shows the forest regenerating from a 1994 storm that left trees snapping and buckling under the weight of a cocoon of ice.

Killens Pond offers the opportunity to hike through a uniquely diverse forest as southern species mingle at the northern edge of their range with northern species reaching their southern boundary. Seven separate species of oak trees share the sandy soil with majestic loblolly pines; American holly jostles with Virginia pine and so on.

Felton, Delaware
(302) 284-4526
www.destateparks.com/park/killens-pond/

Trap Pond State Park

Trap Pond is a small portion of the Great Cypress Swamp and features the northernmost natural stand of baldcypress trees in the Untied States. In the late 1700s a millpond was constructed to power a sawmill to harvest the valuable lumber. During the Depression in the 1930s, the Civilian Conservation Corps put men to work building recreation facilities and in 1951, 14 years after the Delaware legislature authorized the development of the state park system, Trap Pond became the first to welcome visitors.

The 5-mile long *Boundary Trail* completely circles both the 90-acre millpond and the baldcypress swamp. There is a mixture of natural and paved surfaces and the flat trail is very easy for any dog to walk. Stately loblolly pines dominate the forest and gently flowing streams feed the pond. For canine hikers not interested in a complete circumnavigation of Trap Pond there are short atmospheric trails along the edge of the swamp that could be taking place in Louisiana instead of Delaware.

Laurel, Delaware
(302) 875-5153
www.destateparks.com/park/trap-pond/

Cape Henlopen State Park

Cape Henlopen has the distinction of being one of the first parks in America: in 1682 William Penn decreed that Cape Henlopen would be for "the usage of the citizens of Lewes and Sussex County." The area had been Delaware's first permanent settlement 50 years earlier by ill-fated Dutch colonists who were massacred by local Indians. Today the park boasts more than 5,000 acres, including four miles of pristine beaches (dogs allowed in off-season) where the Delaware Bay meets the Atlantic Ocean. It is Delaware's largest state park.

The primary destination for dog owners at Cape Henlopen is the 3.1-mile *Dune Overlook Trail*, located south of the campground. The loop is part natural surface, part paved road through pitch-pine corridors and past old fortifications. Do not skip the two short spur trails! One leads into the spartina marshes typical of the Delaware Bay estuary and the other is a journey onto the 80-foot Great Dune, the highest sand pile on the Atlantic shore between Cape Cod and Cape Hatteras.

Cape Henlopen's strategic location at the mouth of the Delaware Bay led the United States Army to establish Fort Miles among the dunes in 1941. Remnants of Cape Henlopen's military past remain nestled among the massive sand dunes. Bunkers and gun emplacements were camouflaged deep in the sand and concrete observation towers were built along the shoreline to bolster America's coastal defenses during World War II. Lookouts scanned the Atlantic Ocean for German U-boats and although the fort's huge guns were never fired in battle, an enemy submarine did surrender here after the war. These silent sentinels remain scattered along Delaware's beaches and one has been restored to provide visitors with a panoramic view of the park and the ocean.

Lewes, Delaware
(302) 645-8983
www.destateparks.com/park/cape-henlopen/

T☉UR
IDEA #83: DOGGIN' AMERICA'S SMALLEST STATE

Another state where you can make a vacation for your dog in a single area code is Rhode Island, especially a water-loving dog. You are never more than a half-hour drive from salt water in the Ocean State. There are counties larger than Rhode Island, there are parks larger than Rhode Island. But you can spend a holiday visiting all the tail-friendly parks in the state; here are some of the best...

Beavertail State Park

The first lighthouse built at Beavertail was the third in the country when it was lit in 1749 - after only the Boston Harbor Light (1716) and the Great Point Light on Nantucket (1746). Four years later the Newport Light, as it was called, became America's first lighthouse to burn to the ground. The rubble tower that was built next lasted a full century until it was replaced by the current granite lighthouse that guides vessels into Narragansett Bay. The United States Navy took control of this point in World War II and erected Fort Burnside, named to honor Civil War general and Rhode Island governor Ambrose Burnside. In 1980 the state acquired the land as surplus property.

You can hike with your dog from one end of the park to the other atop the rocky shoreline on park roads and a narrow dirt path. If the weather is calm and the seas benign you can include the craggy rocks in your route. The views will be spectacular at almost any point in your hike with four specific overlooks designated. Interpretive signs describe the area, including the Beavertail fault with its geologic story of ancient Rhode Island. Make sure to bring plenty of fresh water for your dog at Beavertail. There isn't much shade out on the point and no drinking water.

Jamestown, Rhode Island
(401) 423-9941
www.riparks.com/beaverta1.htm

Cliff Walk

In the late 1800s wealthy New Yorkers began coming to Newport, Rhode Island to escape the suffocating summer heat in the city. They built the most extravagant "cottages" ever seen in America on the rocky bluffs overlooking the Atlantic Ocean. No matter how impressive the mansion or how rich the owner, however, no one's property could extend all the way to the shoreline. By virtue of "Fisherman's Rights" granted by the Colonial Charter of King Charles II and a provision in the Rhode Island Constitution, the public is always guaranteed the legal right to walk along a small sliver of cliff.

Not that the powerful residents on the other sides of the gate have always agreed with that right. In the past bushes were planted, walls erected and even bulls grazed to discourage use by the public. Other owners embraced the *Cliff Walk* and helped develop it from a mere footpath. Some tunnels were built and flagstones placed in muddy stretches. Eventually the federal government stepped in to help rebuild the path after erosion during hurricanes. In 1975, the *Cliff Walk* was named the first National Recreation Trail in New England.

Today the *Cliff Walk* rambles for about 3.5 miles, about two of which are paved and easy to walk. Dogs are welcome all along the *Cliff Walk* and courtesy bags are even provided at the start on Memorial Boulevard. Continuing past the paved path, the journey turns rustic with some walking on unprotected, open cliff faces and boulder hopping. It requires concentration but any level of canine hiker can negotiate the trip. If you continue to the end you will drop to ocean's edge and small coves where your dog can get a swim. Here you have the option of returning by the same route along the black Atlantic rocks or exiting into the town and walking back on the sidewalks in front of the mansions whose backyards you have just tramped through.

Newport's First Beach, at the start of the *Cliff Walk*, is open to dogs only in the off-season.

Newport, Rhode Island
www.cliffwalk.com/

George Washington Management Area

In the Spring of 1965 over 300 Australian sailors were in the United States awaiting delivery on their guided missile destroyer, the *HMAS Perth*, that was being readied in Bay City, Michigan. The original *HMAS Perth* had been torpedoed in World War II at the Battle of Sunda Strait and sank with the loss of 350 of her crew and three civilians. Another 324 of the *Perth's* crew survived the sinking and were taken prisoner.

With six weeks down time ahead of them the problem arose of how to keep the men occupied. The Division of Forests in Rhode Island had a solution: come and help develop the George Washington Forest. So work groups of 100 Aussie sailors rotated on two-week tours in the Rhode Island wilderness felling trees, building picnic areas and carving trails. By all accounts the sailors had a splendid time with their enforced shore leave. They worked hard and played hard, enjoying swimming in the adjacent Bowdish Reservoir. Visitors have been enjoying their efforts ever since.

After her commission on July 17, 1965 the *HMAS Perth* was deployed in Vietnam and came under fire four times. It was the only Australian ship to be hit by enemy fire and was awarded the United States Navy Meritorious Unit Commendation for her service. On November 24, 2001 the *HMAS Perth* was sunk as a dive wreck off the Western Australian coast.

The *Walkabout Trail* constructed by the Australians is a six-mile loop with several cut-offs to shorten the canine hike. They appear to have done a superior job in scouting the peripatetic route for as you walk along the trail seems to pass through the prettiest scenery on the property. Those surroundings include rock outcroppings, marshlands, a white Cedar swamp and a grove of dark, Eastern hemlocks. This is easy going for any dog with small hillocks and a well-maintained path. There are many other trails that lead off the *Walkabout*, including a spur to Peck Pond to expand your dog's day in the George Washington Memorial State Forest but you will still cover but a fraction of its more than 3,000 acres.

Chepachet, Rhode Island
(401) 568-2013
www.riparks.com/georgewashcamp.htm

Goddard Memorial State Park

In the late 1800s Henry Grinnell Russell, like most of his Rhode Island neighbors, walked around a property that was stripped bare by agriculture and deforestation. Russell, who came by this property when he married his Civil War buddy's sister, wasn't content to lead a treeless life. As he walked the sandy dunes Russell would drop acorns from his pockets, planting them in holes punched with his cane. He would fill the holes with three acorns - one oak for the squirrels, one for the worms, and one to grow.

Henry Russell would add different trees to his Oaks Estate and by the early 1900s foresters from the U.S. Forest Service called this "the finest example of private forestry in America." After Russell died Colonel Robert Hale Ives Goddard came into possession of the Oaks and continued the reforesting project.

When he died in 1927 the estate was left to the state to remain forever in its natural state and opened as a public park on June 1, 1930.

The canine hiking at Goddard Memorial State Park is conducted primarily on bridle paths through the tall forests sandwiched between the bay and the open fields of the picnic areas and golf course. Don't despair about taking your dog down the chewed-up paths often associated with horse trails - these wide, sandy avenues through the forest are packed sand and extremely paw-friendly.

This is easy going throughout on gentle terrain. Pick a trail that leads to a dog-friendly beach. At Long Point your dog can indulge in the gentle waves of Greenwich Cove and you can continue on the sand around to the other side of the main beach. The bridle trail network consists of 18 miles of multi-intersecting short trails.

Warwick, Rhode Island
(401) 884-2010
www.riparks.com/goddard.htm

Weetamoo Woods

This land was originally part of the Massachusetts Bay Colony, known as Pocasset and home to the Wamponoag-Pocasset tribe. The Wamponoag-Pocassets were the Indians of Pilgrim fame who helped the English settlers survive the harsh early days and participated in the first Thanksgiving dinner.

Things were not so civil a half-century later when the warrior Metacom, given the English name Philip by his tribal chief father, led a rebellion against the British. He was aided in his cause by his widowed sister-in-law, Weetamoo, that translates to "sweetheart." During the King Philip War in the summer of 1675 Metacom and Weetamoo used the swamp here to hideout from British patrols. They might well have succeeded in defeating the British were it not for rival tribes in the region and on August 12, 1676 King Philip was killed and the remnants of his tribe dispersed or sold into slavery.

These 450 acres of woodlands were acquired by the town of Tiverton in 1990. The best canine hiking in Weetamoo Woods is along the *Red Trail* that travels part of the way on the Eight Rod Way, surveyed in 1679 as a road between Sakonnet and Plymouth Colony. Today the old road is ideal for your dog to trot down through one of the last large, unbroken forested areas along the New England coast. Look for American holly trees in the understory.

Tiverton, Rhode Island

TOUR

IDEA #84: DOGGIN' AMERICAN ICONS

What better way to dog America than to drop in on classic Americana with your dog...

Cherry Blossoms (Washington D.C./New Jersey)

Most everyone is familiar with the famous cherry blossoms that burst into bloom in early spring around the Tidal Basin in Washington D.C. In Japan the flowering cherry tree is an exalted plant known as a "Sakura." The planting of cherry trees on the National Mall originated in 1912 as a gift of friendship to the United States from the people of Japan. You can take your dog for a hike on the Mall to the cherry blossoms - it is one of the country's most tail-friendly city parks. The very first specimen is across the water from the Jefferson Memorial.

But what is less well-known is that there is another Northeast city that has more varieties and numbers of Japanese cherry trees than Washington D.C...

Branch Brook Park in Newark, New Jersey is America's first county park, opened in 1895. The cherry trees were planted in 1927 as a gift from Mrs. Felix Fuld and the Bamberger family. There are more than 2,000 white and pink flowering cherry trees, unique in their placement to be reminiscent of the Japanese countryside. Branch Brook is listed on the National Register of Historic Places.

The park is an interesting one to hike with your dog. It stretches for almost four miles but is usually less than 400 yards wide. Your dog will be trotting on paved and dirt paths through open meadowland studded with cherry trees and small patches of woodlands. The "branch" of the park's name connects to the Passaic River and still flows through the property. One of the first things done to construct the park was to transform Old Blue Jay Swamp into a lake that still serves as a centerpiece for visitors.

The weekly Cherry Blossom Festival takes place in Branch Brook Park every mid-April, usually a week after the National Cherry Blossom Festival in Washington.

Newark, New Jersey
newark1.com/branchbrook/

Field of Dreams (Iowa)

After scouring Iowa for a farm with just the right features, producers for a movie about an Iowa corn farmer who hears voices telling him to build a baseball field settled on Don Lansing's 100-acre Dyersville spread. A wrap-around porch was constructed on the turn-of-the-century farmhouse and three days were used to transform 2 1/2 acres of cornstalks into a pristine baseball diamond.

Field of Dreams, with star Kevin Costner asking, "Is this Heaven?," opened in 1989 and became one of the most beloved baseball movies ever filmed. Soon fans began arriving in Iowa looking for the magical field. It was decided not to plow it over and plant next year's crops. Today the "Field of Dreams" is open for your dog to run around the bases or just lounge in the outfield grass daily from April to October.

Dyersville, Iowa
(888) 875-8404
www.fieldofdreamsmoviesite.com/

Hollywood Sign (California)

The seeds of one of the world's great city parks were sown with the arrival of Colonel Griffith Jenkins Griffith from Wales in 1865 to make a fortune in California gold mines. In 1882 Griffith came to Los Angeles and purchased 4,071 acres of an original Spanish land grant, Rancho Los Felix. In 1896 he gave more than 3,000 acres of California oaks, wild sage and manzanita to the city as a Christmas present - "a place of relaxation and rest for the masses."

Today Griffith Park is the largest urban wilderness area in America, including 53 miles of trails, fire roads and bridle paths. Many feature views of the famous Hollywood sign - the 6-mile *Mt. Hollywood Trail* climbs to the top. The sign first appeared on the side of Mt. Lee in 1923 and was originally miscast as an advertising sign for a real estate development, "Hollywoodland." Each of the original letters was 30 feet wide and 50 feet tall, stitched together of metal squares, wires and pipes. It featured 4,000 20-watt bulbs spaced eight inches apart. The giant billboard cost $21,000 and was only intended to stand for about 18 months.

Instead the sign trundled on for decades, eventually resembling a Vaudeville act on the road too long. Hollywoodland went bust in the 1940s. The unmaintained sign was propped up by the Chamber of Commerce who dropped the last

four letters but it went on rusting and crumbling for years. In 1978 the old sign
was scrapped and re-born with 194 tons of concrete, enamel and steel and stands
today as the most recognizable icon of American culture to the world.

It is illegal to hike to the sign, perched safely behind restrictive fences, today,
with or without a dog. You will get plenty of time with the sign in Griffith Park,
however. Tail-friendly touches include a dog park adjacent to Ferraro Soccer Field
and rides for dogs on the Los Angeles Live Steamers miniature train.

Los Angeles, California
(323) 913-4688
www.lacity.org/rap/dos/parks/griffithpk/griffith.htm

Punxsutawney Phil (Pennsylvania)

European traditions and superstitions have long centered around February
2, the midway point between the winter solstice and the spring equinox. For
centuries it was believed the weather on this date, known as Candlemas Day,
could foretell the length of the current winter.

In Germany, this forecasting was entrusted to a hedgehog. If the animal
emerged from its burrow and saw its shadow it would become frightened and
scurry back underground. If the hedgehog perceived no shadow, it was time to
stay above ground and spring was near.

In the 1800s restless Western Pennsylvanians in the middle of a long winter
began staging annual groundhog hunts. At some point lost in the mist of history,
Clymer Freas, a newspaper editor in Punxsutawney, tied the groundhog hunt
to Candlemas Day. The hunt morphed into a celebration and the members of
the Punxsutawney Groundhog Club began trekking out to Gobbler's Knob
south of town to mark "Punxsutawney Phil's" prognostication. The first official
Groundhog Day trek was held in 1887.

Today the annual celebration lasts a weekend (a screening of Bill Murray's
Groundhog Day is a staple of the event) and attracts up to 30,000 revelers. That's
too many to squeeze your dog into but Gobbler's Knob is a public park that
welcomes your dog otherwise. There are large grassy fields for a game of fetch,
rough woodland trails, groundhog-themed public art and a permanent stage. No
need to worry about your dog chasing Punxsutawney Phil when you visit - he lives
behind glass on Barclay Square in town.

Punxsutawney, Pennsylvania
www.punxsutawney.com/

Smokey The Bear (New Mexico)

The Lincoln National Forest became famous around the world in May 1950 after an orphaned 5-pound bear cub was discovered clinging to a tree in a forest fire. The two-month old survivor was enlisted as the living symbol for Smokey the Bear, a cartoon caricature created six years earlier to preserve forests for use in World War II. While Smokey lived in the National Zoo in Washington D.C., he reportedly grew to be the second most beloved character in America, behind only Santa Claus. When Smokey died in 1976 he was returned to his home in Capitan, New Mexico and buried in a grave marked by a stone and plaque.

Today, the Lincoln National Forest, where elevations rise to 11,500 feet, comprises over 1.1 million acres across three tracts of land. Days of canine adventure await in any of the tracts; many trailheads are easily located just off main roads. Choose from easy rambles with your dog among the cool pines or tackle strenuous canyons in the desert wilderness.

Lincoln National Forest, New Mexico
(505) 434-7200
fs.fed.us/r3/lincoln/

4

DOGGIN' AMERICA HISTORY

America can be a strange place for dog owners. Places where you would not expect to be able to take your dog, like outdoor historic shrines, often welcome dogs on the grounds while places you would expect to be able to take dogs, like national parks, nearly all ban dogs. It almost feels like we have found a loophole in the system when we take our dogs to some of the most historic grounds in the country.

DOGGIN' AMERICA'S BATTLEFIELDS

The difference between touring Civil War sites and Revolutionary War sites is akin to the number of Americans who follow baseball and those who are cricket enthusiasts. During the American Revolution relatively few battles were fought over seven years of conflict and afterwards it was not in vogue to protect the land involved. Still, you are likely to find the extra effort worth the experience when you travel with your dog to investigate the struggle for independence...

TOUR
IDEA #85: DOGGIN' THE AMERICAN REVOLUTION

Guilford Courthouse National Military Park (North Carolina)

With the Revolutionary War stalemated in the North in 1778, the British strategy to squash the rebellion shifted to the South. Georgia and South Carolina were completely under British control by 1780. Nathanael Greene, an ironmaster by trade, self-taught in the art of war and George Washington's hand-picked commander of the Southern Department, was determined to keep North Carolina out of British hands.

From his base in Virginia Greene harassed the British as their attack spread northward. Pursued by a frenetic Lord Cornwallis, Greene selected sloping ground near Guilford Courthouse to make his stand. He aligned his superior force of 4,000 men - of which scarcely one in five had ever seen battle action - in three lines to receive the British assault on March 15, 1781.

The first line, manned by inexperienced North Carolina militia, was quickly brushed aside and fled. Breaking through the second Patriot line, however, required savage fighting and by the time the Redcoats reached Greene's last line, Cornwallis was becoming desperate. He directed his artillery to fire grapeshot over his own lines into the melee of friend and foe alike. The harsh directive to fire into his own troops dispersed the Americans and saved his army.

Greene retired from the field. Technically the loser, his losses had been light. Cornwallis kept the field but lost the war at Guilford Courthouse. His army limped on to Wilmington, convinced that conquering Virginia would collapse the Revolution. Greene let him go and moved southward to re-conquer South Carolina and Georgia, confident that American troops assembling in Virginia would destroy Cornwallis - which they did seven months later in Yorktown. Begun in 1887, the 220-acre park was later established in 1917 as the first battleground of the American Revolution to be preserved as a national military park.

Guilford Courthouse National Military Park is a local popular dog-walking destination with level, leafy paths in a suburban environment. Nothing remains of either the small wooden courthouse or the community of March 15, 1781 but the grounds are among the most decorated of Revolutionary battlefields, graced by twenty-eight monuments. The most impressive is the large equestrian statue of General Greene, sculpted by Francis H. Packer of New York. Unveiled on July 3, 1915, it bears Greene's words: "We fight, get beat, rise, and fight again."

Greensboro, North Carolina
(336) 288-1776
www.nps.gov/guco/

Kings Mountain National Military Park (South Carolina)

Thomas Jefferson called it, "the turn of the tide of success." For the British, Sir Henry Clinton called the defeat at Kings Mountain, "the first link in a chain of evils that at last ended in the total loss of America." The battle of Kings Mountain, fought October 7, 1780, was the first major Patriot victory to occur after the British invasion of Charleston, in May 1780.

Revolutionary War buffs will certainly want to make the effort to bring the dog to Kings Mountain, site of some of the most vicious American vs. American fighting of the war. Here some 600 "backcountry" men, who had marched over 200 miles, attacked Carolinians loyal to the crown. The Loyalists were under the command of "Bloody" Patrick Ferguson, the only British soldier in the battle.

Ferguson chose to defend his position on traditional high ground, a rocky outcropping surrounded by a hardwood forest. The mountain men, however, worked their way up the slopes, fighting from tree to tree on their way to the summit. The high ground in this case worked against the defenders as they were unable to get clear shots at their attackers.

You can hike with your dog on an interpretive walking trail around Battlefield Ridge. Walking on the thickly wooded mountainside provides an excellent feel for what fighting must have been like on that critical day in the American Revolution. Your canine hike will include an exploration of the spot where Ferguson was killed, marked by a monument and covered with a traditional Scottish stone cairn.

York, South Carolina
(864) 936-7921
www.nps.gov/kimo/

Monmouth Battlefield State Park (New Jersey)

The American Army came of age in 1778 in the Battle of Monmouth, forcing the British from the field in a brilliant counterattack led by George Washington. The General had planned a support role for himself, hoping to deliver a final, fatal blow to the British Army but when he started for the battle he instead discovered 5,000 of his best troops in a confused retreat. A stunned Washington immediately took personal command from Charles Lee, the general he had entrusted the attack to, and stopped the retreat. Eagerly his troops, hardened from their recent experience at Valley Forge, rallied to rout the British in record June heat. It was the last major battle of the Revolution in the north and Washington's finest hour in the field.

Trails, unadorned with historical markers, traverse the scene of some of the most desperate fighting. Most of the canine hiking in the historical park is across open fields with plenty of soft grass for your dog's travels.

Manalapan, New Jersey
(732) 462-9616
www.state.nj.us/dep/parksandforests/parks/monbat.html

Morristown National Historic Park (New Jersey)

Morristown, a village of 250, was a center of iron supply for the American Revolution and even though it lay only 30 miles west of the main British force in New York it was protected by a series of parallel mountain ranges. It was the twin luxuries of a defensible position in close proximity to the enemy that twice brought General Washington to camp his main army here, first in 1777 and again in 1779-1780.

After the Battle of Princeton on January 3, 1777 a worn-down Colonial Army swarmed the tiny town seeking shelter in the few public buildings, private homes, barns and stables then in existence. Steadily Washington rebuilt his flagging troops, overcoming desertion and persistent food shortages.

When here, nothing could have prepared the Continental Army for the worst winter of the 18th century. Twenty-eight blizzards pounded the slopes and whipped through the wooden huts that were cut from 600 acres of hardwood forests here. His greatest foe, however, was disease. An outbreak of smallpox threatened to decimate the small army and Washington ordered the little known and, to many, horrifying procedure of inoculation. Some indeed died but most of his troops did not contract the deadly pox.

Morristown National Historic Park, created in 1933 in the heart of New Jersey, is most attractive for your dog at the Jockey Hollow Encampment Area. You can hike with your dog through open and airy forests with long views through the trees. Four main dog-friendly trails circle the Jockey Hollow Encampment. The 6.5-mile *Grand Loop Trail*, blazed in white, circles the park but doesn't visit any historical attractions without a detour. It is also the only trail that cannot be accessed from the centrally located Trail Center.

The *Aqueduct Loop Trail* and the stacked loop *Primrose Brook Trail* are two of the prettiest rambles with your dog in the park as they trace some of the many gurgling streams that once attracted the Colonial Army. The long-distance *Patriot's Path* links Jockey Hollow to the New Jersey Encampment Area and neighboring parks and contributes mightily to the total of 27 well-groomed miles of Morristown trails.

Morristown, New Jersey
(973) 543-4030
www.nps.gov/morr/

Saratoga National Historic Park (New York)

Saratoga National Historic Park preserves 3,200 acres of battlefield where American revolutionaries, behind General Horatio Gates, prevented British control of the Hudson River in the Fall of 1777. In two battles, three weeks apart, the British suffered 1,000 casualties and General John Burgoyne, awaiting reinforcements that never arrived, was forced to surrender an army of 6,000 men. By thwarting the British initiative to split the Colonies in half, the Americans went a long way towards gaining their independence. Saratoga is one of the most famous and influential battlefields in the world and the National Park Service maintains the ground much as it looked more than 230 years ago.

The *Wilkinson National Recreation Trail* is a 4.2-mile loop across the property, much of which was farmland during the Revolution. The trail is named for the lieutenant who drew maps of the Saratoga Battlefield in 1777. Save for a single dip into the Great Ravine, this is easy canine hiking across rolling grasslands with islands of airy deciduous woods. The route uses part of the roads British troops took to and from the two battles. Interpretive stops include British and German redoubts (outlined in red and white posts).

The .6-mile *Freeman Loop* visits the site of some of the fiercest fighting on John Freeman's farm. If you drive the auto tour road you will find additional short explorations, including a one-mile loop trail that passes the gravesite of Brigadier General Simon Fraser, the spirited core of the British troops. There is no water along the park trails so on hot days a canine canteen will certainly be in order.

Behind the Breymann Redoubt, Station C, on the *Wilkinson Trail*, is the unique Boot Monument. The boot in question belonged to American battle hero Benedict Arnold (before he switched sides to the British). Arnold rode through a cross-fire in front of the defensive position to secure victory and recieved a second wound in his leg. The marble boot monument does not mention the eventual traitor's name.

Stillwater, New York
(518) 664-9821
www.nps.gov/sara/

Valley Forge National Historic Park (Pennsylvania)

The most famous name in the American Revolution comes to us from a small iron forge built along Valley Creek in the 1740s. After a disastrous campaign in the Fall of 1777 George Washington had left Philadelphia in the hands of the British and retreated to a defensible winter campsite out of harm's way but close enough to keep an eye on the British in their toasty Philadelphia homes. During the winter of 1777-78, as Valley Forge grew to be the third largest city in America, hundreds of soldiers died from sickness and disease. No battles were fought here but Valley Forge, the site where the American army was born, became a symbol for the young nation. After the Revolution, the land reverted to fields and Valley Forge was forgotten. America's interest in Valley Forge was rekindled during a Centennial in 1878 and preservation efforts eventually began with the Potts House, now known as Washington's Headquarters.

There are four marked trails in Valley Forge National Historical Park, plus miles of unmarked hikes. The *Multi-Use Trail* loops the Colonial defensive lines and Grand Parade Ground and visits George Washington's headquarters. Panoramic field vistas of the historic grounds are found all along the paved trail's six-mile length. The *Valley Creek Trail* is a flat, linear 1.2-mile walk along Valley Creek, past the original Upper Forge site.

Near the Valley Creek, beginning at the Artificer's Shops on Route 23, is the eastern terminus of the 133-mile *Horse-Shoe Trail* that ends at the *Appalachian Trail* in Hershey, Pennsylvania. In the park, the trail climbs steeply through the woods up Mount Misery, the natural southern defensive boundary of the Valley Forge camp. The historic walking path, so-named as it was built for rider and walker, quickly incorporates back roads and private property and is not worth following outside the park.

Across the Schuylkill River, at Pawlings Farm, a spiderweb of unmarked trails will take your dog away from the tourists; the 3-mile linear *Schuylkill River Trail* hugs the river for its entire route and provides ample access for canine aquatics as it interprets this out-of-the-way area of the encampment.

Valley Forge, Pennsylvania
(610) 783-1077
www.nps.gov/vafo

Yorktown Battlefield (Virginia)

By 1781, fighting in the Revolutionary War had continued for the better part of six years with no real resolution in sight. The British, frustrated by Nathanael Greene's continuing efforts to thwart their southern expedition, contented themselves with raiding parties in the Colonies.

In the summer of 1781 Lord Cornwallis set about fortifying Yorktown and Gloucester Point but on September 5 the French Navy and Admiral Francois de Grasse engaged a British reinforcement fleet and inflicted enough damage to force the British Navy back to New York.

General George Washington followed the French fleet down the coast with an Army of more than 17,000 men and laid siege to Yorktown. Without reinforcements, the 8,300 British soldiers had no choice but to surrender 19 days later, triggering talks that would end the American Revolution.

Yorktown doesn't maintain formal hiking trails - the park is traversed by two driving loops - but there are plenty of opportunities to explore the battlefield with your dog on foot. The historic site is graced by an abundance of trees and rolling hills in a park-like setting. Turnouts and wayside exhibits afford easy access to these canine leg stretchers.

A prime stop is at the reconstructed Redoubts 9 and 10, which anchored the east end of the British line. The Americans under Alexander Hamilton assaulted Redoubt 10 and the French stormed Redoubt 9. After intense hand-to-hand fighting both earthen forts were overrun in less than thirty minutes.

The Battlefield Tour is a 7-mile driving loop that could actually be hiked with your dog; traffic is generally light and there is plenty of room to step off the paved roadway if necessary. Footpaths also connect to the hiking trail system of the adjacent Newport News Park.

Yorktown, Virignia
(757) 898-3400
www.nps.gov/colo

TOUR
IDEA #86: DOGGIN' THE AMERICAN CIVIL WAR

Nothing has a greater hold on the imagination of American history buffs than the Civil War. Travelers can find some remnant of the War Between The States in every state. Civil War battlefield sites are prominent in every southern state and can be found as far west as Arizona. Here are just a few of the important stops you will make when planning a vacation with your dog touring the American Civil War...

Antietam National Battlefield

On September 17, 1862, Robert E. Lee's first attempt to invade the North came to a climax. After his smashing victory at the First Battle of Bull Run in August, General Lee marched his army of 41,000 Southerners against George McClellan's 87,000-man Army of the Potomac.

When silence fell again across the field, Antietam had become "The Bloodiest Day of the Civil War." Federal losses were 12,410, Confederate losses 10,700. The fighting was indecisive, but Lee's initial foray into the North was over. Great Britain now hesitated to recognize the new Confederate government and President Abraham Lincoln had the opportunity he needed to issue the Emancipation Proclamation, freeing all slaves in the states in rebellion.

The 8.5-mile interpretive driving tour of the battlefield is one-way so it is really too far to do on foot with your dog but there are plenty of places to park and get out to explore, including the solemn "Bloody Lane" - an old sunken road separating area farms where the dead and wounded were piled two to five feet deep in the dirt.

One place that demands to be explored on foot is the Burnside Bridge, southeast of Sharpsburg. Union General Ambrose Burnside and his 12,000-man force attempted to cross this 125-foot span over Antietam Creek at 9:30 a.m. on the morning of the battle but were held off by 450 Confederate sharpshooters hidden in the bluffs on the other side of the creek. The federals were not able to cross the bridge until early afternoon. At the Burnside Bridge you can access the *Snavely Ford Trail*, a 2.5-mile footpath that traces the creek and conveys the agrarian feel of the area when two armies clashed here.

Sharpsburg, Maryland
(301) 432-5124
www.nps.gov/anti/

Battlefields of Manassas (Virginia)

The Manassas Gap and the Orange and Alexandria railroads crossed in Manassas, a surveyor's decision in the 1850s that would transform this small farming community into one of America's best-known towns. Twice in the first two years of the Civil War the Northern and Southern armies clashed five miles north of town near a creek called Bull Run, resulting in 30,000 casualties in an attempt to control that railroad junction.

On July 21, 1861 the Civil War was expected to end. The fully-equipped Union Army under General Irvin McDowell was prepared to take the field for the first time at Bull Run. The complete submission of the rebels was such a certainty the Federal troops were accompanied by picnickers and sightseers. After ten hours of bloody fighting the Union Army was in retreat towards Washington and it was apparent this was not going to be a one-battle conflict.

The armies returned to Bull Run a year later, seasoned and spirited. Robert E. Lee's Army of Northern Virginia was at the peak of its power and he outmaneuvered General John Pope's Union Army in three days of struggle beginning August 28. With his masterful victory here Lee was able to carry the war to the North for the first time.

Two trails that interpret the critical clashes over this ground that retains much of its wartime character. Each route covers more than five miles and offers a pleasing mix of open-field and woods hiking over moderate terrain. The *First Manassas Trail* takes in Bull Run and the Stone Bridge where the first shots were fired. It also features more open fields. The *Second Manassas Trail* across the western section of the park is the preferred route to take your dog on a busy day. If time is limited take the one-mile *Henry Hill Loop Trail* around the Visitor Center where the critical fighting in the first battle of the Civil War took place. The trail follows part of the Southern Line where General Thomas J. Jackson stood firm an became immortalized as "Stonewall."

Manassas, Virginia
(703) 361-1339
www.nps.gov/mana

Chickamauga National Military Park (Georgia)

Two desperate battles were fought in this area in the fall of 1863. Twenty-five years after the war ended, President Benjamin Harrison signed a bill on August 19, 1890, establishing this site as America's first national military park. Today it remains the nation's largest with wooded trails and open fields aplenty for your dog to roam on more than 5,400 acres scattered with more than 1,600 markers, monuments, cannons and tablets.

The prize at stake along the Chickamauga Creek was the city of Atlanta and access to the heart of the Confederacy. It was a new type of battle - fought in the woods and heavy underbrush and not in open fields. The Confederate forces of Braxton Brag maneuvered brilliantly and won a victory that forced the Union Army to withdraw from the field. But it came at a terrible cost. Of the 66,000 Southern troops more than 18,000 became casualties; the Union losses surmounted 16,000. The Union forces withdrew to Chattanooga where the Confederate siege almost subdued the Federal army. But on November 23 Ulysses S. Grant directed an all-day attack that opened the city and cleared the way to Atlanta.

The battle grounds can be explored with a 7-mile self-guided driving tour or you can park your vehicle and explore on foot with your dog. Use a combination of wooded footpaths, multi-use concrete walks and open fields to investigate the battlefield. Metal markers (blue and red) are positioned so the field appears as it did to the generals trying to direct their scattered troops through the woods.

Fort Oglethorpe, Georgia
(706) 866-9241
www.nps.gov/chch

Gettysburg National Military Park (Pennsylvania)

Gettysburg National Military Park, where Civil War Union forces halted a Confederate invasion commanded by Robert E. Lee, in south-central Pennsylvania is America's most-visited battlefield. A good way for dog owners to digest the most analyzed three days in American history (July 1-3, 1863) - and escape the crowds - is to leave the auto tour and explore the grounds on foot. The battlefield swallows the town of Gettysburg although most of your walking will take place in quiet farmland and boulder-studded hillsides south of the village where the climactic fighting took place.

A full day to hike with your dog can be crafted on the 9-mile *Billy Yank Trail* and the 3.5-mile *Johnny Reb Trail*. Part of the Gettysburg Heritage Trails Program, printed guides lead the way on these rambles. Shorter canine hikes include the one-mile *High Water Mark Trail* that interprets the final desperate Confederate race across nearly one mile of open ground by the 12,000-man "Pickett's Charge" and an historic climb that twists through the woods to the summit of Big Round Top, a crucial Union position on the top of Cemetery Ridge.

While at Gettysburg, also take time to hike with your dog on informal trails leading to more than 1,400 statues and memorials erected to remember this most historic of American ground, where more men fell than in any battle ever fought in the United States.

Gettysburg, Pennsylvania
(717) 334-1124
www.nps.gov/gett/

Monocacy National Battlefield (Maryland)

In 1847 a farm was cobbled together here from several small tracts that were purchased in 1862 by John Worthington. This farm saw withering action on July 7, 1864 when Union general Lew Wallace, better known as the author of Ben Hur: A Tale of The Christ, took up a defensive position with 2,700 men at Monocacy Junction, planning to check the advance of General Jubal Early and his 18,000 Confederates. The bloody battle that came two days later was a decisive defeat for the outnumbered Federals, but the delay it caused Early probably kept Washington from falling into Confederate hands. In 1928, Glenn Worthington petitioned Congress to create a National Military Park at Monocacy. The bill passed but acquisition of land for preserving the Monocacy National Battlefield did not take place for another half-century.

Much of the battlefield is in private hands but there is still plenty to see in the farm land that is virtually unchanged since the Civil War. At the park Visitor Center an interpretive half-mile trail in light woods leads to the Monocacy River. Down the road, a stacked loop explores the Worthington farm. The park is devoted as much to the natural evolution of the landscape as to remembrance of battles fought. Of particular interest are the gnarly Osage-orange trees that were grown as natural fences. The terrain grows steep in places but overall this is a relaxed hike for your dog on natural trails and graveled farm roads. All told there are more than three miles of trails at Worthington Farm.

Frederick, Maryland
(301) 662-3515
www.nps.gov/mono/

Pea Ridge National Military Park (Arkansas)

On March 7, 1862, snow still covered the frozen ground when the Union Army of the Southwest, 10,500 troops under Brigadier General Samuel R. Curtis, clashed with 16,000 Confederates commanded by Major General Earl Van Dorn. The battle raged at two separate sites: Leetown and Elkhorn Tavern.

The Union, most of whom were Germans who spoke no English, prevailed at Leetown while the outcome at Elkhorn Tavern was less decisive, although Southerners left the field under heavy Union artillery bombardment. When the Battle of Pea Ridge ended the next day, the State of Missouri was secure for the Union.

Dogs are welcome throughout Pea Ridge, the first battlefield west of the Mississippi River to be declared a national military park. It is also the largest. The park's hiking trail is seven miles long and goes through both natural and historic areas of the park. Shorter loops are accessible from the Elkhorn Tavern should your dog desire.

Rogers, Arkansas
(501) 451-8122)
www.nps.gov/peri/

Shiloh National Military Park (Tennessee)

The first major western battle of the Civil War was fought along the Tennessee River on April 6 and 7, 1862. The prize was possession of major railroads and control of the lower Mississippi River valley. General Albert Sidney Johnston led 44,000 Confederates in a surprise attack on Ulysses S. Grant's 40,000 Union troops in the fields and forests surrounding a small log church called "Shiloh meeting house."

The Confederates pushed Grant back two miles that first day, but Johnston was mortally wounded near Peach Orchard. Grant's reinforcements arrived at Pittsburg Landing the next day, enabling him to overwhelm new commander General P.G. T. Beauregard. The two-day carnage claimed 23,746 men recorded killed, wounded or missing. Shiloh was the bloodiest battle since the war began, forcing Grant to conclude, "I gave up all idea of saving the Union except by complete conquest."

Exploration of the military park is primarily via a 9.5-mile driving tour but there are many chances to get your dog out and explore the quiet, wooded hillsides, mostly on historic dirt roads. Riverside Drive rolls down from the Visitor Center to the Tennessee River and visits the Shiloh Indian Mounds, a National Historic Landmark.

Shiloh, Tennessee
(901) 689-5696
www.nps.gov/shil/

TOUR
IDEA #87: DOGGIN' AMERICA'S COASTAL FORTS

The first thing European settlers did when they arrived on our shores was build a fort. From these crude wilderness earthworks and log blockhouses to the massive masonry fortifications of the 19th century, forts played an important role in American defense through World War II. Today forts have morphed into military bases that are cities in their own right. Many of the old forts remain wholly or partially intact, original or restored, and make unique destinations with your dog. Plotting out a fascinating canine tour down the East Coast you would want to hit...

Fort Popham (Maine)

Fort Popham was one of the Third System of coastal fortifications developed by the United States during the first half of the 19th century and characterized by greater structural durability than earlier works. Nearly all of the more than 30 Third System forts built after 1816 still exist.

Popham, begun in 1862 to protect the mouth of the Kennebec River and the Bath Iron Works, was never fully completed although it was garrisoned until World War I. The State of Maine picked up Fort Popham for $6,600 in 1924 and converted it into an historic site.

Today Fort Popham is one of the best places in Maine to bring your dog. The tail-friendly beach extends for more than a mile and a hike here passes not only the semi-circular granite fort but a life-saving station and offshore lighthouses perched on rocky atolls.

Phippsburg, Maine
(207) 389-1335
www.state.me.us/cgi-bin/doc/parks/find_one_name.pl?park_id=40

Fort Wetherill (Rhode Island)

For most of its time in American history these high granite bluffs looking down on the East Passage of Narraganett Bay have led a military life, albeit deactivated for the most part. Colonists built an earthen battery here and when it was known as Dumpling Rock the United States built Fort Dumpling in the early 1800s.

Around 1900 the fortifications were beefed up and the fort was renamed in honor of Captain Alexander Wetherill, a local infantryman killed in the Battle of San Juan in the Spanish American War. During World War II the old fort saw its last active duty - as a training center. It closed in 1946; the guns hidden in the cliffs never used. In 1972 the State of Rhode Island acquired the property for a park.

The canine hiking at Fort Wetherill is mostly on narrow dirt trails out to rocky promontories overlooking the sea. What they lack in distance they more than make up for in aesthetic appeal. At land's end the short hike is to the remains of the old battery. The only marked trail is a Nature Trail but don't get excited - it only goes up and down a small hill between parking lots. Don't neglect it, however, for the views are riveting.

Jamestown, Rhode Island
(401) 423-1771
www.riparks.com/fortweth.htm

Camp Hero (New York)

The federal government first established a base at the strategic tip of Long Island in 1929, naming the fort for Major General Andrew Hero, Jr., who was the Army's Chief of Coast Artillery at the time. During World War II, with German U-boats menacing the East Coast, the installation was bulked up with seaplane hangars, barracks and docks and renamed Camp Hero. All the buildings were built to look like an innocuous New England fishing village. Concrete bunkers had windows painted on them and base buildings sprouted ornamental roofs with fake dormers. The gymnasium was made to look like a church with a false steeple. At its peak, the camp housed 600 enlisted men and 37 officers.

There is plenty of unique wandering to be found for your dog in old Camp Hero. The *Paumanok Path* begins (or ends) its journey across Long Island here. You can explore the buildings still standing in the military area. Bunkers and odd structures are seemingly around every turn. Your dog will find elevation changes as the trails visit the top of fragile bluffs and work down to cobble beaches. Although much of the surface is broken macadam or sandy jeep roads you can also find traditional woods-walking on paths like the *Battery 113 Trail*. Oh, and stick to the roads and trails - it is not impossible to stumble upon unexploded ordnance. The trails lead down to the Atlantic Ocean where the surf is often frisky enough to dissuade all but the most avid dog paddler.

The dominant man-made structure remaining in Camp Hero is a massive AN/FPS-35 long range radar used in the early 1960s. Only 12 of these radars, capable of picking up objects 200 miles away, were ever built. The antennas weighed 70 to 80 tons and were perched on concrete tower bases built 80 feet high. There were numerous bugs with the giant radars and all have been dismantled except for the one at Camp Hero. Boaters on Long Island Sound lobbied to save the installation since it was a better landmark during the day than the lighthouse next door. At least that's the official story. Others believe the radar was used by the government in top-secret time travel experiments called the Montauk Project.

Montauk, New York
(631) 668-3781
nysparks.state.ny.us/parks/info.asp?parkID=82

Fort Mott (New Jersey)

Fort Mott was envisioned as part of a three-fort defense of Philadelphia that dangled across the Delaware River. Following the Civil War, work began on 11 gun emplacements but only two were completed when the fort was abandoned in 1876. In preparation for the Spanish-American War in 1896, Fort Mott, named to honor Major General Gershom Mott, a native of Bordentown, was completed and outfitted with three 10-inch and three 12-inch guns. The fort remained active until 1943, although during its last two decades the guns were dismantled and shipped elsewhere. In 1947 the State of New Jersey purchased Fort Mott as an historic site and opened the state park on June 24, 1951.

Fort Mott features a self-guiding walking tour through the 19th century defensive position that enables your dog to ramble into the gun batteries and ammunition magazines and to clamber on top of the massive protective parapet. This wall was built of concrete poured 35 feet thick with an additional 60 feet of earth piled in front. Landscaping made the fort look like a big hill from the Delaware River. Down by the river your water-loving dog will find a perfect sandy beach, wave action from the Delaware and plenty of driftwood to fetch.

In addition to this unique dog walk there is a groomed trail that winds through twelve-foot high swamp grasses to Finn's Point National Cemetery, the final resting place for 2,436 Confederate soldiers who perished in a Civil War prisoner of war camp at Fort Delaware on Pea Patch Island in the river.

Pennsville, New Jersey
(856) 935-3218
www.state.nj.us/dep/parksandforests/parks/fortmott.html

Fort Howard (Maryland)

The British selected North Point, now part of Fort Howard Park and the southernmost point in Baltimore County, as the landing site for a 6-ship invasion force on September 12, 1814. In the pre-dawn hours 4,700 British marines disembarked here to begin a 17-mile march on Baltimore. Later that day the Americans engaged the force in the Battle of North Point, slowing the invaders and triggering a demoralizing chain of events for the British that hastened the end of the War of 1812. The army returned to North Point in 1899 to build Fort Howard as the headquarters for the coastal defense of Baltimore. The base was turned over to Baltimore County for use as a park in 1973.

The *Endicott Trail* is a paved walk through the "Bulldog at Baltimore's Gate" that enables your dog to wander through the gun batteries, ammunition magazines and earth-covered parapets that are camoflauged from the open water. Although a dummy hand grenade was found in the picnic area in 1988 it is unlikely your dog will sniff out any old ordnance here.

Where else can your dog climb into an actual battery and scan the Patapsco River just like gunnery officers who once aimed guns capable of accurately firing 1,000-pound projectiles eight miles?

North Point, Maryland
(410) 887-7259

Fort McHenry (Maryland)

Francis Scott Key was a 35-year old lawyer selected as an envoy to secure the release of American doctor William Beanes during the War of 1812. Sailing under a flag of truce, Key boarded the British flagship *HMS Tonnant*. His mission was a success but Key was detained as the British bombardment of Fort McHenry, a star-shaped defender of Baltimore Harbor built in the late 1700s, began on the morning of September 13, 1814. After nearly two days of launching 1500 bombshells, the British abandoned their invasion. Properly inspired, amateur poet Key scribbled out the lines to "The Defence of Fort McHenry" on the back of an envelope. It became the "Star-Spangled Banner" when performed by a Baltimore actor a month later and was adopted as America's national anthem on March 3, 1931. Two years later, Fort McHenry came under the direction of the National Park Service and today is the only area designated both a national moument and historic shrine.

Fort McHenry rests on a 43-acre appendage of land in the mouth of Baltimore Harbor. There are large grassy open fields around the brick fort with plenty of room for romping for the dog. Cool breezes from the water and a grove of sycamore trees on the south side provide relief from the sun if needed. A concrete trail runs along all three sides of the seawall to create a loop of the park with plenty of opportunity to soak up historical monuments and shrines. A restored tidal wetland area keeps feeding and migratory birds arriving.

Baltimore, Maryland
(410) 962-4290
www.nps.gov/fomc/

Fort Washington (Maryland)

The first Fort Washington was completed here in 1809 and was the only defense of the nation's capital until the Civil War. Occupying high ground overlooking the Potomac River, the fort was a formidable obstacle to any enemy contemplating a water assault on Washington. When it became obsolete and a defensive installation the post was used as an infantry training facility.

Now a 341-acre recreational park, you can take your dog for a hike through the assorted military structures (not allowed in the masonry fort itself - one of the few seacoast American forts still in its original form) and on trails that lead to views of the nation's capital and the Virginia shore, as well as down to the

Potomac itself. The Fort Washington lighthouse is located near the Potomac River on park property.

Fort Washington, Maryland
(301) 763-4600
www.nps.gov/fowa/

Fort Macon (North Carolina)

The need for the defense of Beaufort Inlet became apparent in the early dawn hours of 1747 when Spanish raiders sacked the town of Beaufort. It took another 50 years for a formal masonry fort to be completed on the tip of Bogue Banks but in 1825 it was washed away by a hurricane. In the 1840s the critical task of keeping back the sea was assigned to a young Army engineer named Robert E. Lee.

At the start of the Civil War, North Carolina quickly took control of the fort but the garrison surrendered on April 26, 1862 to Generals John C. Parke and Ambrose Burnside after a land and sea bombardment. For the duration of the war Fort Macon served as a coaling station for Union navy ships. Afterwards the seacoast brick fort was a federal prison for a time and was eventually abandoned following the Spanish-American War in 1903. The state purchased the property for one dollar in 1924 and it became North Carolina's second state park.

You can bring your dog into the inner court of the pentagonal fort, enclosed by 54-inch thick outer walls of brick and stone, and examine the restored exhibits. Formal hiking at Fort Macon State Park is reserved for the .4-mile *Elliot Coues Nature Trail* that runs through low-lying sand dunes between the Beaufort Inlet and the fort. But this is just an appetizer for your dog in the park.

The prime attraction for canine adventurers here is the best dune-backed beach walking on North Carolina's Crystal Coast. In addition to the wide sand at low tide your dog can explore the shallow waters and crannies around the jetty at the end of the island. And when your dog's thoughts turn to cool grass he is welcome to scramble atop the ramparts of Fort Macon. Dogs are allowed throughout the park except in the bathhouse or at the swimming area.

Atlantic Beach, North Carolina
(252) 726-3775
www.ncparks.gov/Visit/parks/foma/main.php

Fort Fisher (North Carolina)

The largest earthwork fort in the Confederacy was constructed here to keep Wilmington open to blockade runners during the Civil War. Until July 1862, Fort Fisher was little more than several sand batteries mounting fewer than two dozen guns. Colonel William Lamb, working on designs created in Russia for the Crimean War, employed as many as 1,000 men, many of them slaves, to create one mile of sea defense and one-third of a mile of land defense.

The Union had long planned an assault on Fort Fisher but did not feel confident to do so until December 24, 1864. For two days the sand and earth fortifications absorbed Union shells and the force withdrew. On January 12 the fort was bombarded by land and sea and finally capitulated after six hours of fierce fighting. It was considered the greatest land-sea battle of the Civil War and helped seal the ultimate doom of the Confederacy.

Most canine hikers will bring their dogs to Fort Fisher for its seven miles of tail-friendly white sand beaches. Head south from the Visitor Center and you will discover nothing but open, dune-backed beach ahead of you.

But there are a couple of fun options here as well. The *Basin Trail* slips almost unnoticed from the south end of the parking lot into what appears to be a maritime forest. You twist through a maze of wax myrtles for only a few steps, however, before bursting into the open with nothing but a flat expanse of sand in every direction. Forging on, you cross a marsh and soon bring your dog to an old World War II bunker. Further on, your destination is a a platform overlooking The Basin a half-mile away.

On the north boundary of the park is the Fort Fisher State Recreation Area where you can hike among the formidable earthwork mounds that give a clear view of the Cape Fear River and the strategic importance of the site. A captured cannon and relics recovered from sunken blockade runners are among the treasures on display.

In 1955, 62-year old Robert Harrill left behind a wake of failed jobs and relationships in the Carolina mountains for a life of solace at the seashore. He came to settle in the old World War II bunker at Fort Fisher where he would live for 17 years. He was tabbed the "Fort Fisher Hermit" but he was far from alone. He welcomed all visitors and more than 100,000 made the pilgrimage over the years to listen to his philosophies of simple life. In 1969 the state of North Carolina called him the Tarheel State's second largest tourist attraction behind only the battleship *USS North Carolina*. Not that Robert Harrill ever lived truly alone - he often had a dog by his side.

Kure Beach, North Carolina
(910) 458-5798
www.ncparks.gov/Visit/parks/fofi/main.php

Fort Moultrie (South Carolina)

In January 1776 Charlestonians began to defend their town by constructing a fort on Sullivan's Island. Six months later the palmetto log-and-sand fortification showed only two walls facing the harbor and two incomplete walls exposed to the rear. Meanwhile British amphibious forces were massing offshore.

Rather than sail by the meager American defenses into Charleston, Sir Henry Clinton chose to destroy the unnamed fort. Nine powerful warships opened fire on the morning of June 28. The crude fort proved to be an ideal bastion, as the spongy palmetto wood received the cannon balls without splintering. The sand mortar absorbed what the palmetto could not. After nine hours the British fleet and its more than 200 guns was forced to retire. Charleston would remain unmolested for three more years.

The little fort was subsequently named for its commander, William Moultrie. After the Revolution Fort Moultrie was neglected, and by 1791 little remained. Under a nationwide system of seacoast fortifications, Fort Moultrie was rebuilt in 1798 and remained active until World War II.

Dogs are welcome on the grounds but not inside the fort and not on the ferry to Fort Sumter or at Fort Sumter if arriving by private boat. Out on the grounds is the Cannon Walk with artillery pieces dating from the Civil War that tell the story of the evolution of seacoast defense weaponry during a period of rapid technological development. The maze of sand-and-grass paths that wander around Fort Moultrie and Battery Jasper make for an easy open-air exploration for your dog. The real adventure comes when you split a small dune and arrive on the beach at Sullivan's Island. Here your dog can go off-leash much of the year and a couple of miles of sandy beach await. Fort Sumter, where the first shots of the Civil War rang out, is clearly seen in Charleston Harbor from the beach.

Sullivan's Island, South Carolina
(843) 883-3123
www.nps.gov/fosu/historyculture/fort_moultrie.htm

Fort Pulaski (Georgia)

With an estimated 25 million bricks and seven-and-a-half foot thick walls, Fort Pulaski, built on Cockspur Island in the salt marshes near the mouth of the Savannah River, was considered impregnable, ranked as one of the "most spectacular defense structures" ever built in the United States. When it came under attack for the first time the fort succumbed in barely more than one day.

Georgia militia occupied the fort, manned only by an ordnance sergeant and a civilian, without resistance before the Civil War on January 3, 1861. Federal troops launched a bombardment 15 months later using experimental rifled cannons. The new weapons quickly breached Fort Pulaski's walls and threatened to blow up its main magazine containing 40,000 pounds of gunpowder. The Confederates quickly surrendered and defense strategy worldwide was changed forever.

Today Fort Pulaski is one of the best forts to explore with your dog, who can poke around throughout the property. It is one of the best-preserved of America's early masonry forts, including four-foot deep moats crossed on drawbridges and a maze of bulbous earthworks that hide tunnels of powder magazines. Pock-marked walls still display craters where Union artillery tore two feet into the red bricks.

Outside the fort, the *Lighthouse Overlook Trail* moseys a mile through a line of myrtles and palms at the edge of the island on paw-friendly wood chips and soft dirt. At the end your dog can cool off with a dip in the Savannah River in the shadow of the Cockspur Island Lighthouse.

Savannah, Georgia
(912) 786-5787
www.nps.gov/fopu

Fort Clinch (Florida)

Occupied by both Union and Confederate troops during the Civil War, Fort Clinch, named for General Duncan Lamont Clinch of Florida's Seminole Wars fame, was never actually finished and was made obsolete by the rifled barrels used at Fort Pulaski. In the end, although the fort was of strategic importance, neither side ever engaged its guns in battle here.

Converted into a state park in 1935, Fort Clinch is in a remarkable state of preservation. All told the state park encompasses 1,153 acres at the tip of Amelia Island. Your dog is welcome at Fort Clinch but cannot go on the beach.

Fernandina Beach, Florida
(904) 277-7274
www.floridastateparks.org/fortclinch/

Fort Pickens (Florida)

Fort Pickens occupies the western tip of Santa Rosa Island and was the largest of a series of forts built to protect Pensacola harbor. Constructed with 21.5 million bricks, the pentagonal bastion was completed in 1834. It would be occupied off and on until 1947. Fort Pickens saw much early action in the Civil War after the lightly fortified Federal naval yard in Pensacola was given over to the Rebels. Fort Pickens was able to be supplied by sea so the Union company held out. On May 9, 1862, the Confederates abandoned Pensacola, and Fort Pickens, once a linchpin in the Union blockade, became a prison. In the 1880s, Geronimo and other members of the Chiricahua-Apache tribe were prisoners here.

In 2004, Hurricane Ivan, which at the time set a record for 36 consecutive six-hour periods at Category 4 strength, swamped Santa Rosa Island. Fort Pickens Road into the park has been closed ever since with a scheduled re-opening in 2009. In the meantime, dog owners can hike down the road and enjoy the solitude of the barrier island. Dogs are not permitted on the beach.

Pensacola, Florida
(850) 934-2600
www.nps.gov/guis/planyourvisit/fort-pickens.htm

TOUR

IDEA #88: DOGGIN' AMERICA'S LIGHTHOUSES

You say you want to tour the East Coast but forts and military history are a bit grim for you? You're looking for a tour a tad more romantic? Then take out a map and start charting your way via America's lighthouses. Your dog won't be allowed to take standard lighthouse tours, of course, but there is often much more in store for your dog at historic lights like these...

West Quoddy Head Light (Maine)

Perched on 80-foot black rock cliffs, Quoddy Head State Park is the easternmost point of land in the United States. Come early and your dog can be the first dog in America to see the sun rise.

West Quoddy Head Light, built in 1808, still guides ships through the

Grand Manan Channel with its original Fresnel lens. The moist climate around Quoddy Head is frequently foggy and the lighthouse was one of the first to employ a fog bell that was eventually replaced with a steam-powered foghorn. The lawn around the squat, red-and-white striped lighthouse is ideal for relaxing with your dog and scanning the sea for whales in the channel.

Some of the best canine hiking directly on the rocky Maine Coast is found at Quoddy Head State Park. Your dog will love this *Coastal Trail* at land's end; eagerly bounding to the top of the many hillocks to see what awaits on the other side before dropping to water level at Carrying Place Cove where the shallow waters are ideal for a doggie dip. The return trip can be made over the inland *Thompson Trail* through light forests of shallow-rooted white spruce and hardy balsam trees battling the wind and salt spray. Many of these arboreal warriors remain standing after losing the fight, leaving spectral sculptures along the coast. A side trip leads to the Carrying Place Cove Bog, a National Natural Landmark. This subarctic remnant is home to plants that survive in low temperatures and thin, non-nurturing soil. Here carnivorous plants such as the sundew and pitcher plants gobble insects for nutrients unavailable in the soil.

Lubec, Maine
(207) 733-0911
www.state.me.us/cgi-bin/doc/parks/find_one_name.pl?park_id=10

Montauk Point Lighthouse (New York)

At the eastern tip of Long Island the land rises slightly. The Montaukett tribe who reigned over this area called the hill "Womponamon," an Algonquian word meaning "to the east." Great tribal councils were convened from the point.

During the American Revolution the British Royal Navy controlled Montauk Point, lighting enormous fires on the bluff to guide its warships stationed in nearby Gardiner's Bay. When the British departed after the war the American government quickly realized the importance of a lighthouse on Montauk Point. In 1792 Congress appropriated $255.12 to buy land upon which a light was to be built to guide boats past the perilous rocks. The first whale oil was lit in 1797 in New York's first lighthouse and America's fourth. The historic Montauk Lighthouse was the first building seen by millions of immigrants sailing to America.

In Montauk Point State Park dogs can only go west of the concession stand which works out well since that is where the trails are. You didn't really want to

use the playground did you? There are two trailheads here. The red-blazed trail
dives towards the shoreline down a service road and the green-blazed *Money Pond
Trail* starts a little ways up the road.

The Money Pond is where the pirate Captain Kidd supposedly stashed
two treasure chests but no loot has ever been found. Your dog may feel as if he's
discovered gold on this tight, twisty route however. The sandy surface is a delight
on the paw and the many dips and rolls are certain to pique any dog's interest.

The *Money Pond Trail* joins the yellow-blazed *Seal Haulout Trail* for a
longer journey out to Oyster Pond and the red-blazed stem that closes the hiking
loop. The further your dog hikes from the point the sandier the beaches become.

Montauk, New York
(631) 668-36781
nysparks.state.ny.us/parks/info.asp?parkID=136

Sandy Hook Light (New Jersey)

The Sandy Hook Lighthouse has been guiding ships past the nasty shoals off
New Jersey for 240 years. You can walk your dog around the grassy base of this
National Historic Landmark and well-behaved dogs can even sit in on the short
video history of the illumination of New York harbor. While looking at the old
brick sentinel, you can grasp the dynamics of land-building at Sandy Hook - when
first built, the lighthouse was a mere 500 feet from shore and today is more than
one and one-half miles from the northern end of the peninsula.

Ships sailing into New York harbor have always needed to navigate around
the shifting sands of Sandy Hook. The first lighthouse was built from lottery
funds in 1764. The strategic peninsula has been fortified since the War of 1812
and the Hook was the site of the first United States Army Proving Ground. The
last active military base, Fort Hancock, closed in 1974 but the United States
Coast Guard still maintains an active presence at Sandy Hook.

Seven miles of ocean beach curl around to reveal views of the Brooklyn
skyline and the Verrazano Narrows Bridge, the longest suspension bridge in
the world when it opened in 1964. Open all year to dogs are short nature trails
through a 264-acre maritime forest that holds the greatest concentration of
American Holly on the East Coast.

Atlantic Highlands, New Jersey
(718) 338-3988
www.nps.gov/gate/

Cape May Lighthouse (New Jersey)

The clean, white tower at the bottom of New Jersey is the third beacon to guide ships around the tip of Delaware Bay. This one has been standing since 1859; its light at 157 feet was automated in 1946. Visitors can climb 199 steps to the top (no dogs).

The Cape May Light stands at Cape May Point State Park. In the interest of nesting shorebirds dogs are prohibited in the park from April 15 to September 15. But when permitted, this is a primo spot to bring your dog. The wide sandy beach provides hours of hiking time and a trio of short trails wind through the wetlands and marine forest fronting the beach. Cape May is also one of the premier birding spots in America. In the fall hundreds of hawks use this migratory route favored by songbirds, dragonflies and Monarch butterflies.

Cape May Point, New Jersey
(609) 884-2159
www.state.nj.us/dep/parksandforests/parks/capemay.html#links

Cape Hatteras Lighthouse (North Carolina)

There are five lighthouses on the Outer Banks your dog can visit - three in the Cape Hatteras National Seashore. The oldest operating lighthouse in North Carolina is the 75-foot tower on Ocracoke Island and the 150-foot Bodie Island Lighthouse dates to 1872.

The most famous, and America's tallest at 208 feet, is the black-and-white swirl-striped Cape Hatteras Lighthouse. Its light can be seen 20 miles out to sea and has been reported to have been seen from 51 miles. Although your dog can't do it, you can climb the 268 steps to the top. The current location of the Hatteras Light is not the original - in 1999 the entire 208-foot structure was moved a half-mile away from the encroaching ocean. The journey took 23 days.

There is no better place for long hikes with your dog on dune-backed beaches than Cape Hatteras National Seashore but there are also a trio of short nature trails - one on each island - to try with your dog. The best of the lot is in Buxton Woods on Hatteras Island, near the Visitor Center and lighthouse. This trail bounds across gnarled pine and oak-covered dunes with marshy wetlands tossed into the mixto provide a shady respite from a day on the beach with your dog.

Manteo, North Carolina
(252) 473-2111
www.nps.gov/caha/planyourvisit/climbing-the-cape-hatteras-lighthouse.htm

Hunting Island Lighthouse (South Carolina)

The 5000-acre Hunting Island was once a hunting preserve, hence its name. Before that it was a stopover for sailors and pirates. Much of the park was developed as a Depression-era project and its 1120-foot fishing pier is one of the longest on the East Coast.

The lighthouse in the park, built in 1859 and destroyed in the Civil War before being rebuilt with cast iron plates designed to be dismantled and moved, is the only public light in South Carolina. When open, you can climb the 167 steps - without your dog - to the top for a commanding view of the shoreline.

Hunting Island State Park is one of the best places you can bring your dog. Dogs are allowed on the park trails and the ocean beach - four miles of natural sand - is open for long canine hikes beside the Atlantic waves.

There is a good chance that you have already seen Hunting Island. The Viet Nam scenes from the movie *Forrest Gump* were filmed here. The trees come right down to the beach and the lush, tropical feel of the vegetation indeed give off the aura of a jungle. A trail leads along the length of the inland lagoon - man-made from sand dredging - that is where Forrest saved Lieutenant Dan in the movie.

Hunting Island, South Carolina
(843) 838-2011
www.southcarolinaparks.com/park-finder/state-park/1019.aspx

Tybee Island Light Station (Georgia)

Tybee Island, gateway to the Savannah River, has sported a light since 1732, just about from the first day General James Oglethorpe founded the Georgia colony. The present black-and-white parfait lighthouse has been in place since 1916.

The light station stands in a residential area of Tybee Island, on a lot not much bigger than a modern suburban subdivision, and there is not much for your dog to do beyond a game of fetch in the grass. But the Tybee light rates a visit for you traveling companion nonetheless - a fine wood chip-covered dog park is only two short blocks away.

Tybee Island, Georgia
(912) 786-5801
www.tybeelighthouse.org/

St. Marks Lighthouse (Florida)

The St. Marks Lighthouse got off to an inauspicious start in 1830 when its walls were discovered to be hollow instead of solid and the builders were charged with deliberate fraud against the United States. Calvin Knowlton rebuilt the tower (with the only wooden staircase in any Florida lighthouse) and the light was properly commissioned in January 1831.

In 1842, with its base threatened by erosion, the original brick tower was dismantled and rebuilt further inland - just in time for the Great Hurricane of 1843 with angry 10-foot storm surges. Every building in the area was destroyed except the lighthouse. The 82-foot tower has remained stout ever since, even withstanding a Confederate attempt to blow it up during the Civil War. The last keeper retired in 1960 and now an automated St. Marks Light guides mariners across 15 miles of Apalachee Bay.

The Light is now part of the expansive St. Marks National Wildlife Refuge with over 68,000 acres under protection. At the lighthouse the *Levee Trail* and *Cedar Point Trail* introduce more hardy plants adapting to the whipping winds and salt spray. Your dog will only have to deal with the potentially harsh conditions for about one mile. The star walk for canine day hikers is the *Mounds Pool Interpretive Trail* that dips in and out of woods around freshwater and salt marshes. Highlights include close-up looks at Cabbage Palms, the Florida state tree.

St. Marks, Florida
(850) 925-6121
www.fws.gov/saintmarks/

DOGGIN' MOUNT RUSHMORE

Few visitors to the Black Hills in South Dakota leave without at least taking a look at Mount Rushmore. And if you are traveling with a dog, that is about all you will be able to do. Dogs are restricted to the parking lot area in the shadow of the world-famous mountain carving that took sculptor Gutzon Borglum 14 years to complete.

A better vacation for your dog is to actually follow in the footsteps of the four Presidents staring down from that mountain. Here are a few ideas...

TOUR
IDEA #89: DOGGIN' GEORGE WASHINGTON

George Washington is known not only as the "Father of Our Country" but the "Father of the American Foxhound." An avid foxhunter, he sought to breed a new type of dog to course the terrain around his estate at Mount Vernon. He crossed French hounds from his friend the Marquis de Lafayette, with his own smaller black-and-tan English hounds. Washington listed 30 new "American" foxhounds by name in his journal and hounds currently registered with the American Kennel Club are descended from those originals. The Father of Our Country often favored silly names for his beloved dogs: Drunkard, Tipler, Tipsy.

Here's another dog story about George Washington. During the American Revolution, two days after the Battle of Germantown outside of Philadelphia on October 6, 1777 a dog was found wandering in the American Camp. Inspecting the dog's collar it was apparent the dog, whose name and breed is lost to history, belonged to victorious British commander General William Howe, who remained at Germantown. Even with the loss of the Colonial capital of Philadelphia hanging over his head, General George Washington steadfastly adhered to the code of gentlemanly behavior in wartime by returning the dog with a handwritten note: "General Washington's compliments to General Howe. He does himself the pleasure to return him a dog, which accidentally fell into his hands, and by the inscription on the Collar appears to belong to General Howe."

For a fellow who lived almost 300 years ago, even before his life as commander of the Continental Army, George Washington got around quite a bit, both physically and, if we are to believe revelations that Martha Custis was quite the Colonial hottie, socially. You can cobble together an adventurous outdoor trip with your dog by tracing Washington's bootsteps...

George Washington's Birthplace (Virginia)

The Washington family saga in America began in 1657 when seafaring John Washington tarried in the Tidewater region of northern Virginia, befriended Nathaniel Pope and married Pope's daughter, Anne. The couple was given 700 acres on Mattox Creek as a wedding gift to start a tobacco farm. John eventually acquired more than 10,000 acres.

John Washington's grandson, Augustine claimed his inheritance on Bride's Creek and purchased more than 1,000 more acres on Pope's Creek. He fathered four children by Jane Butler who died at the age of 30 in 1729. Washington remarried a year later, taking as his bride Mary Ball, an orphaned daughter of a prominent planter. Their first child, George, was born in 1732 in the manor house at Pope's Creek. Although the family moved away when he was not yet four, George returned many times as an adolescent to work the family plantation.

On Christmas Day, 1779, while Washington was busy guiding the Continental Army, the manor house of his birth burned. It was never rebuilt. The birthplace was excavated in 1936 and the foundations preserved. Its location and dimensions are indicated by an oyster shell outline. A typical Tidewater house of the upper classes of the 1700s has been constructed on the property as a memorial to President George Washington.

The 538-acre George Washington Birthplace National Monument has been developed as a representative tobacco plantation and there is plenty of room to roam with your dog. Packed gravel paths lead around the house, fields, groves of trees and gardens. A wooded nature trail runs for a mile on a wide, leaf-littered natural surface through a coastal mixed pine forest. Plus, there is plenty of grass for your dog to trot on. And you can hike with your dog along the Potomac River beach. All in all, not a bad day for your dog.

Washington's Birthplace, Virginia
(804) 224-1732
www.nps.gov/gewa/

Sky Meadows State Park (Virginia)

When he was 16 years old George Washington joined a surveying expedition to western Virginia, garnering a valuable skill in a colony where land was being settled constantly. He was soon able to begin buying unclaimed wilderness land. One of his speculative parcels today is part of Sky Meadows State Park, a crown jewel in the Virginia state park system on the eastern slopes of the Blue Ridge Mountains.

The real star here for your dog are the meadows - there simply aren't many open-air hikes available across Northern Virginia. Be advised, however, that if you've never gone much beyond your neighborhood walk with your dog, this isn't the place for your first big adventure. Except for the *Snowden Trail* nature loop you will be hiking up a mountain at Sky Meadows.

The trail system offers about ten miles of marked paths that can be molded into canine hiking loops, the most popular being the North Ridge-South Ridge circuit. The *South Ridge Trail* utilizes an old farm road while the *North Ridge Trail* picks its way up the mountain like a traditional hiking trail. You are probably best served by going up the South Ridge since it is not as steep and views are longer coming down the North side.

For those looking for a full day of hiking with your dog the *Appalachian Trail* is 1.7 miles away and there are loop options there as well. If you just want to enjoy the meadows you can confine your dog's explorations to the *Piedmont Overlook Trail* on the North Ridge.

Delaplane, Virginia
(540) 592-3556
www.dcr.virginia.gov/state_parks/sky.shtml

Great Dismal Swamp National Wildlife Refuge (Virginia)

At the age of 21 Washington could be found down on the Virginia-North Carolina border organizing the Dismal Swamp Land Company. His plan was to drain the Dismal Swamp - so named by the English because there was no need for settlers to force Indian tribes off the land since they had already left - and set up logging operations. Over the next 200 years all of the cypress and Atlantic white cedar forests would be logged at least once.

Establishment of the refuge began in 1973 when the Union Camp Corporation donated 49,100 acres of land to The Nature Conservancy.

This land was then conveyed to the Department of the Interior, and the Great Dismal Swamp National Wildlife Refuge was officially established.

If you are looking for a place to disappear with your dog on a hike for hours, this is it. During its logging years, over 140 miles of roads were constructed through the Dismal Swamp. The best place to launch your dog's adventure is the parking lot at the end of Jericho Lane, off Route 642. Your dog will be hiking on firm sand/dirt roads, level and easy everywhere. Shade is at a premium on hot days so pack plenty of water for your outing. You can create a hiking loop from the several ditches that join at Jericho Lane.

The refuge has also developed an interpretive trail at the site of Washington's former camp, Dismal Town. An extensive boardwalk, nearly a mile long with a couple of spurs, snakes through the heart of the swamp. For a full day's adventure with your dog a 4.5-mile hike along the Washington Ditch will get your dog to Lake Drummond, one of only two natural lakes in the state of Virginia.

Suffolk, Virginia
(757) 986-3705
www.fws.gov/northeast/greatdismalswamp/

Fort Necessity National Battlefield (Pennsylvania)

George Washington's military career began in 1754 when the newly commissioned 22-year old lieutenant colonel was sent to the Ohio Valley to build a road and help defend British fortifications against the incursions of the French. Events deteriorated and Washington rapidly constructed a small, circular palisade he named Fort Necessity. When a force of 600 French and 100 Indians fell upon the crude fort, Washington was forced to capitulate, the only time he would ever surrender to an enemy in his career. The confrontation at Fort Necessity was the opening battle in North America of what would become the French and Indian War. It would end in the expulsion of French power from North America and India.

George Washington called Great Meadows, as the area surrounding Fort Necessity was then known, "a charming field for an encounter." You will take away the same impression today as you hike the grounds with your dog - minus the musket fire, of course. The focal point of the battlefield tour is a reconstructed fort built in the exact location of Washington's original stockade.

The interpretive trail traverses open meadows and light woods. Subsequent landowners grew fruit trees here that contribute to the park-like feel of one of

America's oldest battlefields. Part of this easy canine hike trips along traces of the Braddock Road that was first blazed in 1750 by Nemacolin, a Delaware Indian, and built by Washington's expedition. The battlefield tour covers about one mile.

Farmington, Pennsylvania
(724) 329-5512
www.nps.gov/fone/

Mount Vernon (Virginia)

In 1759 George Washington set himself up as a gentleman farmer on 2,000 acres at Mount Vernon. He wrote about his plantation on the Potomac River, "No estate in United America is more pleasantly situated than this." It was with the greatest reluctance that he would leave his life at Mount Vernon when the events of a revolutionary new nation led him to a greater calling in 1775.

Today Mount Vernon is the most visited private estate in America. After picking up a biscuit at the entrance gate, your dog can trot across much of the 500 acres that have been preserved. On the grounds are more than 20 outbuildings and 50 acres of gardens for your dog to explore. She may even meet some grazing livestock.

The *Forest Trail* is a short interpretive walk through a wooded area over a ravine and past an old cobble quarry that was used to create roadways, walkways and the main entrance. This little hike features one steep climb and a wide, groomed path for your dog.

Mount Vernon, Virginia
(703) 780-2000
www.mountvernon.org/

Washington's Crossing (Pennsylvania)

In the American Revolution, Washington's little army had taken one pounding after another as they camped on the western bank of the Delaware River in December 1776. Knowing that upcoming enlistments would expire with the new year and probably reduce his 2,400 men by about a thousand, Washington decided on a bold strike against the British across the river in Trenton before they swarmed into the Colonial capital of Philadelphia.

Using specially designed Durham boats - wide and flat and capable of handling heavy loads - the men started ferrying across the 300-yard river late in the afternoon of Christmas Day. It was not until the following morning that all his men and 18 cannon were on the Jersey side and the successful march on Trenton that would save the Revolution began.

Today the Washington Crossing Historic Park is a quiet riverside plot of manicured lawns and graceful oak trees. Like Washington, your dog can also cross the Delaware - by walking across the river on an open grate steel bridge. After soaking in long views up and down the river, on the Jersey side is extensive hiking on The Delaware & Raritan Canal towpath and in the hills of Washington Crossing State Park.

Washington Crossing, Pennsylvania
(215) 493-4076
www.ushistory.org/washingtoncrossing/

TOUR
IDEA #90: DOGGIN' THOMAS JEFFERSON

Thomas Jefferson was not the dog lover George Washington was. In 1811 he wrote to a colleague attempting to curb dog attacks on sheep, "I participate in all your hostility to dogs and would readily join in any plan of exterminating the whole race." That's harsh. Jefferson, in fact, kept dogs, taking pains to procure French "shepherd dogs" to work his flocks before sailing back from Europe after a stint as Minister to France. At best, he could be said to have regarded all animals, including dogs, with more of a scientific eye than a sentimental one. Setting this aside, you can still take a splendid vacation with your dog chasing Thomas Jefferson across his beloved Virginia...

Tuckahoe Plantation (Virginia)

Young Tom spent much of the first decade of his life in this home of his Randolph cousins, built between 1712 and 1730. The Randolphs were possibly the most powerful family in colonial Virginia and provided Jefferson's entry into learned society. Tuckahoe stands as one of the most architecturally complete plantations remaining from the early 18th century, and among the many dependencies is a tiny brick schoolhouse where Jefferson embarked on a lifelong odyssey of intellectual discovery.

The grounds of Tuckahoe are open for self-guided tours, which you take with your dog. The English boxwood garden was over 200 years of age and one of the most extensive in the country with 29 beds before it was decimated in the 1970s. The Ghost Walk visits the former maze. Other highlights include the herb and vegetable gardens and several family graveyards.

Richmond, Virginia
(804) 784-5736
www.tuckahoeplantation.com/

Colonial Williamsburg (Virginia)

Thomas Jefferson came to "the big city" at the age of 16 to attend the College of William & Mary in 1760. A young man of serious disposition, Jefferson would sometimes refer to Williamsburg as "Devilsburg." He would return again during the American Revolution as governor of Virginia in 1779 and 1780 before moving with the government to Richmond in the latter year. He would later soften his views on Williamsburg, offering that William & Mary was "the finest school of manners and morals that ever existed in America."

By the 1900s American life had essentially passed Williamsburg by. With the help of dog sleds full of Rockefeller family money the town was restored and re-created to reflect the early history of America. Today, Colonial Williamsburg is Virginia's most popular tourist attraction. Your dog is welcome to walk through the cobblestone streets and play on the village greens but can't go in any of the buildings to view the demonstrations.

For an extended outing with your dog, go out west of town to the *Greensprings Greenway* where a two-mile loop circles a 34-acre beaver pond on a wide, soft dirt path that will delight any dog. The trail is stuffed with so many interpretive signs that you almost don't have to visit neighboring Jamestown and Williamsburg to learn about the area's pivotal American history.

Williamsburg, Virginia
www.history.org/

Harpers Ferry National Historic Park (West Virginia)

No place in America packs as much scenic wonder and historical importance into such a small area as Harpers Ferry National Historic Park where the Shenandoah and Potomac rivers join forces. George Washington surveyed here as a young man. Thomas Jefferson, when he visited hailed the confluence as "one of the most stupendous scenes in Nature" and declared it worth a trip across the Atlantic Ocean just to see.

Later Meriwether Lewis prepared for the Corps of Discovery in 1804 by gathering supplies of arms and military stores at Harpers Ferry. A United States Marine Colonel named Robert E. Lee captured abolitionist John Brown at Harpers Ferry when he attempted to raid the United States Arsenal and arm a slave insurrection. General Thomas "Stonewall" Jackson scored one of his greatest military victories here during the Civil War. It was a no-brainer when Congress appropriated funds for a national monument in Harpers Ferry in 1944 and 2,300 acres of Maryland, Virginia and West Virginia were interwoven into the National Historic Park in 1963.

Dogs are welcome in Harpers Ferry National Historic Park and hikes are available for every taste and fitness level. On the Maryland side of the Potomac River is the towpath for the Chesapeake & Ohio Canal, which was completed in 1850 as a 184.5-mile transportation link between Washington D.C. and Cumberland, Maryland. The trail is wide, flat and mostly dirt.

Beside the canal, the Maryland Heights rise dramatically 1,448 feet above the rivers. The *Stone Fort Trail* up the Heights is the area's most strenuous hike and one of the most historic. With the outbreak of the Civil War, the Union Army sought to fortify the strategic Maryland Heights with its commanding views of the waters and busy railroad lines below. The roads leading to the summit were remembered by Union soldiers as "very rocky, steep and crooked and barely wide enough for those wagons."

Wayside exhibits help hikers appreciate the effort involved in dragging guns, mortar and cannon up the mountainside. One 9-inch Dahlgren gun capable of lobbing 100-pound shells weighed 9,700 pounds. Think about hauling five-ton guns up this nearly vertical climb while you are walking a 70-pound dog. The trail leads to the remnants of the Stone Fort which straddles the crest of Maryland Heights at its highest elevation.

A branch off the *Stone Fort Trail* winds down to the Overlook Cliffs, perched directly above the confluence of the Potomac and Shenandoah rivers. The best view of Harpers Ferry is from these rock outcroppings where it is easy to understand the town's importance to transportation in Colonial America, its value to the jockeying of battling armies in the Civil War and its susceptibility to crippling floods. There are no protective fences and dogs should be watched carefully on the open rocks at the Overlook Cliffs.

Access to Lower Town in Harpers Ferry is by National Park Service shuttle bus from the visitor center. Dog owners can best access this area by driving to the Maryland Heights for parking and walking across the Potomac River. The bridge features open grating that can intimidate skittish dogs not familiar with grates.

On the other side of the town of Harpers Ferry in West Virginia, along the Shenandoah River, is Virginus Island and the ruins of a thriving industrial town that finally succumbed to flooding in 1889. The trails that weave through the ruins are flat and shady and connect to the trails in historic Lower Town, where abolitionist John Brown barricaded himself in the fire engine house and battled Federal troops. Finally, climbing up the steep grade out of Lower Town is a short trail to Jefferson Rock, where Thomas Jefferson recorded his impressions in 1783.

Harpers Ferry, West Virginia
(304) 535-6029
www.nps.gov/hafe

Monticello (Virginia)

Thomas Jefferson began planning a house on this site as a young boy and started construction on Monticello in 1769. He continued work on his beloved estate, incorporating features of Palladian architecture he admired in classical European ruins, for more than a half-century despite ongoing financial difficulties, especially in the years after he left the presidency in 1809. For the final 17 years of his life Jefferson scarcely left the shadow of his mountaintop home.

The third president is buried in Monticello's small family burial ground, beneath a simple marker, in accordance with his instructions. The epitaph is his own: "Here was buried Thomas Jefferson/Author of the Declaration of American Independence/Of the Statute of Virginia for religious freedom/And father of the University of Virginia."

The squire of Monticello might be appalled but you can walk your dog on the parkway he developed as a scenic entrance to the house with over 130 species of trees and shrubs that are native to Albemarle County. In Kemper Park dogs can walk a half-mile up the *Saunders-Monticello Trail* that winds for two miles up the side of the steep Carter Mountain serving up views of the Blue Ridge Mountains along the way. You can also take your dog for a spirited journey on the natural wooded paths.

Charlottesville, Virginia
(434) 984-9822
www.monticello.org/

Poplar Forest (Virginia)

Poplar Forest, about 90 miles from Monticello, was Thomas Jefferson's personal retreat. One of only two homes he designed and built for his own use, Jefferson would visit three or four times a year, staying "from a fortnight to a month at a time." He stayed here of the first time in 1809. Jefferson considered the brick octagon plantation house, blending a variety of architectural influences, his personal masterpiece.

Dogs are welcome on the grounds at Poplar Forest. Interpretive brochures lead you through the 61-acre property. Jefferson's intent was for the ornamental elements, agricultural fields, woods and house to meld seamlessly into a harmonious whole. Note that Poplar Forest is open only April through November and closed on Tuesdays.

Forest, Virginia
(434) 525-1806
www.poplarforest.org/

TOUR
IDEA #91: DOGGIN' ABRAHAM LINCOLN

By all accounts Abraham Lincoln was a dog lover ("I care not for a man's religion whose dog and cat are not the better for it," he once said) but did not get his first dog until around 1855 when he was in his late 40s. Fido, a medium-sized yellow mutt, became a familiar sight around Springfield, Illinois trailing Lincoln on his rounds through town. "Fido," incidentally, which became a generic reference for dogs, translates from Latin as "faithful."

When he was elected president in 1860, however, Lincoln decided against bringing Fido, apparently a bit of a nervous dog, to the White House. Fido was left in the care of neighbor boys who were instructed never to leave the dog tied up alone in the yard and to never be scolded for entering the house with muddy paws. Abraham Lincoln and Fido were never reunited - after the Presidential funeral in Springfield in 1865 Fido was brought back to his original home to meet with familiar mourners. He died less than a year later. Your tour of Lincoln sites will take you back to Fido's stomping grounds...

Nancy Hanks Memorial (West Virginia)

For hard-core Lincolnphiles an appropriate place to begin your explorations is at the site of Nancy Hanks' birth in 1784 on the slopes of Saddle Mountain, in then Hampshire County, Virginia but now in West Virginia. Nancy Hanks married a carpenter named Thomas Lincoln is 1806. Abraham was the second of the couple's children to come along, in 1809.

For decades the remote site was marked only by a rustic stone monument but an early-American, one-room cabin was moved to the site in the 1970s. The cabin site is remote (follow small brown signs off US 50, between MD 972 and US 220) and usually surrounded by a healthy bonnet of high grass. But there likely won't be anyone around so it is a good place to let your dog out for a romp.

New Creek, West Virginia
(304) 813-1912

Abraham Lincoln Birthplace National Historic Site (Kentucky)

An impressive Doric-columned marble-and-granite memorial building rises from the site of the birth of America's sixteenth president where Thomas Lincoln purchased a hillside Kentucky homesite in 1808. Each of the 56 steps leading up to the granite and marble memorial represents one year in Lincoln's life. Th e log cabin housed inside was once believed to be the actual cabin of Lincoln's birth, but further research has indicated otherwise. The Memorial Building was built in 1911, financed by contributions from more than 100,000 people.

Lincoln lived the first two-and-a-half years of his life on the 300-acre Sinking Spring farm, which you are allowed to tour on foot with your dog (no buildings, as usual). Highlights on the grounds, which are visited by two easy walking trails, include the site of the Boundary Oak that was living here the same time as the Lincolns and the namesake Sinking Spring that was the family water source.

Hodgenville, Kentucky
(270) 358-3137
www.nps.gov/abli/

Lincoln Boyhood Home (Kentucky)

The Lincoln family moved about six miles north of Hodgenville in 1811. Lincoln later wrote that his earliest memories were of the five years he spent at Knob Creek. Here he attended school for the first time and watched slaves marched to auction. In December 1816, due to squabbles over faulty land titles, the Lincolns left Kentucky for Indiana.

A log cabin made of material of the time, erected in 1800 and moved from an adjacent farm in 1931, represents the Lincoln home that your dog can inspect while touring the property. The construction is typical of the Lincoln era, with a prominent chimney made of logs and mud. The Overlook Trail imparts a sense of life as it was in a backwoods setting along Knob Creek.

Hodgenville, Kentucky
(270) 358-3137
www.nps.gov/abli/

Lincoln Boyhood National Memorial (Indiana)

Certainly no American has ever had his footsteps so carefully dogged as Abraham Lincoln. Here we are in southern Indiana, a rugged wilderness when Thomas Lincoln moved his family here in December 1816. Abraham grew up here, clerking at James Gentry's store in his first job and working the farm until leaving the state at the age of 21.

Your dog need not miss a step in the Abraham Lincoln sage - she is welcome here as well. Walking paths lead around a working farm typical of an early nineteenth-century homestead. One trail of 12 stones, each taken from a structure of importance in Lincoln's life, leads to the grave of Nancy Hanks Lincoln, who died here on October 5, 1818 after becoming "milksick" from drinking the milk of a cow who had grazed on poisonous snakeroot.

Lincoln City, Indiana
(812) 937-4541
www.nps.gov/libo/

Lincoln Log Cabin State Historic Site (Illinois)

In March 1830 the Lincoln family ferried across the Wabash River from Indiana at Lawrenceville (now tiny Lincoln Land State Park). From that moment it seems his every step in the state has been documented. Houses he visited, courthouses he argued cases in, depots he boarded trains at - you can visit them all. The only house that Abraham Lincoln ever owned, in Springfield (413 South Eighth Street), holds no promise for action-loving dogs but is worth a drive-by.

This site in eastern Illinois was the last home of Thomas Lincoln and Sarah Bush Lincoln, his stepmother, where they lived until the 1840s. Your dog can wander around the 86-acre site that contains a replica of the Lincoln house and outbuildings.

Lerna, Illinois
(217) 345-1845
www.lincolnlogcabin.org/

Lincoln's Tomb State Historic Site (Illinois)

Abraham Lincoln was laid to rest in Oak Ridge Cemetery in Springfield, Illinois at the request of Mrs. Lincoln. The imposing 117-foot tomb was sculpted by Larkin Goldsmith Mead and is the final resting place for Mary Todd, Tad, Eddie, and Willie Lincoln. Bronze tablets bear the text of the Gettysburg Address, Lincoln's farewell address in Springfield, and his second inaugural address.

The monument to Lincoln was dedicated on October 15, 1874, on six acres of ground. Mead won the commission worth $206,000, the largest ever received by an American sculptor up to that time. Your dog is welcome to hike the grounds of Oak Ridge Cemetery but can't go into the monument.

Springfield, Illinois
(217) 782-2717
www.illinoishistory.gov/hs/lincoln_tomb.htm

Rock Creek Park (Washington D.C.)

This trail of Abraham Lincoln didn't even reach his days as President, which of course, could consume another vacation. One of the most unique Lincoln sites in Washington D.C. is Fort Stevens. The nation's capital was protected with a ring of 68 forts during the Civil War and Rock Creek Park preserves several military sites. Although technically a national park, Rock Creek Park is more like a city park administered by the National Park Service. How many other national parks boast of ballfields and 30 picnic sites?

Two main parallel hiking trails, run the length of the park from north to south on either side of Rock Creek. The wiser choice for canine hikers is the

Valley Trail (blue blazes) on the east side. In contrast with its twin, the *Western Ridge Trail* (green blazes),there are fewer picnic areas and less competition for the trail. Both are a rooty-and-rocky frolic up and down the slopes of Rock Creek, a superb canine swimming hole. Numerous spur trails and bridle paths connect the two major arteries that connect at the north and south to create a loop about ten miles long.

Your dog can visit the remnants of Fort De Russy, an earthworks fortification returned to its natural state just east of the *Western Ridge Trail* on a bridle path at Oregon Avenue and Military Road. Also near Military Road, three blocks east of the main park on 13th Street, is Fort Stevens. It was here the only fighting of the Civil War took place within the limits of Washington D.C. Union defenders repulsed a Confederate attack from General Jubal Early on July 11-12, 1864.

Abraham Lincoln rode up from the White House and stood on a parapet watching the battle - the only time in United States history that an American president was under fire by enemy guns while in office. A dramatized plaque marks the spot today in the partially reconstructed fort. Your dog will probably be more interested in playing fetch on the grassy grounds however.

Washington, D.C.
(202) 895-6015
www.nps.gov/rocr/

TOUR

IDEA #92: DOGGIN' THEODORE ROOSEVELT

No United States President is associated as strongly with the outdoors and animals as Theodore Roosevelt. The teddy bear was named after the 26th president and so to is a stout, short-legged breed of rat terrier, the Teddy Roosevelt Terrier. The indefatigable Roosevelt was a voracious traveler: the first American president to ride in an automobile and the first to travel outside the country. It would take the better part of years to trace his footsteps on vacation with your dog but here are some spots that hit the highlights...

Mount Roosevelt (South Dakota)

On February 14, 1884, when Theodore Roosevelt was 25 years old and a New York legislator, his wife and mother died, only hours apart. Devastated, Roosevelt abandoned politics and struck out for the Dakota territories where he had first visited as a lad to help cure his asthma. This time he hoped to rebuild his body and restore his spirit with the hard work of ranching. After a blizzard wiped out his prized herd of cattle in 1885, he returned to eastern society. Roosevelt's legacy in the Dakota Territory is memorialized in the Theodore Roosevelt National Park, where dogs are not allowed on the trails. A better choice would be Mount Roosevelt in the Black Hills where Teddy was a regular visitor. In his spare time out West Roosevelt worked as a deputy sheriff hunting outlaws. When bringing in a horse thief one day he met met Black Hills Sheriff Seth Bullock, beginning a lifetime friendship.

When Roosevelt died in 1919, Bullock lobbied to get a favorite peak, Sheep Mountain, renamed Mountain Roosevelt and worked tirelessly to construct the nation's first monument to the great man on its summit, even though he himself was close to death. The cylindrical stone "Friendship Tower" was dedicated just before Bullock passed that very same year. Now part of the Black Hills National Forest, the *Mount Roosevelt Trail* winds in a loop to the summit - an easy romp for your dog even though the entire hike is over one mile high.

Deadwood, South Dakota
(605) 673-9200

Sagamore Hill National Historic Site (New York)

Upon returning to New York after his stay in Dakota Territory, Roosevelt came to Oyster Bay, Long Island where his family had taken summer vacations. He resumed construction of a Queen Anne-style frame house he had commissioned before his wife's death and took up full-time residence at Sagamore Hill in 1887. He would live here the remainder of his life, raising six children with his second wife Edith.

As the park literature stresses, "Pets are as welcome at Sagamore Hill today as they were when the Roosevelts lived here a century ago." Would Teddy Roosevelt be associated with a park that doesn't allow dogs? The 83-acre property is open every day to explore from dawn to dusk. Paths and a nature trail lead through the pastures and orchard down to Cold Spring Harbor.

When he was in residence, Roosevelt often led funerals for his children's pets which included not only dogs but birds, mice and a badger named Josiah. You can view the family pet cemetery on the estate grounds.

Oyster Bay, New York
(516) 922-4792
www.nps.gov/sahi/

Theodore Roosevelt County Park (New York)

Theodore Roosevelt first came to the attention of the American public as a Lieutenant Colonel during the Spanish-American War in 1898. He organized a regiment of cowboys, Indians and Ivy League aristocrats who could all ride and shoot into the First United States Volunteer Cavalry Regiment, soon popularly known as the "Rough Riders."

It was not a figurehead position. Roosevelt's men landed at Daiquiri, Cuba on June 22 and saw battle action on June 24. A week later Roosevelt led two charges up the San Juan Heights, first on horseback and, after his steed was shot from under him, on foot. The capture of San Juan Heights effectively ended the war. However, the toll from tropical disease was becoming more deadly than enemy bullets and the celebrated regiment was sent to Camp Wickoff at the end of Long Island to be quarantined.

Dog-friendly Theodore Roosevelt County Park now covers much of the ground that was once Camp Wickoff; the Third House that serves as park headquarters was camp headquarters a century ago. The park maintains an extensive trail system but dog owners are best served at the *Big Reed Pond Nature Trails*. Here, a triple-stacked loop of colored trails pile up almost three miles of first-rate hiking with your dog. This is one of the few interpretive trails on Long Island. Outer Beach behind the campground on Long Island Sound offers excellent dog paddling - you can hike down a service road to the beach. A small beach on Lake Montauk opposite the trailhead also serves up superb doggie dips.

Montauk, New York
(631) 852-7878
www.co.suffolk.ny.us/webtemp1.cfm?dept=10&id=888

Theodore Roosevelt Island National Memorial (Virginia)

Of the four icons on Mount Rushmore, Theodore Roosevelt is the only one not to have a memorial around the National Mall in Washington, D.C. Instead he has his own island nearby in the Potomac River. During his presidency, Theodore Roosevelt set aside over 234 million acres of public lands as national parks, forests, monuments and wildlife refuges. After his death in 1919, Roosevelt admirers sought a suitable memorial - and what better way to honor his legacy of conservation than by dedicating this wooded, 88-acre island in the Potomac River in his memory?

Access is only from the Virginia side of the Potomac, from a parking lot off the George Washington Parkway. After leading your dog across a footbridge, three curvilinear trails conspire to cover the marsh, swamp and forest of the island. The *Upland Trail* and *Wood Trail* are covered with imbedded yellow stones; the Swamp Trail utilizes a boardwalk. All are extremely wide and ideal when more than one dog is in tow. There is enough elevation change to keep your dog's interest and the thick woods produce a shady haven just yards from the crush of Washington bustle.

Nestled in the center of the island, the Theodore Roosevelt Memorial is dominated by a 17-foot bronze statue by Paul Manship. It overlooks a diorama of fountains and four 21-foot granite tablets, inscribed with the tenets of Roosevelt's thoughts on Nature, Youth, Manhood and the State.

McLean, Virginia
(703) 289-2500
www.nps.gov/this/

DOGGIN' AMERICA BY ROAD, RAIL & AIR

TOUR
IDEA #93: GET MOVIN' WITH YOUR DOG
By road...

Wandering animals, buffalo and deer, were the first to discover this natural break in the daunting Appalachian Mountains. These migratory mammals blazed the trail that American Indian tribes would later follow. American settlers seemed destined to be bottled up on the East Coast until April 1750 when Dr. Thomas Walker discovered the gap through the mountains. Later, Daniel Boone blazed the Wilderness Road through the Cumberland Gap in 1775.

Over the next 20 years, although no wagons rolled through the pass, more than 200,000 people made the journey west into the wilderness of Kentucky and beyond. The Cumberland Gap was honored as a National Historic Park in 1940 and a new tunnel through the mountains will enable the Wilderness Road to one day be restored to its 1700s appearance.

The **Cumberland Gap National Historic Park** encompasses more than 20,000 acres of rich forest lands in the mountains on the Kentucky-Virginia border. The best spot to view the gap is at Pinnacle Overlook, accessible on a 4-mile paved road. Most visitors don't make it beyond the overlook but canine hikers can take off on a wide, rolling walk at the top of mountains with good views through thin trees and from rocky perches. The *Ridge Trail* is an easy walk from the campground. It runs for 19 miles through the woods, rolling across the ridgetop; all told, there are more than 50 miles of marked trails in the park.

To walk on the Wilderness Road, try the *Tri-State Peak Trail*, a steady 1.3-mile climb around the mountain. After a narrow, rocky beginning up switchbacks, the trail goes through the historic gap before heading to the 1,990-foot summit on a wide logging road. From the pavilion on the summit are views of Virginia, Kentucky and Tennessee.

At the base of the *Tri-State Peak Trail* are the remains of a 30-foot-high, charcoal-burning blast furnace that produced iron through much of the 19th century. Built of limestone slid down the mountain, the Newlee Iron Furnace was the focal point for an iron-making community here. The furnace could produce about three tons of iron a day to be shipped down the Powell River to Chattanooga.

Middlesboro, Kentucky
(606) 248-2817
www.nps.gov/cuga/

By rail...

Perhaps nothing as important in American history happened in as remote a location as the completion of the first transcontinental railroad in the Promontory Mountains on May 10, 1869. The **Golden Spike National Historic Site** preserves the spot where East and West were forever linked in the United States.

The highlight here is an easy hike. Your dog can come along on the 1.5-mile *Big Fill Walk*. Building a railroad through the Promontory Mountains to complete the railroad was some of the most difficult work faced by crews in the entire four-year project. Cuts had to be blasted through tough limestone rock and deep ravines needed to be bridged or filled - the story of which is told along this hike through exposed rock to remains of the Big Fill and Big Trestle. The original tracks are long gone but you can drive along the transcontinental railroad right-of- way on a seven-mile auto tour.

The ceremonial gold spike is on display at Stanford University in Palo Alto, California but your dog can stand at the actual last spike site where there is a replica of the original laurel tie and ceremonial plaque.

Brigham City, Utah
(435) 471-2209
www.nps.gov/archive/gosp/home.html

By air...

Early in the 20th century two Dayton, Ohio bicycle mechanics tamed the skies for all humankind at Kitty Hawk. Orville and Wilbur Wright were lured to the Outer Banks - then a near wilderness - to test their experimental fliers by the high dunes, blustery winds and the promise of soft, sandy landings.

The brothers achieved lift-off and powered flight on December 17, 1903. The first flight lasted only 12 seconds but three subsequent flights that day improved their success exponentially. The secretive nature of the brothers kept their achievement from becoming public knowledge for several years when improved flyers were demonstrated for huge crowds in New York and Paris.

The Art Deco-influenced stone memorial to the conquest of the air on Big Kill Devil Hill was designed by the architectural firm of Rodgers and Poor and dedicated in 1932. The **Wright Brothers National Memorial** features a large open area with two walking destinations of interest. Big Kill Devil Hill, where the Wrights conducted glider tests to test their theories of flight, has been stabilized and is laced with paths around and to the top of the 90-foot dune.

Out on the flats you can hike with your dog on rubber mats along the path of the world's first flight. Although it may be tempting to take your dog around the inviting open space, sand spurs and prickly pear are waiting to stab your dog's paws. So stick to the prescribed paths and roadways.

Kitty Hawk, North Carolina
(252) 473-2111
www.nps.gov/wrbr/

DOGGIN' THE OLD WEST

TOUR

IDEA #94: DOGGIN' LEWIS & CLARK

The most famous travelers in American history were Meriwether Lewis and William Clark, who journeyed from St. Joseph, Missouri to the Pacific Ocean to map out just what Thomas Jefferson had bought in his Louisiana Purchase from France. What is less known is Seaman, a Newfoundland dog Lewis bought for $20, joined the Corps of Discovery in Philadelphia. On the expedition, Seaman served the Corps as hunter, sentry, and companion. Upon reaching the Pacific, Seaman became the first dog to travel the breadth of America.

You can trace the steps of the Lewis & Clark expedition - and Seaman - today, more or less. Unless you are boating down the Missouri River you can get a feel for the journey by intersecting key historical locations in your vehicle. Here are a few that will pique your dog's interest as well...

Fort Atkinson State Historical Park (Nebraska)

Early in their expedition, on August 3, 1804 north of what is modern-day Omaha, Captains Lewis and Clark held their "First Council" with chiefs of the the Oto and Missouria Indian nations. In 1820, on the recommendation of the Corps, the first U.S. military post west of the Missouri River, Fort Atkinson, was established here.

Today the frontier outpost has been reconstructed as the Fort Atkinson State Historical Park. Your dog is permitted on the grounds and can hike the two-mile trail that runs though the surrounding grasslands. On the grounds is a statue group depicting participants in the "First Council," including Seaman. It is one of ten statues along the Lewis & Clark Trail that depict the big dog; here it is one of his less noble poses.

Fort Calhoun, Nebraska
(402) 468-5611
www.ngpc.state.ne.us/parks/guides/parksearch/showpark.asp?Area_No=73

Sergeant Floyd Memorial (Iowa)

One of the early significant locations you can visit is a bluff on the Iowa-Nebraska border in Sioux City overlooking the Missouri River. Here, on the upstream journey in the summer of 1804 Sergeant Charles Floyd took sick, most likely stricken by a burst appendix, and died. A funeral was held and Floyd buried on this bluff. For the rest of the expedition - two years - there would not be another death.

In 1901 a 100-foot obelisk of heavy Kettle River sandstone was erected over the remains. In 1960 the Sergeant Floyd Monument was recognized as America's first National Historic Landmark by the U.S. Department of Interior. Today surrounded by a 23-acre park your dog ran scale the bluff and catch a swim in the Missouri River below.

Sioux City, Iowa
www.nps.gov/history/nr/travel/lewisandclark/ser.htm

Pompeys Pillar National Monument (Montana)

This is one of the more whimsical sites on the Lewis & Clark Trail, one that didn't involve life-and-death decisions. After disengaging from Lewis on the return trip, William Clark navigated down the Yellowstone River. On the south side of the river he saw a massive sandstone butte 150 feet high and "400 paces in secumpherance," as Clark described it. He called it "Pompy's Tower" after Sho-shone guide Sacagawea's child and climbed to the top of the navigational landmark as countless others had done for centuries before the Americans' arrival. He inscribed his name and date into the stone; still visible, his mark is probably the only extant on-site evidence of the entire expedition. Now managed by the Bureau of Land Management the site is open to your dog; if the vehicle gate is locked, walk in but there will be no services.

Nibbe, Montana
(406) 896-5013
www.blm.gov/mt/st/en/fo/billings_field_office/Pompeys_Pillar.html

Missouri Headwaters State Park (Montana)

After traveling 2,500 miles Lewis & Clark reached the bewildering confluence of three previously uncharted rivers. They named the trio for President Jefferson and two members of his cabinet, Albert Gallatin and James Madison. That was the easy part. The tougher call was choosing which one to follow. The fate of the entire expedition hung in the balance because should they choose wrongly and be forced to backtrack they faced the deadly prospect of getting caught in a Rocky Mountains winter. After much consternation and some scouting the leaders forged successfully on via the southwest flowing tributary, the Jefferson River.

Today the Three Forks of the Missouri, a National Historic Landmark, is part of Missouri Headwaters State Park. The 500-acre park is an airy, undeveloped slice of Big Sky country ideal for camping and fishing with your dog or hiking the easy-going trails to scenic vistas in the surrounding bluffs. The passage of 200 years has caused little to change in this land; in fact, Meriwether Lewis would no doubt recognize the landscape were he and Seaman to set up camp with you.

Three Forks, Montana
(406) 994-4042
fwp.mt.gov/lands/site_281910.aspx

Travelers' Rest State Park (Montana)

Lewis and Clark were introduced to this idyllic campsite in open meadows beside the free-flowing Lolo Creek by their Shoshone guide. The Corps of Discovery stayed here both going and returning and each time at a critical moment in the expedition. Heading west Lewis and Clark were unable to find a water passage all the way to the Pacific and it was here they regrouped and prepared for an arduous 200-mile overland trek over the Bitterroot Mountains. While recuperating at Travelers' Rest on the way home it was decided, against all military precedent, to split the expedition in order to explore more territory. Lewis and Clark went their separate ways knowing it was likely the forces would never re-unite. Travelers' Rest remains undisturbed and your dog is welcome to take the interpretive trail through the park but camping is no longer allowed here.

Lolo, Montana
(406) 273-4253
fwp.mt.gov/lands/site_2233810.aspx

Fort Clatsop National Memorial (Oregon)

Eighteen months after setting out, the Corps of Discovery reached the Pacific Ocean. With winter on the doorstep they quickly built a shelter of two rows of wooden huts behind the dunes. Lewis and Clark would not leave Fort Clatsop for home until March 23, 1806, having established an American presence in the Pacific Northwest that would lead to the first American settlement at the mouth of the Columbia River by fur trader John Jacob Astor only five years later.

The original Fort Clatsop rotted away by the mid-1800s. The National Park Service rebuilt many of the huts - using frontier tools and methods typical of the age - and it now serves as the linchpin for 12 parks and sites that comprise the Lewis and Clark National Historic Park. Here you can take one of the most historical hikes with your dog anywhere in America - the 6.5-mile *Fort To Sea Trail* that follows the route members of the expedition took to the Pacific Ocean, although you don't have to forge muddy lowlands and bogs. The trail snakes its way through tall forests, sneaks under US 101 and crosses ocean dunes. Makes you wonder how many times Seaman ran this way to get to the Pacific Ocean.

Astoria, Oregon
(503) 861-2471
www.nps.gov/lewi/planyourvisit/fortclatsop.htm

TOUR

IDEA #95: DOGGIN' MOVIE WESTERNS

Are you a fan of movie westerns? If so, why not pack up the dog and get out to explore the "movie sets" where many of those classic sagas were filmed on location...

Monument Valley (Utah)

It will not take long after pulling onto the 17-mile auto tour in Monument Valley for movie buffs to recognize the isolated buttes and exquisitely carved rock formations scattered across the high plateau. Legendary director John Ford was the first to film in the valley, making the iconic *Stagecoach* in 1939. Stagecoach made a star of John Wayne and elevated the Western from B-movie status into the most popular form of American cinema. The action scenes were shot in open desert country known today as Stagecoach Wash. Ford and Wayne returned many times to Monument Valley for *The Searchers*, *She Wore A Yellow Ribbon* and many,

many other oaters.

Today these defining images of the American West belong to a tribal park of the Navajo Nation. There are no formal hiking trails along the auto tour but there are many chances to stop and wander with your dog about such familiar movie backdrops as the Mitten Buttes in *Fort Apache* where Wayne and Henry Fonda clashed over the administration of Army power and the North Window where the body of Chris Hubble is discovered in *Sergeant Rutledge*.

Monument Valley, Utah
(435) 727-5874
www.navajonationparks.org/htm/monumentvalley.htm

Spearfish Canyon (South Dakota)

In 1990 star/director Kevin Costner reinvigorated the movie western with his sprawling *Dances With Wolves* and won a Best Picture Oscar. He replicated the Kansas plains in South Dakota and the opening sequence, where Costner receives his orders at Fort Hays to travel to Fort Sedgewick, was filmed on a private ranch east of Rapid City. Several of the set pieces, including the major's house and the blacksmith shop have been moved to a free tourist spot known as the Fort Hays Dances With Wolves Film Set (four miles south of Rapid City) where you can get out and poke around with your dog.

The Indian winter camp at the center of the movie was set up in Spearfish Canyon in the Black Hills National Forest, said to be six times more ancient that the Grand Canyon. The exact spot of the final scene where Costner and Mary MacDonnell leave the tribe was once marked by signs but have long since succumbed to souvenir-hunters. Even if you don't find it while hiking with your dog the gorgeous limestone cliffs in the heavily vegetated canyon will be more than a consolation. There is easy access to Spearfish Creek for some joyous dog-paddling and in the northeast section of the canyon, across the road from the main park, is Indian Springs where early settlers speared fish in a small spring-fed pond and you can guess the rest.

Black Hills National Forest, South Dakota
(605) 673-9200
www.spearfishcanyon.com/index1.htm

Fisher Towers (Utah)

Restless John Ford introduced the movie world to another western landscape in 1949 when he went searching for a new desert location for his upcoming *Wagon Master* to star Ben Johnson and Ward Bond. He arrived in Moab where he was shown the Professor Valley and the Fisher Towers that rise over 900 feet above the neighboring Colorado River. Ford indeed made *Wagon Master* here and more than 50 feature films would be shot on location around Moab in the next 50 years. To John Wayne, this area always defined the West.

Your dog won't be able to draw a full conclusion to agree or disagree with the Duke - the canine hike at Fisher Towers, part of the Colorado Riverway Recreation Area, ends when a ladder climb scales an awkward rock before reaching the end of the trail. But there is more than enough exploring on these multi-hued sedimentary rock formations to satisfy any canine adventurer.

Just west of Fisher Towers along US 191 on the opposite side of Moab you can visit a half-mile spur on the western side of the Dead Horse Point mesa that leads to an overlook of Shafer Canyon. Across the canyon you can see an open plain that was used to film the famous final scene in the buddy movie *Thelma & Louise* when Susan Sarandon drives a Thunderbird convertible over a cliff. Although there are wrecked automobiles in Shafer Canyon, they were placed there by the Bureau of Land Management to shore up the river bank. The wreckage from the movie was airlifted out of the canyon by helicopter.

Moab, Utah
(435) 259-2100
www.blm.gov/ut/st/en/fo/moab/recreation/recreation_areas/

Alabama Hills (California)

If you have ever watched a western or the opening to the *Lone Ranger* you will know this place as you arrive with your dog. The Alabama Hills consist of rounded, weathered granite boulders piled across a desert flatlands that form a vibrant contrast with the sharply sculptured ridges of the nearby Sierra mountains. These majestic backdrops and rugged rock formations began attracting the attention of Hollywood, 212 miles to the west, in the 1920s.

You can hike with your dog along Movie Flat Road, a wide, dusty dirt passage through the Alabama Hills that is one of the most recognizable movie sets in Hollywood history. Beginning with Tom Mix in the silent era, every major

Western star galloped down the road on horseback at one time or another. Roy Rogers appeared here in his first starring role in *Under Western Stars* and Bill Boyd, known on the screen as Hopalong Cassidy, filmed so many roles in Lone Pine that he moved here.

The Alabama Hills hosted one of the largest location shoots in history when 1,200 extras staged the climactic battle scene in *Gunga Din*. Other notable westerns among the more than 100 films shot here include *The Lone Ranger, How The West Was Won*, and *The Gunfighter*. Although the golden age for Lone Pine has gone the way of the Hollywood western, film crews occasionally still appear. *Bad Day at Black Rock* (Spencer Tracy/Robert Ryan) used the area to build an entire town along the railroad tracks in 1955 and, more recently, Fred Ward and Kevin Bacon battled giant earthworms in the Alabama Hills in *Tremors*. You won't find any canine swimming holes so make sure to bring plenty of drinking water, especially in hot weather (you are less than a two-hour drive from Death Valley).

Lone Pine, California
(760) 872-5000
www.blm.gov/ca/st/en/fo/bishop/scenic_byways/alabamas.html

Vasquez Rocks Natural Area Park (California)

No tour of movie Western filming locations with your dog would be complete without a stop at Vasquez Rocks Natural Area Park, just north of Los Angeles. Both Rin Tin Tin and Lassie, the two biggest canine action heroes in cinematic history, mugged for the camera in these rock formations shaped by the San Andreas Fault over which they rest. The rocks are named for Tiburcio Vásquez, one of California's most notorious stage coach robbers of the 1800s who used the sloping rocks as a hideout.

The Vasquez Rocks are now a Los Angeles County park and popular with climbers and hikers. Your dog is welcome to join in the fun but if you choose to investigate the rocks off the trails make sure to bring a good map. And keep an eye out for movie crews. Your dog may be the next big star.

Agua Dulce, California
(661) 268-0840
parks.co.la.ca.us/vasquez_narea.html

TOUR

IDEA #96: DOGGIN' WESTERN OUTLAWS

In their time these fellows were tracked and chased by many a dog so you will simply be indulging in a time-honored tradition when you set your dog onto the trail of these outlaw legends...

Billy The Kid

As law and order sorted itself out in 1878 and 1879, the Lincoln County Wars agitated America's largest county. A central figure in the conflict was a 17-year old hired gun named William Bonney. Imprisoned for extracting revenge on a sheriff's posse, Billy the Kid was detained in Lincoln before breaking out of jail and killing two guards. Bonney was soon hunted down and killed by Sheriff Pat Garrett.

The entire town of Lincoln - some 150 strong - is today a National Historic Landmark. You and your dog can walk through the one-street town, several blocks long, and study the historically preserved buildings that include the merchandise store owned by murdered Englishman John Tunstull and the courthouse where Billy the Kid made good his daring escape.

After your walking tour you can pile the dog back in the car and take a driving tour on the 84-mile loop around Lincoln dubbed the Billy the Kid National Scenic Byway. It doesn't have much to do with Bonney's travels but you will get a healthy dose of the rugged beauty of the American West and plenty of recreation opportunities for your dog in the Lincoln National Forest.

Lincoln, New Mexico
www.billybyway.com/lincoln-a.html

Jesse James

"Jesse James is the only American bandit who is classical, who is to this country what Robin Hood or Dick Turpin is to England, whose exploits are so close to the mythical and apocryphal"...Carl Sandburg

To jump on the trail of Jesse James you will need a vehicle. A driving tour of Jesses James' outlaw life in Missouri includes such towns as Liberty (the bank where the James gang executed the nation's first successful daytime bank robbery), Winston (site of the "Great Train Robbery"), St. Joseph (the house where he was shot and killed), Kearney (Jesse James' grave) and Independence (jail where brother Frank turned himself in after Jesse's murder).

After all that driving your dog will want to stretch his legs, and the place to do it is in the Mark Twain National Forest that covers 1.5 million acres and stretches across 29 Missouri counties. Although named for Mark Twain, the Missourian most associated with the Ozark hills is not the humorist but outlaw Jesse James. James was reputed to have used the limestone caves as hiding places, including a prominent rock room along the *Berryman Trail* in the Potosi Ranger District. A national recreation trail, this was created as a horse trail and there are no steep climbs as the undulating path switches back and forth up to craggy ridges from dark, leafy hollows.

The James-Younger gang's first Missouri train robbery took place in the Fredericktown District near a small town called Gads Hill when five men robbed the Little Rock Express on its way from St. Louis to Little Rock on January 31, 1874. The gang brought with them a pre-written press-release that was left with the crew on the train to relay to the local newspapers.

Mark Twain National Forest, Missouri
(573) 364-4621
www.fs.fed.us/r9/marktwain/

Butch Cassidy

Tracking Butch Cassidy and the Wild Bunch is no easier today than it was for "those guys" 100 years ago. If you and your dog sign on with this posse, bring a rugged vehicle and some tough paw pads. The most famous hide-out for the gang - and the most famous hide-out in the Old West - was Hole-in-the-Wall, the only break in a red sandstone escarpment that runs for fifty miles through the Big Horn Mountains of Wyoming. The area was remote and accessed only by narrow passes that were easily defended by cattle rustlers and outlaws.

Today the Hole-in-the-Wall is on public land administered by the Buffalo Field Office of the Bureau of Land Management. The trailhead is 32 miles from Interstate 25 and any services, mostly on a primitive two-track road that passes through many livestock gates that must be opened and closed. The hike with your dog into the Hole-in-the-Wall traverses uneven terrain for 2.5 miles.

Cassidy, born Robert LeRoy Parker, utilized other equally remote hideouts along what came to be known as "the Outlaw Trail." Now that you know what is involved in reaching a western outlaw lair you may want to bring your dog to

Brown's Hole, a rugged Green River canyon near the junction of Utah, Colorado and Wyoming and Robbers Roost, a savage stretch of Utah desert sandwiched between the Colorado River, the Green River and the Dirty Devil River.

You can continue on the trail of Butch Cassidy if you wish, although it won't get any easier. While in Utah you can head over to Circleville, just outside Zion National Park, to check on his boyhood home but the ailing house is unmarked. The San Miguel Valley Bank in Telluride, Colorado where Cassidy pulled his first bank robbery in 1889 burned three years later. It was replaced at the corner of Pine and Main streets by the Mahr Building where a Yorkshire Terrier-sized plaque marks the spot. The Bank of Montpelier (Idaho), which was the first robbery attributed to the Wild Bunch in 1896, has most recently been a print shop. Other Western sites attributed to Butch Cassidy may, instead, be just be marking his legend.

Oh, and if you want your dog to see the spot where Paul Newman and Robert Redford "jumped" off the cliff in *Butch Cassidy and the Sundance Kid*, travel to Durango, Colorado and go 13 miles north to Baker's Bridge, off CR 250. The shot was created in three separate stages. Newman and Redford run towards the cliff edge above the Animas River; then stuntman are filmed jumping 30 feet into the gorge, while the camera shoots without the water to create the illusion of a much longer drop; and finally Newman and Redford are shot landing in the water back in California.

Kaycee, Wyoming
(307) 684-1100
www.blm.gov/wy/st/en/field_offices/Buffalo.html

TOUR
IDEA #97: DOGGIN' AMERICA'S GOLD RUSHES

The lure of gold has spurred many an American to travel. You can still chase gold today but your dog will have more fun if you just hunt down the places where gold was discovered in years gone by...

Reed Gold Mine State Historic Site (North Carolina)

On a lazy Sunday in 1799 Conrad Reed played hooky from church and went down to play in Little Meadow Creek on the family farm. Young Conrad found a shiny yellow rock and brought it home. A silversmith in nearby Concord was unable to identify the rock, purported to weigh 17 pounds, so for several years it served as a doorstop in the Reed home.

Finally in 1802 a jeweler recognized the rock as being of gold and the Reed family began searching in the creek for other valuable deposits - but only in late summer after the crops were in. Soon America had its first gold mine and its first gold rush. By 1824 the Reeds had collected an estimated $100,000 worth of gold from their creek and underground mining began. Gold would continue to be removed from the area sporadically until 1912.

Your dog can't take the free mine tour but is welcome on the trails that pick along both lode and placer mining areas. The *Lower Hill Trail* features "Talking Rocks" that describe the mining activities at Reed Gold Mine and various rocks found in the southeastern United States. Numerous locations feature historic mining machinery, and an area on Upper Hill has the chimney and restored foundations of the 1854 mill house. And for a couple of bucks you can rent a pan and try your luck at finding gold.

Midland, North Carolina
(704) 721-4653
www.nchistoricsites.org/Reed/reed.htm

The Switzerland of America (Colorado)

The mountains of southwestern Colorado are so rugged they earned the nickname, "Switzerland of America." Still, the promise of gold and silver brought prospectors to blaze trails and build roads deep into the mountains. In 1892 President Benjamin Harrison created the Grand Mesa National Forest as the third such reserve in America. The Uncompahgre and Gunnison forests soon followed and together the three parcels of public land, managed as one unit, contain more than three million acres - the largest national forest in the Rocky Mountains.

This is the place to come for challenging canine hiking. And there is a surprising amount of hiking and not climbing on some of the highest mountains on the continent. Uncompahgre Peak is a stand-alone "fourteener" at 14,309 feet that can be reached with a seven-mile round-trip ascent. About half the mountain is above the treeline and this is an open hike that begins with a long, steady gain before a steep scramble to the flattish top above the Big Blue Wilderness.

Near the Victorian mining town of Ouray you can test the 4.2-mile *Bear Creek National Recreation Trail*. Steep inclines early in the hike serve up views of town before the trail picks its way through Bear Creek Canyon. Pay attention because the footpath, built by miners, shrinks to two feet wide in places. Your destination is the Yellow Jacket Mine but backpackers can penetrate deeper into the mountains.

Delta, Colorado
(970) 874-6600
www.fs.fed.us/r2/gmug/

Marshall Gold Discovery State Historic Park (California)

If you were able to assemble all the gold ever mined in the history of the earth it would fit comfortably in two Olympic swimming pools. And about 1% of all the above-ground gold ever mined was found in the first five years of the California Gold Rush. Those first shining flecks of gold were spotted in a tailrace for a sawmill James Marshall was building for himself and John Sutter alongside the American River in 1848.

Today you can stop and poke around with your dog at one of America's most historic sites. The discovery of gold at Sutter's Mill triggered the greatest mass migration of people ever seen in the United States and ignited the spectacular growth of the West but ironically, the area today is peaceful and unpopulated. You can still pan for gold in the American River and your dog will find her own treasure playing in the soothing rapids.

Coloma, California
(530) 622-3470
www.parks.ca.gov/?page_id=484

Empire Mine State Historic Park (California)

The Empire Mine was the richest hard-rock mine in California, operating for 106 years and producing almost six million ounces of gold. But it never came easy. Logger George Roberts discovered a quartz outcropping glistening with gold near where the present-day parking lot is shortly after the 1849 Gold Rush began. Miners swarmed the area but to get at the gold they had to dig and blast and by 1851 most of the prospectors sold off their claims to a consortium that consolidated them into the Empire Mine. It would not be until the 1880s that the mine would turn a profit. Eventually 367 miles of tunnels, some over a mile deep, would be excavated at the Empire Mine.

Today you can get a look at the main mine shaft and explore ten miles of wooded trails with your dog. The interpretive *Hardrock Trail* investigates the mills and machinery necessary to mine gold across two miles and 20 trail stations. A one-mile loop off the main drag climbs Osbourne Hill that is sprinkled with old mine sites and foundations. Across Highway 174 from the Visitor Center the *Pipeline Trail* on Union Hill follows the route of a pipe that carried water from a reservoir to power mining machinery.

Grass Valley, California
(530) 273-8522
www.parks.ca.gov/Default.asp?page_id=499

Jacksonville Woodlands (Oregon)

Gold was discovered in Oregon's Jackson Creek in 1851 but it brought neither fame nor fortune to the prospector, a lone miner remembered today only as "Mr. Sykes." Gold fever flared soon enough and within two years there were thousands of men tediously pulling flakes and nuggets from area creek beds. Jacksonville's first brick buildings were in place by 1853 as the town thrived. It even became the county seat but when the Oregon & California Railroad headed for nearby Medford in 1887 and bypassed Jacksonville the good times ground to a halt. Jacksonville residents built their own railroad four years later but the struggling line was dismantled and sold in 1925. During the Depression desperate residents dug deeper into the ground under the town to extract a few dollars of gold to survive. Not much happened in town after that. So little changed, in fact, that the entire downtown was designated a National Historic Landmark in 1966.

In 1989, residents formed the Jacksonville Woodlands Association to preserve and protect the quiet forests on the slopes surrounding the town. Most explorations of the Jacksonville Woodlands will start in town along the *Zigler Trail*, a flat one-mile journey along the Jackson Creek where gold was first discovered. A detailed brochure tells the fascinating story and makes for a prolonged walk with the dog. Strollers will want to turn around at the footbridge and retrace your pawprints but adventurous canine hikers will turn left and climb the ridges and canyons above the town. The 3-mile *Rich Gulch Trail* leads to a panoramic view of Jacksonville and countryside.

After hiking through the peaceful Jacksonville Woodlands, be sure to take your dog on a walk through town. More than 80 original brick and wooden buildings from the 1800s are listed on the National Register of Historic Places. Dogs are as welcome in Jacksonville today as they were in the mining camps of yesteryear - there is a water bowl placed for dogs outside the Visitor kiosk.

Fifteen miles south of Jacksonville on Upple Applegate Road you can continue your dog's quest for gold on the *Gin Lin Trail*. In 1881 Gin Lin, a Chinese mining boss who had already successfully mined in other areas of the Applegate Valley, purchased mining claims in the "Palmer Creek Diggings" area. Results of hydraulic mining operations are evident along this trail. Gin Lin reportedly took up to $2 million in gold from his claims in the Applegate Valley. Jealous of his success, other miners lobbied for new laws to tax those of Oriental descent which caused Gin Lin to retire from Oregon. His trail is lost to history at this point.

Jacksonville, Oregon
(541) 899-8118
www.jacksonvilleoregon.org/

TOUR

IDEA #98: DOGGIN GHOST TOWNS

You say that when you travel with your dog you are tired of hearing people tell you "That dog can't come in here." Sounds like you need a ghost town. When you go hunting ghost towns with your dog you will find that "ghost" is a broad term. Some ghost towns still have a handful of people living in them; others are tourist attractions with actors and gift shops. Here are some ghost towns that are administered by state and federal governments as parks that look more or less the way they looked when abandoned...

Bodie (California)

William Bodey dug gold out of these barren hills in 1859 but he died in a blizzard that winter and never saw the town his strike would spawn. More gold was discovered in the surrounding hills and by 1880 the town was bustling with 10,000 residents. It was reported that there were 65 saloons operating in Bodie, to go along with the brothels, gambling halls and opium dens. Legend has it that there was a man killed in Bodie every day.

After the gold played out the town soldiered on, tapping into the timber resources in the nearby mountains. Electricity even came to Bodie in 1911. But avalanches and fires crippled the town and, unlike other boom towns, endured a slow death. The National Park Service declared Bodie an Historic District and the State of California took over in 1962 to create a State Historic Park, preserving the remains of the town in a state of "arrested decay." As a result, Bodie is one of the largest and best preserved ghost towns in the United States, with 170 buildings standing.

Despite a 17-mile drive down a dusty road there is not unfettered access to Bodie as you can only go in during park hours, weather permitting. But this is no tourist trap - there are no re-creations in Bodie and no food and water for sale. The only business that intrudes on the ghost town aura is a small museum. You can bring your dog into the townsite and walk the gravelly streets peering into store windows with shelves still stocked and poolhalls with balls still racked on dusty, ornate tables.

Bodie, California
(760) 647-6445
www.parks.ca.gov/?page_id=509

Rhyolite (Nevada)

The old mining town of Rhyolite fulfills every image you have ever had of a ghost town - abandoned buildings of some substance, stark desert surroundings and the feeling that you are the first person to visit the town in years. Aside from being remote Rhyolite is amazingly accessible - a paved road takes you straight into town.

Although considered the "Queen City" of Death Valley, Rhyolite flamed up and burned out quickly, surviving little more than a decade. When quartz - an indicator of gold - was found all over a hillside in 1904 there were soon 2000 claims in a 30-mile radius of the townsite. Soon the population approached 10,000; the railroad arrived and the town was electrified. There were hotels, a hospital, a school for 250 children, a stock exchange and even an opera. The financial Panic of 1907 decimated the town and by 1916 the light and power were turned off forever in Rhyolite.

Rhyolite is in Death Valley but not part of the national park; it is on Bureau of Land Management land so when you pull up, open the door and just let your dog out. There likely won't be anyone around to say differently. Numerous ruins include a nearly intact train depot and the walls of a three-story bank. The highlight is The Bottle House, that a miner built from 50,000 beer and whiskey bottles - it was restored by Paramount Pictures in 1925.

Rhyolite, Nevada
www.nps.gov/deva/historyculture/rhyolite-ghost-town.htm

Bannack (Montana)

Bannack is the site of Montana's first major gold discovery, where John White pulled placer deposits out of Grasshopper Creek on July 28, 1862. The town population swelled immediately to 3,000 and was named as Territorial Capital of Montana. In a familiar tale with placer gold rushes, the people drifted away quickly as the streams played out. But unlike other Western boom towns that fell off the map, more than 50 log and frame buildings still line Main Street, protected by the state of Montana as a park.

While the goal of Bannack State Park is to preserve the site as a "real" ghost town there is a Visitor Center and tours but if you are looking for that ghost town-feel come to explore outside the summer months. This is the best preserved of all Montana ghost towns and you can bring your dog through the townsite and walk into any of the buildings that are not locked. Included in your explorations are the old cemetery, stripped of most grave markers; a crushing mill; a Masons Lodge; and an old gallows where Sheriff Henry Plummer, reputed stage coach thief and murderer, was hanged without a drop by vigilantes in 1864.

Dillon, Montana
(406) 834-3413
www.bannack.org/

Elkhorn (Montana)

Elkhorn boomed behind the discovery of silver by Swiss-born Peter Wys in 1870. Over the years almost nine million ounces of silver were extracted from Elkhorn Mine. After the railroad arrived in 1887 it was estimated that more than $30,000 a day worth of silver was being shipped out of Elkhorn. When the silver market crashed in the 1890s most of the people living in the town and gulches moved on to the next strike.

A handful of people still live in Elkhorn and most of the buildings are privately owned but you are welcome to visit and follow the self-guided walking tour with your dog. Elkhorn Ghost Town State Park preserves two outstanding examples of frontier architecture side-by-side: Fraternity Hall and Gillian Hall.

West Helena, Montana
(406) 495-3270
fwp.mt.gov/lands/site_281892.aspx

Custer (Idaho)

This mining town was founded the same year its namesake, George Armstrong Custer, was killed at the Battle of Little Bighorn, 1876. Custer and its sister city Bonanza flourished as the support center for the General Custer, Lucky Boy and other rich mines. Bonanza met a sudden end when it burned in 1897 while Custer's demise was only a bit more prolonged. As the local mines played out one by one it was a ghost town by 1910.

The Challis National Forest that administers 800,000 acres and is the gateway to the largest wilderness area in the lower 48 states took ownership of the townsite in 1966. Today a walking tour of wooden cabins, businesses and a school line a classic old Western one-street town.

Challis, Idaho
(208) 879-4100
www.fs.fed.us/r4/sc/yankeefork/index.shtml

DOGGIN' THE END

TOUR
IDEA #99: DOGGIN' DINOSAUR BONES

Dinosaurs were probably the first animals to travel long-distances across America and you can make a vacation out of chasing their footsteps with your dog...

Agate Fossil Beds National Monument (Nebraska)

During the Miocene Era, some 20 million years ago, the High Plains of Nebraska resembled today's endless grass savanna of the Serengeti Plains in Africa. During the 1890s, scientists rediscovered what the Lakota Sioux already knew - bones preserved in one of the most complete Miocene mammal sites in the world. There are remnants of the ancient grasses and hoofprints of prehistoric animals in sediments preserved in the park, as well as layers of fossilized bones.

These include strange beasts like the "terrible pig" Dinohyus, land beavers, snarling beardogs, and dwarf rhinos in abundance. Some of these creatures are on display in the Visitor Center (off-limits to your dog) and in outdoor exhibits along the park trails (your dog is welcome). Much of this geologic history is recorded in the park's natural features, including fossils exposed in the bluffs above the Niobrara River. Most of the hikes in the park are shortish, clocking in from one to three miles. For those with more time, short hikes from one to three miles allow the opportunity to explore the natural history of the Niobrara River Valley and its current and past wildlife.

Harrison, Nebraska
(308) 668-2211
www.nps.gov/agfo/

Berlin-Ichthyosaur State Park (Nevada)

When an ocean covered western Nevada the biggest and meanest creature swimming about with an indiscriminate appetite was the Ichthyosaur. Like the whale today, the fish-like sea creatures were the biggest animals on the planet at the time. The specimens found in the park on the slopes of the Shoshone Mountains are among the largest specimens ever discovered, reaching 50 feet in length.

The fossilized remains of Ichthyosaurs discovered here in 1928 proved to be the most abundant concentration in North America. Excavations began in 1954 and Berlin-Ichthyosaur State Park was established to protect and display the remains of about 40 sea monsters. The "Berlin" of the park is a turn-of-the-century silver mining town that died in 1911. Unlike many small Western ghost towns, Berlin was never wiped out by fire. In the dry Nevada desert the small collection of wooden buildings look much like they did when the solid rock Diana Mine, also preserved in the park, was spewing out ore cars full of silver. Dinosaurs and a ghost town - your dog gets a two-fer when you steer off the main Nevada highway.

Austin, Nevada
(775) 964-2440
parks.nv.gov/bi.htm

Big Bone Lick State Park (Kentucky)

During the Pleistocene Epoch, over 15,000 years ago, a huge ice sheet covered the ground from Canada down to the Ohio River. On the edges of this ice sheet, great herds of giant mastodons, wooly mammoths and ground sloths gathered at warm salt springs that still bubble from the earth at Big Bone Lick State Park.

The salty marsh that attracted these prehistoric visitors sometimes proved to be a fatal attraction. Animals became trapped and perished in what the early pioneers called "jelly ground." The fossilized remains of these prehistoric animals here were discovered in 1739. Explorers to the area reported using enormous ribs of mastodons for tent poles. The scientific community recognizes the site as the "Birthplace of American Vertebrate Paleontology."

Today, as part of the state park, there is an outdoor museum and a small lake with over three miles of trails to explore with your dog. Dogs are also permitted in the park campground.

Union, Kentucky
(859) 384-3522
parks.ky.gov/findparks/recparks/bb/

Cleveland-Lloyd Dinosaur Quarry (Utah)

No one knows for sure how this barren, rock-strewn landscape can be such a rich depository for the remains of dead dinosaurs but more than 12,000 bones and one dinosaur egg have been excavated from these prolific fossil beds. The Cleveland-Lloyd (Cleveland is the location, Lloyd a wealthy expedition backer) Dinosaur Quarry contains the densest concentration of Jurassic-aged dinosaur bones ever found and there are more museums around the world displaying material from this quarry than any other. Recognized as the best spot for fossilized bones from the flesh-eating Allosaur, the quarry was designated a National Natural Landmark in 1966. Bones from 74 different animals have been found here.

Your dog is allowed to sniff out some dinosaur bones as well (but not to take home). Several paths lead out into the desert, most prominently the self-guided *Rock Walk Interpretive Trail*. This 1.4-mile loop points out the geology, natural history, and human history of the quarry. If your dog is feeling frisky climb up to Raptor Point that gains 180 feet in less than a half-mile. The *Rim Walk* takes off from here for another scenic mile before looping and returning.

Cleveland, Utah
(435) 636-3600
www.blm.gov/ut/st/en/fo/price/recreation/quarry.html

Dinosaur National Monument (Colorado)

"Dinosaur" is a quick and easy umbrella rubric for the fossil treasures preserved in the sands of an ancient river in present-day northwestern Colorado. Sea creatures a hundred million years older than the dinosaurs are found in the rocky cliffs here. When the Rocky Mountains were uplifted the animal remains preserved in the sandbar became stranded a mile in the sky.

Beginning in 1909 more complete dinosaur skeletons and well-preserved skulls have been excavated and sent to museums from this site than any other. There are still more to see and the National Park Service reopened the Dinosaur Quarry as an on-site fossil exhibit. The cliff face has 1,500 dinosaur bones embedded in the side of a mountain.

Your dog will never see this as the quarry is accessed from the Visitor Center via a shuttle bus (and for the time being, people won't see it either as the ground has been deemed unstable). But there is more for the canine explorer at Dinosaur National Monument than old bones. The remote canyons of the Green and Yampa rivers were added to the original park in 1938, introducing dramatic canyon scenery into the visitation experience. As usual, your dog is banned from the hiking trails. But there is plenty of off-trail exploration available for your dog across this arid, sculpted land, even if you just wander in the vicinity of the canyon overlooks.

Dinosaur, Colorado
(970) 374-3000
www.nps.gov/dino

Dinosaur Valley State Park (Texas)

Some of the best evidence of dinosaur habitation occurs in the layered rocks of the Palaxy River. About 113 million years ago this mid-Texas site was tidal flats of the Gulf of Mexico where large reptiles left deeply impressed tracks in the soft, slimy mud. The rock hardened over millions of years and the Palaxy River went to work cutting at resistant rock and exposing the ancient footprints now preserved in rocky molds.

The first tracks were noticed in 1909 but not much thought was given to them until 1938 when Roland T. Bird of the American Museum of Natural History visited the river loop and identified a rare double set of tracks indicating a giant plant-eating dinosaur being chased by a carnivorous pursuer. He dug up the record of the prehistoric hunt and sent it to New York to be displayed.

Today your dog is welcome to walk in dinosaur prints that can be seen at several locations along the Palaxy River when water levels permit. To get the best views you will be splashing through the water with your dog to examine the exposed rock ledges. There are another dozen or so miles of tail-friendly, multi-use trails available as well. Oh, and the two dinosaurs you see in the park are fiberglass refugees from the 1964 World's Fair. New York got the footprints and Texas got the fiberglass display dinos.

Glen Rose, Texas
(254) 897-4588
www.tpwd.state.tx.us/spdest/findadest/parks/dinosaur_valley/

Dry Mesa Dinosaur Quarry (Colorado)

Bones of 23 different dinosaurs - including some of the largest skeletons ever found - have been unearthed in the Uncompahgre National Forest since their discovery in 1971. Large plant-eating sauropods, with intimidating names like Supersaurus and Ultrasaurus, came to feed at a remnant watering hole in an ancient dry lake bed when a severe drought resulted in a mass mortality.

You can visit the Dry Mesa Dinosaur Quarry near the east fork of Escalante Creek (on gravel roads with vehicles of high clearance) anytime with your dog although the fossils are buried when researchers are not present. Free guided hikes of the fossil beds are offered on Fridays and Saturdays when digs are in process.

Delta, Colorado
(970) 874-6600
http://www.fs.fed.us/r2/gmug/

Fossil Butte National Monument (Wyoming)

Looking around at the sagebrush and bone-dry desert in this 9,000-acre park it takes imagination to picture this as the Great Lakes region of America 50 million years ago. There isn't even anything to eat here - Fossil Butte National Monument is one of a few areas in southwestern Wyoming not grazed by cattle and sheep. But long ago there were three major lakes in what is today Colorado, Utah and Wyoming. This one, Fossil Lake, spread across 1,000 square miles. The animals that lived here enjoyed sub-tropical weather. Their remains piled up in the bottom of the lake and fossilized into a rock layer of laminated limestone and volcanic ash.

No dinosaurs here but few places on earth can match the fossils of Fossil Lake for sheer abundance, crystalline preservation and remarkable variety of fish, mammals, plants, reptiles and birds. The two interpretive trails that take your dog into the fossil beds are among the best in American archeological tourism. The *Historic Quarry Trail* gains 600 feet in elevation over 2.5 miles as you climb back in time millions of years through parts of the Wasatch and Green River formations. A short side loop leads to the site of an historic fossil quarry on Fossil Butte and wayside exhibits explain it all. For a change of pace the *Fossil Lake Trail* introduces a spring-fed aspen forest of a high-desert oasis. You are advised to be on the lookout for wildlife here - there are more pronghorn antelope than people in the state of Wyoming and a herd 100 strong roam the national monument.

Kemmerer, Wyoming
(307) 877-4455
www.nps.gov/fobu/

John Day Fossil Beds (Oregon)

The deep ravines and eroded formations of northeast Oregon's Blue Mountains display one of the longest and most continuous records of evolutionary change in the United States. Fossils of land plants and animals dating back 6 to 54 million years have been unearthed in these federally protected fossil beds. Evidence uncovered here tells us that desert-like eastern Oregon was once a tropical environment where crocodiles and palm trees flourished.

Your dog is welcome on all the dusty trails in the national monument, many of which are short interpretive outings where you can learn about the passage of time. The only trail you can find fossils in the rocks is the *Trail of Fossils* in the Clarno District.

The marquee canine hike at John Day Fossil Beds is a sometimes-grueling 600-foot ascent on the *Blue Basin Overlook Trail* at the Sheep Rock Unit. The purchase on this three-miler is an unforgettable look across the John Day River Valley. Less vigorous canine explorers will find a series of trails through fossil-bearing foundations, including layers of volcanic ash. Another picturesque hike is the *Carroll Rim Trail* at the Painted Hills Unit that overlooks the entire area of red and gold claystone hills.

And if it gets hot, as it tends to do in eastern Oregon, take your dog for a splash in the John Day River, the longest undammed tributary of the Columbia River. And who was John Day? He was an unfortunate fur trader who became separated from his expedition party along the Columbia River in 1810. Day was robbed by Indians who took all his possessions, including his clothes. Subsequent travelers would point out the spot where the incident took place and the river eventually became named for him.

Kimberly, Oregon
(541) 987-2333
www.nps.gov/joda

La Brea Tar Pits (California)

One of the world's most famous fossil sites is the La Brea Tar Pits in Los Angeles and your dog can visit as well. The tar pits are oil seeps that bubble to the surface and heat into a sticky asphalt. There are no dinosaurs in the La Brea pits - the animals preserved here were entrapped only between 40,000 and 10,000 years ago. But since 1906, more than one million bones have been pulled from the black ooze representing 231 species of vertebrates and 234 kinds of invertebrates. The most common large mammals are dire wolves and saber-toothed cats with the remains of thousands of individuals of each of these Ice Age species having been identified.

Outside the museum in Hancock Park, where your dog can roam, are life-size replicas of several extinct mammals. But keep a close eye on your dog as you walk through the park - about 10 gallons a day of sticky goo still bubbles to the surface in the La Brea Tar Pits.

Los Angeles, California
(323) 934-7243
www.tarpits.org/

TOUR

IDEA #100: DOGGIN' AMERICA'S GRAVEYARDS

Cemeteries were America's first parks. In many towns the local burying ground may still be the area's most significant greenspace. Respectful dogs are often welcome in graveyards and if you are looking for an offbeat outdoor experience you can share with your dog, a tour of America's cemeteries may be for you. One famous cemetery that does not allow dogs is Forest Lawn in Hollywood, California, final resting place to countless stars. Another is Mount Auburn Cemetery, America's first landscaped garden cemetery, in Cambridge, Massachusetts. But here are some of our most notable graveyards to visit with your dog...

Arlington National Cemetery (Virginia)

When the Marquis de Lafayette visited the 1,000-acre estate of George Washington Parke Custis, the step-grandson of George Washington, in 1824 he declared the view across the Potomac River the finest in the world. In 1831 the property became the home of Robert E. Lee. When the general turned down command of the Union Army before the Civil War and cast his lot with the rebel Confederacy, Lee's family left, never to return. The land was confiscated after the war began and it was proposed as the Arlington National Cemetery.

In 1882 Custis Lee, the general's oldest son, successfully sued the United States for the return of his ancestral land, but by then the hillside was covered with headstones. He accepted $150,000 for the property. Today Arlington is the largest and most famous of the more than 100-plus national burying grounds. Your dog is welcome to trot across more than 400 landscaped acres and past the graves of 225,000 war veterans.

Arlington, Virginia
(703) 607-8585
www.arlingtoncemetery.org/

Hollywood Cemetery (Virginia)

In 1847, influential Philadelphia architect John Notman, credited with introducing the Italianate style to America, was commissioned to create a burial ground overlooking the James River. Notman arranged the gravesites and paths to wind gracefully across the property studded with holly trees and created one of the country's most beautiful rural cemeteries. With the advent of the Civil War, Hollywood Cemetery also became one of the most historic. Thousands of Confederate soldiers are interred here along with 22 Confederate generals, six Virginia governors and two United States presidents.

Dogs are not permitted as regular visitors but occasionally Hollywood Cemetery opens its gates to lucky canine adventurers as part of the History Hounds walking tours sponsored by the Richmond SPCA and Historic Richmond Tours.

Richmond, Virginia
(804) 649-0711
www.richmondhistorycenter.com

Hope Cemetery (Vermont)

The first thing that strikes you upon driving into Hope Cemetery is the visual harmony presented across the 85-acre hillside graveyard. Every one of the more than 10,000 monuments is crafted of identical gray stone and that is because Barre, Vermont is the "Granite Capital of the World." Most of the granite for America's headstones in harvested here, a few miles away in the Rock of Ages Quarry. Since the 1800s master stonecarvers, many from Italy, have migrated to Barre and their handiwork is on display above the graves in Hope Cemetery that opened in 1895.

As you wander through this open, outdoor sculpture garden with your dog you'll notice exquisitely scripted bas relief artwork on standard issue headstones but also whimsical monuments such as a half-scale race-car, an elephantine soccer ball, a bi-plane steered towards the heavens and a gravity-defying cube balanced on one corner. This is one graveyard visit with your dog you won't shortly forget.

Barre, Vermont
(802) 229-4619
www.central-vt.com/web/hope/index.html

Saint Louis Cemetery (Louisiana)

Your dog is welcome on the grounds of America's most unique, and some contend, the most haunted, burial ground - the three Roman Catholic graveyards of Saint Louis Cemetery. The grounds are lined in a maze of above-ground tombs in the fashion of the world's most famous cemetery, Pere Lachaise in Paris. The tombs are more a result of their French and Spanish origins than the troublesome

New Orleans water table. The cemeteries were flooded following Hurricane Katrina in 2005 but did not suffer much damage.

St. Louis Cemetery #1 is the oldest and most notorious of the trio. It opened in 1789 just outside the city's French Quarter and is the resting place for over 100,000 New Orleanians, including some of the city's most colorful characters. The wealthy French-Creole playboy Bernard de Marigny, who introduced the game of craps to the United States, is buried here. So too is Etienne de Bore, American-born French Musketeer and sugar baron who was the first Mayor of New Orleans. Oh, and the remains of mystical Voodoo priestess Marie Laveau are believed to be interred in the Glapion family crypt, which cements St. Louis' spot atop the rankings of "most haunted graveyards." Her spirit has been reported inside of the cemetery, walking between the tombs wearing a red-and-white turban with seven knots in it. So if you notice your dog acting oddly for no apparent reason, pay close attention.

New Orleans, Louisiana

Sleepy Hollow Cemetery (New York)

The small three-acre churchyard of the Old Dutch Church on a hillside above the Hudson River was just another small town burial ground until Washington Irving had his Headless Horseman ride through in the "Legend of Sleepy Hollow" in 1820. In 1849 an adjacent graveyard, the Tarrytown Cemetery, opened and when Irving was interred twelve years later its name was changed to Sleepy Hollow Cemetery to honor the author's request.

Irving was the first American to become wealthy solely through his pen and it is appropriate that some of the country's wealthiest folks came to be buried along with him at Sleepy Hollow including members of the Astor family, Andrew Carnegie, Walter Chrysler, William Rockefeller and Leona Helmsley who famously bequeathed $12 million to her dog when she passed in 2007. Luckily Trouble the Maltese can visit her here and get quite a workout walking through the hilly 90-acre graveyard.

Tarrytown, New York
(914) 631-0081
sleepyhollowcemetery.org/

5

RULES FOR DOGS IN 100 OF THE MOST POPULAR NATIONAL PARK SERVICE LANDS...

1. Blue Ridge Parkway   *(21,646,864 visits)*
Dogs are allowed on most trails and in all 9 campgrounds.

2. Golden Gate National Recreation Area   *(13,806,766)*
Dogs are welcome on most of the nearly two dozen parcels of Federal land. No dogs are permitted in Tennessee Valley, China Beach, Muir Woods, Alcatraz and the Phleger Estate.

3. Great Smoky Mountains National Park   *(9,215,806)*
Dogs are prohibited from all park trails except the 2-mile trail from Park Headquarters to Gatlinburg and the 2-mile trail between Cherokee and the Oconaluftee Visitor Center. Dogs are allowed in the picnic areas and campgrounds.

4. Gateway National Recreation Area   *(8,955,609)*
At Sandy Hook dogs are allowed on the beach from Labor Day to March 15 and throughout other areas of the park at any time; no dogs are allowed on Jacob Riis Park from Memorial Day weekend through Labor Day weekend and no dogs are allowed at the Breezy Point Tip from March 15 through August.

5. Lake Mead National Recreation Area   *(7,627,906)*
Dogs are allowed on trails but not on the beaches.

6. Delaware Water Gap National Recreation Area   *(5,248,958)*
Dogs are welcome on trails and most locations within the recreation area. No dogs are allowed at Milford Beach, Hidden Lake Beach, Smithfield Beach or on the mowed areas at Kittatinny Point Visitor Center, Bushkill Visitor Center, Watergate Recreation Site or Hialeah Picnic Area.

7. Gulf Islands National Seashore   *(4,572,364)*
Dogs are not permitted on the beaches or in the picnic pavilions.

8. Cape Cod National Seashore   *(4,431,059)*
Dogs are prohibited from nature trails, shorebird nesting areas and all lifeguardprotected beaches. In addition to non-protected beaches, canine hikers can use seashore fire roads and the West and Sunset horse trails in the Province Lands. Dogs are welcome at the seashore fresh water ponds from October 16 through May 14.

9. Grand Canyon National Park   *(3,936,823)*
Dogs are allowed on trails throughout developed areas of the South Rim but never below the rim. On the North Rim, dogs are allowed only on the bridle trails that connects the lodge with the North Kaibab Trail.

10. Olympic National Park   (3,654,022)
Dogs are not permitted on park trails or meadows. Dogs are not allowed on any beaches except Rialto Beach north to Ellen Creek and on the Kalaloch beach strip between the Hoh and Quinault Indian reservation. Dogs are allowed in the campgrounds.

11. Cape Hatteras National Seashore   (3,651,066)
Dogs are allowed throughout the park except on designated swimming beaches.

12. Chesapeake & Ohio Canal National Historical Park   (3,477,090)
Dogs are allowed along the towpath and on most trails. No dogs are permitted on the boardwalk trails on the Olmsted Island Bridges and on the Billy Goat "A" Trail around Bear Island.

13. Colonial National Historical Park   (3,320,873)
Dogs are allowed to walk the battlefield at Yorktown and play on the beach at Cape Henry. Dogs are also welcome in Colonial Williamsburg.

14. Yosemite National Park   (3,305,631)
Dogs are not allowed on any park trail or in any picnic area. Dogs are permitted anywhere on the Yosemite Valley floor between the Happy Isles Nature Center or Mirror Lake parking lot and the Pohona bridge. Dogs are not permitted on any slope above the Valley floor. Several campgrounds allow dogs.

15. Cuyahoga Valley National Park   (3,191,359)
Dogs are allowed on all park lands.

16. Rocky Mountain National Park   (3,005,524)
Dogs are not allowed on any park trail. Dogs are allowed in parking areas, picnic areas and campgrounds.

17. Yellowstone National Park   (2,969,868)
Dogs are not allowed on trails or boardwalks. Dogs are permitted within 100 feet of roads, parking areas and campgrounds.

18. Chattahoochee River National Recreation Area   (2,712,783)
Dogs are permitted across park lands.

19. Grand Teton National Park   (2,606,492)
Dogs are not allowed on park trails; dogs can walk on roads and road shoulders, parking lots, picnic areas and campgrounds.

20. Acadia National Park   (2,550,586)
Dogs are allowed everywhere in the park except Sand Beach, Echo Lake Beach, the Isle au Haut campground and the "ladder" trails.

21. Zion National Park   (2,510,627)
Dogs are allowed on only one trail: the Pa'rus Trail. Dogs are allowed in campgrounds and along roadways.

22. Point Reyes National Seashore   (2,254,465)
Dogs are not permitted on trails or in campgrounds. Dogs are allowed on the south end of Limantour Beach, Point Reyes Beach North and Point Reyes Beach South.

23. Mount Rushmore National Memorial   (2,159,189)
Dogs are not allowed anywhere in the park except in the pet exercise area at the end of the upper parking ramp.

24. Glen Canyon National Recreation Area   (2,127,265)
Dogs are allowed in the park.

25. Assateague Island National Seashore   (2,107,032)
In Maryland, dogs are allowed on the beach and in campgrounds, but not on the trails. In Virginia, dogs are not allowed in the park - even in a car.

26. Rock Creek Park   (2,099,504)
Dogs are allowed on trails throughout the park.

27. Mammoth Cave National Park   (1,898,817)
Dogs are allowed on the above-ground trails in the park.

28. Glacier National Park   (1,864,822)
Dogs are not allowed on park trails but can stay in drive-in campgrounds and visit picnic areas.

29. Indiana Dunes National Lakeshore   (1,834,435)
Dogs are allowed on most park trails.

30. Gettysburg National Military Park   (1,829,790)
Dogs are permitted outside park buildings.

31. Chickasaw National Recreation Area   (1,511,522)
Dogs are allowed on park trails except on paths leading into the Environmental Study Area (east of the Travertine Nature Center).

32. Hot Springs National Park   (1,438,043)
Dogs are allowed on the trails and other areas outside buildings in the park.

33. Sequoia & Kings Canyon National Park   (1,418,512)
Dogs are not allowed on park trails; dogs can visit the picnic areas and campgrounds.

34. Mount Rainier National Park   (1,267,044)
Dogs are allowed on no trails except a small portion of the Pacific Crest Trail near the park's eastern boundary.

35. Valley Forge National Historical Park   (1,190,893)
Dogs are allowed on all park trails.

35. Valley Forge National Historical Park   (1,190,893)
Dogs are allowed on all park trails.

36. Sleeping Bear Dunes National Lakeshore   (1,190,748)
Dogs are allowed on most park trails but cannot make the Dune Climb. Dogs are not allowed on North or South Manitou Island.

37. Joshua Tree National Park   (1,174,142)
Dogs are not allowed on the trails but can be in the campgrounds.

38. Vicksburg National Military Park   (1,067,130)
Dogs are allowed in the park.

39. Lake Meredith National Recreation Area   (1,043,380)
Dogs are permitted throughout the park.

40. Canaveral National Seashore   (1,042,090)
Dogs are not allowed on the beach or beyond the parking lots.

41. Amistad National Recreation Area   (952,096)
Dogs are allowed on trails and in most areas of the park.

42. Everglades National Park   (940,482)
Dogs are allowed in parking lots and campgrounds but not on trails.

43. Cumberland Gap National Historical Park   (928,596)
Dogs are allowed on park trails.

44. Badlands National Park   (906,868)
Dogs are allowed only in developed areas such as campgrounds, parking areas and along roads - not on any trails.

45. Big South Fork National Recreation Area   (901,419)
Dogs are allowed on most park trails.

46. Bryce National Park   (899,408)
Dogs are not allowed on park trails; dogs can visit the picnic areas and campgrounds.

47. Curecanti National Recreation Area   (892,408)
Dogs are allowed on the trails.

48. Chickamauga & Chattanooga National Military Park   (845,037)
Dogs are allowed in the park.

49. Manassas National Battlefield   (790,086)
Dogs are allowed throughout the park.

50. Fire Island National Seashore   (779,241)
Dogs are prohibited from swimming beaches and other posted areas.

49. Manassas National Battlefield   (790,086)
Dogs are allowed throughout the park.

50. Fire Island National Seashore   (779,241)
Dogs are prohibited from swimming beaches and other posted areas.

51. Canyon de Chelly National Monument   (764,186)
Dogs are allowed on overlook trails but not below the rim.

52. Arches National Park   (761,861)
Dogs are not allowed on any hiking trails but are permitted in campgrounds.

53. Guilford Courthouse National Military Park   (757,267)
Dogs are allowed on park trails.

54. Whiskeytown National Recreation Area   (704,747)
Dogs are allowed on most park trails.

55. Wind Cave National Park   (696,402)
Two trails allow dogs within the park: the Elk Mountain Nature Trail takes off around the campground and the Prairie Valley Trail near the Visitor Center.

56. Cape Lookout National Seashore   (643,507)
Dogs are permitted in the park year-round.

57. Saguaro National Park   (642,457)
Dogs are not allowed on unpaved trails.

58. Petrified Forest National Park   (575,650)
Dogs are not allowed on unpaved trails in the park.

59. Cedar Breaks National Monument   (558,454)
Dogs are not allowed on park trails.

60. Padre Island National Seashore   (534,484)
Dogs are allowed anywhere except on the deck at Malaquite Beach and in front of the Visitor Center at the swimming beach.

61. Capitol Reef National Park   (516,379)
Dogs are not allowed on any park trails.

62. White Sands National Monument   (509,480)
Dogs are allowed on trails throughout the park.

63. Carlsbad Caverns National Park   (472,670)
Dogs are not permitted on park trails above or below ground.

64. Theodore Roosevelt National Park   (471,210)
Dogs are prohibited on all park trails.

63. Carlsbad Caverns National Park   (472,670)
Dogs are not permitted on park trails above or below ground.

64. Theodore Roosevelt National Park   (471,210)
Dogs are prohibited on all park trails.

65. Santa Monica Mountains National Recreation Area   (468,977)
Dogs are allowed on many park trails; dogs are not permitted on trails that run into state park land.

66. Fredericksburg & Spotsylvania National Military Park   (455,826)
Dogs are not allowed in most areas of the park.

67. Crater Lake National Park   (455,648)
Dogs are not allowed on park trails but are permitted in the picnic areas.

68. *Catoctin Mountain Park*   (453,302)
Dogs are allowed on park trails.

69. *Pictured Rocks National Lakeshore*   (428,390)
Dogs are welcome in designated developed areas and on most primary front country trails but not in the backcountry or selected posted lakeshore trails.

70. *Little Bighorn Battlefield National Memorial*   (418,755)
Dogs are allowed to explore the park.

71. *Mesa Verde National Park*   (411,399)
Dogs are not allowed on park trails.

72. *Devil's Tower National Monument*   (407,688)
Dogs are not allowed on park trails.

73. *Redwoods National Park*   (398,973)
Dogs are not allowed on any trails but are allowed at Crescent and Gold Bluffs beaches. Dogs are permitted in picnic areas, campgrounds and at the Freshwater Lagoon Spit.

74. *North Cascades National Park*   (390,277)
Dogs are not allowed on park trails.

75. *Lassen Volcanic National Park*   (387,480)
Dogs are not allowed on park trails.

76. *Morristown National Historical Park*   (384,303)
Dogs are permitted to hike on park trails.

77. *Canyonlands National Park*   (366,861)
Dogs are banned from all trails.

78. *Big Bend National Park*   (322,329)
Dogs are not allowed on trails, off roads, or on the Rio Grande River. Dogs can stay in campgrounds.

78. *White Sands National Monument*   (509,480)
Dogs are allowed on trails throughout the park.

79. *Antietam National Battlefield*   (313,201)
Dogs are not allowed on trails across the park.

80. *Harpers Ferry National Historical Park*   *(310,489)*
Dogs are allowed on park trails in Maryland, Virginia and West Virginia.

81. *Bandelier National Monument*   *(300,760)*
Dogs are not allowed on park trails but can stay in campgrounds.

82. *Dinosaur National Monument*   *(299,622)*
Dogs are allowed on most of the park trails.

83. *Organ Pipe Cactus National Monument*   *(295,080)*
Dogs are allowed on two trails: the Palo Verde Trail and the Campground Perimeter Trail. Dogs are allowed in the campground.

84. *San Juan Island National Historical Park*   *(276,018)*
Dogs are allowed on park trails and mutt mitts are provided at trailheads.

85. *Kings Mountain National Military Park*   *(265,673)*
Dogs are allowed on park trails.

86. *Fort Donelson National Battlefield*   *(237,063)*
Dogs are allowed on park trails.

87. *Great Sand Dunes National Monument*   *(235,535)*
Dogs are welcome outdoors anywhere in the park.

88. *Voyageurs National Park*   *(233,825)*
Dogs are not allowed on any park trails but can stay in campgrounds on the four main lakes. Dogs can also visit picnic areas and boat launch ramps.

89. *Guadalupe Mountains National Park*   *(216,095)*
Dogs are allowed only on the trail between the campground and the Visitor Center and the Pinery Trail at the Visitor Center. Dogs are also permitted in the campgrounds.

90. *Cowpens National Battlefield*   *(213,629)*
Dogs are allowed on park trails.

91. *Craters of the Moon National Memorial*   *(182,789)*
Dogs are not allowed off the pavement onto trails.

92. *Bighorn Canyon National Recreation Area*   *(177,441)*
Dogs are allowed on most park trails.

93. Petersburg National Battlefield   (176,311)
Dogs are allowed throughout the park.

94. Black Canyon of the Gunnison National Park   (174,346)
Dogs are allowed on overlook trails, some of which are nearly a mile, but are not permitted below the rim. Dogs are also prohibited from the Warner Nature Trail.

95. Apostle Islands National Lakeshore   (172,871)
Dogs are allowed on the islands.

96. Pinnacles National Monument   (165,011)
Dogs are allowed only on roads and in parking and picnic areas.

97. Saratoga National Historical Park   (148,490)
Dogs are permitted on trails throughout the park.

98. Jewel Cave National Monument   (131,481)
Dogs are allowed on above-ground trails in the park.

99. Lava Beds National Monument   (114,418)
Dogs are not allowed in the wilderness area.

100. Scotts Bluff National Monument   (113,885)
Dogs are allowed on park trails.

6

INDEX

As a young lawyer, 19th century Senator George Graham Vest of Missouri, addressed the jury on behalf of his client, suing a neighbor who had killed his dog. Vest's speech has come to be known as "Tribute to the Dog."

The best friend a man has in the world may turn against him and become his enemy. His son or daughter that he has reared with loving care may prove ungrateful. Those who are nearest and dearest to us, those whom we trust with our happiness and our good name may become traitors to their faith. The money that a man has, he may lose. It flies away from him, perhaps when he needs it most. A man's reputation may be sacrificed in a moment of ill-considered action. The people who are prone to fall on their knees to do us honor when success is with us may be the first to throw the stone of malice when failure settles its cloud upon our heads.

The one absolutely unselfish friend that man can have in this selfish world, the one that never deserts him, the one that never proves ungrateful or treacherous is his dog. A man's dog stands by him in prosperity and in poverty, in health and in sickness. He will sleep on the cold ground, where the wintry winds blow and the snow drives fiercely, if only he may be near his master's side. He will kiss the hand that has no food to offer; he will lick the wounds and sores that come in an encounter with the roughness of the world. He guards the sleep of his pauper master as if he were a prince. When all other friends desert, he remains. When riches take wings, and reputation falls to pieces, he is as constant in his love as the sun in its journey through the heavens. If fortune drives the master forth an outcast in the world, friendless and homeless, the faithful dog asks no higher privilege than that of accompanying him, to guard him against danger, to fight against his enemies. And when the last scene of all comes, and death takes his master in its embrace and his body is laid away in the cold ground, no matter if all other friends pursue their way, there by the graveside will the noble dog be found, his head between his paws, his eyes sad, but open in alert watchfulness, faithful and true even in death.

ABOUT THE AUTHOR

Doug Gelbert has written over 20 books including *So Who The Heck Was Oscar Mayer?*, guides to the Civil War and American Revolution, and more than a dozen books on hiking with your dog.

Gelbert also leads hiking tours with your dog and is a columnist for *Fido-Friendly* magazine.

Cruden Bay Books has been a leading publisher of guidebooks to adventure with your dog since 1998 with over 30 titles in print in the A BARK IN THE PARK series and DOGGIN' AMERICA series. For additional information visit our website at: *www.hikewithyourdog.com*.

Made in the USA
Middletown, DE
28 June 2023

34110535R00205